History as a Translation of the Past

History as a Translation of the Past

Case Studies from the West

Edited by
Luigi Alonzi

BLOOMSBURY ACADEMIC
LONDON • NEW YORK • OXFORD • NEW DELHI • SYDNEY

BLOOMSBURY ACADEMIC
Bloomsbury Publishing Plc
50 Bedford Square, London, WC1B 3DP, UK
1385 Broadway, New York, NY 10018, USA
29 Earlsfort Terrace, Dublin 2, Ireland

BLOOMSBURY, BLOOMSBURY ACADEMIC and the Diana logo are
trademarks of Bloomsbury Publishing Plc

First published in Great Britain 2023
Paperback publication year is 2025

Copyright © Luigi Alonzi 2023

Luigi Alonzi has asserted his right under the Copyright,
Designs and Patents Act, 1988, to be identified as Editor of this work.

Cover image: Old books pages, © R.Tsubin / Getty Images

Bloomsbury Publishing Plc does not have any control over, or responsibility for, any third-party websites referred to or in this book. All internet addresses given in this book were correct at the time of going to press. The author and publisher regret any inconvenience caused if addresses have changed or sites have ceased to exist, but can accept no responsibility for any such changes.

Every effort has been made to trace the copyright holders and obtain permission to reproduce the copyright material. Please do get in touch with any enquiries or any information relating to such material or the rights holder. We would be pleased to rectify any omissions in subsequent editions of this publication should they be drawn to our attention.

A catalogue record for this book is available from the British Library.

A catalog record for this book is available from the Library of Congress.

Library of Congress Cataloging-in-Publication Data

Names: Alonzi, Luigi, editor.
Title: History as a translation of the past : case studies from the West / edited by Luigi Alonzi.
Other titles: Case studies from the West
Description: London ; New York : Bloomsbury Academic, 2023. | Includes bibliographical references and index. | Summary: "Combining elements of cultural history and translation studies, this book explores a new theoretical approach which recognises history as a translation of historical deeds with present language"– Provided by publisher.
Identifiers: LCCN 2023026332 (print) | LCCN 2023026333 (ebook) | ISBN 9781350338210 (hardback) | ISBN 9781350338258 (paperback) | ISBN 9781350338227 (epdf) | ISBN 9781350338234 (ebook)
Subjects: LCSH: Historiography. | Translating and interpreting.
Classification: LCC D13 .H5796 2023 (print) | LCC D13 (ebook) | DDC 907.2–dc23/eng/20230624
LC record available at https://lccn.loc.gov/2023026332
LC ebook record available at https://lccn.loc.gov/2023026333

ISBN: HB: 978-1-3503-3821-0
PB: 978-1-3503-3825-8
ePDF: 978-1-3503-3822-7
eBook: 978-1-3503-3823-4

Typeset by Integra Software Services Pvt. Ltd.

To find out more about our authors and books visit www.bloomsbury.com
and sign up for our newsletters.

Contents

List of contributors		vi
Acknowledgements		ix
Introduction: Translating the past *Luigi Alonzi*		1
1	Herodotus translating the past *Richard P. Martin*	25
2	Translation and temporalities in classical reception histories: Narratives, genres, forms and the agency of translators *Lorna Hardwick*	49
3	Flesh made word: Translational processes in the production of the synoptic gospels *Karen Bennett*	69
4	The historian's dilemma: Domestication or foreignizing? *Peter Burke*	91
5	'*Chance*' in Max Weber's later writings *Keith Tribe*	107
6	'We politicians': Translation, rhetoric and conceptual change *Kari Palonen*	121
7	Translated history and historical time: Transtemporal understandings of Greek and Roman concepts *Alexandra Lianeri*	141
8	'Just ask the stones': Eco-translation, natural history and geomedia *Karin Littau*	167
9	The historian as translator of the past *Luigi Alonzi*	191
Name Index		214

Contributors

Richard P. Martin is Antony and Isabelle Raubitschek Professor at Stanford and has previously taught Classics for eighteen years at Princeton University. He is working on several books, concerning Homeric religion, Old Comedy and ancient poetry in performance. He interprets Greek poetry in the light of performance traditions and social practices. His primary interests are in Homeric epic, Greek comedy, mythology and ancient religion. His research is informed by comparative evidence ranging from fieldwork on oral traditions in contemporary Crete to studies in medieval Irish literature.

Among his major publications are *Healing, Sacrifice, and Battle: Amechania and Related Concepts in Early Greek Poetry* (1983) and *The Language of Heroes: Speech and Performance in the Iliad* (1989). He has also published books for general audiences (*Classical Mythology: The Basics*, 2016; *Myths of the Ancient Greeks*, 2003; *Bulfinch's Mythology*, edit. 1991) and a number of articles on Greek, Latin and Irish literature.

Lorna Hardwick is Professor Emerita of Classical Studies at the Open University (UK) and an Honorary Research Associate at the Archive of Performances of Greek and Roman Drama at the University of Oxford. She is (with Professor James Porter) the editor of the *Classical Presences* series (Oxford University Press) and was the founding editor of the *Classical Receptions Journal* and of the open access online journal *Practitioners' Voices in Classical Reception Studies*. She is Director of the Reception of Classical Texts Research Project and has published extensively on Homer, Athenian cultural history, Greek Tragedy and its modern reception and on translation theory and practice. Her books include: *Translating Words, Translating Cultures* (2000), *Reception Studies* (2003, also translated into Greek), *Classics in Post-Colonial Worlds* (2007, edited with Carol Gillespie), *Companion to Classical Receptions* (2007, edited with Christopher Stray), *Classics in the Modern World: A 'Democratic Turn'?* (2013, edited with Stephen Harrison). She is the convenor of the research network Classics and Poetry Now (CAPN) and is the joint editor, with Professor Elizabeth Vandiver and Professor Stephen Harrison, of the Oxford University Press digital and print project Oxford Classical Reception Commentaries (OCRC).

Karen Bennett is Associate Professor in Translation at Nova University, Lisbon, and a researcher with the Centre for English, Translation and Anglo-Portuguese Studies (CETAPS), where she coordinates the Translationality strand. She is a general editor of the journal *Translation Matters* and a member of the editorial board of the Brill series *Approaches to Translation Studies*. She is currently preparing a three-volume mini-series for Routledge, titled *Multilingualism, Lingua Franca and Translation in the Early Modern Period*.

Peter Burke is Professor Emeritus of Cultural History at the Emmanuel College, University of Cambridge. Educated by the Jesuits and at Oxford (St John's and St Antony's), Peter Burke taught in the School of European Studies, University of Sussex from 1962 to 1979 as Assistant Lecturer and Lecturer in History and as Reader in Intellectual History. He moved to Cambridge to become Lecturer in History and subsequently Reader in and then Professor of Cultural History. He has published twenty-three books, including *The Italian Renaissance* (1972), *Popular Culture in Early Modern Europe* (1978), *The Fabrication of Louis XIV* (1992), *The Art of Conversation* (1993), *A Social History of Knowledge* (2000), *Eyewitnessing* (2000), *What Is Cultural History?* (2004) and *Languages and Communities in Early Modern Europe* (2004) and has been translated into twenty-eight languages. His studies of historiography include *The Renaissance Sense of the Past* (1969) and *The French Historical Revolution* (1990). He has also published important articles on the history of translation and edited, with Ronnie Po-chia Hsia, *Cultural Translations in Early Modern Europe*, 2007.

Keith Tribe is Associate Professor of History at Tartu University (Estonia) working with Marten Seppel on research into 'Concepts of Change in Early Modern Europe', supported by the Estonian Research Council. His principal research interest involves the integration of the study of economic and political discourse with early modern European economic history, an interest that runs back to his doctoral work during the 1970s on the agrarian foundation of English political economy. Besides his new translation of Max Weber's *Wirtschaft und Gesellschaft Teil I* (Max Weber, *Economy and Society. A New Translation*. 2019), he has also published a translation of Max Weber's 1893 Address to the Verein für Socialpolitik. His new book, *Constructing Economic Science. The Invention of a Discipline 1850-1950*, has been published in November 2021. Among his recent publications are 'Capitalism, Contingency and Economic Development', in *The Routledge International Handbook on Max Weber*, edited by Alan Sica, 2022; *Political Reason and Language of Change: Reform and Improvement in Early Modern Europe*, edited by Adriana Luna-Fabritius, Ere Nokkala, Marten Seppel and Keith Tribe, 2022; and 'Framing *The Wealth of Nations*', *History of Political Economy*, 54 (5), 2022: 951–73.

Kari Palonen is Professor Emeritus of Political Science at the University of Jyväskylä, Finland.

His major publications are on the fields of the conceptual history of politics, on the principles and practices of conceptual history, in the political thought and methodology of Max Weber as well in the parliamentary studies with the focus on concepts, procedure and rhetoric. Among his recent publications are 'Max Weber on Parliamentarism and Democracy', in *The Routledge International Handbook on Max Weber*, edited by Alan Sica, 2022; *Rhetoric and Bricolage in European Politics and Beyond: The Political Mind in Action*, edited by Niilo Kauppi and Kari Palonen, 2022; and 'Politicisation as a Speech Act: A Repertoire for Analysing Politicisation in Parliamentary Plenary Debates', in *Palgrave Studies in European Political Sociology*, edited by Haapala Taru and Oleart Álvaro, 2022.

Alexandra Lianeri completed her PhD at the University of Warwick in 2001 and worked as Junior Research Fellow at the Institute of Hellenic and Roman Studies, University of Bristol, and Moses Finley Fellow at the University of Cambridge. She joined the classics department of the University of Thessaloniki in 2011. She has been a visiting scholar at the Harvard Centre of Hellenic Studies.

Her research explores the role of classics in modern European intellectual history with a focus on the history of political thought and the relation between ancient and modern historiography. She is further interested in the theory of translation and reception of classical antiquity and is author of *A Democracy of the Past: Translating Dēmokratia in Nineteenth-Century Britain*, forthcoming.

Karin Littau is Professor of English and Comparative Literature at the University of Essex, UK. She has published on book and film history, adaptation, translation and reception studies. Her articles on translation have appeared in journals such as *Comparative Critical Studies, Forum for Modern Language Studies, MLN, Translation Studies, TTR* and, most recently, in *IJoC* and *SubStance*. Her next book is a history of the relations between literature and film; others include *Theories of Reading: Books, Bodies and Bibliomania* (2006; translated by Manantial into Spanish in 2008), *A Companion to Translation Studies* (2007, with Piotr Kuhiwczak) and *Cinematicity in Media History* (2013, with Jeffrey Geiger).

Luigi Alonzi is Associate Professor of History at the University of Palermo. He achieved his PhD at the University of Basilicata and later continued his research activity at the universities of Salerno and Rome (La Sapienza). In recent years he has paid growing attention to the history of words/concepts and to historical method, cognitive linguistics, historical semantics. Among his recent works are: 'The Term "Political Oeconomy" in Adam Smith', *Intellectual History Review* 31 (2), 2021: 321–39; *'Economy' in European History. Words, Contexts and Change over Time*, Bloomsbury Academic, 2022; "'Oeconomy' and 'political oeconomy' in *The Theory of Moral Sentiments* and in *The Wealth of Nations*', *Adam Smith Review* 13, 2023: 184-202.

Acknowledgements

My first acknowledgment goes to the contributors to this volume who are among the foremost scholars in their respective fields of study; I thank them for their kindness in accepting my editing and for the penetrating insights provided in their fascinating chapters. I cannot forget Sarah Maitland, Mark and Ruth Phillipps who had enthusiastically accepted to take part in the volume but, for different reasons, have not been able to perform their contribution; their proposals and participation have been inspiring. Many thanks also to Rhodri Mogford and the entire Bloomsbury Academic staff for their support and professionalism. For many years now, I have the privilege of enjoining a constant intellectual dialogue with Peter Burke and Keith Tribe; once again, they have not failed to give me their help and suggestions. I wish to express my deep gratitude and appreciation to them.

Introduction: Translating the past

Luigi Alonzi

I.1. Cultural history and cultural translation

Historical interpretation of the past can be considered an act of translation, epistemologically and cognitively. Before encountering a concept or finding a meaning, the eyes and brain of historians encounter a sign, in many cases a concrete written/printed word. This does not provide any explicit meaning or immediate conceptual reference, besides the meaning or concept related to this word that he/she had already in his/her mind. To grasp the meaning of a word and to outline the conceptual content of a word in different times and places, historians must indeed firstly reconstruct the unique linguistic contexts in which such a word was used and, as far as possible, delineate the history of this word, seeking to clarify its different meanings and conceptual references through time. The same can be said for images and archaeological remains, whose (historical) meanings are represented by historians and archaeologists through an act of translation, defined also as an act of transmutation.

In fact, words, images, remains can all be considered as objects deserving the same treatment on the part of historians and archaeologists, whose task consists exactly in translating their past meanings into present language. This act of translation is also an act of synchronization which connects past, present, and future, disrupting and resetting time, as well as creating complex temporalities differing from linear chronology. In this vein, the study of the different forms through which the past is constantly translated leads to the central problem of historical inquiry, that is, to the concept of anachronism. The task of the historian therefore consists in establishing the framework in which this cultural encounter between past and present occurs, making the rules governing this encounter as clear as possible. To this extent the historian's work could be compared to that performed by translator. Peter Burke, working within a discourse on translation in early modern Europe, has observed:

> If the past is a foreign country it follows that even the most monoglot historian is a translator. Historians mediate between the past and the present and face the same dilemmas as other translators, serving two masters and attempting to reconcile fidelity to the original with intelligibility to their readers.
>
> (Burke 2007a: 7; see also Burke 2007b)

Burke appealed to the anthropological tradition inaugurated by Edward E. Evans-Pritchard, who had criticized the approach of Malinowski and Radcliffe-Brown to social anthropology as one based on the model of natural sciences in search of universal laws. Evans-Pritchard sought a closer relationship between history and anthropology, focused on a study of encounters between cultures and on the specificity of the cultural history of single communities. According to Burke, the term-concept 'cultural translation' was

> originally coined by anthropologists in the circle of Evans-Pritchard, to describe what happens in cultural encounters when each side tries to make sense of the actions of the others [...] Working as they often do in situations where the cultural distance between themselves and their informants is unusually great, anthropologists are well-aware of the problem of untranslatable terms [...], as well as the more general problem of communication between natives of one culture and natives of another. They are becoming increasingly conscious of both the linguistic and the wider cultural problems involved in turning conversation with informants into their own academic prose.
>
> (Burke 2007a: 8; see also Burke 2007b)[1]

It was in this framework that studies on cultural translation developed, and a growing interconnection between historians and anthropologists was established. Reflecting on the relationships between history and anthropology, Alan Macfarlane (1988) argued that in its analysis of myth, legend and history, [anthropology] suggests that history and historians need to be constantly aware of the ways in which their own insights are legitimations which are subtly affected by political, economic and social worlds which they inhabit. The anthropology of historical research has still to be written, but it would be a fruitful area of study. There can be little doubt that of all the disciplines which lie adjacent to history, anthropology has had the most marked influence in the period between 1960 and 1985.

Soon afterwards studies developed along the lines sketched by Walter Benjamin, progressively widening the notion of 'translation' from a linguistic perspective to that of social sciences, flourishing particularly in post-modernist and post-colonial studies. In particular, *The Task of the Translator* became a mandatory point of departure for anyone seeking to cope with the 'translatability' of texts, that is, for anyone trying to come 'to terms with the foreignness of languages to each other' (Rendall 1997: 157).[2] Thanks also to other writings by Walter Benjamin (see, especially, in this context, the essay on the concept of history),[3] this perspective was progressively enlarged to include different forms of cultural translation and to meet the different problems raised by cultural encounters, especially those linked to the relations of powers between 'dominant translators' and 'cultures translated'. In a critical essay published in 1986 devoted to the concept of cultural translation in British social anthropology, Talal Asad (1986: 164) remarked that

> the anthropological enterprise of cultural translation may be vitiated by the fact that there are asymmetrical tendencies and pressures in the language of dominated

and dominant societies. And I have suggested that anthropologists need to explore these processes in order to determine how far they go in defining the possibilities and limits of effective translation.

During the following decade there was a significant increase in the number of scholars linking translation studies to cultural studies. Susan Bassnett, observing a cultural turn in translation studies, also detected an ongoing translation turn in cultural studies, inviting scholars to focusing much more on 'cultural plurality'. This of course referred to the well-known works by Homi Bhabha and Tejaswini Niranjana, and concluded by pointing out the necessity (a) of investigating 'the acculturation process that takes place between cultures' and 'the way in which different cultures construct their image of writers and texts', (b) of carrying out 'more comparative study of the ways in which texts became cultural capital across cultural boundaries', (c) of fulfilling 'greater investigation of what Venuti has called "the ethnocentric violence of translation" and much more research on into the politics of translating', and finally (d) of promoting 'a pooling of resources to extend research into intercultural training and the implication of such training in today's world' (Bassnett 1998: 138).[4]

Centred on the notion of 'cultural translation', this new trend was common in post-modern and post-colonial studies and was based on two key notions, 'negotiation' and 'cultural hybridity'. These were variously criticized and questioned. If there are not two different cultures, if on the contrary there are two hybrid cultural spaces already 'translated' in which people are continuously in the act of translating and being translated, then translation is not at all possible; in other words, this perspective placed the very notion of 'translation' at stake, since it was absorbed into the notion of culture, removing the linguistic substratum of the notion of translation. As Harish Trivedi (1995; 2007) noted,

> if there is one thing that Cultural Translation is not, it is the translation of culture. In fact, it spells, as I shall go on to argue, the very extinction and erasure of translation as we have always known and practised it.

As he clearly showed, the notion of 'cultural translation' elaborated in post-modernist and post-colonial studies intersected with the problem of the cultural identities and also affected the renewal of gender studies and the general issues linked to the use of English in the globalization processes (see also Snell-Hornby 1999; *The Translator* 2017). While there is much to be valued in Trivedi's arguments, I think that the notion of 'cultural translation' can be maintained with appropriate clarifications.[5]

It could be observed that the use of the term 'cultural translation' is itself an example of metaphorical translation and linguistic transformation. What other term should historians, philosophers and writers have used to express the idea of a 'passage' from a starting to an end point if not the term 'cultural translation'? What other term could be used to indicate the act performed by each person when assimilating and expressing 'Others' ideas if not 'cultural translation'? Certainly, synonyms could have been used, but perhaps translation is what best renders the idea. Evidently, as with every word, the word 'translation' has no universal and permanent meaning. It is thus significant that during the final decade of the twentieth century many scholars from different disciplines felt the need to use the term 'cultural translation', considering that it appropriately expressed an idea they had in their mind; at the same time, these scholars enriched this term with new meanings and semantics prompted by the cultural contexts into which they lived.

No scholar can definitively say what the meaning of the term 'cultural translation' is, and no disciplinary area can claim an exclusive right of use of this term; everyone can use the terms as they see fit: the important thing being that the semantic nucleus of words is carefully identified. The use of a word is linked to a semantic vector which in the course of its transmission necessarily loses some of its parts and acquires others conferred on it by those who receive it. The translation of words and concepts must for the same reason be considered a creative act, and the notions of 'equivalence' and 'faithfulness' applied to translations must be understood within this analytical framework. This is how language works: we must accept that in communication, as Luigi Pirandello masterfully taught more than a century ago, words and signs are never unambiguous, since everyone receives them in the context of differing references and inferences related to their cultural background. On the other hand, this reference to Pirandello, which for me is obvious, for other is not so at all – demonstrating how, when approaching this issue, I have in my intellectual toolbox different tools for understanding words than others.

Sarah Maitland takes a broad sociocultural and cognitive perspective in emphasizing the hermeneutic foundation of the concept of 'cultural translation' and its constitutive relationship with the processes of conferring meaning to the world and understanding of otherness. While she highlights the negative aspects in the recent overuse of the concept of 'cultural translation', she has urged scholars to focus on the creative function of translation as an act of appropriation and signification in the encounters between different cultures. Surveying the different issues raised by an excessive metaphorical extension of the concept of 'cultural translation', Maitland has identified two main problems that were supposed to derive from an unclear definition of the concept of 'cultural translation': an ethical problem, the treasonable function of the translator as a cultural mediator, and a methodological problem, the departure from the practice of interlingual translation. Maitland has observed that no one can in fact claim the prerogative of determining the legitimate definition of 'cultural translation' and that, by its nature, this concept remains vague and open to the different uses of the various disciplines.

That said, Sarah Maitland concludes that cultural translation and linguistic translation are two sides of the same coin since they are both part of the same act of interpreting reality through the appropriation of otherness and the integration of differences. Furthermore, she argues that what is valid for interlingual translation is also valid for translations within the same language in different times and places, since the translator's task is not so much aimed at grasping the author's intentions as at making the text understandable for the audience it is addressed to. Starting from these premises she argues:

> To say that cultural translation eschews linguistic paradigms of translation in favour of 'cultural processes' does not mean that we cannot detect movements

we associate most closely with the linguistic work of translation, for, as I have already discussed, every understanding that takes place in the world is actively interpretative, in the sense that all things can and do mean more or less than they appear. We must never forget that the textual and linguistic problems with which interlingual translation deals start *before* we address the problem of transferring texts from one language to another, for the same mode of interpretation we associate with translation between languages also take place in the one language alone.

(Maitland 2017: 25)[6]

It is interesting to note that Sarah Maitland proposes a hermeneutic approach in which historiographical literature is almost completely absent; yet her analysis broadly aligns with the argument developed in this book. This is all the more true considering that the two pillars on which her analysis is based, George Steiner and Paul Ricoeur, are also two authors of central importance to the construction of perspectives elaborated here. Their contribution to the analysis of the concept of translation will be treated below from a historical perspective.

I.2. Present language and historical past

To clarify what is meant by the term 'translation' in this book, it needs to be pointed out that it refers not only to the relationships between two different languages but also to the linguistic and cultural relationships existing within the same language in different times. To be even more precise, it can be added that it is not even referred uniquely to the intralingual translation or *rewording* conceived by Roman Jakobson as 'an interpretation of verbal signs by means of other signs of the same language';[7] in fact, often the greatest problems for the historians arise when they have to use the same words or signs and then have to explain how they have changed their meanings over time. On a cognitive basis, it is precisely the use of the same word or sign that can make interpretation difficult for the reader, since very often (but not always) historians use the same words without specifying their actual and past meanings; it is at this moment that the *rewording* evoked by Jakobson could be needed, since a historian must 'translate' past words using synonymous words and/or, more often, entire definitions to render their difference with successive uses of the same word. Evidently, at the highest level this is not simply a grammatical and syntactic question, but it implies a proper linguistic and cultural translation of past texts/events.

Of course, historians are constantly engaged in interlingual translation and intersemiotic translation, but in this case the work of translation is consciously undertaken and perceived; the same cannot be said for the work that historians usually perform when simply writing, which is eminently a work of cultural translation between past and present. Fortunately, I do not need to insist too much on explaining this central point. Much of what I want to say has already been brilliantly outlined, firstly by George Steiner and then by Paul Ricoeur. In my opinion, all historians should read carefully the pages devoted by George Steiner to the concept of translation as an act of interpretation. To begin I would like to quote a dense passage from *After Babel*, our compass in this short summary, highlighting in bold some terms used by Steiner to convey the idea of the creative act that takes place every time a work/text is reproduced, both musically, artistically or literarily (italics are, instead, those used by Steiner).

> **When the most thorough interpretation occurs**, where our sensibility appropriates its objects while, in this appropriation, guarding, quickening that object's autonomous life, **the process is one of original repetition**. We **re-enact**, in the bounds of our own secondary but momentarily heightened, educated consciousness, the creation by the artist. We **retrace**, both in the image of a man drawing and of one following an uncertain path, the coming into form of the poet. Ultimate connoisseurship is a kind of finite *mimesis*: through it the painting or the literary text is made new – though obviously in that reflected, dependent sense which Plato gave to the concept of 'imitation'. The degree of **re-creative immediacy** varies. It is most radically life-giving in the case of musical performance. Every musical realization is a new *poiesis*. It differs from all the other performances of the same composition. Its ontological relationship to the original scores and to all **previous renditions** is twofold: **it is at the same time reproductive and innovatory** […]
>
> 'Interpretation' as that which gives language life beyond the moment and place of immediate utterance or transcription, is what I am concerned with. The French word *interprète* concentrates all the relevant values. An actor is *interprète* of Racine; a pianist gives *une interprétation* a Beethoven sonata. Through engagement of his own identity, a critic becomes an *interprète* – a life-giving performer – of Montaigne or Mallarmé. As it does not include the world of the actor, and includes that of the musician only by analogy, the English term interpreter is less strong. But it is congruent with French when reaching out in another crucial direction. ***Interprète/interpreter* are commonly used to mean *translator*. This, I believe, is the vital starting point.**
>
> When we read or hear any language-statement of the past, be it Leviticus or last-year's best seller, we translate. **Reader, actor, editor are translators of language out of time.**
>
> (Steiner 1975: 26–8)

We should reflect on this last profound statement, speaking to the deep relationship between anachronism, translation and the work performed by the historian. Steiner's conceptualization continues in terms which would have deserved to be written entirely in bold, containing the best synthesis of the work of the historian as a cultural translator and, particularly, as a 'translator within'.

The schematic model of translation is one in which a massage from a source-language passes into a receptor-language via a transformational process. The barrier is the obvious fact that the one language differs from the other, that an interpretative transfer, sometimes, albeit misleadingly, described as encoding and decoding, must occurs so that the massage 'gets through'. Exactly the same model – and this is what is rarely stressed – is operative within a single language. But here the barrier or distance between source and receptor is time. As we have seen, the tools employed in both operations are correlate: both the 'external' and 'internal' translator/*interprète* have recourse to lexica, historical grammars, glossaries of particular periods, professions, or social milieux, dictionaries of argot, manuals of technical terminology. In either case the means of penetration are a complex aggregate of knowledge, familiarity, and re-creative intuition. In either case also, as we shall see, there are characteristic penumbras and margins of failure. Certain elements will elude complete comprehension and revival. The time-barrier may be more intractable than that of linguistic difference. Any bilingual translator his acquainted with the phenomenon of 'false friends' […] The 'translator within' has to cope with subtler treasons. Words rarely show any outward mark of altered meaning, they body forth their history only in a full established context. Where a passage is historically remote, say in Chaucer, the business of internal translation tends towards being a bilingual process: eye and ear are kept alert to the necessity of decipherment. The more seemingly standardized the language […] the more covert are indices of semantic dating. We read as if time has had a stop.

(Steiner 1975: 28–9)[8]

If the historian does not make this point clear the entire reconstruction risks being founded on a misleading assumption. History is a linguistic and cultural textile weaved by the thread of translations; indeed, texts and events are constantly re-translated through new 'actual' languages in order to be understood. The same can be said for the re-translations of classics:

As every generation retranslates the classics, out of a vital compulsion for immediacy and precise echo, so every generation uses language to build its own resonant past.

(Steiner 1975: 29–30)

We have not a single Dante or Shakespeare, but many different interpretations/translations of Dante and Shakespeare:

Literature, whose genius stems from what Éluard called *le dur désir de durer*, has no chance of life outside constant translation within its own language […] In short, the existence of art and literature, the reality of felt history in a community, depend on a never-ending, though very often unconscious, act of internal translation. It is no overstatement to say that we possess civilization because we have learned to translate out of time.

(Steiner 1975: 30–1)

Once again, Steiner's argument culminates with a reference to translation as an act performed 'out of time', which resets historical time, or better, historical time (in all its complexity) is entirely contained in the present act of translating. By narrating past events, the historian makes them present; but what is the relationship between the 'reality of historical past' and the narrative constructed by the historian? Reflecting on this issue, Paul Ricoeur has identified three main ways elaborated by historians and philosophers to relate narratives to the 'reality of historical past', using as titles 'Under the Sign of the "Same": Re-enacting the Past in the Present', with reference especially to Robin Collingwood; 'Under the Sign of the "Other": A negative ontology of the past', with reference especially to Jacques Derrida; and 'Under the Sign of the "Analogue": a tropological approach', with reference especially to Hyden White.[9]

As Ricoeur observed, the idea of re-enactment, formulated unequivocally by Collingwood in the first paragraph of the *Epilegomena*, 'abolishes the historical distance between past and present'; in Ricoeur's view, the problem of the 'identity thesis', advanced by Collingwood, is that the process of re-enactment retraced by the historian would allegedly abolish any distance from the original creation, making it impossible to think of this process as a re-creation. More radically, this process would have prevented historians thinking of the past as 'Other'; this latter perspective has instead been taken to extreme by philosophers such as Michel de Certeau, Gilles Deleuze and Jacques Derrida, whose hermeneutic theories would on the contrary lead to disbelief in the 'translatability' of the historical past in terms of the present. According to Ricoeur, for these authors (especially for Derrida) the historical past is radically different from the present, and this would have made it impossible to conceptualize the 'otherness' of the historical past, paradoxically making the enigma of temporal distance even more opaque.

A possible solution to this problem was found by Ricoeur in the tropological approach elaborated by Hyden White, who has made 'available to us a *rhetorical* theory, and in this rhetoric, a theory of *tropes* in which the similar is mobilized by the strategy of discourse under the figure of *metaphor*' (Ricoeur 1984: 27; italics are in the text); this tropological treatment would have allowed Ricoeur to build a bridge between his theory of narrative and his theory of metaphor, and in particular to give a more satisfactorily solution to the leading historiographical problem of 'representing' the past with present words, which take the place of past events. In this perspective, 'the historian's work then consists in making the narrative structure a "model", an "icon" of the past, capable of "representing" it' (Ricoeur 1984: 29); in this sense, White's tropological theory would recalibrate the two previous theories centred on the concepts of 'sameness' and 'otherness', simply by saying to us that past events 'must have happened *as* it is stated in the narrative considered' (Ricoeur 1984: 33).

That said, Ricoeur argues that without taking carefully into account the two previous theories, 'the recourse to the theory of trope runs the risk of erasing the dividing line between *fiction* and *history*', although historians are no longer under the illusion they restore the past as it really happened, for historical events cannot be entirely re-constructed without constraints, as in fiction.

> In other words, a certain tropological arbitrariness must not make us forget the kind of constraint that the past exerted on historical discourse through known documents, by demanding an endless *rectification* on its part. The relation between

history and fiction is certainly more complex than we can ever say. Of course, we must combat the prejudice that the historian's language could be made entirely transparent, so that the facts would speak for themselves.

(Ricoeur 1984: 34–5)

In sum, Ricoeur seems to hesitantly conclude that the only possible way out to pay our debt to the past, to do justice to the 'reality of the past', would consist in subsuming the categories of 'sameness' and 'otherness' into the category of the 'analogue', shifting from a proud 'really' to the humble 'as such'; 'the analogue, precisely, holds within it the force of re-enactment and of distancing, to the extent that being as is both being and not being' (Ricoeur 1984: 36). These concluding words, though representing an advance, leave a sense of incompleteness that was certainly felt by Paul Ricoeur himself who, not surprisingly, in subsequent years returned on different occasions on this subject, significantly in lectures dedicated to the analysis of the act of translating and to the semantic structure of translation (Ricoeur 2004).[10]

Note that in his reflections on this subject, Ricoeur does not refer to the task of the historian but, as we shall see, his considerations conform with what he had stated in the small book mentioned above, representing a refinement and a development of it;[11] since the first lecture in Stuttgart in 1997, he emphasized that the act of translating, as it was stated for the act of historical reconstruction, is based on a binary relationship between 'Sameness' and 'Otherness', resolved at the level of the 'Analogue'. The translator, just like the historian, is a mediator between an author or an oeuvre and a readership; the characteristic of this mediation is that the (past) authors or oeuvre use an 'Other' language in respect to the translator, who uses the 'Same' language of his readership.[12]

The anguish with which the previous book on the reality of historical past ended is here coherently taken up and sublimated in the 'bonheur' of the translator, who matching the 'Otherness' of the different (of the past) must practice a 'hospitality of language' (*hospitalité langagière*); the previous acceptance of the level of the 'Analogue', which appeared to be hesitant and resigned, now seems to be resolved more convincingly in a semantic structure characterized by a 'correspondence without equivalence' (*correspondence sans adequation*). This would be exactly the act of translating performed by the translator, and by historians acting as cultural translators; after all, as Ricoeur stated in the opening lesson held the following year in Paris, the translator/historian can only aim at an alleged equivalence, which cannot be based on a demonstrable identity. Once again, the translation is conceptualized as an equivalence without identity.[13]

At this point, Ricoeur turns to what we have identified as the central question for the task of the historian as a cultural translator: the question of intra-linguistic translation. As we have already seen with George Steiner, this issue seems to be the core not only of any theory of translation (although, as is known, Steiner did not like the concept of 'theory') but of any rigorous hermeneutics and philosophy of language. At bottom, intralinguistic and interlinguistic translation, called by Ricoeur *traduction interne* and *traduction externe*, imply the same act of understanding the 'Otherness' and trying to render this 'Otherness' understandable through the means of words, whether belonging to other languages or to the same language. Translating – Ricoeur states – is to say the same thing with other words, and in this vein the act of translating is perfectly associable to the act of explaining and understanding, for when we have to explain something to others in a better way we attempt to say the same thing with other words.[14]

Finally, stimulated by the book of the Hellenist Marcel Detienne (2008) on 'comparing the incomparable', Ricoeur deals with the problem of the translatability of words, texts and cultures; he clarifies from the beginning that when translating the translator does not start from the word but from the language. Summing up his previous reflections, Ricoeur concludes that the translation does not necessarily occur between two comparable words, texts or cultures; the greatest challenge for the translator, as for the historian, consists precisely in trying to translate the *intraduisible*, the 'Otherness'. In this case too, Ricoeur argument is perfectly consistent with Steiner's: the act of translating is a creative act which is repeated any time that a 'text' is translated.[15] Every time that a text is translated the translator gives it new life, enabling his linguistic community to understand it with new words and to appropriate it; otherwise, the reason for continually re-translate texts would be incomprehensible.[16]

This is in general an exact conceptualization of the work performed by the historian when confronting with past languages; the entire terminology used by the historian when reconstructing the past, also in the language of the historian's own linguistic community, is based on 'comparable' terms. Using present concepts and his own language, the historian restores concepts and languages of the past. Not, of course, as they 'really' were, an enterprise that would be impossible, but by using '*des équivalents sans identité*'. It needs to be pointed out that in this '*contruction de comparables*' the historian cannot simply render sense with sense, but must come to terms with the historical weight of language, with the constant tension between present language and historical past. With reference to ancient history, Neville Morley (1999: 81–2) has perceptively argued that

> we can come to understand the ancient world (and any other period of history, and any other culture) only through translation, finding equivalents in our language for their words, concepts and ideas. Inevitably, there is a risk of missing something important, or introducing something new by mistake, but this risk is inherent in *every* attempt at understanding the past [...] History involves a constant tension between sameness and difference; we have to translate antiquity into our own terms at the same time as we emphasise the difference between us and them.

I.3. From history and translation to history as translation

Taking stock of the difficult relationships between history and social theories at the end of the twentieth century, Peter Burke (1992: 21) noted that 'we are living in an age of blurred lines and open intellectual frontiers, an age which is at once exciting and confusing'; the traditional contribution given by linguistics, hermeneutics and semiology to the theoretical reflections in historiography has found new paths of research among those 'blurred lines'. In his now classic study *History and Social Theories*, Burke foregrounded the suspicious approach of historians to theory and their frequent recourse to the theoretical tools, concepts and models elaborated by sociologists, anthropologists, psychologists, economists, geographers and so on; it is worth noting that around the same time he was writing his text, Susan Bassnett and André Lefevere (1990) edited a collection of essays titled *Translation, History, and Culture*, followed two years later by a sourcebook on *Translation/History/Culture* (Lefevere 1992). Reflecting on this passage, Susann Bassnett (1998) argued that these publications testified to a 'cultural turn in translation studies'; she also urged undertaking a 'translation turn in cultural studies', which should be interdisciplinary in its approach, in line with postcolonial studies and gender studies.

After more than twenty years we can say that these wishes have largely come true and that the 'translation turn' has attracted the attention of scholars of various disciplines, with the differences and distances that always characterize a change of paradigms or simply shifts of perspective. At the end of her book devoted to this subject, Mary Snell-Hornby (2006) invited scholars in different disciplines to 'make dialogue, not war', resuming the title of a lecture she gave in November 2003 on the theme 'The Translation Turn in Cultural Studies'. On the whole, we have moved from a restricted and linguistic notion of translation to a broader and metaphorical one, which is more productive on a theoretical and transdisciplinary level,[17] but for which there is inevitably no lack of criticism. Rainer Guldin (2022: 26) has argued that scholars in translation studies should avoid limiting the concept of translation to a restricted linguistic horizon; while this must be considered more correct and pure, it is important to accept the possibility of having other metaphorical and extended notions of translation in different disciplinary domains, characterized by different presuppositions and different ends (see also Guldin 2018).

One of the major trends in this latter direction has touched on the relationships between history and translation, developed especially in the field of translation history. In a recent debate over the significance of translation history Theo Hermans (2021: 18) emphasized that he 'tried to find angles to look at translation from different viewpoints, including some that at first sight look very unpromising like, for example, [Niklas] Luhmann, who never talked about translation at all [...] And so, reading historians writing about historiography, I noticed that in recent decades they, too, have discovered translation'. It is an important and interesting testimony, considering the fact that historians and translators have developed their interests on the subject almost always independently from each other and that translation history has been a privileged field of studies for translation scholars; at the first international conference organized by the Translation and History Network, held in Tallinn (25–28 May 2022), participants were still mostly translation scholars.[18] Some years ago, Sergia Adamo (2006: 85) observed that the flourishing of translation history occurred in the course of a wide-ranging process of transformation of historiographical methods and theories; as a consequence, she invited scholars in translation studies to be aware of the fact that 'different methods of historiography and historical theories relate to different objects of studies'.

In fact, Anthony Pym (1992) long ago complained about the lack of history in translation history, at a time when this field of inquiry had not yet reached any clear definition, and some years later he devoted an entire monograph to *Method in Translation History* (1998). Only in 2001 did Liven D'hulst (2001) present an account on why and how translation histories should be written, since when the field of translation history has begun to acquire a more definite shape and some awareness of its methods and ends. Of course, scholars initially engaged in translation history worked especially in linguistic and literary environments, without a specific commitment in history, and their focus was generally assumed to be the reconstruction of the role played by translators and translations in history. In charting the future of translation history, Paul F. Bandia (2006: 46) maintained that a good starting point for translation historians could be 'to start viewing themselves as such – that is, as historians – rather than as translator scholars or practitioners masquerading as historians'. Evidently, this would require the creation of a new and interdisciplinary space not yet existing, based on a different training and having also different ends; according to Chris Rundle (2012: 239), translation historians should ask themselves 'not what history can tell us about translation but what translation can tell us about history'.

In subsequent studies Rundle (2014) has outlined the difficulties existing in approaching both research communities, historians and translators, also highlighting the significant absence of any thorough discussion of the philosophical implications of history in translation studies (Rundle 2021). All the same, in recent years studies under the label 'translating the past' have multiplied, ranging from medieval tales (Hedeman 2009), literature (Beal 2012), narratives (Santos 2019) and architecture (Hoppe 2019) to modern activities (Hernes 2020), from South Africa (Coombes 2000) to India (Zutshi 2011; Krishna Mehrotra 2019). In the meantime, here have been several special issues of translation journal and reviews (*Meta* 2004–2005; *Translation Studies* 2012; *Methis* 2012; *MonTi* 2013; *The Translator* 2014; *Przekładaniec* 2019; *Translating and Interpreting* 2019) devoted to the subject of translation history (see Rundle 2022); recently a new journal has been founded with the aim of contributing to the ongoing interdisciplinary conversation on translation and interpreting history (*Chronotopos. A Journal of Translation History*: 2019–). Julia Richter (2020), who is member of the editorial team of this journal, has also provided an insightful overview of the perspectives and methods of translation history.

For reasons of space, it is not possible to provide a complete outline of the problems, achievements and outcomes characterizing this newly formed disciplinary domain (for an early critical overview of studies in translation history, see Howland 2003). However, I cannot conclude my remarks here without mentioning two outstanding achievements within translation history, representing two major theoretical pillars in the construction of a more solid bridge between translators and historians. I refer to Theo Hermans' (2022) textbook *Translation and History* and to the monograph *La Traducción y La(s) Historia(s)* by M.ª Carmen África Vidal Claramonte (2018). In fact, the first represents more than a textbook for students and scholars, as stated in the preface; it contains not only important insights concerning translation history but also important clarifications regarding the conception of history as seen through the lens of translation. Indeed, Hermans' approach to history and translation is based on the essential consideration that history and translation are an integral part of our lived experience of the world, since

> history writings and the study of history deal with the past but are anchored in the present. This is partly because all we have for making sense of the past are our contemporary ideas and concepts, and partly because the primary data for historical studies are those traces from the past that are still with us today, whether in the form of memories, of existing knowledge or of material items such as documents or other objects.
>
> (Hermans 2022: i)

Divided into six chapters rich in theoretical insights, this textbook can be considered a big step from 'history and translation' towards 'history as translation'.

Without doubt the most clear and important monograph in this direction is Vidal Claramonte's *La Traducción y La(s) Historia(s)*, where it is plainly stated that the act of translation is an act of interpretation, and to interpret means to live. Thus she takes as point of departure the following definition: writing history is like re-writing realities, and in this process the historian becomes an intralingual translator.[19] Referring to Hayden White and Alun Muslow, Vidal Claramonte states that 'el historiador es un traductor', adding that the translator is an author who re-writes, taking into account the first translator, the historian, who has already provided an interpretation of reality.[20] Some brief considerations can be introduced here. Vidal Claramonte places herself along an interpretative line starting from Walter Benjamin and running through French intellectuals like Derrida, Lyotard, Barthes, Bourdieu, Foucault and de Certeau; on the contrary, the contributions by the German conceptual historians and by the 'Cambridge School' of Intellectual History figures much less. Also as a consequence of this choice she advances a conception of history essentially interpreted as a history of winners and losers, as if all writings of history were inspired by the prevailing (hidden or open) political, cultural and economic dominant interests; this post-structuralist vision of history assumes a structuralist vision of society conceived as a never-ending struggle for power between classes and groups in society, something that is widespread in post-colonial and gender studies as well as in other recent historiographical currents.

However, the conception of history as translation of the past is not motivated by ideological bias but is an epistemological and cognitive achievement; in his preface to Vidal Claramonte's book, recapitulating some of his thoughts on translation and rewriting in the age of post-translation studies (Gentzler 2016), Edwin Gentzler suggests that historians and translators, while trying to be 'objective' in their writings, reproduce their individual points of view unconsciously.[21] However, these unintended behaviours are not always the outcome of power relations but are, instead, the normal relationship that historians and translators establish with historical sources and actors. Historians and translators inevitably 'translate' in the act of speaking and writing, simply because they use their language, which is placed in a specific historical context, regardless of their ideological choices; in this process they must try to be increasingly aware of what explain the actions performed by historical actors and what determines their own reconstructions, at the epistemological and cognitive level. Perhaps a contribution in this direction could be made by the flourishing fields of cognitive translation studies (CTS) and cognitive translations and interpretative studies (CTIS), but the results are still to come; introducing a recent collection of articles in *Linguistica Antverpiensa*, Xiao (2020: 10) and Muñoz Martín conclude that 'sixty years of works have had a modest impact on translator and interpreter training, but we still face challenges such as the need to build and test theoretical models to account for the peculiarities of translational cognition, and the critical assessment and streamlining of our research methods'.[22]

Taking inspiration from the conviction that the writing of history can be considered as an act of translation, epistemologically and cognitively, this book brought together historians with specialisms in different eras and disciplinary areas and scholars in translation studies with a keen interest in history and theory. The main focus of the volume is to examine sources and historical actors as 'translators' between past and present, relating the significance of their presence in history to the different historical contexts in which they occurred and were re-enacted. This perspective involves a strict consideration of the interlingual and intralingual problems raised in different historical contexts, as well as an analysis of para-texts and the different forms of transplantation and multimodal translations. Taking into account recent debates on temporality and 'regimes of historicity', the individual contributions to this volume outline a new conception of history as translation of the past, offering some practical and theoretical examples of historical analysis deriving from this conception. As argued by Peter Burke (2010) developing a concept elaborated by Mikhail Bakhtin, a 'polyphonic history' is needed, in which the voices of the different historical actors are heard and foregrounded; thinking of the epistemological and cognitive aspects emphasized in this volume, it is also possible to state that a 'general theory of relativity' in history, mixing times and spaces in complex relationships, is to be hoped for the future.

There could not be a better starting point for this volume than Herodotus, whose historical method intended as 'translation of the past' is illustrated by Richard P. Martin in the first chapter. Of course, Herodotus was a cultural translator as well, inevitably given his place in the translational nodes of an eastern Mediterranean cultural amalgam, and it is just this double position as diachronic translator, between past and present, and synchronic translator, between languages and cultures, that makes his role as a Greek historian interesting and complex. According to Martin, it is possible to suppose that Herodotus intuited the etymology of *historiê* – the art, not of 'research' in our sense but of viewing as a witness. Indeed, he judged the authenticity and faithfulness of 'his sources' on the base of a double criterion: as *hermêneus*, that is, as contemporary interpreters of languages and historical deeds, and as 'oracles' which were not only considered prophecies for the future but also, in hindsight, witnesses of past events. Especially in this latter case, the historian was required to be skilled in 'translating metaphorically' the divine message received and to interpret it correctly. Although, as Martin observes, the oracular utterances within the *Histories* have prompted many studies, they have not been scrutinized in relation to translation, which requires that one think more abstractly about the semiotic mechanisms that make them work. Herodotus as a historian is an example of multimodal translator, since his *Histories* 'translate' oral testimonies, gestures, images, epigraphs, signs, oracles, writing them 'all down for an unknown – even Greekless – future'.

The attention to the future reception of classical texts and to the different literary and theatrical contexts into which they were 'transplanted' is at the core of Lorna Hardwick's contribution in the second chapter, which focuses on two subjects and three authors/translators. The two subjects are on the one hand the traditional theme of 'fidelity', refreshed in a new perspective, and, on the other, the related area of 'authenticity', addressed in the light of the different contexts into which narratives were placed. The three authors reviewed are Aeschylus (in his *Persians*), Homer and Thucydides (in his *History of the Peloponnesian War*), respectively, interpreted by the scholar/translator Edith Hall, by the poet/translator Alice Oswald and by the dramaturg/translator John Barton. Hardwick's analysis concentrates on the different temporalities which affect, epistemologically and cognitively, the different narratives, genres and forms of translation, and on the meta-narratives intended as 'shorthand for how the work is rightly or wrongly perceived and categorized subsequently, both in itself (e.g. the *Iliad* as poem of war) AND in relation to wider categories (e.g. the impact of war on human suffering and behaviour, lament, memory studies, memorialization)'. For example, she highlights how the destruction of the Acropolis became the subject for 'transhistorical studies of recovery from trauma', how the death of Homeric heroes furthered meta-narratives 'about the notion of a "good death" and about the relationship between memorialization and the realities of war', and finally how episodes from the Peloponnesian War were framed into the narratives of the recent invasion of Iraq.

Karen Bennett scrutinizes the translational processes at work '*upstream*' of the New Testament in Chapter 3, where she focuses on the chains of transmission that led from those that had witnessed the Jesus events at first hand, passing through untold numbers of scribes, editors, translators and commentators, to the actual authors of the gospels. In fact, the Four Evangelists transformed the flesh-and-blood man that was the historical Jesus into the Son of God, saviour of mankind, and this goal was achieved through multiple translational processes which Karen Bennett retraces in detail. Firstly, she introduces the different theories advanced with regard to the chronological and logical priorities between the gospels and their possible sources, observing that in the vertical processes of intralingual (in Greek) or interlingual (from Aramaic and Coptic) translations 'we can expect there to have been some level of adjustment', due to their different constraints and norms; Mark, for example, is considered by many the author of the first gospel and the 'interpreter' (*hermēneutēs*) of Peter, providing different forms of translations or adaptations in this role, though he tried to be faithful to the word received (heard or read). By the same token, the Gospels of Matthew and Luke are considered in their specific literary traditions and cultural contexts, respectively, as expressions of Jewish and Hellenistic 'translations' of the life of Jesus; after that, attention is devoted to the translational processes involved in oral traditions, which would have tended to favour the transmutation of the original narratives, 'as elements are added, omitted and reconfigured to suit new contexts of reception', and to the constraints present in the transmission of the Jesus stories (perception, language, style and genre, patronage, universe of discourse).

These set of norms and constraints are integral part of what Peter Burke calls 'cultures of translation', which face a fundamental dilemma between 'domestication' and 'foreignizing'. Chapter 4 is devoted to exploring the different strategies adopted by historians and translators in facing this dilemma; here Burke introduces an extensive literature ranging from the fifteenth century to the present day. The Renaissance sense of the past was functional to the formation of a new 'culture of translation' more attentive to the discovery of forgery, especially through the analysis of styles and genres; of course, this implied a more acute awareness of the different forms of anachronism operating in the act of translation and, therefore, of the costs of the choices between 'domestication' and 'foreignizing'. Distance of time is similar to distance of place, and as a consequence anthropologists and missionaries were forced to face the same dilemma, starting from the translation of the word 'God', as in the case of China and India, where early modern Jesuits such as Matteo Ricci and Roberto De' Nobili might be described 'as free translators of Christianity'; in a similar fashion, anthropologists such as Edward Evans-Pritchard considered the objective of their discipline to be a 'translation from one culture to another', requiring 'to translate a foreign culture into the language of one's own'. In the case of temporal distance, some authors and translators are inclined to historical renderings which would favour a more direct contact with the past, thus privileging forms of archaism, while others prefer to be more understandable to contemporary audiences, picking out modern terms for their translations; one possible way out for historians who meet the dilemma of translating the past without committing 'violence', Burke notes, is to adopt a form of 'polyphonic history', which also includes forms of 'careful anachronism'.

Chapters 5 and 6 have been entrusted to two of the most authoritative interpreters of Max Weber and Reinhart Koselleck, respectively, to Keith Tribe and Kari Palonen. In Chapter 5 Tribe deals with the use of the term-concept '*Chance*' in Max Weber's *Economy and Society* and with the different problems raised by the translation and interpretation of this term/concept; his contribution shows how central the problem of translatability is for historical inquiry and historical understanding. Indeed, in his influential 'Americanization' of Weber's thought, Talcott Parsons opted to paraphrase the word '*Chance*', or simply translate it by 'advantage' and 'expectation', obliterating the word '*Chance*' from Weber's vocabulary. Forty-five years after Parsons' translation of *Economy and Society*, Ralph Dahrendof drew attention to the extensive use of the word '*Chance*' in the original edition, and in recent years different scholars have emphasized the importance of this term-concept in the Weberian theoretical perspective. In joining this debate, Tribe shows that Weber's use of '*Chance*' emerged from a dispute on historical method involving Eduard Meyer at the beginning of the twentieth century. To achieve an adequate understanding of the fundamental concepts of causality and probability in Max Weber's writings, Tribe identifies the shifts in the meaning of '*Chance*' as used by German scholars in the later nineteenth century. Crucial in this context were Johannes von Kries' writings about probabilistic causality and the associated concept of *Spielräume*. Kries had formerly been a colleague of Weber in Freiburg, and Weber drew on Kries' argument about probability in developing his concept of '*Chance*' as a theoretical tool to address the relationship between motivation and causal explanation.

In Chapter 6 Kari Palonen provides a thorough analysis of the expression 'We Politicians', reconstructing the parliamentary plenary debates of particular European countries and languages through which the term 'politicians' started to be used in a positive sense; to do this he has recourse to the theoretical tool of 'paradiastole' elaborated by Quentin Skinner for historical inquiry, interpreted in particular as a 'neutralizing translation practice' reached by means of rhetorical redescriptions of terms. Palonen follows different paths and stages, beginning with the replacement of 'the advisors to princes of the ancient and early-modern period with parliamentary politicians'; between the nineteenth and twentieth centuries the general process of neutralization of the term 'politicians' would have to pass through a prism formed of the interconnected processes of democratization, parliamentarization and bureaucratization, professionalizing politics. Two major issues were at stake: party patronage and the payment of 'politicians'. In the Francophone area this process of neutralization occurred through the distinction between *hommes politiques* and *politiciens*. In the French Third Republic and in contemporary Belgium *politicien* remained mostly a pejorative term; after the Second World War the term *politicien* seems to have become obsolete in France, while the French-speaking Swiss parliamentarians had no problem with referring to themselves as *politiciens*. Lastly, Palonen examines the phases through which the expression 'we politicians' became a speech act intended to neutralize the pejorative meaning of the term 'politician', thanks especially to the shared identity of parliamentarians.

The following two chapters, by Alexandra Lianeri and Karin Littau, deal with theoretical issues linked to temporality, translation and history. Lianeri's contribution (Chapter 7) delves into the 'the temporal relatedness and excess of concepts and metanarratives of historical understanding' in translated history; it explores how the idea of translating the past affects the structure of historical understanding in the analysis of Greek and Roman concepts, which are considered 'not external to categories of understanding but, also, internal to them'. In other words, these concepts have a transtemporal life and live into our historiographical categories, overcoming spatio-temporal and logical-linguistic borders; at last, they are mixed with our categories of understanding and delivered to the future, in a continuous movement which creatively modifies norms and constraints through infinite acts of translation-transmission. Lianeri critically discusses the different approaches to the problem of translation in history laid out by Arthur Lovejoy, by the Cambridge Group of political thought (Quentin Skinner and John Pocock) and by Reinhart Koselleck; her analysis of history as translation of the past focuses on the following issues: '(a) the thick time of conceptuality in and through which historical understanding is performed, (b) the distribution and redistribution of borders of time that establish antiquity's distance or proximity and (c) the construction of historical sensibilities involving distributions of the sensible in a moving present'. Along this line of reasoning, Lianeri further refines the analysis of 'a regime of untraslatables' provided in a previous study, insisting on the complex temporal tension into which the work of the historian as a translator between past, present and future is performed; she plainly claims that 'concept's unveiling of multiple times in a specific historical present may be conceptualized as translated history'.

In Chapter 8 Littau extends the breadth and depth of the concept of translation, incorporating the idea that 'translation itself emerges from the earth'; indeed, she does not so much consider the translation of literary texts as the translational processes inscribed in nature. This approach takes inspiration from Novalis' theory of translation and connects it with recent debates on the Anthropocene; in so doing, Littau aims to overcome the nature/culture divide and to free scholars from an 'anthrocentric worldview'. Material objects are no longer media which affect cultural expressions and translations, as in her previous studies, but are themselves agents with their own voices and languages; the entire world, made up by animate and inanimate agents, has diverse natural languages which evolve *in* time through never-ending 'translations' of materials. It is this 'entangledness' (*Verbundenseyn*) of the human and the natural that makes it possible to imagine 'communicative possibilities with nature that also involve translation', as in the case of Ursula Le Guin, and allow to speak of eco-translation, biosemiotic translation, geo-linguistics, geo-media and geo-translation (Cronin); this perspective leads to a natural history of translation and media, in which the process of translation is seen as a stratification process entailing that 'we open the book of nature to pay attention not only to what is there written, but to what it is written upon', as literally expressed by the German word *Übersetzung*. Human time is embedded in the deeper time of the earth, which grows strata by strata and trans-forms stones, trees, mountains and so on; all these elements have languages which need to be correctly interpreted and which materially 'translate' themselves from one form into another.[23]

The stratigraphic metaphor of history, derived by Reinhart Koselleck, is also examined by Luigi Alonzi, who in Chapter 9 proposes an interpretation of the historian's task as a translation of the past; starting from the concept of history as contemporary history, as developed by Benedetto Croce and disseminated in the English-speaking world by Robin Collingwood, Alonzi takes into consideration the arguments regarding the relationships between history and translation advanced by eminent historians such as Quentin Skinner, John Pocock and Peter Burke. Then, taking inspiration from an essay by Kari Palonen, particular attention is devoted to Koselleck's theoretical assumption according to which there is (or, at least, there should be) a meta-language which would constitute a necessary term of comparison for the translation of past words and concepts; the thesis put forward in this chapter is that, in fact, such a meta-language does not exist and could not exist, our own language being the only means through which we can translate past words and concepts. The distinction between onomasiology and semasiology, originally introduced in linguistic studies and adopted by Koselleck for historical analysis, could be of help in coping with this issue; if exploited in all its implications, it would avoid some possible epistemological aporias in the conception of history as a translation of the past. Above all, this should lead to awareness of the fact that the act of writing history, that is, the act of translating past words and concepts, is constitutively and unavoidably anachronistic, and that the only way out of this impasse is a form of conscious and careful anachronism. Furthermore, this anachronism should be conceived as a form of synchronism, since language in action continually resets and suspends time, linking past, present and future.

Notes

1. In the 1950 Robert Ranulf Marett Lecture, entitled *Social Anthropology: Past and Present*, while criticizing Malinowski's and Radcliffe-Brown's social anthropology, Evans-Pritchard sought a more rigorous relationship between history and anthropology; he returned on the subject in 1961, in a presentation titled *Anthropology and History* (see Evans-Pritchard 1961).
2. The essay was first published as a preface to Charles Baudelaire's *Tableaux Parisiens* (1923); its translation first appeared in *Illuminations* (1968) – a posthumous collection of essays edited by Hannah Arendt: see, for the references, Mathelinda Nabougodi (2021).
3. Walter Benjamin, *Über den Begriff der Geschichte* (1940), posthumously published in 1950 and reproduced in *Walter Benjamin gesammelte Schriften*, vol. I–2, Suhrkamp, Frankfurt am Main, 1974, pp. 693–704.
4. The quotation comes from Venuti (1995). I also refer here to the introduction to Susan Bassnett, André Lefevere (eds), *Translation, History & Culture*, Pinter Publishers, London, 1990 (reprinted Cassel 1995), co-written by Susan Bassnett and André Lefevere and titled 'The Cultural Turn in Translation Studies'.
5. On the subject see Macedo (2006); Sturge (2009); Muñoz-Calvo (2010); Conway (2012); Harding (2018); Rubel (2020).
6. On this book see the review by Conway (2019).
7. Jakobson (1971: 233): 'We distinguish three ways of interpreting a verbal sign: it may be translated into another sign of the same language, into another language, or into another, nonverbal system of symbols. These three kinds of translation are to be differently labelled:
   1) Intralingual translation or *rewording* is an interpretation of verbal signs by means of other signs of the same language.
   2) Interlingual translation or *translating proper* is an interpretation of verbal signs by means of some other languages.
   3) Intersemiotic translation or transmutation is an interpretation of verbal signs of nonverbal signs systems.'
8. This conceptualization has been summarized by Steiner in his important preface to the third edition (1998: xii).
9. These are the titles of the chapters constituting the book of Paul Ricoeur, *The Reality of Historical Past*, Marquette University Press, [Milwaukee (Wisconsin)] 1984. This small book is generally neglected and contains an excellent synthesis of the subjects dealt with by Ricoeur in the much better known three-volume work *Temps et récit*, Seuil, Paris, 1983–5, translated into English by Kathleen Blamey and David Pellauer as *Time and Narrative*, The University of Chicago Press, Chicago and London, 1984–8; a section of the third volume bears the title *The Reality of the Past*.
10. The first chapter of his book *Sur la traduction* (2004) contains the lecture held at the Institut historique allemand in Stuttgart (15 April 1997), the second chapter is the opening lesson to the Faculté de théologie protestante in Paris (October 1998), while the third chapter was an unpublished essay. See also Ricoeur (2006).
11. Ricoeur's intellectual itinerary after 'the reality of historical past' has been recently retraced following a different path, centred on *La mémoire, l'histoire et l'oubli* and on *Soi-même comme un autre*, by Jeffrey Andrew Barash (2017); see also Sabina Loriga (2001), and Lisa Foran (2012).

12 Ricoeur (2004: 9): 'Auteur étranger, lectur habitant la même langue que le traducteur'.
13 Ricoeur 2004: 40: 'une bonne traduction ne peut viser qu'à une *équivalence* présumé, non fondé dans une *identité* de sens démontrable. Une équivalence sans identité'.
14 Ricoeur 2004: 45–6: 'Je partirai de ce fait massif charctéristique de l'usage de nos langue: il est toujours possible de *dire la même chose autrement*. C'est ce que nous faison quand nous définissent en mot par un autre du même lexique, comme font tous les dictionnaires. Peirce, dans sa science sémiotique, place se phénomène au centre de la réflexivité du language sur lui-même. Mais c'est aussi ce que nous faison quand nous reformulons un argument qui n'a pas été compris. Nous disons que nous l'expliquons, c'est-à-dire que nous en déployons les plis. Or dire la même chose autrement – *autrement dit* – c'est ce que faisait tout à l'heure le traducteur de langue étrangère. Nous retrouvons ainsi, à l'intérieur de notre communauté languagière, la même énigme du même, de la signification même, l'introuvable sans identité, censé rendre équivalente les deux versions du même propos [...] En même temps, un pont est jeté entre la traduction interne, je l'appelle ainsi, et la traduction externe, à savoir que à l'intérieur de la même communauté, la compréhension demande au moins deux interlocuteurs: ce ne sont pas certes des étrangers, mais déjà des autres, des autres proches, si l'on veut; c'est ainsi que Husserl, parlant de la connaissance d'autrui, appelle l'autre quotidien *der Fremde*, l'étranger. Il y a de l'étranger dans tout autres. C'est à pluseirus qu'on définit, qu'on reformule, qu'on explique, qu'on cherche à *dire la même chose autrement*'.
15 Ricoeur 2004: 66: 'Grandeur de la traduction, risque de la traduction: trahison créatrice de l'original, appropriation également créatrice par la langue d'acceuil; *contruction du comparable* [...] Mais n'est-ce pas ce qui était arrivé à plusieurs époque de notre propre culture, lorsque les Septante ont traduit en grec la *Bible* hébraïque, dans ce que nous appellons la «*Septante*», et que peuvent à loisir critiquer les specialistes de l'hébreu seul. Et saint Jérôme récidive avec la *Vulgate*, construction d'un comparable latin. Mais avant Jérôme, les Latin avaient créé des comparable, en décidant pour nous tous que *arêtê* se traduit par *virtus*, *polis* par *urbs* et *politès* par *cives*. Pour rester dans le domain biblique, on peut dire que Luther a non seulement construit un comparable en traduisant en allemande la Bible, en la «germanisant», comme il osait dire, face au latin de saint Jérôme, mais qu'il a créé la langue allemande, comme comparable au latin, au grec de la *Septante*, et à l'hébreu de la Bible'.
16 As regards the creative value of re-translations, see also Venuti (2005), and Venuti (2013).
17 Think, for example, of the foundation of *Translation. A transdisciplinary journal* in 2011.
18 Two very recent book series devoted to translation history came from within translation studies, one published by Springer (2019–) and one by Routledge (2021–).
19 Vidal Claramonte (2018: 13): 'Traducir es interpretar. Interpretar es vivir. Esta es la definición que tomaré como punto de partida: escribir la historia es reescribir realidades, y en ese proceso el historiador se torna de traductor intralingüístico'.
20 Vidal Claramonte (2018: 15): 'Las teorías sobre la historiografía de Hayden White, Alun Muslow y otros muchos utilizan ese verbo, "traducir", y arguyen que lo *historiador es un traductor*. Yo me atrevería a añadir que el traductor es un reescritor que deberá tener en cuenta el primer traductor, el historiador, que ya a hecho una lectura de la realidad'.

21 Vidal Claramonte (2018: ix–x): 'Por muy "objetivos" que intenden ser los historiadores, no pueden evitar manipular los retratos que hacen del pasado para sustener así sus propria creencias personales sobre el presente. Lo mismo lo occurre a muchos traductores que dicen ser neutrales pero que inconscientemente introducen elementos de sus proprias visiones del mundo an el proceso de traducción'.
22 Among the recent initiatives in this field, there is an international network – *Translation/Research/Empiricism/Cognition (TREC)* – which has since 2017 organized a biennial international conference on Translation, Interpreting, and Cognition. See also on the subject, at least, Rojo (2015); Yi (2020); Muñoz Martín (2020); Hong (2021).
23 On this subject see the recent volume edited by Jordheim (2022b).

References

Adamo, Sergia (2006), 'Microhistory of Translation', in Georges L. Bastin and Paul F. Bandia (eds.), *Charting the Future of Translation History*, 81–100, Ottawa: University of Ottawa Press.

Asad, Talal (1986), 'The Concept of Cultural Translation in British Social Anthropology', in James Clifford and George E. Marcus (eds.), *Writing Culture: The Poetics and Politics of Ethnography*, 141–64, Berkeley: University of California Press.

Bandia, Paul F. (2006), 'The Impact of Postmodern Discourse in the History of Translation', in Georges L. Bastin and Paul F. Bandia (eds.), *Charting the Future of Translation History*, 45–58, Ottawa: University of Ottawa Press.

Barash, Jeffrey Andrew (2017), 'Qu'est-ce que la "réalité" du passé historique? Réflexions à partir de la théorie de l'histoire chez Ricoeur', *Le Télémaque*, 51 (1): 89–106.

Bassnett, Susan (1998), 'The Translation Turn in Cultural Studies', in Susan Bassnett and André Lefevere (eds.), *Constructing Cultures. Essays on Literary Translation*, 123–40, Bristol: Multilingual Matters.

Bassnett, Susan André Lefevere (eds.) (1990), *Translation, History & Culture*, London: Pinter Publishers.

Beal, Jane and Mark Bradshaw Busebee (eds.) (2012), *Translating the Past: Essays on Medieval Literature in Honour of Marijane Osborn*, Tempe: Arizona Center for Medieval and Renaissance Studies Press.

Benjamin, Walter (1974), 'Über den Begriff der Geschichte (1940)', in *Walter Benjamin gesammelte Schriften*, vol. I-2, 693–704, Frankfurt am Main: Suhrkamp.

Burke, Peter (1992), *History and Social Theory*, Cambridge: Polity Press.

Burke, Peter (2007a), 'Cultures of Translation in Early Modern Europe', in Peter Burke and Ronnie Po-chia Hsia (eds.), *Cultural Translation in Early Modern Europe*, Cambridge: Cambridge University Press.

Burke, Peter (2007b), 'Lost (and found) in Translation: A Cultural History of Translators and Translating in Early Modern Europe', *European Review*, 15 (1): 83–94.

Burke, Peter (2010), 'Cultural History as Polyphonic History', *Arbor*, 186 (743): 479–86.

Conway, Kyle (2012), 'Cultural Translation', in Yves Gambier and Luc van Doorslaer (eds.), *Handbook of Translation Studies*, vol. 3, 21–5, Amsterdam: John Benjamins.

Conway, Kyle (2019), 'What Is Cultural Translation?', *Journal of Cultural Analysis and Social Change*, 4 (2): 17.

Coombes, Annie E. (2000), 'Translating the Past: Apartheid Monuments in Post-apartheid South-Africa', in Avtar Brah and Annie Coombes (eds.), *Hybridity and Its Discontent. Politics, Science, Culture*, 173–97, New York: Routledge.
Detienne, Marcel (2008), *Comparing the Incomparable*, translated by Janet Lloyd, Stanford: Stanford University Press.
D'hulst, Liven (2001), 'Why and How to Write Translation Histories', *CROP*, 6: 21–32.
Evans-Pritchard E. E. (1961), *Anthropology and History*, Manchester: Manchester University Press.
Foran, Lisa (2012), 'Translation as a Path to the Other: Derrida and Ricoeur', in Arnd Witte and Theo Harden (eds.), *Intercultural Studies and Foreign Language Learning*, vol. 2, 75–86, Oxford: Peter Lang.
Gentzler, Edwin (2016), *Translation and Rewriting in the Age of Post-Translation Studies*, Abingdon: Routlegde.
Guldin, Rainer (2018), *Translation as Metaphor*, London and New York: Routledge.
Guldin, Rainer (2022), 'Translation as Metaphor Revisited. On the Promises and Pitfalls of Semantic and Epistemological Overflowing', in Mona Baker (ed.), *Unsettling Translation. Studies in Honour of Theo Hermans*, 15–28, Abingdon: Routledge.
Harding, Sue-Ann and Ovidi Carbonell Cortés (eds.) (2018), *The Routledge Handbook of Translation and Culture*, New York: Routledge.
Hedeman, Anne D. (2009), *Translating the Past. Laurent De Premierfait and Boccaccio's De Casibus*, Los Angeles: Jean Paul Getty Museums Publications.
Hermans, Theo (2022), *Translation and History: A Textbook*, Abingdon: Routledge.
Hermans, Theo and Chris Rundle (2021), 'The Significance of Translation History – A Roundtable Discussion', *Chronotopos*, 3 (1): 17–30.
Hernes, Tor and Majken Schultz (2020), 'Translating the Distant into the Present: How Actors Address Distant Past and Future Events through Situated Activity', *Organization Theory*, https://doi.org/10.1177/2631797719900999.
Hong, Wenije and Caroline Rossi (2021), 'The Cognitive Turn in Metaphor Translation Studies: A Critical Overview', *Journal of Translation Studies*, 5 (2): 83–115.
Hoppe, Stephan (2019), 'Translating the Past: Local Romanesque Architecture in Germany and Its Fifteenth Century Reinterpretation', in Karl A. E. Henenkeland and Konrad A. Ottenheim (eds.), *The Quest for an Appropriate Past in Literature, Art and Architecture*, 511–85, Leiden: Brill.
Howland, Douglas (2003), 'The Predicament of Ideas in Culture: Translation and Historiography', *History and Theory (Forum on Translation and Historiography)*, 42 (1): 45–60.
Jakobson, Roman (1971), 'On the Linguistic Aspects of Translation', in *Words and Language*, vol. 2 of Roman Jakobson, *Selected Writings*, The Hague-Paris: Mouton.
Jordheim, Helge (ed.) (2022b), 'Fossilization, or the Matter of Historical Future', *History and Theory*, 61 (1): 4–26.
Krishna Mehrotra, Arvind (2019), *Translating the Indian Past: And Other Literary Histories*, Delhi: Permanent Black.
Lefevere, André (ed.) (1992), *Translation/History/Culture. A Sourcebook*, London and New York: Routledge.
Loriga, Sabina (2001), 'Paul Ricoeur e il compito dello storico', *Aperture*, 10: 15–34.
Macedo, Ana Gabriela and Margarida Esteves Pereira (eds.) (2006), *Identity and Cultural Translation. Women's Writings in English in a European Context*, Oxford: Peter Lang.
Macfarlane, Alan (1988), 'Anthropology and History', in John Cannon et al. (eds.), *The Blackwell Dictionary of Historians*, Oxford: Blackwell.

Maitland, Sarah (2017), *What Is Cultural Translation?*, London: Bloomsbury.
Morley, Neville (1999), *Writing Ancient History*, Ithaca, NY: Cornell University Press.
Muñoz-Calvo, Micaela and Carmen Buesa Gomez (eds.) (2010), *Translation and Cultural Identity: Selected Essays on Translation and Cross-Cultural Communication*, Newcastle upon Tyne: Cambridge Scholars publishing.
Muñoz Martín, Ricardo and S. L. Halverson (eds.) (2020), *Multilungual Mediated Communication and Cognition*, Abingdon: Routledge.
Nabougodi, Mathelinda (2021), 'Pure Language', in Mona Baker and Gabriela Saldanha (eds.), *Routledge Encyclopedia of Translations Studies*, 3rd edn, Abingdon: Routledge.
Pym, Anthony (1992), 'Complaint concerning the Lack of History in Translation Histories', *Livivs*, 1: 1–11.
Pym, Anthony (1998), *Method in Translation History*, Manchester: St. Jerome Publishing (2nd edn 2014), Abingdon: Routledge.
Rendall, Steven (1997), 'The Translator's Task, Walter Benjamin (Translation)', *TTR: Traduction, Terminologie, Rédaction*, 10 (2): 151–65.
Richter, Julia (2020), *Translationshistoriographie. Perspektiven & Methoden*, Wien – Hamburg: New Academic Press.
Ricoeur, Paul (1983–5), *Temps et récit*, Paris: Seuil.
Ricoeur, Paul (1984), *The Reality of Historical Past*, Milwaukee, WI: Marquette University Press.
Ricoeur, Paul (1984–8), *Time and Narrative*, English translated by Kathleen Blamey and David Pellauer, Chicago and London: The University of Chicago Press.
Ricoeur, Paul (2004), *Sur la traduction*, Paris: Bayard.
Ricoeur, Paul (2006), *On Translation*, translated by Eileen Brennan, with an introduction by Richard Kearney, London and New York: Routledge.
Rojo, Ana (2015), 'Translation Meets Cognitive Science: The Imprint of Translation in Cognitive Processing', *Multilingua*, 34 (6): 721–46.
Rubel, Paula G. and Abraham Rosman (eds.) (2020), *Translating Cultures: Perspectives on Translation and Anthropology*, New York: Routledge.
Rundle, Chris (2012), 'Translation as an Approach to History', *Translation Studies*, 5 (2): 232–40.
Rundle, Chris (2014), 'Theories and Methodologies of Translation History: The Value of an Interdisciplinary Approach', *The Translator* (special issue on 'Theories and Methodologies of Translation History'), 20 (1): 2–8.
Rundle, Chris (2021), 'Historiography', in Mona Baker and Gabriela Saldanha (eds.), *Routledge Encyclopedia of Translations Studies*, 3rd edn, Abingdon: Routledge.
Rundle, Christopher (2022), 'Introduction. The Historiography of Translation and Interpreting', in Christopher Rundle (ed.), *The Routledge Handbook of Translation History*, Abingdon: Routledge.
Santos, Spenser (2019), *Translating the Past: Medieval English Exodus narratives*, PhD thesis, University of Iowa, https://doi.org/10.17077/etd.3ak5-ork1.
Snell-Hornby, Mary (1999), 'Communicating in the Global Village: On Language, Translation, and Cultural Identity', *Current Issues In Language and Society*, 6 (2): 103–20.
Snell-Hornby, Mary (2006), *The Turns of Translation Studies. New Paradigms or Shifting Viewpoints?*, Amsterdam/Philadelphia: John Benjamins Publishing Company.
Steiner, George (1975), *After Babel. Aspects of Language and Translation*, Oxford: Oxford University Press.
Steiner, George (1998), *After Babel. Aspects of Language and Translation*, 3rd edn, Oxford: Oxford University Press.

Sturge, Kate (2009), 'Cultural Translation', in Mona Baker and Gabriela Saldanha (eds.), *Routledge Encyclopedia of Translation Studies*, 2nd edn, 67–70, London and New York: Routledge.
The Translator (2017), special issue 'International English and Translation', edited by Karen Bennett and Rita Queiroz de Barros, 23 (4).
Trivedi, Harish (1995), 'Translating Culture vs Cultural Translation', *91st meridian*, 4 (1) (spring 2005). iwp.uiowa.edu/91st/vol4-num1/Translating Culture vs Cultural Translation.
Trivedi, Harish (2007), 'Translating Culture vs Cultural Translation', in Paul St-Pierre and Prafulla C. Kar (eds.), *In Translation – Reflections, Refractions, Transformations*, 277–87, Amsterdam/Philadelphia: John Benjamins Publishing Company.
Venuti, Lawrence (1995), *The Translator's Invisibility*, London and New York: Routledge.
Venuti, Lawrence (2005), 'Translation, History, Narrative', *Meta*, 50 (3): 800–16.
Venuti, Lawrence (2013), 'Retranslations. The Creative Value', in *Translations Change Everything: Theory and Practice*, 96–108, London and New York: Routledge.
Vidal Claramonte, M.ª Carmen África (2018), *La traducción y la(s) historia(s). Nuevas vías para la investigación*, Granada: Editorial Comares.
Xiao, Kairong and Ricardo Muñoz Martín (2020), 'Cognitive Translation Studies: Models and Methods at the Cutting Edge', *Linguistica Antverpiensa*, 19: 1–24.
Yi, Chen (2020), 'An Overview of Cognitive Translation Studies', *Canadian Social Science*, 16 (5): 39–43.
Zutshi, Chitralekha (2011), 'Translating the Past: Rethinking Rajatarangini Narratives in Colonial India', *The Journal of Asian Studies*, 70 (1): 5–27.

1

Herodotus translating the past

Richard P. Martin

Is the past a foreign language? Does the historian operate like a bilingual go-between? Can the metaphor of 'translation' clarify the cognitive processes of those who somehow come to understand and transmit events they never personally experienced?

Re-reading Herodotus paves an approach to such questions. His *Histories* would seem to have necessitated translation in several senses, as they mix oral lore, political myths and professional scribal records, from tribes, empires and city-states. Moreover, he himself embodies the translational nodes of an eastern Mediterranean cultural amalgam, not just in his travels but even in his genealogy. An 'Ionised Dorian of Karian offspring', born in the southwest Anatolian Greek city-state of Halicarnassus (modern Bodrum), his ties to the indigenous non-Greek population of the hinterland are suggested by his father's name Lyxes (cf. the Carian deity Lukhsu) and the Carian name of his uncle (or cousin) Panyassis. Odds are he could understand the Carian language.[1]

Of course, first we need to historicize questions and terms. The modern conception of historiography as grounded in documentation is largely a product of those regimes, especially empires, that happened to generate reams of writing. While the 'epigraphic habit' of ancient Athenian democracy may offer a glimmer of the later norm, reasoned analysis about the past was only in its infancy when Herodotus undertook to explain the Persian Wars, while traditions remained largely oral, or if written, came down in poetic form (Homeric epic partaking of both modes).[2] Whatever 'translating' of any documents might have been done by the historian is invisible: he never mentions personal *reading* of non-Greek materials; in general, reading of any sort is rarely alluded to, although Herodotus sometimes mentions inscriptions (in Greek and other languages) or poems (including some now lost, like the autobiographical epic by the shaman Aristeas of Proconnesus: 4.13).[3] Therefore, one's first urge – to explicate Herodotean 'translation' of the past by studying his own acts of cross-linguistic work – proves impossible. We must resort to his accounts of a related (but in one crucial way divergent) procedure, the act of interpreting. If historical 'translation' is essentially diachronic, an act of exploring the recent or distant past through written texts in another language, 'interpreting' is vitally synchronic, a real-time interaction with speakers of another tongue either directly (e.g. by a bilingual historian) or through an interpreter – in Greek, *hermêneus* (root of 'hermeneutics').[4] The latter procedure allows speakers to pursue leads, follow up on what remains obscure and get answers quickly: as Plato's Socrates insisted, people talk back, but texts remain mute (*Phaedrus*, 275d-e). On the other hand, Herodotus' contemporaries probably lacked knowledge beyond a few generations earlier, 200 years (what descends from a grandfather's grandfather) being the usual life span for accurate orally transmitted information (Vansina 1971). Interpreting (in the narrower linguistic sense) nevertheless can provide a handle on the historian's 'interpretation' (broadest sense) of the past, and signal blind spots. After considering it, I shall turn to the invisibility of translational transactions in the *Histories* to the cognitive templates that might explain this blank space in the text.

1.1. Pyramids, rock carvings, interpretation

In only one passage does Herodotus make explicit mention of personal interaction with an interpreter, while describing the pyramids at Giza (2.125.6–7):

> There are writings on the pyramid in Egyptian characters [σεσήμανται δὲ διὰ γραμμάτων Αἰγυπτίων] indicating how much was spent on radishes and onions and garlic for the workmen; and I am sure that [ὡς ἐμὲ εὖ μεμνῆσθαι] when he read me the writing, the interpreter said that sixteen hundred talents of silver had been paid. Now if that is so how much must have been spent on the iron with which they worked, and the workmen's food and clothing, considering that the time aforesaid was spent in building, while hewing and carrying the stone and digging out the underground parts was, as I suppose [ὡς ἐγὼ δοκέω], a business of long duration.[5]

For all its brevity, the passage contains intriguing hints. First, historian and interpreter exist on different planes: the latter apparently translates the centuries-old inscription, but the former does not, as it seems, bother to then write down the details of all he is told. Instead, Herodotus trusts his *memory* of the total payment relayed to him orally by the interpreter-translator. The expression ('if my memory serves me well', as Waterfield more naturally translates it) sounds odd: why include this slight authorial uncertainty about a fairly minor detail? Perhaps it relates to a second notable feature, the manner in which Herodotus proceeds to calculate on his own (as so often), speculating about further outlays for supplies and costs of pre-construction preparations. The accounting is framed by two other expressions of uncertain supposition. '*If* these things are like this' [εἰ δ' ἐστὶ οὕτως ἔχοντα ταῦτα], Herodotus says, it would be an expensively drawn-out process, 'as I suppose'. Why the conditional statement? Does he doubt the inscription's veracity? Or the interpreter's rendition? And why not just ask the interpreter concerning those further man-hour details?

An answer may peer out from the historian's own testimony about methods and sources in the Egyptian *logos*, articulated half-way through his report:

> So far, all I have said is the record of my own autopsy and judgment and inquiry [ὄψις τε ἐμὴ καὶ γνώμη καὶ ἱστορίη ταῦτα λέγουσα ἐστί]. Henceforth I will record

Egyptian chronicles [Αἰγυπτίους ... λόγους], according to what I have heard, adding something of what I myself have seen. The priests told me [ἔλεγον] that Min was the first king of Egypt.

(2.99)

Once more, the precise Greek wording merits attention. That triple font of knowledge – autopsy, judgment, inquiry – literally 'talks', as the participle (λέγουσα) attached to the third and most privileged item (ἱστορίη, 'investigation') applies to all three terms. The author as agent is displaced, represented only by some cognitive faculties and his persistent interrogations; the Greek does not specify that he actually *wrote* something, as if the process of getting information in person and transmitting it was unmediated, instantly enacted orally.[6] The root of the Greek word 'tell' then crops up in the noun that describes Egyptian accounts (λόγους – literally 'tellings' – the root is that of the verb). And, finally, the verb form reappears as Herodotus switches to his newly added source of information – what the Egyptian priests told him. The mention of priestly accounts, whether purely oral communications or recitations from their papyrus scrolls, will offer explicit section markers for the rest of Book Two (cf. 2.110.1, 101.1, 102.2, 107.1, 109.1, 111.1, etc.), pegging the Greek syntax of indirect discourse to repeated speech-acts. Put another way, the priests' discourse adds a fourth channel to the three that Herodotus is already listening to, one different only in volume, but a form of 'telling' just as his native triad (autopsy, judgment, inquiry) has 'told' him all the facts thus far.

Most significant for the point I have been emphasizing – the diminished role of the interpreter in Herodotus' Egyptian account – is this capacity to 'tell', and moreover, to do so interactively. Herodotus questions the priests, gets answers and makes conclusions. This happens vividly at the very moment the historian seeks to question his own culture's narratives (2.118):

But, when I asked the priests whether the Greek account of what happened at Troy were idle or not [εἰ μάταιον λόγον λέγουσι], they gave me the following answer, saying that they had inquired and knew [ἱστορίῃσι φάμενοι εἰδέναι] from Menelaus himself.

As he admits shortly later, Herodotus believes the priestly investigations (*historiai*) confirming the story (a minority opinion, for Greeks) that Helen never went to Troy, a god-crafted facsimile having been sent in her place (2.120.1):[7]

The Egyptians' priests said this, and I myself believe their story about Helen, for I reason thus [τάδε ἐπιλεγόμενος]: had Helen been in Ilion, then with or without the will of Alexander she would have been given back to the Greeks.

After listing some further counterfactuals to support his conclusion, Herodotus ends with a theological assertion coupled with a strong expression of his own thinking (2.120.5):

But since they did not have Helen there to give back, and since the Greeks would not believe them although they spoke the truth – I am convinced and declare [ὡς μὲν ἐγὼ γνώμην ἀποφαίνομαι] – the divine powers provided that the Trojans, perishing in utter destruction, should make this clear to all mankind: that retribution from the gods for terrible wrongdoing is also terrible.

The evidentiary chain in its schematic essentials runs: Herodotus writing contemporary ethnography (the first 98 chapters of Book 2) relies on his own *gnomê* and *historiê*. Entering the diachronic dimension, however – that is, when he needs to learn the 'history' of Egypt in our sense – he relies heavily, if not exclusively, on the *historiai* of *others*, the priestly caste. It is their investigations, in turn, that lead him to produce and display publicly (*apophainomai*) a further *gnomê* (opinion, rule of thumb, idea). In short, the interpreter, in the view of Herodotus, is really a low-level knowledge producer, in contrast to the highest-level authorities, the priests of Heliopolis (whose accounts he has cross-checked). The imbalance in this configuration, between on-site *hermêneus* and distant hieratic knowledge-purveyors, is neatly summed up by the way the verb *epilegomai* gets deployed in two passages just a few pages apart. At 2.125.6, Herodotus said the interpreter stated the content of the pyramid inscription while 'reading' the letters (ἐπιλεγόμενος τὰ γράμματα). Yet the same verb was used to describe his own activity a bit earlier in introducing his reasoning about the legend of Helen's abduction (2.120.1): the Egyptians' priests said this, and 'I myself believe their story about Helen, *for I reason thus* (τάδε ἐπιλεγόμενος)'. When Herodotus applies the verb *epilegomai* to himself, it means something like 'pick out and acknowledge the sequential points of an *argument*'; the same notion of selection and choosing underlies the semantic development of this verb to mean 'read', since it is conceived as a process of picking each letter in sequence. Both uses have already been deployed in the *Histories* by this point (at 1.78.1: Croesus *reasons* about the plans of Cyrus; at 1.124.1: Cyrus *reads* a message concealed inside a dead hare).[8]

In sum, Herodotus credits the oral but interactive reports from Egyptian priests (derived sometimes from written records) while downplaying whatever facts he acquired from interpreters. Whether or not the man at Giza who 'read' to Herodotus the costs of garlic provisions had been trained to understand early inscriptions (or himself learned the text's supposed meaning from some local purveyors of oral traditions) there is a touch of bias – status or even class-based – on the historian's part, as he shifts from local exegete towards nationally acknowledged religious experts. It is tempting to connect this difference with another detail in the Egyptian logos (2.164.1) concerning distinctions – that all Egyptians are divided into seven classes (γένεα) according to occupation, from priests and warriors to merchants, interpreters (ἑρμηνέες), and boat pilots. What is more, all interpreters in Egypt trace their origin to a cohort once entrusted to erstwhile Ionian and Carian allies whom the king Psammetichus had settled near the Nile (2.154.2):

Moreover, he put Egyptian boys in their hands to be taught Greek [τὴν Ἑλλάδα γλῶσσαν ἐκδιδάσκεσθαι], and from these, who learned the language, are descended the present-day Egyptian interpreters.

Yet in the same passage, Herodotus goes on to mention another channel of communication, established at the same time, due to the same settlement (2.154.4):

> It is a result of our communication with these settlers in Egypt (the first of foreign speech [ἀλλόγλωσσοι] to settle in that country) that we Greeks have exact knowledge [ἐπιστάμεθα ἀτρεκέως] of the history of Egypt from the reign of Psammetichus onwards.

Somewhat paradoxically, therefore, from the seventh century BC onwards Greeks possessed *two* sources of information about Egypt: contemporary fellow Greeks originally from Asia Minor, but also the interpreters who supposedly traced their language skills back to the group of youths once taught by the ancestors of those very Greeks. This adds yet another motivation to place the *hermêneus* lowest on the list of historically informed resources: Herodotus can rely on getting information from two higher nodes, one more closely affiliated to his own personal identity in terms of ethnicity (Greeks), the other by class (priests). That Herodotus, therefore, must *not* feel the need to highlight any reliance on translators and interpreters – indeed, seems to elide any such mediation, apart from the passage just examined – is itself rooted in historical and sociopolitical circumstances.

Thanks to this fluent erasure of intermediaries, we are lulled into taking at face value whatever the historian recounts, even when a moment's reflection would have us doubt how he knows certain 'facts'. Only in rare cases can we challenge (millennia later) alleged Herodotean readings. The Egyptian *logos* contains an interesting example of mis-translation in retrospect. Herodotus continues the priestly account about Sesostris (*aka* Rameses II) and his series of conquests (2.102.4–5):

> When those that he met were valiant men and strove hard for freedom, he set up pillars in their land, the inscription on which showed his own name and his country's, and how he had overcome them with his own power; but when the cities had made no resistance and been easily taken, then he put an inscription on the pillars just as he had done where the nations were brave; but he also drew on them the private parts of a woman, wishing to show clearly that the people were cowardly.

The pharaoh's binary response says much about the semiotics of language and the non-verbal in Herodotus, a topic of prime importance.[9] From both classes of foe (valorous and cowardly), he appropriates spots to penetrate the ground with permanent markers of his power – a kind of lithic aggression – but only the former class deserves human speech.[10] After a brief digression on the relationship between Colchians and Egyptians, Herodotus reports (2.106.1–4):

> Also, there are in Ionia two figures of this man carved in rock, one on the road from Ephesus to Phocaea, and the other on that from Sardis to Smyrna. In both places, the figure is over twenty feet high … and right across the breast from one

shoulder to the other a text is cut in the Egyptian sacred characters [γράμματα ἱρὰ Αἰγύπτια], saying: 'I myself won this land with the strength of my shoulders'.

Ironically, even though Herodotus self-confidently points out a misidentification by other viewers, what seems to be presented as *his own* translation has recently been found erroneous. What Herodotus took for 'Egyptian' script was actually hieroglyphic Hittite (a distinct indigenous form) and the relief of 'Sesostris', still visible in the Karabel pass (20 km. east of Izmir), in reality represents Tarkasnawa king of Mira in western Anatolia. Furthermore, what Herodotus took as a proud assertion of personal power by the ancient conqueror is simply the king's title, name and names of ancestors (Hawkins 1998).

Did Herodotus rely on a local interpreter to discover what the writing supposedly conveyed? If so, we have another example of an erased middle-man's oral account of a written document.

1.2. Interpreters within the text

The noun *hermêneus* occurs only eight times in Herodotus. Apart from the three about Egypt (2.125, 154, 164), a fourth (below) relates to the Scythians, and the remaining four occurrences cluster around three major narratives involving interpretation.[11] (Another key episode, also to be examined below, features a periphrasis, rather than the noun.) These 'interpreter' scenes in which the historian does *not* himself figure fill in the broader context for the interpretation of the pyramid inscription, while furthering the initial question: is doing *historiê* like translating?

Clearly, Herodotus is aware of a language world sprawling far beyond the Mediterranean littoral.[12] This becomes vivid in passages like the description of the Argippaei, the bald, snub-nosed people living to the northeast of the steppe-dwelling Scythians (perhaps in foothills of the Urals). In Herodotus' account, they represent an epistemological barrier, the limits of attainable knowledge. Meticulously backing up his ethnographic sources (4.24), the historian writes that 'as far as the land of these bald men, we have full knowledge [πολλὴ περιφάνεια] of the country and the nations on the near side of them'. That he possesses such detailed information has indeed just been demonstrated (4.23) in his sketch of the Argippean lifestyle, from their Scythian clothes, to their fruit-based drinks and cakes, yurt-like winter shelters, sacral status and welcoming attitude towards fugitives. On the other hand, beyond the Argippaei 'what lies north of the bald men no one can say with exact knowledge [ἀτρεκέως ... φράσαι]', as impassable mountains intervene. Knowledge of what lies beyond erodes into implausible story-telling, in the writer's view: 'These bald men say (although I do not believe them) that the mountains are inhabited by men with goats' feet, and that beyond these are men who sleep for six months of the twelve. This I cannot accept as true at all'. Such strange reports by the bald men must themselves have been indirectly transmitted to Herodotus, who has revealed shortly before this how the tribe's existence is known (4.24): 'some of the Scythians make their way to them, from whom it is easy to get knowledge, and from some of the Greeks, too, from the Borysthenes port and the other ports of Pontus; such Scythians as visit them transact their business with seven interpreters [ἑρμηνέων] and in seven languages [γλωσσέων].' The astounding multiplicity of linguistic skills is needed not just to deal with the Argippaei (who speak their own language: φωνὴν ... ἰδίην, 4.23.2) but for the many other *ethnea* one has to pass through to reach them. Of further interest, each *ethnos* requires its own interpreter – no notion arises here of multilingual professionals, or shared comprehension of closely related dialects.[13]

Power, self-assertion and reciprocity emerge as principal themes in the scenes of cross-linguistic manoeuvring. To put it another way, in the *Histories* explicit language mediation highlights moments particularly dense with more critical negotiations. It is not a casual event. The express need for interpreters becomes a textual marker for those perilous periods when cultures might grind past one another like tectonic plates. Whether the acts of mutual understanding are successful depends not on the interpreters' competence (never doubted – there are no 'bad' language mediators in Herodotus) but on the ability of the authority figures, who commissioned certain instances of interpretation, to fully understand what they hear back. In these exchanges, a power differential proves to be the determining factor. Three moments in Book Three sum up this problematic. All three revolve around Persian potentates – Cambyses (once) and Darius (twice).

In the first instance, Herodotus has just finished re-telling the story of the Sun's Table (3.19) and launches into describing the further desires of the impulsive Cambyses.[14] The king has determined to get information by means of spies and so despatches messengers to the city of Elephantine to recruit those among the Fish-Eaters who understood Ethiopian. He then provides them with a cover, sending them 'to see what truth there was in the story of a Table of the Sun in that country, and to spy out all else besides, under the pretext of bringing gifts for the Ethiopian king' (3.17.2). Already, interpreting looks tainted. At the same time, however, Cambyses shares something of Herodotus' own motivation to know the truth, especially that about marvellous objects and behaviours. King and historian are (uncomfortably, for modern sensibilities) alike – a phenomenon we shall observe several more times.[15] Yet another layer of ambiguity and false impressions is woven into the very story of the Table of the Sun (3.18):

> There is a meadow outside the city, filled with the boiled flesh of all four-footed things; here during the night [τὰς μὲν νύκτας] the men of authority among the townsmen are careful to set out the meat, and all day [τὰς δὲ ἡμέρας] whoever wishes [τὸν βουλόμενον] comes and feasts on it. These meats, say the people of the country, are ever produced by the earth of itself.

Godley's English translation does not quite bring out the marked contrast of behaviours and power structures. The night (*men*) is the time for those in authority to set out carefully all those boiled meats that during the day (*de*) chance-comers can consume. The contrast of some sort of magistrates (*en telei*) with ordinary citizens resembles that of a Greek polis, particularly Athens, where the phrase *ho boulomenos* ('whoever wants') had by the fifth century developed a precise legal meaning. But what happens in this diurnal cycle of Ethiopian nurture appears to be the opposite of transparent democratic procedures. It is, instead, a type of institutionalized sacrificial deception. Those who consume the meat – presumably the community of *boulomenoi* – are the locals (*epikhôrioi*) who simultaneously assert that it is the earth itself, in a mythopoeic Golden Age profusion, that in fact affords them their daily animal portions.

The bizarre combination of an Earth that produces *cooked* food perhaps sounds funny to a Greek audience of the later fifth century: the trope of endless free food provision, after all, furnished material for comic dramas in which food cooks itself.[16] On the other hand, as Herodotus' readers would recall from Homer and Hesiod, automatic food production is itself an ambiguous good: it marks the Golden Age (*Works and Days* 117–18), but also the barbarous domain of the Cyclops (*Od*.9.106–11). Furthermore, readers might retain the memory of another Odyssean episode, the Cattle of the Sun – does one really want to risk eating such apparently easy meat?[17]

A bigger question arising from the ethnographic description here is: do the local beneficiaries of the Table believe their food is divinely given, when in fact it is humanly and surreptitiously set forth? Or is this an instance of mass suspension of disbelief, the crowd playing along in a theatrical mode?[18] In any event, the interesting contrasts and ambiguities within this vignette counterpoint the deceptive behaviour of Cambyses, as he sets out to find the truth of the matter. Herodotus might imply that the 'truth' of the wondrous table is actually a kind of benignant lie.

The subsequent encounter described by Herodotus is distanced from any statement of veracity on his part by the constant reference to the Fish-Eaters as the interpreters. On their own initiative, it appears, they explain artefacts of Persian culture for their interlocutors. Now Ethiopians play the role of judgemental ethnographers with the Fish-Eaters as informants.[19] Purple dye and incense, once the processes that produce them are described, are dismissed as deceptive; gold jewellery is simply ineffective, when interpreted by the Ethiopians as a failed attempt to fashion handcuffs and neck restraints (3.22.1–3). In this case, it is the Persians who are deceived, if they really think to bind humans with such fripperies. Much more could be said about the semiotics of foodways embedded in the rest of this episode (the Fish-Eaters playing Lévi-Straussian mediators in this regard, as well as linguistic middle men). But it is worth underlining how the appearance of interpreters in this episode is above all stage-lighted thematically by concealment, deception and contested meanings.

The second example in which interpretation appears also marks a crucial moment of culture clash, as framed within the most famous explicit statement in Herodotus about the relativity of social values. The narrative segues from the madness of Cambyses, who by wounding the Apis bull has violated a universal rule concerning cultural norms – that each *ethnos* cherishes its own, which therefore must be respected. The proof adduced by Herodotus is an experiment by Darius, who asked a group of Greeks 'for what price they would eat their fathers' dead bodies' (3.38.3), and then asked some Indians (eaters of parents) what would induce them to practice cremation. 'The Indians cried aloud, that he should not speak of so horrid an act.' Herodotus continues: 'So firmly rooted are these beliefs; and it is, I think, rightly said in Pindar's poem that custom is lord of all [νόμον πάντων βασιλέα ... εἶναι].'

This fraught moment is highlighted within the text as a discursive turn-taking mediated overtly through interpreters – but in an oddly asymmetrical manner.[20] Darius communicates with the Greeks (in what language is not stated) *without* explicit intervention by *hermêneis*. He then interrogates the Indians – again, no language barrier is mentioned – but *their* response is subject to interpreting for the sake of the Greeks (3.38.4): 'the Greeks being present and understanding through an interpreter [δι' ἑρμηνέος] what was said'. Perhaps this detail explains how a Greek historian eventually obtained the anecdote. But its effect in the narration is to make more isolated one group in the cultural clash (Greeks do not understand without mediation), even as the overall message given has to do with the equality of both parties. Then again, we are not told whether the Indians were present when the Greeks were quizzed, or what *they* understood of the answer.

A further complication: once either side has clearly understood the question (through interpreters or not), we reach the limit of comprehension: neither can truly fathom the depths of depravity implied by the behaviour of those who do things differently (bury vs. consume corpses). In sum, the experiment not only proves the relativity of cultural norms, and (at a higher level) a universal *law* of relativity (a seeming paradox); it also reaffirms the gap between understanding the systems of signifiers (what people say – accessible to professional interpreters) and signified – the weird and upsetting things people do, a gulf that cannot be bridged by language experts. Herodotus chooses to deflect any attention to his own investment in the iron-clad rule by summing up his telling of the anecdote with a gesture towards *another* text already in circulation, Pindar's poem on Heracles' defeat of the monster Geryon (3.38.4). This is not to say that Herodotus 'translates' Pindar in any literal way, but he does indeed carry over and apply the pre-text to a new instantiation of the old principle – another sort of language-internal *translatio*.

What can this interpreting scene say about Herodotus' own practice of historical interpretation? First, that it *is* easy enough (provided one has royally paid interpreters) to bring together otherwise far-flung and mutually repellent communities and make them linguistically transparent to one another. Notionally, given the right sources and resources, one can recover what people say about the past. But, second, the results of inquiry remain stubbornly disparate. There will always be deep cultural incomprehension, the very existence of which leads to such things as the Persian clash with Hellenes. Third – an optimistic twist – Herodotus can nevertheless bring his readers to *understand* incomprehension. Through his textual stand-in 'Darius', with the help of an interpreter, the historian achieves clarity about the effort it takes to clarify – and the natural limitations thereto. We might say, for anyone concerned with history, that this is the beginning of wisdom.

A third passage from Book Three, also about Darius, combines themes of imperial power and personal relations. Once more, mention of interpreters emerges at a pivotal point (as in the Ethiopian *logos*), focused on clashes that will ultimately cause subversion and suffering. Syloson, exiled brother of the Greek tyrant of Samos, had once gifted his flashy red cloak to the young bodyguard Darius in Memphis (3.139). Later, after Darius has become monarch, the Greek comes to the palace in Susa. Interpretation (again, by royal employees) headlines the whole sequence to come (3.140.3): 'The doorkeeper brought Syloson in and the interpreters asked him as he stood there who he was and what he had done to call himself the king's benefactor'.

One notices, right off, that at least one narratively suppressed act of cross-linguistic interpretation has *already* occurred, as somehow Syloson has made clear to the Persians that he desires to be called 'king's benefactor' – an extremely lucrative position, as Herodotus shows later when he cites the Persian word for these (*orosangai*, 8.85.3). Thus, the formal interpretation session starts as a second-order activity, probing Syloson's apparently self-assigned title. The meaning of Greek 'benefactor' [εὐεργέτης] must have been understood by someone on the ground in order for this next interrogation to transpire. Prompted by Persian officials, Syloson recounts his tale; the interpreters at this point fade into the background. As usual, once the linguistic channel has been tuned in correctly, the focus is purely on message. It thus seems natural that Darius converses with Syloson without intermediary. As if certifying the transparency of the interaction, Darius immediately accepts his visitor's back-story. There is no identity testing; in the narrative vicinity of the crazy saga of the 'false Smerdis' (3.61–79), this signals either deep empathy or reckless naiveté on the monarch's part.

Tellingly, Darius' first move is to assign a cash value to the past favour, promising in return 'abundance of gold and silver' (3.140.4). At this point, we might expect the story to end with both sides happy. But the next move underlines cultural difference, a power differential and impending doom (since audience members already know about the subsequent destruction of Samos). The power imbalance is alluded to directly by Darius, who speaks of his lack of *dunamis* when young, which had meant Syloson's gift, though small, represented genuine generosity. But now, to this Persian confidence that any deed can be cashed out in terms of precious metals, the Greek responds using other terms (3.140.5):

> Do not give me gold, O king, or silver, but Samos, my country, which our slave has now that my brother Polycrates has been killed by Oroetes; give me this without killing or enslaving.

Syloson, too, addresses a power differential – the unjust replacement, in his view, of his tyrant brother by an upstart 'slave' (in reality a *free* man but subject to a tyrant – a viewpoint the autocrat Darius would appreciate).[21] But like Achilles in the *Iliad*, he prefers revenge to rewards.

Discussion of relative values leads to the most elaborate scene of interpreter activity. Croesus is the primary figure in Book One's garden of forking paths; through the Lydian's experiences, Herodotus raises the deepest questions not only about how the past determines the present, but also the conditions for narrating any story of the past. His story is also about communication, its failures and eventual breakthroughs, both timely and belated.[22] It could be framed in terms of 'translation', in the broader sense (transference of meaningful ideas), although the narrower sense (linguistic understanding) also becomes explicit at the very end of the account. By then, the mention of interpretation functions, as in my previous examples, to highlight the much larger, problematic nature of cross-cultural understanding, at the same time as it fulfils the purely narrative creation of suspense. To appreciate the full impact, we shall need to touch on several plot-points as they unfold, which will also prove significant when we return to question Herodotus' apparent transparency.

Fusing the first and last modules of the story is the figure of Solon, one of the renowned Seven Sages. He is not, however, the first Greek wise man to journey to the capital of Lydia; Herodotus takes care to mention two other archaic sages as he starts the account of Croesus, tying them to a cunning rhetorical stratagem that put an end to the king's ambitious plans to conquer Aegean islands. As is typical with Sage lore, it is difficult to pin down the exact celebrity source for the triumphant verbal performance.[23] Herodotus writes (1.27.2–3): 'either Bias of Priene or Pittacus of Mytilene (the story is told of both)' reported to Croesus that the islanders whom he intended to attack 'are buying ten thousand horse, intending to march to Sardis against you'.

Croesus is at first delighted at the prospect, presuming that these novice horsemen cannot possibly defeat the polished equestrian Lydians – until the sage flips the script by pointing out that the 'natural wish' of Croesus to meet the enemy *on land* is more than matched by the islanders' own well-placed confidence that *they* will handily defeat the Lydians *at sea*. In other words, Bias (or Pittacus) has brilliantly 'translated' the military equipment of the opposing forces, exchanging Greek 'ships' and Lydian 'horses' at a conceptual level, in order to press home the point: Croesus cannot win. The sage is not technically an interpreter, but rather acts like a master of metaphor in mediating the potential conflict. Croesus, pleased, proceeds to befriend the islanders.

This brief episode previews the continuing focus in Book One on a Greek source whose communication is poorly understood. Here, misunderstanding by the Lydian is almost instantly overcome; later, there will be dangerous lag-times. It also might lead us to ponder the linguistic texture of the exchange. If Bias was the sage on the spot, we could imagine that both parties, king and consultant, spoke Lydian. It would not have been an impossible accomplishment for one living in Priene, 150 kilometres to the west of Sardis, to learn the language. Even Mytilene, some 220 kilometres to the northwest of Croesus' capital, could harbour Lydian speakers – perhaps Pittacus, tyrant of Lesbos, was one. The poetess Sappho, his contemporary living on the same island, mentions Lydia with telling detail in a number of compositions, as in the poem (fr. 16) that expresses longing for her absent Anaktoria, whose lovely step and shining countenance Sappho prefers to the impressive spectacle of Lydian chariots and fighting men on foot. Most conspicuously, for one attuned to translation, Herodotus never mentions linguistic difficulty, instead dwelling only on the conceptual glitch – Croesus' initial inability to comprehend the cognitive gulf between expert seafarers and land-based warriors.

Given this neat rhetorical lesson by the Greek sage, the audience is on the alert for language manipulation when Solon comes to the fore. We would not expect him, as Athenian, to have learned Lydian, and yet there is still no mention of linguistic opacity in the encounter. Once more, 'conceptual' discrepancy is prominent, rooted in the situational disparity of a popular politician (by the era of Herodotus, Solon symbolized democracy) advising an Eastern despot. With two Greek examples, Solon subverts his host's smugness; instead of being flattered and told that he, *qua* fabulously wealthy tyrant, is certainly most fortunate of men, Croesus gets rated beneath an ordinary

Athenian who had a good life (Tellus) and two athletic brothers from Argos (Cleobis and Biton) heroized after their young deaths for their filial devotion. Solon explains his approach in terms of potential change over time: 'To me you seem to be very rich and to be king of many people, but I cannot answer your question before I learn that you ended your life well' (1.32.5). That is, he takes an historian's view of volatile fortunes.

Confirmation comes soon after Solon departs, when Croesus' favourite son Atys is killed in a hunting accident, despite obsessive precautions. The communication (even, 'translation') error, in this case, involves a prophetic dream that clearly showed Atys would be killed by an iron spear-tip. Rather than misread dream-symbolism, Croesus simply allows himself to be persuaded that it will not apply to a hunt from which he has sought to bar Atys (boars not being equipped with hands or spears, as his son protests). In changing his mind (1.40: μεταγινώσκω) under the influence of a bad argument, Croesus repeats the pattern of dismissing good advice transmitted to him by extraordinary means (a Greek sage, a dream); Atys then dies when struck by an errant spear thrown at a boar by Adrastus, a fugitive Phrygian prince whom Croesus had sheltered. The grief-maddened response of Croesus has an interesting communicative dimension. He cries out to Zeus 'by three names – Zeus the Purifier [*katharsios*], Zeus of the Hearth [*epistios*], Zeus of Comrades [*hetairêios*]: the first, because he wanted the god to know what evil his guest had done him; the second, because he had received the guest into his house and thus unwittingly entertained the murderer of his son; and the third, because he had found his worst enemy in the man whom he had sent as a protector'. The invocations are thus in effect transformed into terms of abuse, in this context, as Croesus seeks to demonstrate how Zeus does not fulfil the promise of his cult-titles. The implication is that divine names do not fit reality; they are *not* translated into deeds but rather mark a failure to live up to semantic roles.

The third and most extended misunderstanding (after the sage-visits and son's death) involves oracles, in particular Croesus' interpretation of an ambiguous message from the Pythia, Apollo's mouthpiece at Delphi. Told that if he went to war with Cyrus of Persia, he would destroy a great empire (1.53.3), Croesus assumed it would be his enemy's – not, as it happened, his own. His lack of understanding also characterizes his reading of an auxiliary utterance that indicated he would rule until such time as the Medes 'have a mule as king' (1.55). Whereas Croesus' first misinterpretation pivoted on an ambiguous noun phrase (the 'great empire'), his second stems from inability to think through metaphors. His double mistake is later spelt out by the Pythia, to whose oracle he complained after his humiliating subjugation (1.90.4). Apollo's spokesperson replies, 'he ought, if he had wanted to plan well, to have sent and asked whether the god spoke of Croesus' or of Cyrus' empire. But he did not understood what was spoken, or make further inquiry: for which now let him blame himself', and adds that a 'mule' did in fact come to rule – Cyrus, whose mother was a royal Mede and father a Persian commoner (a 'lesser' breed, from a subject people).

This narrative of missed cues and haywire communication wraps itself around the one dramatic mention of interpreters in the Croesus story, the final passage I will examine in this section. While he was depicted as communicating with Greeks without mediation, with the Persians who conquered his city Sardis it is another story entirely. As flames begin to lick round the edges of the pyre on which Cyrus has placed the conquered despot, Croesus recalls the wisdom of Solon concerning who can finally be called fortunate, and exclaims his name three times (echoing his earlier threefold invocation of Zeus) at 1.86.4:

> Cyrus heard and ordered the interpreters [ἑρμηνέας] to ask Croesus who he was invoking. They approached and asked, but Croesus kept quiet at their questioning, until finally they forced him and he said, 'I would prefer to great wealth his coming into discourse with all despots'. Since what he said was unintelligible [ἄσημα – literally "without signs"], they again asked what he had said.

Unlike the name of Zeus, known to all, but which Croesus indignantly deconstructed, 'Solon' is unfamiliar to the Persian, nor does the context provide clues as to the word's applicability. Interpreters are needed. Ironically, they would most likely have assumed it was a Lydian word, but it turns out, when Croesus explains his recollection of the sage's advice, that 'Solon' is Greek. The full explanation is only forthcoming after a second effort by the interpreters to get at the meaning, since Croesus, after an extended silence, still did not make explicit the connection between his desire and the name he has been uttering; his only gloss, after the first round of questions, had taken the form of a clause with a deictic pronoun (masculine accusative – so that the interpreters must at least now realize that a male human is signified): 'that one [τὸν] I would have preferred, more than great wealth, to have entered into conversation with all tyrants' (1.86.4).

If we seek analogues for how the historical enterprise resembles 'translation', this scene stands out. What the *hermêneis* initially seek is a synchronic explanation, just as Herodotus himself in his ethnographic explorations seeks either to equate, or differentiate, customs and habits of Egyptians, Scythians, Persians and the rest. What is 'Solon', in context, is a question equivalent to 'what does the Egyptian word *piromis* mean?' (2.143.4). Balked in their initial attempt to find an equivalent term for 'Solon' or even contextual clues, the interpreters then switch to the diachronic axis. 'He' – the man Croesus thinks should illuminate all tyrants – must have a back-story, a history; they naturally take it as their mission from Cyrus to determine it. The difficulty of getting accurate facts about the past and the sort of social interaction that this involves are pictured in miniature as the interpreters then press their informant. To get at Croesus' unintelligible first response (ἄσημα) 'they again asked what he had said persistently harassing him [λιπαρεόντων δὲ αὐτῶν καὶ ὄχλον παρεχόντων]'. The Greek text uses two verbs for the questioners' insistency: they literally 'make a bother' as well as 'persevere'. The latter verb (λιπαρεω) is used a few pages after this passage to describe the determined endurance of the Lydians themselves when struck with famine (1.94.3); much further on, the Athenians use it to emphasize how they will hold out to extremes rather than make peace with Xerxes (8.144.4). Much closer in pragmatic terms to the present passage, however, is the phrase describing the tyrant Periander's interrogation of his son, whom he suspects has learnt from his maternal grandfather that Periander had killed the boy's mother (3.51):

> The boy told him that Procles [the grandfather] had treated them kindly, but did not mention what he had said at parting; for he had paid no attention. Periander

said that by no means could Procles not have dropped some hint, and interrogated him persistently [ἐλιπάρεέ τε ἱστορέων] until the boy remembered, and told him.

Here, persistent questioning about what occurred in the past is overtly tied to the key verb 'inquire', which encapsulates Herodotus' own history-writing: 'This is the display of the inquiry [ἱστορίης] of Herodotus of Halicarnassus' (Proem to Book 1). The similarly intense questioning at 1.86, the effort to uncover the past by interpreters serving a monarch, leads also to a revelation by the central actor. Croesus 'explained that first Solon the Athenian had come and seen all his fortune and spoken as if he despised it', and proceeds to re-animate the Athenian's enduring wisdom by quoting the sage. This vivid recollection of the past, presented in terms of a remembered speech-act, resembles Herodotean technique (as also its Homeric predecessor) throughout the work. In short, we can see two sides of the fifth-century historian at work (interpreter and re-presenter) in his depiction of the sixth-century event. What is more, the proverb-like opinion that he makes Croesus echo from Solon is shown to have an immediate effect on its internal audience. Cyrus, hearing from his interpreters what has transpired, 'relented and considered that he, a human being, was burning alive another human being, one his equal in good fortune' (1.8.6.). Allowing his captured enemy to step down alive from his pyre is also depicted as Cyrus' cautious avoidance of righteous vengeance (*tisis*) from the gods – something his Persian successors never learn, as Herodotus will take pains to point out later.[24]

If we pull back from this scene to the metalevel – the historian's own practice – the suspenseful vignette about interpretation looks like instruction for the Athenian audience; Herodotus might well believe that his own opinions about the past will reverberate like Solon's words that he has so memorably enshrined, and protect *them* from error.[25] In keeping with this theme – the life-saving force of words well understood – a significant coda is the episode immediately preceding the pyre-scene. Croesus' son, mute since birth (ἄφωνος), for the first time breaks into speech (ἔρρηξε φωνήν) upon seeing an invading Persian about to kill his father, saying, 'Man, do not kill Croesus!' (1.85.4). This brief 'first utterance' story will find a parallel in the story of Psammetichus later (see below), but in its immediate context functions as yet another confirmation of an oracle: the Pythia, consulted years earlier about the boy's disability, had warned Croesus 'on an unlucky day shall he first speak'. At the same time, the neat match-up of oracle and event parallels the secular, democratic message of Solon (itself like an oracular utterance), similarly brought to fulfilment in the conquest of Sardis. This satisfying narrative turn, when speech and event in fullness of time click into place, clarifies the general lack of 'translation' complexities in Herodotus: his theory of discourse is in fact epitomized by oracles. Before explaining this, however, I must turn to stress further the 'transparency' that I am claiming for his text.

1.3. Erasure, identity

To start with a paradox: on the one hand, Herodotus shows keen awareness about the mutual lack of understanding between cultures and their emblematic representatives – sages and kings. At key points, we are shown that this requires interpreters. On the other hand, he seems assured that his own interpretation of past events is *not* irreparably constrained by the sort of slippage he himself reports as having occurred at earlier times. Yet, when we consider the huge variety of personal and textual interactions that must underlie Herodotus' *historiê*, this confidence seems unwarranted. What is the source of the historian's faith in the legibility of the past, its basic translatability?

That faith is obvious even in the very opening of the work:

This is the display [ἀπόδεξις] of the inquiry of Herodotus of Halicarnassus, so that things done by man not be forgotten in time, and that great and marvelous deeds, some displayed [ἀποδεχθέντα] by the Hellenes, some by the barbarians, not lose their glory, including among others what was the cause of their waging war on each other.

To preserve the memory of what the two groups did is to make a 'display' about things 'displayed'. The verb *apodeiknumi*, with its strong visual thrust, already implies that voice-over is not needed. One can *see* what happened; all it takes is a good viewer to record it. We sense that Herodotus intuits the etymology of *historiê* – the art, not of 'research' in our sense but of viewing as a witness.[26] But since one group, the *barbaroi*, speak, by definition, in a way that Greeks cannot understand, unless Herodotus has personally witnessed every event he narrates, or all information tied to the wars was visually displayed, or everything already was memorialized in Greek, translation had to take place.[27] Where is it?

The next sentences sharpen the question: 'The Persian learned men [λόγιοι] say that the Phoenicians were the cause of the dispute.' A young woman from Argos 'whose name was Io (according to Persians and Greeks alike)' was abducted – but Greek and Persian versions of how she came to Egypt fail to tally. The Persian sources dominate the tale of successive abductions (Medea, Helen), until a Phoenician version about Io is finally acknowledged (1.5.2), just before Herodotus pivots to his own Hellenocentric task of pinpointing the blameworthy party (1.5.3). How did Herodotus obtain Persian or Phoenician material without knowing the languages? Who were the hermeneutic middlemen? None of this is answered. The focus is instead on discursive similarities and differences. It is a real achievement, without doubt, that the early historian can so deftly marshal the slight inflections on each side's account, and even foregrounds these ethnic contestations rather than trying to smooth things over in some unified account. Consequently, even modern readers develop the sense that his sourcing is reliable (being multiple), which forestalls further doubts about the original informants and their idioms. What is more, Herodotus *does* at time name sources, whether as a class (Egyptian priests), ethnic group ('the Lydians' who related Cyrus' change of heart, 1.87) or even named individuals (Archias, whose grandfather died a hero in Samos, 3.55). The ease with which he acquired information about the war on Greek soil, from various Greek-speaking sources, perhaps provided the frictionless model for rendering accounts from *non*-Greek informants. Moreover, the influential example of Homeric epic gave precedent for representing linguistically distinct groups free from problems.[28]

Rosaria Munson, in her sophisticated study of Herodotus' engagement with foreign languages, usefully shifts discussion away from positivist speculation about what languages he knew to the narrator reflected in the text, 'a multilingual character, familiar with the principal languages, at ease with languages, and interested in the world's heteroglossia in the linguistic, as in the cultural, sphere' (Munson 2005: 29). From the rich evidence that she surveys, we can tease out one strand that might have a bearing on history-as-translation: a concern with *identity*, in dual senses that, to my mind, are only superficially different. First, there is the recurring issue of language in relation to ethnic self-presentation – *sociopolitical* identity. Second, there is the frequent mention of equivalence between Greek and foreign words – *lexical* identity.

A group's language, in the *Histories*, embodies its history. Knowledge of what it now speaks and has spoken in the past uncovers a palimpsest of invasions, migrations and interactions. The Athenians are a case in point. In an excursus on early Greek history, within the Croesus tale, the difference between Doric and Ionian Greeks (the latter originating from Athens) is elaborated in terms of movement (wandering 'Hellenes' vs. fixed indigenous 'Pelasgians') and language. Surprisingly, the Athenians originally spoke 'Pelasgian'. This, by Herodotus' quite sophisticated reasoning (noting language shared by contemporary Pelasgian communities in Thrace and the Hellespont region that once emigrated from Attica), was not Greek (1.57). His further conclusion, that 'the Attic nation, being of Pelasgian blood, must have changed its language too [τὴν γλῶσσαν μετέμαθε] at the time when it became part of the Hellenes', shows that the historian is not a linguistic essentialist. People learn the speech of others by contact; there is no immutable bond between race and language. At the same time, once established in a community, a language *does* become the primary signifier of communal identity; thus, Herodotus can continue with an assertion that the 'Hellenic' component (by which he means the now-Hellenized Athenians) has always had the same language since its beginning'. In other words, identity and language are equated; even though it started out 'Pelasgian', the existing group's genesis can be traced to the moment it adopted Greek.[29] Of course, in the thick of the struggle with Persia, a sense of shared identity beyond the individual city-state makes it all the more crucial that a common language serve as a rallying point. The Athenians pledging never to sue unilaterally for peace hold up to the Spartans 'the kinship of all Greeks in blood and speech [ὅμαιμόν τε καὶ ὁμόγλωσσον], and the shrines of gods and the sacrifices that we have in common, and the likeness of our way of life' (8.144.2). Language becomes a key marker in the fourfold description of Hellenic solidarity. If the latter two – ritual and life-style – are matters of convention, the first two, more prominent by their positioning, come closer to being naturally determined conditions.

This view of *langue* as a distinctive identifier finds a parallel at the level of *parole*, where the identification of individual terms from the lexicon of Persian, Scythian, Egyptian or other language relies on a similar sense that there is *one* right match, as there is globally between ethnos and speech. Such a 'glossographical' approach to language comparison, of course, seems natural at the level of objects, tools or animals in a shared realm of discourse: if Greeks and Medes both recognize dogs, each language will have a term (and only one) for dog (*kuôn* in Greek, *spax* in Median: 1.110.1). 'Fit' characterizes the way Persian names describe their bearers, for they 'agree with the nature of their persons and their nobility' (1.139), Herodotus believes (with some accuracy, although his further claim that 'all end in the same letter, that which the

Dorians call *san*, and the Ionians *sigma*' only applies to their nominatives in Greek form).[30] Less naturally, even in less concrete realms Herodotus displays confidence about the appropriateness of a foreign word's 'fit' – as if he knows the right slot for it in the target tongue. The word for the Persian king's birthday feast (*tukta*) equates to the Greek 'perfect' (9.110.2: τέλειον). His push beyond terminological equivalences, into Persian etymology, hints that *tukta*, to Herodotus, forms a correct 'conceptual' match with Greek – although whether the feast's perfection stems from rounding off an annual cycle or expressing the ideal monarch's status is unstated (Munson 2005: 61). At another point, Herodotus is more explicit about his method (4.59.2):

> In the Scythian tongue, Hestia is called Tabiti; Zeus (in my judgment [γνώμην] most correctly so called) Papaeus; Earth is Apia; Apollo Goetosyrus; the Heavenly Aphrodite Argimpasa; Poseidon Thagimasadas.

No doubt, he hears in the Scythian name for Zeus the Greek word for 'Daddy', *pap(p)as* (πάππας). So the Scythians 'most correctly [ὀρθότατα]' named the father of gods and men, since a Greek speaker can grasp their concept. Although there is no space here to develop the point in detail by analysing the Psammetichus experiment (2.2), we can note a similar attitude. The Egyptian king's quest to identify the oldest language leads him to conclude that the 'first utterance' of two contact-deprived toddlers (the word *bekos*) indicates a *signified* 'bread', matches the Phrygian *signifier* for bread (the glossographic assumption) and proves that Phrygian is older than Egyptian (thus, Egyptians are not the earliest people).[31] Again, the overarching assumption is that one can always discover the proper one-to-one linguistic 'fit'. Starting from Herodotus' remarks on the names of Egyptian gods, Walter Burkert has convincingly argued that his theory of language operates on similar principles of 'natural' appropriateness like those fully on display in Plato's *Cratylus* (Burkert 2013).[32] The sheer profusion of such one-to-one matches in the *Histories*, whether terms for objects or more abstract words, not only shapes our perception of Herodotean expertise but also works to entrench a world view that extends well beyond language.[33] That view has consequences for the historian's attitude towards the past, and originates, I submit, within a distinctive religious-verbal institution: oracles.

1.4. Oracular hermeneutics

The oracular utterances within the *Histories* have prompted many studies but have not been scrutinized in relation to translation, which requires that one think more abstractly about the semiotic mechanisms that make them work.[34]

At first sight, oracles appear polysemous. 'A great empire' is either Persia or Lydia, depending on one's confirmation bias. But this apparently unfettered signification is anything but free. In the oracle given to Croesus, for example there is *one* right answer, just one referent for 'great empire'. The first interpretive requirement, that is to say, is like the contest between empires, a zero-sum game where only one prevails. This logic accords with the Herodotean view of language that I sketched above. Names are not conventions so much as conveniences; that is, when two or more names refer to the same signified, the emphasis is not on linguistic relativity or the arbitrary nature of the sign but on appropriateness within the bounds of a language, which makes the name uniquely irreplaceable (synonymy not being considered a problem).

Take the striking example of an intentionally bilingual proclamation (in Herodotus' view) by the Pythia. 'A son of weak and stammering speech' (ἰσχόφωνος καὶ τραυλός) born to Polymnestus of Thera sought help from Delphi for his problem (4.155.3) but received instead the command from Apollo to found a colony. Herodotus states his opinion that it was only upon being addressed by the Pythia as Battus ('stammerer'), and departing for Libya, that the young man adopted this name (μετωνομάσθη) from his earlier one (in other sources, 'Aristotle').

> For the Libyan word for king is 'Battus', and this (I believe) is why the Pythian priestess called him so in her prophecy, using a Libyan name because she knew that he was to be king in Libya.

Proleptically, the oracle adopts the language of Battus' future realm, instead of addressing him with the Greek equivalent *basileus* (4.155.3). On closer examination, the story sounds as though it wrestles with an ethnocentric back-formation. Battus *did* become 'king' of the Libyan region Cyrene and so got properly titled, but on the assumption that this was *always* the man's name, a Greek would imagine that a term of abuse ('stammerer') had somehow been transformed into an honorific. The folktale motif seen in the sudden utterance by Croesus' mute son here is modified and applied to Battus' almost magical upgrade in status, in contrast to local Theran and Cyrenaean narratives.[35] Herodotus' preferred version instead recognizes the panoptic universality of the Pythia that ignores the local convention and instead assigns Battus his name and position in life simultaneously. The principle remains: there is *one* true name given one's true place. A corollary: history reveals it.

Another view of the way in which oracles are perceived to 'fit' reality emerges in the account of a royal descendant of the original Battus (4.163). The exiled Arcesilaus is told by the Pythia that Apollo has allowed his family to rule Cyrene for a maximum of eight generations: he should return there in peace, 'but if you find the oven full of amphoras, do not bake the amphoras' and 'do not go into the tidal place [τὴν ἀμφίρρυτον]; for if you do, then you shall be killed yourself, and also the bull that is fairest of the herd'. Arcesilaus promptly forgets the oracular warning, incinerates a number of opponents in a tower (the symbolic 'amphorae' as he tardily realizes), flees the spot he interprets as the 'tidal place' and ends up assassinated with his father-in-law (the 'bull') in the latter's city (another tide-washed spot). This failure of 'translating' signifiers into the world of things is twofold, inasmuch as the first slip comes from not thinking in terms of metaphor, while the second results from prematurely assigning a generic epithet to a specific locale – a different type of misreading.[36] But the larger point remains: divine discourse employs infinite equivalences (through symbolization or generic language) but to encode *one* and only one intended meaning. Perhaps the most telling remark is that which Herodotus uses to conclude the episode: 'Arcesilaus whether with or without intent missed the meaning of the oracle [εἴτε ἑκὼν εἴτε ἀέκων ἁμαρτὼν τοῦ χρησμοῦ] and fulfilled his destiny'. Unlike so many oracles blithely taken amiss by biased interpreters like Croesus, this one, the historian hints, might have been subject to intentional *hamartia* ('missing of the mark') – the ultimate insult to Apollo.

For our larger investigation, this raises the analogous possibility that translators of the past, such as Herodotus, can also choose – from whatever motives – to get it wrong. That Herodotus does *not* do this can be extrapolated from his continual assurances about the good-faith efforts he has put into gaining information, whether from authorities, travellers, eye-witnesses or the descendants of people involved in key events. But it is also apparent in the way he speaks of oracular knowledge. In the midst of his account of the all-important battle of Salamis, Herodotus somewhat abruptly addresses the reader (8.77.1–2): 'I cannot say against oracles that they are not true, and I do not wish to try to discredit them when they speak plainly [ἐναργέως λέγοντας]', and proceeds to quote eight poetic lines attributed to the legendary Boeotian prophet Bakis that unambiguously refer to a naval blockade and sack of Athens while predicting Greek victory in a battle at sea. The event is framed, in the diction of archaic wisdom-poetry, as the triumph of Zeus' will and divine justice (*Dikê*) over insatiable aggression (*Hubris*). For the historian, the truth of the entire utterance is now a matter of record, as Salamis clearly represents such a victory.[37]

This pivotal passage, then, combines and distils an entire theology and philosophy of history. It invites a more nuanced view of the historian, as being less a researcher and more a witness to how fate and the will of the gods (not always distinguished) come to shape human affairs – a different 'seer'. At the same time, it turns the historian into a secondary author, if we take as primary the god or seer who first uttered the words predicting an event; Herodotus is the latter-day exegete, whose business it is to confirm in his own text that the first 'text' (the oracular) remains operative. Given this distinctive approach, Herodotus does indeed 'translate' the past, though never explicitly making the analogy.

To find a figure within the *Histories* for such a textualizing translator, we might do worse than recall a man named 'Mouse' (*Mys*). When he entered the oracular site of Apollo Ptoios in Boeotia 'straightway the diviner prophesied in a foreign tongue' to the dismay of three Thebans who accompanied him. Mys, undeterred, 'snatched from them the tablet which they carried and wrote on it that which was spoken by the prophet, saying that the words of the oracle were Carian. After writing everything down, he went back to Thessaly'. Herodotus, too, connoisseur of speech, understands the language of the divine, its patterns and results, and writes it all down for an unknown – even Greekless – future.'[38]

Notes

1. Quoted from Herda (2013: 424). Mandell (1990) presumes ability in Carian; Harrison (1998:3) is sceptical.
2. On what Athenian epigraphic habits afforded the fifth-century historian, see Faraguna (2017), with extensive bibliography. Poems on the history of Ionia were composed by Herodotus' relative Panyassis (*Suda*, s.v. Panyasis).

3   On the inscriptions, see Haywood (2021), West (1985).
4   On the term, with further references, see Schirripa (2015).
5   All translations from Godley (1920) unless otherwise noted.
6   Compare Waterfield (1998: 132): 'my account … *has been dictated by* my own observation'.
7   The priests are as scrupulous as the historian in separating local traditions from knowledge acquired by 'investigations' (2.119.3): 'The priests told me that they had learned some of this by inquiry [ἱστορίῃσι], but that they were sure of [ἀτρεκέως ἐπιστάμενοι λέγειν] what had happened in their own country.'
8   On *epilegomai* see *LSJ* s.v. III.1 and III.2; for the etymology (and further cognates) see Chantraine (1968: 625). That these diverse senses can fit one Greek verb is further clarified by usage of the Greek simplex form *lego*, as in the sentence cited above at 1.124.1: Cyrus 'read' a slip of papyrus (ἐπελέγετο) and the letters 'said (ἔλεγε) the following …'. In other words, the reader in this scenario simply *adds to* (*epi-*) a process already inherent in the text. English 'read' (from a Germanic root meaning 'advise, interpret' – cf. German *Rat*) and, similarly, the development of English 'tell' (from a root meaning 'count, recount' – cf. German *zählen*) illustrate similar clustering of notions related to interpretation, calculation and verbal performance.
9   On which see the brilliant study Hollmann (2011).
10 Typologically, his action echoes a Greek cultural habit, marking key sites and dominating territory with 'herms' (ithyphallic statues of Hermes), which Burkert (1979: 39–41) has compared to monkeys' aggressive genital displays.
11 Brandwood (2020) surveys these without making connections to history-writing. I agree with his central point that interpreters 'help to define and focalize the roles of both the *histôr* and his audience, while also marking points in the *Histories*' narrative of cultural translation that require the intervention of the work's arch-translator, Herodotus himself' (2020: 17).
12 Harrison (1998) provides an incisive survey of the topic.
13 For similar situations, see the diverse, often mutually incomprehensible aboriginal languages of northeast Australia experienced by Dixon (1989).
14 On Cambyses, the 'paradigm of human dysfunction' and Herodotus' view of universal truths, see Munson (1991).
15 On inquisitive kings, see Christ (1994), who stresses crucial differences with Herodotus.
16 E.g. *Amphictyons* of Telecleides (fr.1 KA); related plays mentioned in Athenaeus (6.267e–270a).
17 On the alimentary code that governs both the Table of the Sun and the Cattle of the Sun, see Vernant (1989); on the special status of Ethiopians as close to gods like the Sun, see MacLachlan (1992).
18 A prime example of which has already been set forth, sceptically, at 1.60.3–5 (the return of Pisistratus with 'Athena').
19 It works both ways: Munson (2005: 74) notes 'the innocent and respectful Icthyophagi are also, vis-à-vis the recipient of the *Histories*, surrogate-ethnographers for Herodotus himself.'
20 Brandwood (2020: 20–1) pinpoints some of the confusions.
21 On the sociolinguistic nicety, see Asheri et al. (2007: 518).
22 An overview of the topic in this tale, see Sebeok & Brady (1979).
23 On multiple Sage stories, sources and wisdom as performance, see Martin (1993).

24 Munson (2005: 75) nicely sums up: 'Only after Croesus relates, and the interpreters translate, the whole story of Solon's visit to Croesus, Cyrus understands – as Croesus himself had not at the time – the "human" (*anthrôpinon*), that is to say, the cross-cultural, meaning of Solon's words. Solon is the real interpreter, who translates from the particular to the general, and his words are for the whole human race'.
25 On the Athenian audience as his specific addressee, see Ostwald (2011: 265–77).
26 Excellent extended treatment of the evolution of the word: Darbo-Peschanski (2007: 21–110).
27 On *barbaros* see Munson (2005: 1–2 and 65–6).
28 Greek-Trojan interactions do not require translation, whereas the Trojan allies' diverse tongues are sometimes mentioned: further discussion in Munson (2005: 2–3) and, more expansively, Mackie (1996).
29 On the linguistic complexities of the entire passage, see Laird (1933). Persistent language identities characterize the Geloni (4.108), Eretrians (6.119.4), Attic women abducted to Lemnos (6.138.2) and possibly the Caunians (1.172).
30 Asheri et al. (2007: 171)) note that Persian names (other than theophoric) often denoted physical characteristics.
31 Full-scale analysis is in Gera (2003). Cf. Munson (2005: 21): '*Bekos* is a plausible sound for both human infants and animals, and ancient readers already explained it as the children's imitation of the only *phônê* (or "voice") they have heard, the bleating of the goats.'
32 Chamberlain (1999) connects Herodotean theorizing with broader approaches to speech and text seen in ancient materialist thought.
33 Harrison (1998: 44–5) lists forty-five translation pairs; for full discussion of each item, see Miletti (2008: 87–97).
34 On oracles in Herodotus, see Crahay (1956); Kirchberg (1965) and Kindt (2006).
35 Munson (2005: 83) notes that his home communities identify Battus 'with a linguistic handicap that corresponds to his social and political marginality in a Greek context' – he is without a strong *citizen* voice.
36 A common motif: cf. Cleomenes at 'Argos' (6. 80), Cambyses at 'Ecbatana' (3.64.3–5).
37 On clarity in this passage, see Harrison (2000: 130–2).
38 On intricate Herodotean appropriation of oracular voices, see Barker (2006). Larger problems of oracular interpretability are emblematized by the complicated linguistic history of Dodona (2.54–57, starting point for Munson 2005).

References

Asheri, David, Alan Lloyd and Aldo Corcella (2007), *A Commentary on Herodotus Books I–IV*, edited by Oswyn Murray and Alfonso Moreno, Oxford: Oxford University Press.

Barker, Elton (2006), 'Paging the Oracle: Interpretation, Identity and Performance in Herodotus' History', *Greece & Rome*, 53: 1–28.

Brandwood, Steven (2020), 'Herodotus' *Hermēneus* and the Translation of Culture in the *Histories*', in Thomas Figueira and Carmen Soares (eds.), *Ethnicity and Identity in Herodotus*, 15–42, New York: Routledge.

Burkert, Walter (1979), *Structure and History in Greek Mythology and Ritual*, Berkeley: University of California Press.

Burkert, Walter (2013), 'Herodotus on the Names of the Gods: Polytheism as a Historical Problem' (1st edn 1985), in Rosaria Vignolo Munson (ed.), *Herodotus: Volume 2: Herodotus and the World*, 198–209, Oxford: Oxford University Press.
Chamberlain, David (1999), 'On Atomics Onomastic and Metarhythmic Translations in Herodotus', *Arethusa*, 32 (3): 263–312.
Chantraine, Pierre (1968), *Dictionnaire étymologique de la langue grecque: histoire des mots*. Paris: Klincksieck.
Christ, Matthew (1994), 'Herodotean Kings and Historical Inquiry', *Classical Antiquity*, 13 (2): 167–202.
Crahay, Roland (1956), *La littérature oraculaire chez Hérodote*, Paris: Les Belles Lettres.
Darbo-Peschanski, Catherine (2007), *"L'Historia": commencements grecs*, Paris: Gallimard.
Dixon, Robert (1989), *Searching for Aboriginal Languages: Memoirs of a Field Worker*, Chicago: University of Chicago Press.
Faraguna, Michele (2017), 'Documents, Public Information and the Historian: Perspectives on Fifth-Century Athens', *Historiká*, 7, https://doi.org/10.13135/2039-4985/2589.
Gera, Deborah (2003), *Ancient Greek Ideas on Speech, Language, and Civilization*, Oxford: Oxford University Press.
Godley, Alfred (1920), *Herodotus*, Cambridge, MA: Harvard University Press.
Harrison, Thomas (1998), 'Herodotus' Conception of Foreign Languages', *Histos*, 2: 1–45.
Harrison, Thomas (2000), *Divinity and History: The Religion of Herodotus*. Oxford: Clarendon Press.
Hawkins, John (1998), 'Tarkasnawa King of Mira 'Tarkondemos', Boğazköy Sealings and Karabel', *Anatolian Studies*, 48: 1–31.
Haywood, Jan (2021), 'The Use(s) of Inscriptions in Herodotus' Histories', *American Journal of Philology*, 142 (2): 217–57.
Herda, Alexander (2013), 'Greek (and Our) Views on the Karians', in A. Mouton, I. Rutherford and I. Yakubovich (eds.), *Luwian Identities: Culture, Language and Religion between Anatolia and the Aegean*, 421–506, Leiden: Brill.
Hollmann, Alexander (2011), *The Master of Signs: Signs and the Interpretation of Signs in Herodotus' Histories*, Washington, DC: Center for Hellenic Studies.
Kindt, Julia (2006), 'Delphic Oracle Stories and the Beginning of Historiography: Herodotus' Croesus Logos', *Classical Philology*, 101 (1): 34–51.
Kirchberg, Jutta (1965), *Die Funktion der Orakel im Werke Herodots*, Hamburg: Vandenhoeck & Ruprecht.
Laird, A. G. (1933), 'Herodotus on the Pelasgians in Attica', *The American Journal of Philology*, 54 (2): 97–119.
Mackie, Hillary (1996), *Talking Trojan: Speech and Community in the Iliad*, Lanham, MD: Rowman and Littlefield Publishers.
MacLachlan, Bonnie (1992), 'Feasting with Ethiopians: Life on the Fringe', *Quaderni Urbinati di Cultura Classica*, 40 (1): 15–33.
Mandell, Sara (1990), 'The Language, Eastern Sources, and Literary Posture of Herodotus', *Ancient World*, 21: 103–8.
Martin, Richard (1993), 'The Seven Sages as Performers of Wisdom', in C. Dougherty and L. Kurke (eds.), *Cultural Poetics in Archaic Greece: Cult, Performance, Politics*, 108–28, Cambridge: Cambridge University Press.
Miletti, Lorenzo (2008), *Linguaggio e metalinguaggio in Erodoto*, Pisa: Fabrizio Serra.
Munson, Rosaria (1991), 'The Madness of Cambyses (Herodotus 3.16-38)', *Arethusa*, 24: 43–65.
Munson, Rosaria (2005), *Black Doves Speak: Herodotus and the Languages of Barbarians*, Washington, DC: The Center for Hellenic Studies.

Ostwald, Martin (2011), *Language and History in Ancient Greek Culture*, Philadelphia: University of Pennsylvania Press.
Schirripa, Pino (2015), 'ἑρμηνεύς, esegeta, traduttore, portavoce', in C. Ampolo, U. Fantasia and L. Porciani (eds.), *Lexicon Historiographicum Graecum et Latinum*, vol. 3 (β-ζ), 201–8, Pisa: Edizioni della Normale.
Sebeok, Thomas and Erika Brady (1979), 'The Two Sons of Croesus. A Myth about Communication in Herodotus', *Quaderni Urbinati di Cultura Classica*, 1: 7–22.
Vansina, Jan (1971), 'Once upon a Time: Oral Traditions as History in Africa', *Daedalus*, 100 (2): 442–68.
Vernant, Jean Pierre (1989), 'Food in the Countries of the Sun' (1st edn 1979), in M. Detienne and J. P. Vernant (eds.), *The Cuisine of Sacrifice among the Greeks*, translated by P. Wissing, 164–9, Chicago: The University of Chicago Press.
Waterfield, Robin (1998), *Herodotus: The Histories*, Oxford: Oxford University Press.
West, Stephanie (1985), 'Herodotus' Epigraphical Interests', *Classical Quarterly*, 35 (2): 278–305.

2

Translation and temporalities in classical reception histories: Narratives, genres, forms and the agency of translators

Lorna Hardwick

2.1. Introduction

This chapter discusses examples of translation of Greek texts as a way to scrutinize how 'time sites' are created, transplanted, reinterpreted and augmented in the cultural histories of texts.[1]

Translations are often perceived as bridging times as well as places and languages. This can be a fruitful topic but needs further refinement. Two aspects will provide the underlying critical dimension in my discussion: (i) the problematics of fidelity analysis in translations. Notions of translational 'fidelity' have become unpopular conceptually and practically (often for good reasons, since they may imply that meaning is 'fixed'). However, revisiting this problem is part of analysing whether narratives that are grounded in 'history' carry an implication of 'truth', and if they do, how that is to be interpreted, both in terms of the ancient text itself and in terms of how it can best be communicated in translations; and (ii) the associated area of 'authenticity'. This issue embraces all types of text, including those that do not claim to present a historical narrative but that have nevertheless been created in relation to historical contexts (their pasts; their presents). In texts that are primarily literary, 'truth' and 'authenticity' may be defined in formal and linguistic terms, making cognitive and affective claims that purport to convince readers and/or spectators to take them seriously.

Translations themselves are in a sense counter-texts. They challenge arguments that, for example, Greek and Latin texts can only be accessed by those who can read them in the original languages. More broadly, translations challenge the view that the histories of particular groups can only be created and communicated by members of those groups. As Ngugi wa Thiong'o put it in his Welleck Library Lectures:

> Translation is the language of languages. It opens the gates of national and linguistic prisons. It is thus one of the most important allies of world literature and global consciousness .... [Globalectic reading] means breaking open the prison house of imagination built by theories and outlooks that would seem to signify the content

within is classified, open to only a few [...] this may also mean the act of reading becoming also a process of self-examination.

(Ngugi 2012: 61)[2]

The translator's task is thus to enlarge the constituency of people who can both empathize with and deliberate upon the content of the texts. The growing appreciation of the importance of translation and the changes in the recognition of the translator's role (no longer invisible, but creative and engaged) have energized a number of research projects, some of which acknowledge the role of translations of Greek and Roman material.[3]

In selecting examples for discussion, I have started from the main aims of this edited collection, but have also adapted and augmented them. In the Introduction to this volume, the editor has emphasized that:

1. *The act through which historians interpret the past can be considered as an act of translation, epistemologically and cognitively.* I thoroughly endorse this claim, but have extended its remit to include critics and practitioners in other genres, such as epic poetry and drama, that also engage with the past (literally or figuratively). I have also added 'affect' to the epistemological and cognitive criteria. This is because in all genres (including historiography) writers deploy many strategies for capturing the intellectual and imaginative assent of readers and spectators.
2. *This act of translation is also an act of synchronization which connects past, present and future, disrupting and resetting time, as well as creating complex temporalities differing from any linear chronology.* The editor's insight provided a crucial stimulus to me to think about how what is done and thought in the present affects interpretation of the past, and of texts produced in the past, and how interpretation of the past in turn affects what people think and do in the present and how they envisage and create the future.[4]
3. *Hence the study of the different forms through which the past is constantly translated leads to the central problem of historical inquiry: to the concept of anachronism.* Recent attention to this set of problems has resulted in the broadening and deepening of the concept of translation (by resorting, for example, to the concept of transplantation). In my discussion I take the view that anachronism is not only an inevitable but actually a desirable feature of translation and that the relationship between anachronism and the creation of authenticity can be mutually enhancing. This is the case with concepts as well as with allusions and lexical choices. Concepts present particular challenges for the translator's task in moving across and between different contexts and value systems and in identifying and communicating shifts and ambivalences in meaning and association, within and between texts (an issue discussed in depth by Lianeri in the volume). In addition, there is a dual directional aspect to the impact of concepts. Modern translators and critics use, whether explicitly or implicitly, notions such 'heightened receptivity', 'simultaneity', 'low and high intensity' of beliefs and values (see further Hardwick 2018a, 2022 and *forthcoming* a). Such concepts influence the translator's selection of texts, the arrangement of material and the register and idiom of the

language used in order to enhance communication with the target readers and audiences.[5] Paramaterial, such as translators' prefaces, notes and interviews, has become increasingly important as a source of evidence about the agency of the translator (Batchelor 2022).

Two further aspects of my choices need a brief explanation here. First, all of the examples to be discussed in detail engage with trauma in the sense that traumatic events provide the context for the ancient text and for its structure and language. The modern translator engages not only with that but also with the implications for modern equivalents and the associations that might be made with contemporary trauma. This is a significant field for the relationship between temporalities and bears on translation theory and practice in several ways. It is a means of 'seriously working on the past', to borrow Adorno's phrase (Adorno 2005, quoted and discussed Gopal 2019: 453). It is also a necessary part of what I like to characterize as 'seriously working upon the present', as well as on the future, and brings into translation analysis questions about the sociopathologies of societies ancient and modern, and the construction of cultural memory (in antiquity and subsequently, including the nexus between the two). The paradigm of trauma also directs attention to the sometimes protean relationship between rational and affective in the language and structure of texts and in their interpretation and translation.[6]

Second, I have chosen 'narratives' as the framework for the discussion. Narratives are of several different kinds and their differences and inter-relationships are central to the activity of the translator. (i) *Narratives within the work* – these may include both the 'what' and the 'how', that is: the 'story', the development of the 'plot', the sequence of events and episodes, narrative techniques of focalization (if any), authorial intervention or *metalepsis* (the presence of the author in the text) and other 'shaping' techniques.[7] The narrative within the work includes communication with audiences within the text (internal). (ii) *Narrative directed to the immediate co-present audiences outside the work* (e.g. readers/spectators) and to future readers and audiences. Both the first and second dimensions of narrative include directions of the gaze, and the translator has to engage with those aspects, plus ensuring that the historical contexts and aesthetic techniques used in directing the gaze in the source text are communicated to the additional readers/audiences that are the target of the translation. In both the ante-text and the translation *all* these gazes are constituent parts in the construction of individual, social and community memory (of the text, its values and the contexts to which it relates).

Both the first two categories of narrative and their trajectories link across to the third one: (iii) *metanarrative*. I use this term as shorthand for how the work is rightly or wrongly perceived and categorized subsequently, both in itself (e.g. the *Iliad* as poem of war) *and* in relation to wider categories (e.g. the impact of war on human suffering and behaviour, lament, memory studies, memorialization). Translators/adapters have to engage with all these types of narrative, both in terms of their interpretation of the source text and in terms of their communication of their new text to their assumed readers and audiences. This means that translators, in different degrees, are involved with translation as commentary and as creativity.[8]

For those reasons, I have chosen three types of translation/translators for discussion in the extended examples. The first is the scholar/translator. Edith Hall's edition of

Aeschylus' *Persians* (1996) includes Greek text and translation on facing pages. Hall's Introduction and Commentary are sensitive to form and contexts as well as to language, lexical and tonal choices. Hall explains and justifies her interpretative judgements, and discusses the ancient audience and context of performance. Aeschylus' play and the approach taken by Hall as scholar-translator inform understanding and critical analysis of the three levels of narrative, within the play, beyond the play and in conjunction with metanarratives. Metanarratives include how the Athenians responded to victory and trauma in the Persian War; how they constructed their role in Greece; how the play, and the narratives it carries with it through translation, has been used subsequently; and how the suffering of enemies resonates with the perspectives of the victors.

My second example is the work of a poet-translator. Alice Oswald's *Memorial* (2011) combines detailed knowledge of Homer's Greek with an autonomous poetic voice. It is of special interest because of its disruption of elements of Homeric narrative and its adaptation of similes, while it retains the overall structure of the Homeric poem and its register, and explores transcultural sensitivity to lament. Oswald's translational technique results in an original work that also revises metanarratives about the notion of a 'good death' and about the relationship between memorialization and the realities of war.

My third example is drawn from historiography. I focus on some of the challenges and opportunities presented to the translator by Thucydides' *History of the Peloponnesian War*. The section includes brief discussion of the work of the dramaturg/translator John Barton, who selected and reworked extracts from Thucydides' narrative in the context of the heightened receptivity to metanarratives that characterized readers and audiences at the time of the Iraq wars in the late twentieth and early twenty-first centuries.

2.2. Aeschylus *Persians*: The scholar-translator

Tragedy raises special issues for how translators handle the intersections between historical context and aesthetics because its settings are largely mythological. Ancient tragedians transposed some contemporary issues away from Athens in place, time and mythological narratives, although they embedded hints about the relationship between the remote settings and contemporary events.[9] This also impacts on analysis of narratives and metanarratives. The few extant exceptions of specific referencing of events to do with recent history are, however, revealing. The best known is the play by Phrynichos, *The Capture of Miletos*. This referred to the sack of the Ionian Greek city by the Persians in 494 BCE. The sack took place in the final phase of the Ionian revolt of the Greek island cities against Persian domination in 494 BCE. The play is thought to have been performed in 493/2 but this is not absolutely certain (Hall 1996, 7, with n. 37; Mac Sweeney 2021).[10] According to Herodotus (6.21.2), audiences in Athens were moved to tears at the play's portrayal of the suffering people of a city with which they had cultural, economic, ethnic, religious and economic ties. Most of the male Milesians were killed, and the women and children enslaved. Survivors were taken to Susa; the city was in effect ethnically and politically 'cleansed' (Herodotus 6. 21).

The play was deemed to have been excessive in reminding the Athenians of 'evil happenings' (*kaka*), and the playwright was fined by the authorities. An order was made that no one should stage the play again. However, after a gap of some fifteen years Phrynichos again alluded to contemporary issues in *Phoenician Women*, which referenced the more cheering recent victories by the Greeks and marked a turning point in the acceptability of allusions to recent history (Cartledge 1996: 24, 32). Nevertheless, this new acceptability may have depended on a new context of victory.

The victory of the Greeks over the Persians at Marathon (490 BCE) was iconic in Athenian memory.[11] A second invasion by the Persians took place in 480 and involved the battles of Artemisium (sea) and Thermopylae (land, after which Xerxes laid waste central Greece and destroyed the Acropolis, *agora* and *kerameikos* in Athens). These were followed by the battles of Salamis in 480 (sea) and Plataea (land) in 479. Aeschylus' *Persians* followed in 472 BCE, and the trilogy of which it was a part was awarded first prize. The play offers some unique insights into how recent history was handled through the formal elements of tragedy and in its staging for the citizen spectators, many of whom would have had first-hand fighting experience, including memories of the actual battle of Salamis. In this respect, the key formal elements in the narrative presented in the play are the Messenger Speech (purporting to give a first-hand account of events that occurred off-stage), together with the interventions by the Chorus. Also crucial is the *rhesis* (solo speech), the lament by the Persian queen Atossa. The events at Salamis and the aftermath are ostensibly narrated in the play from the point of view of the defeated Persians. That presentation has shaped how the play has been received in scholarship, especially in causing keen debates about the extent to which play permitted or even encouraged the Athenian spectators to gloat in victory and to seize the main credit for the defeat of Persia, rather than honouring the role of other members of the Greek coalition.[12] A further strand in scholarly debate interprets the play as also encoding a warning to the Athenians against *hybris*, overweening pride and violence that would lead to complacency and damage them in the future. All these issues hinge on the nature and tone of the narrative presented in the play, and the scholar-translator's work is shaped by this. The narratives within the play also feed into the construction of metanarratives. These influence future receptions and staging of the play, including adaptations.[13] The metanarratives are also integral to historical studies of the construction of the role of Athens in the Persian wars. For example, Aeschylus' play has been adduced as evidence of the Athenian desire to elevate the naval battle at Salamis, with its role for the Athenian sailors, over the Spartan-led land battle at Plataea.[14] There is a further metanarrative that concerns the recovery of the Athenians from the trauma of successive invasions, especially the destruction of the Acropolis, and the construction of images of (Athenian) leadership as a psychosocial aid to recovery. This becomes one example in transhistorical studies of recovery from trauma (Proietti 2019).[15]

In discussing Aeschylus' play, therefore, concerns range from issues of historical 'truth'/plausibility in relation to the audience within the play, in relation to the audience in the theatre at the time of performance, and in relation to future readers, audiences and scholarly debates. To consider how these issues were approached by the scholar-translator, I will focus on one extended passage. I will not be addressing the question of the accuracy or otherwise of the play's ethnic and cultural depiction of the Persians (discussed in Hall 1996: 21–5; in Hall 1989; and in Harrison 2000). The concern will be with the 'truth' claims that might be made about the plausibility of the narrative of the battle and its aftermath, about the effects of the focus on the experience and feelings of the Persians, and about how the play might be situated in associated metanarratives.

Edith Hall's text, translation and commentary on Persians were published in 1996. As a scholar-translator, Hall (1996: 25–8) comments in the Introduction on the survival and manuscript transmission of the text, together with textual issues. She also makes clear that in the commentary she was concerned less with military history than with 'visual and performative dimensions of the play, its emotional impact, its metaphors, symbols, imagery and psychological registers'. She emphasizes her aims in the commentary to reveal the tension between 'the tragedy's "translation" of authentic Persian practices and blatant misrepresentations emanating from its ethnocentric Athenian perspective' (Hall 1996: 28). Taken together, the text, translation and commentary help to explain what the defeat of Xerxes meant to the victors. The Introduction takes as its opening gambit: 'One of the many themes to have been neglected by critics in Aeschylus' *Persians* is memory' (Hall 1996: 1).

The setting of the play is by the tomb of Dareios, the Persian ruler who had led the first invasion of Greece and was defeated at Marathon. His son Xerxes led a second invasion and was defeated at Plataea and Salamis, after which he fled back to Asia. This occasions a key sequence in Persians, the Messenger Speech which is delivered to the Queen Atossa (mother of Xerxes) and to the Chorus of Persian Elders (*Persians* lines 249–514, with facing translation pages 53–69). It is the longest Messenger speech in extant tragedy. The Messenger Speech convention enabled focalized narratives of events that took place off-stage to become part of the texture and emotional world of the play, both for the 'internal' audiences who heard the Messenger and the 'external' spectators in the theatre (at the time and subsequently). Because the context in this play was one of recent history, the Messenger's apparently 'factual' narrative had to be plausible to the spectators, many of whom would have had the events in their own memories. It also had to colour and energize the dynamics of the play.[16] The Chorus specifically notes that 'you will soon be in possession of a full and truthful report', even if what it contains is disastrous news (*kakon* – possibly an allusion to the response of the Athenian audience to Phrynichos' *Fall of Miletos*, and an indication to the spectators that the boot is now on the other foot). In the Greek text used by Hall, the Messenger's Speech starts with a summary of the extent of the disaster and then gives more detail in three main sections: a roll-call of the names of the dead Persian commanders, a contrast with Greek democratic practice; a second narrative covering the size of the respective fleets, with a theological closing section on religion and the protection of Athens by a combination of Pallas Athene and the citizens – 'while men remain to a city its defences are secure' (line 349, tr. Hall 1996: 59, which renders 'safe' as 'secure'); and the third section of the speech recounts the actual naval battle.

The most important aspects of the narrative include its embedded evidence-based approach, for example, emphasis on eye-witness testimony, which also echoes the language of the law courts – as in line 266, tr. page 55, in which the Messenger says that his account does not depend on hearsay. The impact of this 'factual' thread is deepened by the emotional effect of the lament that introduces it and by the appeal to the senses of the visual images of the Persian dead in shipwrecks. In the Chorus' lament these recall the fate of the Greeks returning from Troy.[17] The lament also pictures the grief of the bereaved families, weeping widows, parents bereft in their old age (lines 533–90, with facing translation pages 71–2). These are conventions of lamentation in Greek literature. What is significant here is that the sympathy evoked is for the Persian defeated and yet that also has to be viewed through the prism of Greek values, which held that it was good to harm enemies. However, it is also worth noting that in the *Iliad* Homer gives at least equal weight to the sufferings of the Trojans (notionally the enemies of the Greeks).[18] There is an underlying Homeric parallel with Aeschylus' treatment of the Persians in that the revered old ruler (Dareios/Priam) is presented with respect and the blame attached to an impetuous son (Xerxes/Paris). Since Aeschylus' work is pervaded by allusions to Homer as well as to the settings of the Trojan War, it is reasonable to think the ambivalence in *Persians* is there for a purpose, an example perhaps of how Aeschylus was working with the remote 'past' as well as with recent events.

The Chorus' response to the Messenger's narrative is also intertwined with accusations against Xerxes and implied celebration of some kind of 'liberation' of Ionian Greeks (and possibly Persians themselves) from the threat of his yoke. The episode is prescient with notes of warning – warnings against impiety and against the violence and arrogance associated with *hybris* that are articulated by the ghost of Dareios later in the play (lines 808, 821–2, with translation at page 87, in which Hall leaves *hybris* untranslated and instead glosses the transliterated concept in the commentary, ad loc., implying its untranslatability into modern English usage).[19] The importance of the whole Messenger sequence is underlined by the apparent inclusion of antiphonal singing, which is unusual for the role of characters who are not protagonists in the plays. Its depth and complexity both accommodate and hold in tension the different strands of historical narrative, performative transformation of perspectives and metanarrative, which in its turn fed into the Athenians' construction of their recovery from the trauma of Persian invasion. There are also implications for how the play has been received and staged in the modern period.[20] The conflicting emotions of lament for suffering and triumphalism for its infliction present challenges for translators and dramaturgs as well as opening up the possibilities for readers and spectators to experience overlapping affinities with invaders and invaded, and with victors and the defeated. Hall's combination of text, facing-page translation and commentary provides the raw material for exploring the subtleties of Aeschylus' use of narrative and the possibilities for metanarratives.

2.3. Alice Oswald *Memorial*: The poet-translator

Alice Oswald's *Memorial* was published in 2011.[21] It is a work that is both a new poem in its own right and also a 'translation' of aspects of Homer's *Iliad*.[22] *Memorial* has been performed by Oswald in many venues and to different types of audience. In the author's Preface to the printed text, Oswald began by saying that 'this is a translation of the *Iliad*'s atmosphere, not its story' (Oswald 2011: 1). Her emphasis on *atmosphere* raises a number of critical points – how the atmosphere in the Homeric source text is depicted and how that relates to Oswald's poem (how this shapes the poem aesthetically and temporally, including the dominant themes, the formal elements and diction); the relationship between atmosphere and narrative *between* both poems and within them, especially the shifts brought about by the selection of material and forms, as well as the tonality created by Oswald; the impact of modern performance of epic on how spectators and listeners experience the poem; the ways in which the subject matter of the Homeric and the Oswald poems feeds into individual and collective memory, ancient and modern; and the extent to which metanarratives about the *Iliad* and about death in war are revised or reinforced.

The first claim in Oswald's preface concerns the removal of the conventional label of 'nobility' that critics (at least since Matthew Arnold) have attached to Homer's *Iliad*, and which has been instrumental in creating affinities in subsequent literature and public imagination between the deaths of Homeric heroes and the lasting fame of a 'good death' (*kleos*). A good death will in a sense immortalize a dead soldier. Provided that he is accorded heroic status, his exploits will live on in the public memory and imagination.[23] Rather than accepting that the *Iliad* is a celebration of a particular kind of nobility, Oswald prefers the term used by critics in antiquity, *enargeia* ('bright unbearable reality'). She is attracted by this term because it is the word used when the gods come to earth as themselves and not in disguise. That is, it carries associations of truth, however hard to bear that truth may be. Oswald described the poem that was left after the removal of Homer's narrative and episodic structure as 'bipolar [...] made of similes and short biographies of soldiers'. In using that embedded metaphor she not only suggested a tension between art forms but also referenced a relationship between two poetic traditions in Greek poetry: pastoral lyric (in which the metre of similes is sometimes compressed as part of the shorter lyric form), and the biographical elements in lament poetry (Oswald 2011: 1). When the body of the dead person was laid out, the mourning was led by a professional poet and was 'antiphonally answered' by women who offered personal biographies of the dead person. In Oswald's response to these elements of the *Iliad*, the 'biographies' are paraphrases of the Greek and the similes are translations (Oswald 2011: 2).

However, the term 'translations' needs qualification. Oswald categorized her approach to translation as 'fairly irreverent'. Although she worked closely with the Greek, she avoided 'carrying words over into English', instead using the Greek to provide 'openings through which to see what Homer was looking at' (Oswald 2011: 2). This introduces a layer of interpretation and commentary that underpins her poem.[24] The capacity of poetry and poetic translation to provide 'openings' is a favourite metaphor for Oswald. For example, in her May Lecture 'Sidelong Glances' in her Oxford Professor of Poetry Series (27 May 2021) she discussed how literature has 'a back door'. Oswald identified aurality and orality (often exemplified by subaltern groups such as women and ethnically marginalized groups) as rich sources of unexpected ways into a poem. On the basis of her discussion of 'sidelong glances', she also proposed that when poets sing, 'the dead will turn up and sing with you' – a suggestion relevant to epic in performance and therefore to the reception of

Homer. In her Lecture, Oswald also argued that traditional processes of storytelling can provide an alternative to traditions of literary language. In contrast to those traditions, Oswald's 'glancing' is a lateral and associative movement, allowing poetry to be made from a patchwork of remarks and voices, rather than relying on poetry being a link in a great chain of literary development. The points made in the Lecture directly illuminate Oswald's sensitivity to the spirit and atmosphere of oral poetry, which she regards as 'never stable, but always adapting itself to a new audience, as if its language, unlike written language, was still alive and kicking'. Her poem offers 'a series of memories and similes laid side by side: an antiphonal account of man in his world' (Oswald 2011: 2).[25]

There are two key aspects to Oswald's presentation of this 'account'. The first is the selection of the material that is presented to readers via the printed text and to the listeners/spectators at her performances and radio readings. The second key aspect is the communication in her performances of the orality and aurality of the impact of the *Iliad* and of *Memorial*. In the selection of material from Homer, she not only removes the authorial narrative and its associated focalizations but also refocuses the biographies and varies the locations and repetitions of the similes attached to dead soldiers – including soldiers who were not accorded extended treatment in Homer.[26] The list of the dead takes up eight printed pages, functioning as a prelude to the main text and resembling the inscriptions of names on a war memorial. The list is presented in order of their deaths, starting with Protesilaus ('The first to die was PROTESILAUS [...] He died in mid-air jumping to be the first ashore/There was his house half-built', Oswald 2011: 13) and ending with Hector 'And HECTOR died like everyone else .... He always knew it would happen' (Oswald 2011: 71).

In her discussion of modern repositioning of Homer from epic to lyric, Georgina Paul has pointed out that it is misleading to emphasize the centrality of narrative to epic at the expense of non-narrative aspects, and that Oswald redresses that imbalance in awareness by retaining the structure of the *Iliad* and the order of deaths but also allowing lyric, especially pastoral and choral lyric, to infuse the similes. These are sometimes repositioned as 'free units', lifted out of their original context and relocated in new ones (Paul 2018: 141–4). An example is the case of the opening simile of *Iliad* XVI, 5–13 (in which Achilles calls Patroclus 'girlish'). This simile is transferred to portray the dying Scamandrius as a dependent child (Oswald 2011: 18–19).[27] The movement provides both an instance of 'repetition with a difference' and a use of the content of a Homeric simile as a kind of 'hanging motif' that can be connected and reconnected, in this case to add an emotional aspect to the instant of death.[28] The emotional associations (with grief, families and their feelings) are present in Homer but are amplified and reworked by Oswald to include the feelings of those who are dying. The overall effect is to deepen and extend the range of poetic 'truths' in the poem. Plausibility is intensified in performance through the body language, breathing, tonality and gesture of the rhapsody, all of which bring the audience into the poem, emotionally and physically. Hearing, seeing, moving and thinking are part of a process of experiencing, engaging and understanding that brings together the performer and the audience members. Epic poetry is especially dynamic in creating that kind of crossover. It has the capacity to accommodate and sustain change without losing its own identity. This capacity is sometimes theorized as 'self-difference' and underlies much of the creative practice that is central to classical receptions in the literary, filmic and performing arts. Self-difference has also been conceptualized as a key characteristic in translation studies, providing another way of mapping the mutuality of the two areas (see Hardwick 2018a: 571, with further references).

Oswald's poem is also an implicit commentary on memorialization. Recent research in memory studies has problematized the inter-relationships between individual and social/communal memory: 'individual memory cannot be detached from the memory of others, since the definition and verification of a memory often implies an awareness of others' memories: our memories are vivified, completed and guaranteed only in relation to those of others. Memory, therefore, is neither exclusively nor intrinsically individual' (Giangiulio 2019a: 19). In framing her poem as a roll-call for the dead that links the experiences of the dying and the emotional impact on their families through the lyric and formal tonalities of lament, Oswald redraws the relationship between individual members of a community (ancient or modern) and the members of the 'imagined community', constructed by memorials, material and poetic (Canevaro 2019: 341). Oswald's poem diminishes the role of one aspect of Homer's narrative, the focalized sequential development of the story of the war, but retains the descriptions of the experiences of death, including the mourning by families. Those aspects are present in Homer but moved to the centre by Oswald, especially through the emotional and affective impact of lyric and lament. The overall effect is to undermine the metanarrative of *kleos* as *telos*, its subsequent domination of perspectives on Homer as 'the poet of war', and its impact on the ideas and practices associated with memorials.

2.4. Evidence, analysis and narratives: The dramaturg as translator of Thucydides

Thucydides' *History of the Peloponnesian War* recorded and interpreted the events and outcomes of the war between the Athenians and the Spartans and their allies in the second half of the fifth century BCE. It has become a foundational text not only for ancient historians and students of historiography but also for a range of disciplines in the social sciences, such as political science, international relations and strategic studies (Harloe and Morley (2012); Lee and Morley (2015): 1–10; Morley 2014; Rengakos and Tsakmakis 2006). This range of impact has necessarily involved many translations (complicated by Thucydides' compressed and sometimes obscure Greek). These translations have become the main source for modern engagement with his ideas and methods. Thucydides included some first-person material, authorial interventions in which he commented self-reflexively about his methods and the formal structure of his work and about the underlying causes and effects of the war.[29]

Emily Greenwood has observed the remarkable lack of detailed discussion of the history of translations of Thucydides. To help remedy this lack, she analysed fourteen different translations of Thucydides, commenting in particular on their relationships to normative translation theory and suggested that 'Translation is reception in the sense that the translator interprets an author in the light of several different contexts: cultural, historical, literary, academic/scholarly, and in conscious engagement with existing translation'. She also concluded that adaptation of Thucydides is an under-researched area, especially since adaptations encode how Thucydides continues to function as an intermediary and intercultural site, including permitting and even inviting affective as well as rationalist responses (Greenwood 2015: 92, 114–15). To this I would add that Thucydides' text embeds conscious engagement with a range of narratives, including metanarratives, and that this in turn energizes further metanarratives.

To lay a foundation for addressing those complexities, it is useful to identify three layers in his writing: (i) Thucydides' perspective on evidence and historical truth, (ii) the formal and structural elements that frame his *History* and (iii) how these aspects converge in the narratives within and beyond his text. Thucydides' *History* is an example of a text in which the author is working to explain the recent past in a way that informs (his) present and which he hopes will also inform future analysts. However, the sophisticated layering of his text has also influenced how future events, unknown to Thucydides, have been interpreted (including how agency has been conceptualized in contexts unimagined by Thucydides).

In the opening book of his History, Thucydides claimed that the war between the Athenians and the Spartans was 'the greatest war of all' (1.21), beyond even the Persian War because of its length and because of the unprecedented suffering it caused: 'never before had so many cities been captured and then devastated ... never had there been so many exiles, never such loss of life, both in the actual warfare and in internal revolutions (*staseis*)' (Thuc. 1.23). He also claimed that the relevance of his account went beyond the present since, assuming human nature remained the same, similar events would be likely to occur in the future (1.22). He also emphasized that his account was evidence based, derived from his own experience or that of eye-witnesses, and that his methods focused on reporting the facts (*erga*). However, he swiftly went on to concede that so far as the deliberations in policy debates were concerned, the words (*logoi*) he attributed to speakers were what he considered the occasion demanded (1.22). This is a covert way of saying that his representation of these speeches was based on his own analysis of the strategic contexts in which they took place. That strand in the work represents another dimension to *logos*. Moreover, most of Thucydides' shaping of the extended narrative of events is highlighted by debates and speeches. Those that are directly related to decisions about the conduct of the war include the Mytilene Debate of 427 BCE, in which the Athenian Assembly changed its mind about the command to kill and enslave the inhabitants of a defeated city (3.36-50); the Melian Dialogue of 416/5, in which the leaders of the city of Melos failed to persuade the Athenians that they should be allowed to remain neutral, with the result that after a siege 'the Melians surrendered unconditionally to the Athenians, who put to death all the men of military age whom they took, and sold the women as slaves', sending out five hundred men as permanent occupiers (5. 84-115); and the debate preceding the sending of the disastrous and hybristic Athenian expedition to Sicily in 415 (6.8-32). Key speeches also include the *epitaphios* (Funeral Speech) attributed to Pericles on the occasion of the communal funeral given to those killed in the first year of the war, in which the Athenian leader celebrated the citizen democracy, the Athenian *arche* (sea-empire) and the glorious buildings financed from tribute money from the 'allies' (2.34-46); the 'Last

Speech' by Pericles (2.60-65), in which the *strategos* justified the exercise of Athenian power: 'your empire (*arche*) is now like a tyranny; it may have been wrong to take it but it is certainly dangerous to let it go.'[30] Thucydides carefully juxtaposed these set-piece speeches with prose accounts of crucial events; for example, the plague that ravaged the Athenians and almost destroyed their sense of communal solidarity is described immediately after the triumphalist *epitaphios* (2.47-55). The prose account of the civil strife of 427 in another Greek city, Corcyra (3. 80-84), demonstrates the relationship between external war (*polemos*) and internal war (*stasis*) and includes discussion of how the very meanings attached to words change swiftly in times of crisis. That episode precedes the account of the factional rivalry in Athens that led to the decision to send the expedition to Sicily.

It will be clear from this very brief outline that Thucydides' *History* is structured to present much more than a simple narrative. Thucydides scholars have problematized simplistic notions that he was either a 'scientific' historian or a 'tragic' historian, demonstrating instead that he used literary and theatrical techniques to manipulate juxtaposition of speeches and narrative, to embed allusions, to flash forward and backwards, to question complacencies and to direct readers' attention to metanarratives beyond the sequence of events in the war (see Hesk 2015, with extensive citations of modern scholarship in political science as well as in ancient history). There is an epistemological gap between Thucydides' authoritative focus on giving an accurate account of events and his admission that he focalized speakers to say 'what the occasion demanded', which brings to the fore the formal and allusive features of his work. This presents multiple challenges to translators, and justifies Greenwood's insistence on comparing different translations (Greenwood 2015, 2021). In the case of Thucydides, comparing translations helps scholars (and students) to uncover the political lenses through which translators perceived and expressed Thucydides' concepts.[31] Translators also have to disentangle his sometimes coded language and to attempt to find target language equivalents for concepts that might otherwise have been left transliterated with glosses supplied. The translator's task is complex but underlines the richness of the narratives and metanarratives that can be retrieved.

Recent geopolitical events have continued to inspire different ways of commenting on and reworking Thucydides' special combination of *logos* and *ergon* as interrelated spheres of human activity. These have included some different approaches to using Thucydides as a text (usually excerpted) to provide a site for thinking and for transformation of perspectives. A performative example was the 2006 performance in London, directed by John Barton in collaboration with the Royal Shakespeare Company, of *The War that Still Goes On*, a 'one-off' performed reading of a sequence of episodes from Thucydides (published text Barton 2006, description and analysis in Hardwick 2015b).[32] The occasion attracted an audience of some five hundred people on a Sunday afternoon at the Aldwych Theatre. The casually dressed cast sat on stacking chairs in a semi-circle. The actor who spoke Thucydides' authorial interventions sat at the side. Many audience members were not familiar with Thucydides, and the performed reading was punctuated by sometimes incredulous gasps from audience members who saw and felt connections between Thucydides' depiction of, for example, the ancient power politics of the Melian Dialogue and the recent invasion of Iraq by a coalition of forces led by the US and including the UK.[33] These responses were sometimes prompted and intensified by Barton's use of modern idiom. This element was in some respect problematic because the selection of episodes and the language and register used by Barton tended to activate correspondences with the present and to filter out historical and contextual differences. The performance was followed by a panel discussion composed of academics, prompting the audience to think about the influence of modes of performance on understanding and critical thinking. This redressed the balance somewhat as it created a deliberative association between 'performing' Thucydides and discussing how transhistorical analysis and debate might be fostered.[34] In that respect, appreciation of the interplay in Thucydides' *History* between narratives and metanarratives was crucial, as was awareness of the additional layer of metanarratives and the desire to create connectivities that were brought by the audience in the theatre and fostered by Barton's excerpted translations.

This examination of the interfaces between textuality, translation and reception indicates that alternative types of 'fidelity' theory need to be developed. These would take account not only of the generic 'historical/historiographical' frames but also of the ways in which literature (oral and written) and dramatic texts are seeded into, and in their turn create dense temporalities that are anachronistic and timely as well as rooted in the contexts and aesthetic forms of the ante-texts. The dual function of translators – as agents who excavate ancient texts and also produce new texts with multi-directional reach – creates new transactional sites. These include internal, external and metanarratives which can sometimes challenge fixed hegemonic notions about the cultural trajectories of ancient texts and contexts. Without analysis of this density of translational temporalities, it is impossible to 'seriously work upon the past' (as Adorno put it), or, indeed, to work upon the present and the future.

Notes

1 I would like to thank the volume editor most warmly both for his invitation to contribute to the discussions and for his encouragement and patience during the writing process. I also thank Alexandra Lianeri and Richard Armstrong for ongoing discussions on many aspects of translation theory and practice.
2 Of the two most progressive recent discussion of the cultural history and future of the study of Greek and Roman antiquity, Bromberg (2021) gives translation a core role in his call for global approaches. The PostClassicisms Collective (2020) surprisingly devotes very little attention either to the theory of translation or to its impact. The extent of the cultural mapping promoted by study of translations is discussed in Lianeri (2008). De Pourcq (2020) considers the impact of different frames used in classical reception studies (including Hardwick 2020).
3 The work of Josephine Balmer (2009, 2013) on translation and creativity and of Susan Bassnett (2014) on histories and theories of translation have been especially important. Baker (2022) problematizes key issues and contains important essays on translation as commentary (Batchelor) and on performance and literary agency (Saldanha).

4   Variations on this theme include the concept of simultaneity put forward by the poet and dramatist Derek Walcott, notably in his exploration of the interwoven resonances between Homeric *nostos*, desire to return home, and the failed attempt of Achille (in *Omeros*) to return to his African roots and be recognized (Walcott 1990). See also Holmes (2016) on *cosmopoiesis* and its relationship to the creation of the future(s).

5   Unfortunately lack of space precludes discussion of this aspect (which would merit a whole chapter). Examples might include Tony Harrison's combination of elevated and vernacular diction in his film poem *Prometheus* (discussed in Stead 2022; Hall 2021 ch. 7 discusses Harrison's filmic work more widely), Blake Morrison's rural Yorkshire setting of his version of Sophocles' tragedies for performance in a cattle market by Northern Broadsides (Morrison 2003) and Seamus Heaney's religious and demotic registers in translations of episodes from Aeschylus and Virgil and in his full translation of *Aeneid* VI (Heaney 2009 and 2016. Discussion in Hardwick *forthcoming* c).

6   Andrew Bowie's recently published introduction to Adorno discusses how Adorno engaged with key ideas in history, philosophy, sociology and critical history. Adorno's project was motivated by the Holocaust (Bowie 2022). See also the discussion in Klooster and Kuin (2020). Hardwick (2019) surveys some examples in antiquity and its modern receptions.

7   On *metalepsis*, see Matzner (2020). On *metalepsis* in the reworking and translation of Greek and Roman texts by Michael Longley, see Hardwick (2009).

8   This tripartite division has affinities with recent work in classical reception studies; for example, Haywood and Mac Sweeney (2018) identify detail, theme and metapoetics as key aspects of the reception of the topic of the Trojan War but are less focused on readers and spectators as agents in translation.

9   For example, Sophocles' *Antigone*, which debated issues about burial and the conflicts between *polis* and family funerary rites; also Euripides' *The Women of Troy*, which was performed in 415 BCE after the Athenian atrocities in the defeat of Melos in 416 (although, taking into account the time necessary for being granted a chorus and rehearsals, the writing of the play may have been underway before that event. The issue would have been at the front of the spectators' minds; the trilogy was awarded only the second prize).

10 Mac Sweeney rightly points out that the precise associations that underlay the response of the Athenian spectators depend to some extent on whether the play was staged before or after the Persian sack of the Acropolis at Athens in 480/79.

11 Aeschylus served as a hoplite soldier at Marathon and was again called on in 480/79 (Salamis and Plataea). His brother was killed at Marathon ([Ion of Chios], *Life of Aeschylus*, 4).

12 Hall (1996: 9–15) discusses the celebration in other art forms of victory over the Persians, the various kinds of evidence available to Aeschylus and the political context in Athens.

13 Examples are included on the database of the *Archive of Performances of Greek Drama*, based at the University of Oxford and are freely accessible at www.apgrd.ox.ac.uk. On the relationship between translations and adaptations, see further Hardwick (2021a).

14 See Harrison (2000) for the political and cultural investment in Athenian identity as leader in Greece. Yates (2019: especially 5 and 166) notes the overall lack of

15   coherence in the sources concerning hegemony among the Greeks, which was to some extent a retrospective construction.
15   At the time of writing, Professor Proietti has further work in preparation on the topic 'Coping with War Trauma in Ancient Greece'. I am grateful to her for kindly sending me bibliographical material (Proietti 2021).
16   It is likely that some of the Chorus members themselves, performers who were not professional actors but were drawn from the citizen body, might have had personal recollections of the battle, either in respect of their own participation or that of their friends and family members.
17   Aeschylus also imaged death at sea in the speech of the Herald in *Agamemnon* (lines 637ff) in which the water 'blossomed' with corpses as the Greeks returned from Troy.
18   In contrast with Homer, Aeschylus does differentiate strongly between Greeks and their oriental enemies in descriptions of dress, culture and speech (Hall makes much of this in the Introduction and Commentary; see further pages 19–25). However, she does not deduce from this that the suffering of the Persians is devalued or loses dramatic impact.
19   The concept of *hybris* indicated violent assault, physical or verbal, attacking the honour of someone else, human or divine, and leading to disaster caused by overweening pride of the perpetrator. It is a major theme in fifth-century-BCE tragedy and historiography.
20   The performance history of *Persians* is documented at www.apgrd.ox.ac.uk.
21   *Memorial* was awarded the Warwick Literary Prize in 2013, the first volume of poetry to win the award.
22   Oswald was trained as a classicist at the University of Oxford and reads Homer in the original language. Her *oeuvre* as a poet is extensive. In interaction with classical themes and texts, she draws on her own observations of the natural world in the West of England (e.g. in *Dart* 2002, which won the T. S. Eliot Prize for Poetry).
23   The effect on, for example, public awareness and attitudes to the war created by the poetry written during and after the slaughter of soldiers in the First World War has been the subject of considerable analysis by scholars and historians. For associations with classical material, see further Vandiver (2010), Hardwick in Pender (2018b) and Hardwick, Harrison and Vandiver (*forthcoming*).
24   It also avoids some of the 'pitfalls of translation' that are challenging to translators who seek exact equivalence between ancient Greek and modern English concepts; see Vandiver (2022: discussing Herodotus).
25   Interestingly, 'An Account of Homer's Iliad' is the subtitle of Christopher Logue's *War Music* (Logue 2015). However, the meaning suggested by the word 'Account' in Logue is very different from that in Oswald's translational approach (for Logue, see Greenwood 2007).
26   On repetition with a difference as a literary technique in classical receptions, see further Hardwick (2016; 2022).
27   Emily Greenwood (2018: 277–8) has cited this usage to point out that Oswald's concept of the bard (*aoidos*) is to a certain extent historicized.
28   Paul also draws attention to how Oswald brings into the poem her expertise as a horticulturalist, for instance in the simile of the olive tree, deployed by Homer to mark the death of Euphorbas (*Iliad* XV11.52–60; Oswald 2011: 31; Paul 2018: 143). The contribution of ecocriticism to classical reception and translation studies is increasingly recognized (see further Hardwick, Harrison and Vandiver (*forthcoming*).

29 Thucydides himself had been appointed to a military command as general, but in 424 BCE he was accused of failing to carry out his mission and dismissed. He commented that this and his subsequent exile enabled him to obtain evidence from all sides (4.104–7).
30 The structuring of Book 2 reads like a commentary on Thucydides' assertion at the beginning of his work that war is the result of fear, self-interest, rivalry, greed and the desire for lasting reputation (1.76.2). Translations quoted here are from Rex Warner's version (first published in 1954, London: Penguin).
31 This is important for any reader but especially so because of the use made of Thucydides' text and concepts in other disciplinary contexts, such as international relations and political science, where users are less likely to have detailed knowledge of the Greek.
32 John Barton (1928–2018) had a long history of responses to and re-arrangement of ancient material, for example, in *Tantalus; An Ancient Myth for a New Millenium*, a 'blockbuster' collaboration with the theatre director Peter Hall (1930–2017). *Tantalus* consisted of ten plays, performed in sequence, which drew on Greek poetry and plays about the Trojan War (published text Barton 2000). An earlier collaboration with Kenneth Cavander resulted in *The Greeks*, an adaptation of ten plays on the *Oresteia* theme which was staged in 1980 (published text Barton and Cavander 1981).
33 There was a performative irony in that in the Mytilene debate the Athenian demagogue Cleon was depicted by Thucydides as accusing the members of the Athenian Assembly of behaving 'like spectators at a show' who were irrationally persuaded by colourful rhetoric to change their minds (3.38).
34 A productive attempt to foster that kind of dialogue took place at Bristol University in 2013 at a workshop titled 'Might Is Right? Ancient and Modern Debates', organized by Neville Morley. A short dramatization of Thucydides' Melian Dialogue was performed by four drama students, facing each other in pairs across a table. The discussion that followed considered scripting and performance aspects (including bodily movement and gesture) as well as the political and ethical issues (see further Hardwick 2015: 296–7).

References

Adorno, Theodor W. (2005), 'The Meaning of Working through the Past', in Theodor W. Adorno, *Critical Models: Interventions and Catchwords*, trans. Henry W. Pickford, 89–103, New York: Columbia University Press.

Baker, Mona (ed.) (2022), *Unsettling Translation: Studies in Honour of Theo Hermans*, London: Routledge. Open Access, https://www.taylorfrancis.com/books/oa-edit/10.4324/9781003134633/unsettling-translation-mona-baker (accessed 5 June 2022).

Balmer, Jospehine (2009), *The Word for Sorrow*, Cambridge: Salt.

Balmer, Josephine (2013), *Piecing Together the Fragments: Translating Classical Verse, Creating Contemporary Poetry*, Oxford: Oxford University Press.

Barton, John (2000), *Tantalus*, London: Oberon Books.

Barton, John (2006), *The War that Still Goes On: Adapted from Thucydides' History of the Peloponnesian War and Plato's Dialogue with Alcibiades*, London: Oberon Books.

Barton, John and Kenneth Cavander (1981), *The Greeks: The War, the Murders, the Gods. Ten Greek Plays Given as a Trilogy by the Royal Shakespeare Company*, London: Heinemann.

Bassnett, Susan (2014), *Translation*, London: Routledge.
Batchelor, Katrhyn (2022), 'Translation as Commentary. Paratext, Hypertext, Metatext', in Baker (2022: 48–61), http://www.taylorfrancis.com.
Bowie, Andrew (2022), *Theodor Adorno: A Very Short Introduction*, Oxford: Oxford University Press.
Bromberg, Jacques A. (2021), *Global Classics*, London and New York: Routledge.
Butler, Shane (ed.) (2016), *Deep Classics: Rethinking Classical Reception*, London: Bloomsbury.
Byrne, Sandie (ed.) (2022), *Tony Harrison and the Classics*, Oxford: Oxford University Press.
Canevaro, Mirko (2019), 'Courage in War and the Courage of the War Dead – Ancient and Modern Reflections', in Giangiulio (2019b: 187–205).
Cartledge, Paul (1996), 'Deep Plays': Theatre as Process in Greek Civic Life', in Pat E. Easterling (ed.), *The Cambridge Companion to Greek Tragedy*, 3–35, Cambridge: Cambridge University Press.
De Pourcq, M. Maarten, Nathalie de Haan and David Rijser (2020), *Framing Classical Reception Studies: Different Perspectives on a Developing Field*, Metaforms: Studies in the Reception of Classical Antiquity, Leiden: Brill.
Giangiulio, Maurizio (2019a), 'Do Societies Remember? The Notion of Collective Memory: Paradigms and Problems (from Maurice Halbwachs on)', in Giangiulio (2019b: 17–33).
Giangiulio, Maurizio, Elena Franchi and Giorgia Proietti (eds.) (2019b), *Commemorating War and War Dead: Ancient and Modern*, Stuttgart: Franz Steiner Verlag.
Gopal, Pryiamvada (2019), *Insurgent Empire: Anticolonial Resistance and British Dissent*, London and New York: Verso.
Greenwood, Emily (2005), *Thucydides and the Shaping of History*, London: Duckworth.
Greenwood, Emily (2007), 'Logue's TeleVision: Reading Homer from a Distance', in Barbara Graziosi and Emily Greenwood (eds.), *Homer in the Twentieth Century: Between World Literature and the Western Canon*, 145–76, Oxford: Oxford University Press.
Greenwood, Emily (2015), 'On Translating Thucydides', in Lee and Morley (2015: 91–121).
Greenwood, Emily (2018), 'Multimodal Twenty-First-Century Bards: From Live Performance to Audiobook in the Homeric Adaptations of Simon Armitage and Alice Oswald', in Macintosh (2018: 275–88).
Greenwood, Emily (2021), 'Herodotus, Anti-colonialism, Diversity, and Black Traditions in the Modern World', Herodotus Helpline, 24 March, https://www.herodotushelpline.org/seminar-schedule, with videolink (accessed 23 September 2022).
Hall, E. (1989), *Inventing the Barbarian: Greek Self-definition through Tragedy*, Oxford: Oxford University Press.
Hall, Edith (ed., intr., tr., and comm.) (1996), *Aeschylus Persians*, Warminster: Aris and Phillips.
Hall, Edith (2021), *Tony Harrison: Poet of Radical Classicism*, London: Bloomsbury.
Hardwick, Lorna (2009), 'Is the 'Silken Thread' Worth More Than 'a fart in a bearskin'? Or How Translation Practice Matters in Poetry and Drama', in S. J. Harrison (2009: 172–93).
Hardwick, Lorna (2015), 'Thucydidean Concepts', in Lee and Morley (2015: 493–511).
Hardwick, Lorna (2016), 'Homer, Repetition and Reception', in A. Efstathiou and I. Karamanou (eds.), *Homeric Reception across Generic and Cultural Contexts*, *Trends in Classics* Supplementary Volume 37, 15–30, Berlin: De Gruyter.
Hardwick, Lorna (2018a), 'Epilogue. Voices, Bodies, Silences and Media: Heightened Receptivities in Epic in Performance', in F. Macintosh (2018: 558–72).
Hardwick, Lorna (2018b), 'The Poetics of Cultural Memory: World War 1 Refractions of Ancient Peace', in Elizabeth Pender (ed.), *Classical Receptions Journal Special Issue: Classics and Classicists in World War 1*, 10 (4): 393–414.

Hardwick, Lorna (2019), 'Classics in Extremis: The Edges of Classical Reception' in Edmund Richardson (ed.), *Classics in Extremis*, 13–24, London: Bloomsbury.
Hardwick, Lorna (2020), 'Aspirations and Mantras in Classical Reception Research: Can There Really Be Dialogue between Ancient and Modern?', in De Pourcq (2020: 15–32).
Hardwick, Lorna (2021a), 'Translation and/as Adaptation', in Vayos Liapis and Avra Sidiropoulou (eds.), *Adapting Greek Tragedy: Contemporary Contexts for Ancient Texts*, 110–30, Cambridge: Cambridge University Press.
Hardwick, Lorna (2021b), 'Tracking Classical Scholarship: Myth, Evidence and Epistemology', in S. J. Harrison and C. Pelling (eds.), *Classical Scholarship and Its History: Essays in Honour of Christopher Stray*, 9–31, Berlin and Boston: De Gruyter.
Hardwick, Lorna (2022), 'Heightened Receptivities: When Ancient and Modern Meet in Greek Tragedy', in I. Karamanou (ed.), *Ancient Theatre: Proceedings of the Nafplion Conference on Otherness*, 283–95, Tripoli, GR: University of the Peloponnese.
Hardwick, Lorna (2023 forthcoming a), 'Cultural Hegemonies: Subaltern Agency through Greek and Roman Texts', in Gramsci Network (ed.), *Class and Classics: Historiography, Reception, Challenges; Towards a Democratization of Classical Studies*, Trends in Classics Supp. Vol., Berlin and Boston: De Gruyter.
Hardwick, Lorna (2023 forthcoming b), 'What's behind the Label?', in J. Krasilnikov, V. Nørskov and C. Thrue Djurslev (eds.), *Popular Receptions of Classical Antiquity*, Aarhus.
Hardwick, Lorna (2023 forthcoming c), 'Seamus Heaney's Religious Palette: Catholic, Roman, Greek', in C. Murray (ed.), *Cambridge Themes in Irish Literature and Culture: Religion*, Cambridge: Cambridge University Press.
Hardwick, Lorna, Stephen J. Harrison and Elizabeth Vandiver (forthcoming), *Greek and Roman Antiquity in First World War Poetry: Making Connections*, Oxford: Oxford University Press.
Harloe, Katherine and Neville Morley (eds.) (2012), *Thucydides and the Modern World: Reception, Reinterpretation and Influence from the Renaissance to the Present*, Cambridge: Cambridge University Press.
Harrison, Stephen J. (ed.) (2009), *Living Classics: Greece and Rome in Contemporary Poetry in English*, Oxford: Oxford University Press.
Harrison, Thomas (2000), *The Emptiness of Asia: Aeschylus' Persians and the History of the Fifth Century*, London: Bloomsbury.
Harrison, Tony (1998), *Prometheus*, London: Faber.
Haywood, Jan and Naoíse Mac Sweeney (2018), *Homer's Iliad and the Trojan War: Dialogues of Tradition*, London: Bloomsbury Academic.
Heaney, Seamus (2009), 'Title Deeds: Translating a Classic', in Harrison (2009: 122–39).
Heaney, Seamus (2016), *Aeneid Book VI*, London: Faber.
Hesk, Jon (2015), 'Thucydides in the Twentieth and Twenty-First Centuries', in Lee and Morley (2015: 218–37).
Holmes, Brooke (2016), '*Cosmopoiesis* in the Field of "The Classical"', in Butler (2016: 269–89).
Hornblower, Simon (1991–2008), *A Commentary on Thucydides*, 3 vols., Oxford: Oxford University Press.
Klooster, Jacqueline and Inger Kuin (eds.) (2020), *After the Crisis: Remembrance, Re-anchoring and Recovery in Ancient Greece and Rome*, London: Bloomsbury.
Koselleck, Reinhart (2004), *Futures Past: On the Semantics of Historical Time*, translated and introduced by K. Tribe, New York: Columbia University Press.
Lee, Christine and Neville Morley (eds.) (2015), *A Handbook to the Reception of Thucydides*, Malden MA and Oxford: Wiley-Blackwell.

Lianeri, Alexandra and Vanda Zajko (eds.) (2008), *Translation and the Classic: Identity as Change in the History of Culture*, Oxford: Oxford University Press.
Logue, Christopher (2015), *War Music: An Account of Homer's Iliad*, London: Faber.
Mac Sweeney, Naoíse (2021), 'Remembering the Persian Sack of Miletos', *Herodotus Helpline*, 27 January. www.herodotushelpline.org/seminar-schedule (accessed 15 July 2022).
Macintosh, Fiona, Justine McConnell, Stephen Harrison and Claire Kenward (2018), *Epic Performances: from the Middle Ages into the Twenty-First Century*, Oxford: Oxford University Press.
Matzner, Sebastian and Gail Trimble (eds.) (2020), *Metalepsis: Ancient Texts, New Perspectives*, Oxford: Oxford University Press.
Morley, Neville (2014), *Thucydides and the Idea of History*, London: I.B. Tauris.
Morrison, Blake (2003), *Oedipus and Antigone, by Sophocles, Versions*, Halifax: Northern Broadsides.
Ngugi wa Thiong'o (2012), *Globalectics: Theory and the Politics of Knowing*, Welleck Lectures 2010, New York: Columbia University Press.
Oswald, Alice (2002), *Dart*, London: Faber.
Oswald, Alice (2011), *Memorial*, London: Faber.
Oswald, Alice (2021), 'Sidelong Glances', Oxford Professor of Poetry Lecture (27 May).
Paul, Georgina (2018), 'From Epic to Lyric: Oswald and Kohler', in Macintosh (2018: 133–48).
Postclassicisms Collective (2020), *Postclassicisms*, Chicago and London: University of Chicago Press.
Proietti, Giorgia (2019), 'Can an Ancient Truth Become an Old Lie? A Few Methodological Remarks Concerning Current Comparative Research on War and Its Aftermath', in Giangiulio (2019: 71–92).
Proietti, Giorgia (2021), 'Herodotus, the Persian Wars and the Greeks' Intentional (hi) stories', 3 November, *Herodotus Helpline*. www.herodotushelpline.org/seminar-schedule (accessed 15 July 2022).
Rengakos, Antonios and Antonis Tsakmakis (eds.) (2006), *Brill's Companion to Thucydides*, Leiden: Brill.
Saldanha, Gabriela (2022), 'From Voice to Performance: The Artistic Agency of Literary Translations', in Baker (2022: 97–111).
Stead, Henry (2022), 'Fire, Fennel and the Future of Socialism: Tony Harrison's *Prometheus*', in Byrne (2022: 202–21).
Vandiver, Elizabeth (2010), *Stand in the Trench Achilles: Classical Receptions in British Poetry of the Great War*, Oxford: Oxford University Press.
Vandiver, Elizabeth (2022), 'Controversies and Pitfalls of Translation: Herodotus in Contentious Times', *Herodotus Helpline*, 16 March 2022, https://herodotushelpline.org/seminarschedule/ (accessed 20 July 2022).
Walcott, Derek (1990), *Omeros*, London: Faber.
Yates, David (2019), *States of Memory: The Polis, Panhellenism and the Persian War*, Oxford: Oxford University Press.

3

Flesh made word: Translational processes in the production of the synoptic gospels

Karen Bennett

The history of Bible translation has fascinated scholars since long before translation studies (TS) was formally inaugurated as a discipline. The seventy translators of the Septuagint, Jerome and the Vulgate, the vernacular Bibles of the sixteenth and seventeenth centuries – the narrative of these successive superimpositions has become general knowledge for anyone interested in cultural history or the history of ideas. And when translation first began to acquire legitimacy as an autonomous field of study in the 1970s and 1980s, the Bible featured heavily in many of the early histories and introductions that appeared (Steiner 1975; Kelly 1979; Bassnett 1980).

Much less is known, however, about the translational processes at work *upstream* of the New Testament, the chain of transmission that led from those that had witnessed the Jesus events at first hand, passing through untold numbers of scribes, editors, translators and commentators, to the actual authors of the gospels. Yet these are all very important because, somewhere along the line, over the course of these various retellings, the flesh-and-blood man that was the historical Jesus was transformed into the Son of God, saviour of mankind, with all the consequences that this implies. The operation was mythopoeic, of course, but it was also *historiographical* in the sense that multiple sources, both oral and written, will have been consulted and selected to produce the coherent accounts that have come down to us. And now that historiography is finally coming to be understood as translational (in the sense that it involves processes of interpretation, selection and rewriting analogous to what the interlingual translator has always done when she reproduces texts in another language), the study of those processes has started to fall under the purview of the translation scholar.

Hence, this chapter will attempt to apply some of the concepts and theories developed in translation studies to the synoptic gospels in order to try to determine just when and how the historical Jesus was transformed into the saviour of legend. This is a difficult proposition, of course. The subject is so complex, and the existing Bible scholarship already so extensive and polyvocal, that it cannot hope to be achieved in a short chapter such as this. What I hope to show, however, is that this is a field worthy of the attention of translation scholars, irrespective of the languages involved.

Nevertheless, it is clear from the outset that there were indeed many translational processes at work, even in the traditional understanding of the term. The New Testament was written in Koine Greek, the lingua franca in the region at the time, but Jesus and his apostles would have spoken Aramaic;[1] this means that somewhere classic *interlingual* translation will have taken place (when? how? by whom?). There will also have been *intralingual* translation, as oral accounts were converted to written form, and piecemeal records of oral sayings, known as *logia*, were edited into an organized narrative. And if we consider the role of iconography[2] in the transmission of the gospel stories, there is likely to have been *intersemiotic* translation too. Also, the process will be primarily *vertical* rather than horizontal, in that it involves chains of transmission across time. This is the form of translation that was dominant in the medieval period,[3] but was sidelined in modern translation theory because it inevitably involved transformation, incompatible with the expectations of semantic invariance.[4]

However, now translation scholars are awakening to the fact that translational processes play an important role in the constitution of knowledge, cultures and systems (Blumczynski 2017; Gentzler 2017; Bassnett and Johnston 2019; Bennett forthcoming), and that these processes are susceptible to analysis using the tools that have been developed in descriptive translation studies (DTS) (Lambert and van Gorp 1985; Toury 2012). DTS is grounded in the understanding that texts inevitably serve different purposes in different contexts of reception, and that it is this repurposing that drives the translation process. Hence, it should theoretically be possible to examine how the Jesus stories were transported from context to context by comparing source and target versions in the light of the constraints (Lefevere 1985; 1992) and norms (Toury 2012) operating on them at the time, as well as the network of values and beliefs, conscious or unconscious, that will have conditioned the translator-chronicler-historian's interpretations. The starting point for such a project will of course be the vast body of Bible scholarship that already exists, and in this chapter I will consider insights provided by strands such as form criticism,[5] redaction criticism,[6] literary criticism,[7] social scientific criticism[8] as well as the more recent eyewitness approach.[9] I should point out, however, that, in view of the sheer volume of scholarship available and the complexity of the debates that are already under way, this is necessarily a very superficial reconnaissance, designed merely to gauge if translation scholars have indeed something to offer the many other specialists working in the field.

3.1. The synoptic gospels

This chapter is concerned with the synoptic gospels – those of Matthew, Mark and Luke – so-called because they have things in common[10] that are not shared by the Gospel of John or the various non-canonical gospels. In fact, the narrative they tell is so similar, as regards both scope and language, that there was clearly some interdependence in their production. According to a statistical study produced by Honoré (1968), over three-quarters of Mark's content is found in both Matthew and Luke, while 97 per cent of Mark is found in at least one of the other two synoptic gospels.

There are also passages in which the wording is almost the same, indicating borrowing or a common source. For example, in the account of the healing of the leper, told in Mt. 8.2-3, Mk 1.40-42 and Lk. 5.12-13, more than half the wording in Greek is identical, though each version includes words absent in the other two and omits something included by the other two (Smith 2022). The similarity is even more striking in the passage about the preaching of John the Baptist recorded in Matthew (3.7-10) and Luke (3.7-9). Here the two accounts agree almost verbatim for a span of over sixty words.

These similarities have led to the question that Bible scholars call the 'synoptic problem', concerning the order in which the gospels were written and who influenced whom. Though the ancient sources disagreed about the precise chronology,[11] the canonical order of Matthew, Mark, Luke and John, supported by Augustine of Hippo, for a long time went unquestioned. This changed in 1776, when German scholar Johann Jakob Griesbach published a version of the synoptic gospels in which they were displayed side by side, making their similarities and differences apparent, and put forward the theory (the 'two-gospel hypothesis') that the Gospel of Matthew was written before the Gospel of Luke and that Mark was written with knowledge of both of them.

In the nineteenth century, however, German scholars began to apply the tools of literary criticism to the biblical texts, hypothesizing about the existence of a proto-gospel (*Ur-Gospel*), possibly in Aramaic. From this emerged the theory of Markan priority, according to which Mark was written first and used as a source for the other two. Today, the most widely accepted theory is the 'two-source hypothesis', which supports Markan priority, but holds that Matthew and Luke also made use of another document called Q,[12] a hypothetical written collection in Greek of (primarily) Jesus' sayings (λόγια: *logia*). If this in fact existed, it would account for material that is common to the gospels of Matthew and Luke but which does not appear in the Gospel of Mark.

As for the *logia*, these will have been drawn from the early church's oral gospel traditions (preserved and transmitted through formal or informal mechanisms). More recently, another theory has emerged (the 'common-sayings source') which holds that both Q and the extra-canonical Gospel of Thomas,[13] which appear to have had great similarities, were redactions of an earlier collection of sayings (*logia*), done by different groups to serve their own needs. Thus, we can already see emerging a complex chain of transmission, running from the common-sayings source, through Q (and Thomas), joining Mark, and then passing on to Matthew and Luke. These vertical translations may have taken place exclusively in Greek, or may have involved other languages, such as Aramaic and Coptic. In either case, we can expect there to have been some level of adjustment made to the text as the document was adapted to different conditions of reception, despite mechanisms put in place to maintain the tradition intact (see below).

In what follows, I will look at each of the three gospels in turn in order to try to identify some of the translational processes that may have occurred upstream of them, before going on to discuss these issues in more general terms. I am interested in where the authors of the gospels got their information (from whom and in what language or form), and the degree of interpretation that was required in order to transform it into the canonical version that has come down to us.

3.2. The Gospel of Mark

It makes sense to begin with the Gospel of Mark since, as we have seen, most scholars believe it to have been a source for the other two. Probably written in or around the year 70 CE – that is, around the time of the destruction of the Temple by the Romans,[14] it tells of the ministry of Jesus from his baptism up to the discovery of the empty tomb, with Jesus presented as teacher, exorcist, healer and miracle worker. Interestingly, there is no mention of the virgin birth or (in its original version[15]) of the resurrection appearances, and indeed, Jesus keeps his messianic nature secret, instructing his followers on various occasions to keep silent about this mission.[16]

But there is another reason for giving this gospel special attention in this chapter. Mark is explicitly described in the ancient sources[17] as the 'interpreter' (*hermēneutēs*) of Peter, which immediately posits a translational relationship of some kind. The Greek word *hermēneutēs* is frequently used for 'translator' in the interlingual sense,[18] and indeed it is possible that Mark might have had this role. Peter probably spoke Aramaic, and as the gospels were written in Greek, there will have had to have been translation somewhere along the line. But the concept of translation was not restricted to the interlingual variety in ancient times, and the word also had a number of other senses (Auvrayes-Assayas et al. 2014: 1339–40). It might, therefore, mean simply that he explained what Peter had said (i.e. passed it on, conveyed the message) without interlingual translation specifically.[19]

Let us look back at the original source of this claim. We find it in the writings of Papias, a Greek Apostolic Father, Bishop of Hierapolis, who lived in the second half of the first century. Papias is a pivotal figure in the transmission process as he was the last-known living connection with the Apostles, a third-generation Christian. He is described by Irenaeus as the companion of Polycarp (69–155), who in turn was said to have heard John the Evangelist.

According to Eusebius (*Church History* 3. 39), in the early part of his life (i.e. in around 80 CE, the period in which the gospels of Matthew, Luke and John were most likely being written), Papias went around collecting oral reports of the words and deeds of Jesus, some from actual eyewitnesses, which he later (*c.* 130 CE) collected and ordered[20] into a five-volume work *Exposition of the Sayings of the Lord* (Greek: Λογίων Κυριακῶν Ἐξήγησις). This work has been lost, but brief excerpts survive as quotations in the works of two later historians, Irenaeus of Lyons and Eusebius of Caesarea. Let as look more closely at a passage from Eusebius's *Church History* (*c.* 320), in which he quotes Papias on the origins of the gospels of Mark and Matthew. Eusebius reveals a complex and indirect chain of transmission:

> We must now add to his [Papias'] statements quoted above a tradition about Mark, who wrote the Gospel, which has been set forth in these words: 'The Elder used to say: Mark, in his capacity as Peter's interpreter [*hermēneutēs*], wrote down accurately as many things as he [Peter or Mark?] recalled from memory – though not in an ordered form [*ou mentoi taxei*] – of the things either said or done by the Lord'.
>
> (Eusebius, *Church History* 3.39.14–16)

That is to say, Eusebius is quoting Papias, who in turn is invoking 'the Elder' (believed to be 'John the Elder', whom Papias claims was personal disciple of Jesus) about the process of writing the Gospel of Mark. What is more, someone, probably Peter, is recalling from memory,[21] which means that it is never going to be a verbatim rendition of Jesus' words. We know from psychology that there will always be some (largely unconscious) selection involved in the process of recall, even before those memories are put into words,[22] and that when those remembrances are verbalized, they will in turn be shaped by rhetorical patterns and genre configurations circulating in the culture at the time.[23] Something like this seems to be indicated in the passage that follows:

> For he [Mark] neither heard or accompanied the Lord, but later, as I said, [he heard and accompanied] Peter, who **used to give his teachings in the form of *chreiai*** but had **no intention of providing an ordered arrangement [*suntaxin*] of the *logia* of the Lord**. Consequently, Mark did nothing wrong when he wrote down some individual items just as he related them from memory. For he made it his one concern not to omit anything he had heard or to falsify anything. This, then, is the account given by Papias about Mark.
> (Eusebius, *Church History* 3.39.14–16, 16, my emphasis)

The *chreiai*, mentioned in this passage, were brief useful (χρεἰβα means 'use') anecdotes about a particular character, shorter in length than a narration – often as short as a single sentence – and usually conforming to one of a few patterns.[24] They were sufficiently standardized to be used in Greek education, not only in rhetoric[25] but also in the teaching of reading and writing at the lowest level (Hock 2002: 102; Moeser 2002). Thus, the form may have come naturally to Peter, much in the way that the formulae used in certain popular genres today are reproduced quite unreflectingly by individuals today. This then represents an initial imposition of structure, though language, upon the primary perception that will have been Peter's memories of Jesus's ministries.

Papias (in Eusebius's account) tells us that these *chreiai* were written down/translated by Mark in the way they were received – that is to say, accurately and without any editorial intervention – which in fact offers one explanation for the rather fragmented nature of Mark's gospel.[26] Another has been supplied by the form critics (Schmidt 1919 cit. Bauckham 2017: 242), who give little credence to Papias, and instead argue that the short units that make up this gospel (called 'pericopes' in their terminology) pre-existed the gospel as distinct oral traditions, and were transmitted orally until Mark put them in writing and supplied the 'string' onto which they are now 'threaded like pearls'. That is to say, Mark's gospel, for these scholars, is a kind of oral literature that incorporates pre-existing oral traditions and whose framework and ordering are determined by 'topical and other non-historical considerations' (Schmidt 1919 cit. Bauckham 2017: 242).[27]

Only the Passion story seems to have had some pre-existing structure, since it presumes a sequence of events leading up to and following Jesus's death. Indeed, White (in White and Koester 1998a) goes as far as to suggest that Mark's gospel is 'a passion narrative with an extended introduction' and that 'Mark tells the story by thinking about the death and letting all the events that lead up to that death move toward it and through it' (White 1998a) (this claim will be explored in more detail below).

Let us now contrast this with what our same source (Papias quoted by Eusebius) says about Matthew.

3.3. The Gospel of Matthew

Matthew is understood by tradition to have been one of the twelve apostles himself (the former tax collector, Levi), so we might expect his account of Jesus to be more direct than Mark's. However, immediately after the passage of Papias about Mark, quoted above, there is a reference which suggests that, unlike Mark, Matthew might have done some editing of the raw material. As the textual coherence is important here,[28] I will repeat part of what was cited before:

> ... Mark, in his capacity as Peter's interpreter, wrote down accurately as many things as he recalled from memory – though not in an ordered form [*ou mentoi taxei*] – of the things either said or done by the Lord. **But about Matthew the following was said**: Therefore Matthew put the *logia* in an ordered arrangement [*sunetaxato*] in the Hebrew language [*hebraidi dialecto*], but each person [*hekastos*] interpreted [*hērmēneusen*] them as best he could.

It appears from this that Matthew might have ordered (i.e. edited) the sayings of the Lord precisely because Mark had not,[29] and what is more, he did so in Hebrew. If so, this begs the question, who translated his gospel into Greek?

Once again, this passage has been interpreted differently by different scholars. The Greek phrase *hebraidi dialecto* could mean Hebrew or Aramaic (Thomas 1998) – and indeed there are theories that the Gospel of Matthew was written first in a Semitic language and then translated into Greek, either by Matthew himself or by others.[30] Alternatively, the phrase could refer instead to a Semitic style of Greek (Kürzinger 1983, cit. Bauckham 2017: 105), which modern linguists have concluded is an accurate description of the variety (Duling 2010: 299–300).[31]

Most modern scholars, however, reject Papias' attribution of authorship of this gospel to Matthew the Apostle (Burkett 2002; Saunders 2009: 293; Duling 2010) and instead believe that it was written by an anonymous Jew, perhaps a scribe (Mellowes 1998c; Duling 2010: 303), versed in the technical and legal aspects of the scriptures, who was writing for a Jewish Christian community in northern Galilee or Syria.[32] It is 'the most Jewish of all the gospels' (White in Koester and White 1998), displaying a somewhat negative attitude towards gentiles[33] and a mission charge to pray only to Jews[34] (Burkett 2002). Thus, it is not surprising that Jesus' Jewish lineage is emphasized in a way that it wasn't in Mark,[35] and there is much use of Jewish symbolism, including overt rewritings of passages from the Old Testament, such as Moses' Mount Sinai episode in the Sermon on the Mount in which Jesus is explicitly portrayed as a new Moses.[36] The fact that the Pharisees are (anachronistically) portrayed as Jesus' main opponents in Matthew's gospel reflects these tensions in the culture of reception, White (in Koester and White 1998) argues, since it was in this context that the Pharisean movement gradually acquired prominence in the struggle for the future of Judaism.[37]

Another interesting feature about the Gospel of Matthew, significant for our purpose here, is that unlike Mark, it portrays Jesus as divine from the outset. He is shown to be the Son of God, the product of a miraculous birth to a virgin mother,[38] and resurrects at the end. Hence, it would seem that the author of the gospel is going out of his way to present Jesus as the fulfilment of the various messianic prophecies of the Hebrew Bible.

3.4. The Gospel of Luke

If Matthew is the Jewish gospel, Luke is a much more Hellenistic one, and is thought to have been produced for a predominantly gentile audience[39] between 80 and 90 CE in a Hellenistic centre such as Antioch. His Greek is exemplary (Allen 2009: 326), and there is plentiful evidence of artistry, such as the use of a style that echoes the Septuagint, while at the same time linking the narrative to the extratextual world outside the Roman Empire[40] (Allen 2009: 327; Thompson 2010: 329). It is usually considered to be the first part of a two-volume narrative, often referred to as Luke-Acts.

In this work, Jesus emerges as, primarily, a teacher of ethical wisdom, interested in inculcating values of compassion and forgiveness among his followers. He is cultured and literate,[41] to the extent that there may have been an intention to assimilate him to the ideal of the Greek philosopher, someone like Socrates, particularly in the way he dies the calm martyr's death (White in Attridge et al. 1998, Mellowes 1998d),[42] or to the Graeco-Roman concept of the 'divine man' (Koester in Attridge et al. 1998).[43] This may have been because the author was writing for a cultured gentile audience, and was thus trying to combat the image of the Christians as incendiaries and revolutionaries (let us not forget that Jesus was executed as a political criminal), by suggesting that they could be good citizens of the Roman Empire.[44]

Our knowledge of the origins of this gospel comes from the Muratorian Canon,[45] from which we learn that Luke was recruited by Paul in a kind of secretarial capacity,[46] because he was educated and could write, and that he was not an eyewitness himself but reported (i.e. translated in the broader sense of the term) other sources.

> The third book of the gospel is according to Luke. Luke the physician, when Paul had taken him with him after the ascension of Christ, as one skilled in writing, wrote from report in his own name, though he did not himself see the Lord in the flesh and on that account, as he was able to ascertain [events], so [he set them down]. So he began his story from the birth of John.
> (*Muratorian Canon*, cit. Bauckham 2017: 426)

If Luke was indeed a kind of secretary or clerk for Paul, this begs the question of whether he was paid for the service, raising the issue of patronage (an important constraint in descriptive translation studies, as we know from Lefevere 1985, 1992).

The presence of a patron is actually suggested in Luke's own account of the genesis of the project from his preface, which, like the Acts of the Apostles, is addressed to someone called Theophilus:

> Since many have undertaken to set down an orderly account of the events that have been fulfilled among us, just as they were handed on to us by those who from the beginning were eyewitnesses (*autoptai*) and servants of the word (*kathos paredosan h3min hoi ap' arch3s autoptai kai hup3retai genomenoi tou logou*), I too decided, after investigating (*parekolouth 3koti*) everything carefully from the very first (*anothen*), to write an orderly account for you, **most excellent Theophilus**, so that you may know the truth concerning the things about which you have been instructed.
>
> (Lk. 1.1-4, my emphasis)

But who was Theophilus? No one knows for sure beyond that he will have been a high-ranking or influential Gentile (the name is Greek) – perhaps a wealthy benefactor who supported Paul, or even Paul's Roman lawyer, for whom Luke wanted to provide a detailed, historical account of Christ and the spread of the gospel throughout the Roman Empire (Pawson 2007). Allen (2009: 325), on the other hand, argues that Theophilus might not be a real person at all, but that it could refer to a generic gentile reader that was already within the faith (*theo+philus* means 'god-lover') and would therefore have known the story of Jesus already.[47]

From Luke's preface, we also learn more about his sources. The Greek word *autoptai*, also used in Acts 1.21-22, suggests he is relying on account from those that had witnessed events first-hand, while the reference to 'servants of the word' may imply the disciples.[48] If so, then Luke's reportage is likely to have involved classic interlingual translation, given that they will have spoken Aramaic, as we have seen. We also know from this passage that he wrote 'an orderly account', which suggests that he did not record verbatim, as Mark appears to have done, but edited the raw testimony that he received in the manner of a historiographer.[49]

But Luke did not receive all his material orally from eyewitnesses. Though 25 per cent of the material in his gospel is specific to it (i.e. not shared by either of the other synoptic gospels), 50 per cent is shared with Mark and the remaining 25 per cent with Matthew (perhaps with its ultimate source in Q). Comparisons that have already been undertaken between versions have shown that Luke critiqued these sources theologically, omitting material, reworking it and subtly reordering the narrative plot, presumably to show evidence of divine providence (Allen 2009: 325–7).

Indeed, to the extent that Luke imposes a linear narrative upon the Jesus story and uses prophetic patterning to imply that the gentile church is the fulfilment of God's promise to Israel (Allen 2009: 328), he can be seen as translating the gospel story as it was already known (through Matthew and Mark and various non-canonical sources) for a new purpose and readership. For Allen (2009: 325), he is not writing to convert people, but instead to shape the faith and theology of the late first-century gentile church (Allen 2009: 325).

3.5. Informal and formal transmission mechanisms

Between the death of Jesus in c. 30–3 CE and the writing of the first gospel, some forty years elapsed, during which time the Jesus stories will have been told and retold within the oral tradition. We know from oral history that stories tend to be passed along in easily remembered units, and that these units will have been put together in different orders and combinations at different times. Thus, the miracle stories and some of the teachings probably circulated independently of each other. Although some of them were written down in the form of *logia* for the purposes of record and communication between traditions (Koester in White and Koester 1998b), they seem only to have been formally threaded together into a coherent story when Mark created the narrative apparatus to enable this to happen.

By the time of Paul's epistles (48–56 CE), some of this material was already established as part of the communities' traditions and had been subjected to interpretation and discussion (Koester 1990: 54). Though Paul does not really refer much to Jesus' teachings – he is more interested in the 'eschatalogical event' that was 'the death and resurrection of Jesus as the turning-point of the ages' (Koester 1990: 54) – his letters bear witness to the development of these materials, some units of which will have reappeared in Q and the sayings source specific to Mark (Koester 1990: 54).

Koester (in White and Koester 1998b) also sheds some light on the way in which oral traditions develop. Such stories are not, he says, attempts to reconstruct exactly what actually happened – this only occurs later at the formal historiographic stage – but rather they serve to explain certain community practices that will already have developed amongst the Jesus followers (such as hymns, prayers and rituals), using symbols from the tradition. The Passion narrative, in particular, is likely to have developed for liturgical purposes to enable the early Christians to ritually relive the last days of their Messiah (Aslan 2014: 154; Bauckham 2017: 243)[50] and probably acquired a narrative structure quite early on (perhaps as early as the forties).[51] Indeed, for some authors (e.g. Clark in Pagels et al. 1998), the whole function of the gospels was to endorse the Eucharist as the central ritual of the Christian faith, which suggests that the material from the *logia* was effectively added on afterwards.

As we know, the translational processes involved in oral tradition would tend to favour the transmutation of these narratives, as elements are added, omitted and reconfigured to suit new contexts of reception. Indeed, we have seen evidence of this, with a gentile tradition developing in the Hellenistic churches founded by Paul that was distinct in many ways from the Jewish tradition centred on Jerusalem.[52] However, there may also have been mechanisms in place to limit deviations. Gerhardsson (1961), following a major study of oral transmission in Rabbinic Judaism, argues that the early Christians would have adopted methods of tradition preservation similar to those used by the Jews, who were trained to memorize their master's words exactly, using mnemonic techniques and other controls to ensure perfect reproduction. Bauckham (2017: 264–71), for his part, suggests that Paul's letters in fact show evidence of, if not verbatim memorization, 'some process of teaching and learning so that what is communicated will be retained', envisaging the presence of an authorized tradent/traditioner.[53] Hence, there seems to have been something of an interplay going on between the informal collective transmission processes centred upon different Christian communities, which would have been conducive to change and adaptation over time, and the agency of certain authoritative individuals (such as Paul and our synoptic gospel writers) in establishing and fixing that tradition.

It is clear, however, that the writing down of the traditions, whether in the form of *logia* or the more structured gospels, was not in itself a safeguard against mutability. In fact, there was a proliferation of Jesus narratives circulating in the second and third centuries,[54] each of which imagined Jesus differently in accordance with the identities and objectives of the movements that spawned them (Mack 1995).[55] It was only in the fourth century, with the institutionalization of Christianity under Constantine and Theodosius, that the texts that we now know as the New Testament were finally canonized and joined to the Jewish scriptures to form the Christian Bible.

In what follows, I shall consider how the notion of *constraints*, developed by Lefevere (1985; 1992)[56] and Toury (2012)[57] for the study of interlingual translations, might contribute to our understanding of these transmission mechanisms and shed light upon how the historical Jesus gradually evolved into the Lord of myth.

3.6. Constraints on the transmission of the Jesus stories

As we have seen, the term that is predominantly used for interlingual translation in both Greek (*hermenuein*) and Latin (*interpres*) is not restricted to interlingual translation, as today, but is used much more broadly to refer to interpretation in general. Historiography itself can thus be regarded as a translational process in that it involves the rewriting of information that has been culled (from records, chronicles, testimony and other sources) in the light of particular cognitive, social and textual constraints. This section will attempt to categorize the various kinds of constraints that will have operated upon the transmission of the Jesus stories, culminating in the production of the synoptic gospels.

The first of these is the cognitive constraint of *perception*, which operates at all levels in the process. We know that eyewitness accounts of the same event may diverge sharply in terms of what was reportedly seen, revealing differences in focus in accordance with the motivations and emotional status of the observers[58] and that these inaccuracies are then exacerbated by *memory*.[59] But the same cognitive restrictions apply to the way that oral testimony was interpreted by those that produced the collections of *logia*, as well as the way that these were used by the gospel writers. And the process does not stop there. Even historiographers that do not have an overt religious or ideological motive but are committed to the quest for objective truth are to some extent at the mercy of their own cognition in that they will inevitably select and focus on particular aspects of their sources at the expense of others – an observation that applies as much to the contemporary historiographers in my bibliography as to the ancient sources that they drew upon.[60]

Added to this constraint imposed by individual subjectivity are the collective subjectivities embodied in language and culture. As soon as primary perception is encoded in *language*, whether for the purpose of oral transmission or written record, it becomes subject to the constraints imposed by that language – its grammatical structure, lexical availability, idiomaticity and so on. Translation into another language (or indeed translation between oral and written varieties of the same language) will therefore force a change of lens, leading to inevitable alterations in the way the content is presented. This occurs even when control mechanisms are in place to fix the tradition, but it is obviously going to be even more evident in the case of informal transmission processes.

Related to this are considerations of *style and genre*, that is to say, the kind of shaping that takes place to present the account in a form that is recognizable to the culture of reception. We have seen how the ancient genres of biography and historiography provided frameworks within which the gospel authors worked, determining not only the material was ordered and structured but also the literary devices that were used within it.[61] But even on the level of the material that form the raw material for the structured accounts – the *chreia* of Matthew or the *logia* of Thomas and Q – some kind of rhetorical structuring is in evidence, determined by convention.

The question of *patronage*, so central to Lefevere's theory (1985, 1992), may also be evident in some of the more formal accounts of the Jesus stories, particularly the gospels of Matthew and Luke, where we perhaps glimpse the presence of a shadowy authority that might have influenced the rewriter/translator's output through ideological or even financial impositions. These authorities may have been patrons in the conventional sense (as in the case of the hypothetical Theophilus) or merely elders of the different communities, invested with the status of tradent.

It is from the late second century, however, that we start to see the ideological component of patronage really coming into play with measures to restrict the proliferation of narratives.[62] The Muratorian canon (*c.* 170 CE), mentioned above, was an early attempt to systematize a list of approved writings[63] and, though apparently not an official church document, does seem to reflect the belief of a mainstream of early Christian opinion that the gospels of Matthew, Mark, Luke and John had an apostolic source and were therefore the most reliable of the various gospels in circulation. The apostolic tradition was also fiercely defended by Irenaeus, Bishop of Lyon, in his work *Against Heresies* (*c.* 180), which took a stance against more marginal cults such as the Valentinians and Marcionites, who were eventually excluded from the canon. There were also attempts to harmonize the various versions by merging them into a single coherent narrative, such as the *Diatesseron*, created by Tatian in around 160–175 CE, in either Greek or Syriac, and widely used by the Syrian Church for up to two centuries. However, the different churches of antiquity had their own canon lists, and it was not until the fourth century that the list of works to be included in the New Testament was formally accepted in a series of church councils.[64] Ultimately, though, there was no claim made that the four gospels that were finally included in the New Testament canon were all saying the same thing. As Koester (cit. Mellowes 1998e) has pointed out, it was rather an attempt to bring together as many Christian communities as possible into one broad church.

Finally, Lefevere's constraint of *universe of discourse* may have played a crucial role in how different authors have interpreted the biblical sources. Aslan (2014) has mounted a very convincing argument to prove that many of the terms used by and about Jesus in the sources will have had a very different meaning within the historical context of his time to what they acquired in the hands of Paul and the evangelists[65] and that they point to a historical figure that was more of a subversive revolutionary, crucified primarily for acts of sedition against Rome,[66] than the ethereal pacifist he was to become. It may be that, following the Jewish Revolt and destruction of the Temple in 70 CE by the Romans, the evangelists were seeking precisely to distance him from the revolutionary image that he may have had in his own day.

3.7. Conclusion

We are now in a position to draw some tentative conclusions about the question that formed the overriding aim of this chapter – the process by means of which Jesus, the teacher, healer, exorcist and (according to Aslan 2014) revolutionary, was gradually transformed into the Son of God, incarnated on earth in order to save mankind. As we have seen, this transformation is essentially historiographic as successive rewritings gradually moulded the narratives told by the earliest sources to suit new real-world purposes, and in doing so lifted Jesus out of living memory into the realm of myth.

What do we actually know about the real-life Jesus? Historians that have tried to find concrete evidence of his existence in contemporary records and chronicles reveal that there is little information about his life prior to his entry into Jerusalem on a donkey in around 30 CE, his cleansing of the Temple the next day and the subsequent unfolding of the sequence of events that became known as the Passion (Aslan 2014: 73–9). Most of the rest of the material that found its way into the synoptic gospels about his teachings and healing activities were added from the *logia*, while the accounts in Matthew and Luke of his miraculous birth, early life and resurrection were largely fabricated to serve the real-life purpose or *Skopos* (as translation scholars, such as Vermeer 1989, call it) of their author.[67]

Within the synoptic gospels, the most significant transformations seem to have occurred somewhere between the Gospel of Mark and the gospels of Matthew and Luke, probably in response to the demands of specific contexts of reception. That is to say, in the case of Matthew, writing for a Jewish Christian community struggling to find its identity in the wake of the Jewish War, there was clearly a need to emphasize Jesus's Jewish lineage and present him as the fulfilment of the Old Testament prophecies. For Luke, on the other hand, whose audience was predominantly gentile, there seems to be a concern to present him as a philosopher or 'divine man' figure within the Hellenistic tradition.

However, for Aslan (2014: 214–16), the catalyst was actually a figure that we have given scanty attention to in this chapter, but one who seems singlehandedly to have created the image of Jesus that eventually became the version espoused by the institutionalized church. I am of course referring to Paul of Tarsus, epistle-writer and founder of Christian centres across the Hellenistic world, whose theology influenced all three synoptic gospels and came to full fruition in the Gospel of John.[68] What Paul essentially did was to wrest Jesus away from his Jewish roots and transform this rather provincial messiah into a transcendental figure that would be meaningful throughout the whole of the Roman Empire. The implications were immense, not only for spread of Christianity but also for the development of Western semiotics and the translation theory that derived from it (Bennett 2018: 104; Bennett 2022).

Any future translation-based study of the development of the gospel narratives will therefore have to give a better account of the role played by this pivotal figure, looking more closely at how he transformed the inherited tradition and passed it on to the evangelists in a fully translatable form. This work has already been started, with attempts to compare the historical material in the book of Acts to related data in the writings of Paul.[69] But there is still much to be done, not least as regards the reconfiguration of Jesus himself.

Let me close my chapter reflecting a little further on the translational nature of historiography. The historiographer, drawing on records, chronicles and the testimony of eyewitnesses (whether living or dead), selects, interprets and orders that material in the light of her Skopos (and also to comply with genre and discourse expectations in the target culture). We see this at work in the gospel authors themselves and in the *logia*-compilations that they drew on. But we also see it at work in the historiographers downstream of them – Irenaeus, Eusebius, Jerome – and after them, the generations of scholars that have perused the biblical sources for answers right up to the contemporary scholars that have provided the sources for my own chapter. We are all translators in a vertical process that passes through successive texts in a variety of languages and genres, bringing voices out of the mists of time and making them relevant for the world in which we live.

Notes

1. Palestine at the time of Jesus was a multilingual society. The demotic language was Aramaic, with Hebrew used in the synagogues and by scribes and scholars of the law. Greek was the lingua franca of the region, spoken by the Hellenized elite and priestly aristocracy. Curiously, Latin was the language least spoken in this part of the Roman Empire, except perhaps by the soldiers and officials sent out to protect and administer the territory (Aslan 2014: 34–5). The fact that the gospels were written in Greek is actually curious in itself, particularly as the more recent Dead Sea Scrolls, whose themes are close to those of the New Testament, are almost exclusively in Hebrew and Aramaic (Aslan 2014: 243).
2. See, for example, Attridge in Pagels et al. (1998).
3. As in the concept *translatio studii* (Stierle 1996).
4. See Bennett (2022).
5. This approach, which began in Germany with the work of Karl Ludwig Schmidt, Martin Dibelius and Rudolf Bultmann, hinges on the assumption that the Jesus traditions passed through a long period of oral transmission in the early Christian communities (in the manner of folklore) and that the gospels reflect this process of collective production. It uses a method of biblical analysis which classifies

units of scripture by literary pattern and then attempts to trace each type to a particular period of oral transmission to determine a unit's original form and the historical context of production. See Aune (2010a) and Bauckham (2017: 241–8).

6   This approach was derived from form criticism but focuses on the author of the text as editor(redactor) of the source materials, therefore giving greater weight to individual agency. It is perhaps closest to the translational approach proposed here since it proceeds by comparing accounts to see what has been added, omitted or changed, though focusing on how the redactor shaped and moulded the narrative to express theological and ideological goals. See Perrin (1969).

7   This approach treats the Bible as a literary text and approaches it using tools from literary criticism. See Aune (2010b).

8   This is interested in the various codes (religious, geographical, historical, economic and social) operating in the social system of the culture of production. See Neyrey (2010).

9   This is based on the principle that eyewitnesses to events were interpreters as well as observers, and looks at how their accounts were incorporated into historians' writings. In particular, it opposes the form-critical assumption that eyewitness origins of the gospel traditions would have been lost in the anonymity of collective transmission by the time the gospels were written. See Byrskog (2002) and Bauckham (2017).

10 The word 'synoptic' comes from the Greek σύνοψις, 'synopsis', meaning '(a) seeing all together'. The Gospel of John is substantially different in content and in wording, and thus warrants independent treatment.

11 The fourth-century historian Eusebius of Caesarea, in his *Church History* (*c.* 324) records that Clement of Alexandria (*c.* 150–215 CE) believed that the Gospel of Matthew came first, Luke second and Mark third (Bk 6, Ch. 14, §§ 6–10), while Origen (*c.* 185–253) argued for Matthew, Mark, Luke (Book 6, Chapter 25, §§ 3–6). Tertullian (*c.*155–220), for his part, claims in *Against Marcion* (Bk 4 Ch 5) that John and Matthew were first and Mark and Luke came later.

12 From German *Quelle*, meaning 'source'. For more on the Q Gospel, see Piper (2010), Mack (1993), Mellowes (1998a).

13 This consists of 114 sayings attributed to Jesus, thought to have been composed in Greek between 200 and 250 CE. A complete Coptic version of this document was discovered near Nag Hammadi in Egypt in 1945.

14 This cataclysmic event was the culmination of the Jewish-Roman War of 66–73 CE, the first of three major rebellions by Jews against the Roman Empire. Many contemporary historiographers believe that the experience of destruction and displacement suffered by the Jews in the context of the Roman clampdown will have coloured the version of Jesus put about by the gospel writers.

15 Mark's gospel originally ended with two women entering the tomb, and seeing a young man dressed in white, who explains that Jesus has been raised, and instructs them to tell Peter and the other disciples. The women flee in terror. The canonical ending was added by later authors (Mellowes 1998b; Aslan 2014: 229–230).

16 The motif known as the Messianic Secret was first proposed by German theologian William Wrede in 1901 and is based upon the identification of statements by Jesus to his followers instructing them not to reveal his messianic status to others and preventing demons from doing so. Wrede also suggested that it was not historical but had been added by the author of Mark's gospel. See Koester in White and Koester (1998a).

17 Irenaeus (*Against Heresies* 3.1.1); Clement of Alexandria (*Stromata* 7.106.4); Origen (1 Pt 5:13); Eusebius (*Church History* 6.14.5–7); Tertullian (*Against Marcion* 4.5); Jerome (*Illustrious Men* 8); Augustine (*Consensus of the Gospels* 1.2.4).
18 For example, it is the term used by Philo Judaeus about the seventy translators of the Septuagint.
19 See Bauckham (2017: 205–10) for a summary of the various arguments put forward to support and refute the idea that Mark was Peter's translator.
20 *Synkatataxai* (Eusebius, 3.39.3).
21 Though it is not clear from the structure of this sentence whether the pronoun 'he' refers to Peter or Mark, Justin Martyr's description of Mark's Gospel as 'the memoirs' (*apomnēmoneumata*) of Peter (in *Dialogue* 106.3) seems to clarify the matter: in it he notes Papias' statement that Mark 'wrote down some individual items just as [Peter] related them from memory (*apomnēmoneusen*)'. See Bauckham (2017: 212–14), Koester (1990: 37–40).
22 See, for example, Le Cunff (2022).
23 A phenomenon known as 'verbal overshadowing'. See, for example, McGill (2020).
24 The most common of these was "On seeing ..." (ιδών or *cum vidisset*), "On being asked ..." (ἐρωτηθείς or *interrogatus*), and "He said ..." (ἔφη or *dixit*) (Bauckham 2017: 214–17).
25 According to Aelius Theon (*Progymnasmata* 3.2–3), a *chreia* is a 'concise and pointed account of something said or done, attributed to some particular person'. Theon provided eight exercises for students of rhetoric to do with *chreiai*, including memorizing, commenting on, confirming and refuting (Moeser 2002).
26 Bauckham (2017: 230–5) argues that Mark's gospel is only unstructured if viewed within the framework of Greek and Roman historiography, which is what Papias seems to be doing. Bryan (1993: 48–9) has suggested that it might better be viewed within the genre of ancient biography, while Dewey (1994) argues that it was designed for oral performance. See also Schröter (2010: 280–1).
27 On the subject of the oral tradition, see also White and Koester (1998b); Kelber and Byrskog (2009).
28 That is, assuming that Eusebius is reproducing Papias' original report fairly faithfully (*Church History*. 3.39.6). However, as Bauckham (2017: 222) points out, we do not know if the sentence about Matthew follows directly from the one about Mark in Papias or if there was some intervening material that Eusebius has left out. This could make a difference as to how the linker 'therefore' [*oun*] is understood (see footnote 29 below).
29 This is the interpretation put forward by Gundry (1994: 614), due to the presence of the linker 'therefore' [*oun*].
30 See, for example, Jerome's assessment: 'Matthew, also called Levi, apostle and aforetime publican, composed a gospel of Christ at first published in Judea in Hebrew for the sake of those of the circumcision who believed, but this was afterwards translated into Greek, though by what author is uncertain' (Jerome, *Lives of Illustrious Men*, Chapter 3).
31 Bauckham (2017: 224), for his part, reads the last section of this passage ('each person interpreted ...') as evidence that Papias believed there to have been more than one translation of Matthew's *logia*, and that he was probably referring to the non-canonical gospels of the Nazarenes and Ebionites, used by Jewish Christians in Syria and Palestine, and considered by many to be related to the canonical Gospel of Matthew.

32 According to Saunders (2009: 295), it was meant to be performed orally in its entirety within the worshipping assembles of early Christians.
33 Mt. 5.47, 6.7, 18.17.
34 Mt. 10.5-6, 23.
35 Matthew 1.
36 Matthew 5,6,7. See also the transfiguration scene in Mt. 17.2 (Aslan 2014: 261).
37 The Rabbinical movement, which would control the Jewish tradition right through to our own times, developed out of this early Pharisee tradition. See also Mellowes (1998c) and Saunders (2009: 293).
38 We must remember that Isaiah (17.4) prophesied that the messiah would be born of a virgin, though Bible scholarship has proved, more or less definitively, that this is the result of mistranslation into Greek, and that the original Hebrew word *alma* meant only 'young woman'.
39 The Jews are portrayed rather more negatively in Luke-Acts than they are in Matthew, and the universality of salvation, including for gentiles, is emphasized (Thompson 2010: 322–3).
40 For example, the references to the Roman imperial authorities in Lk. 2.1-3 and 3.1-2.
41 For example, in Luke 4, Jesus goes into the synagogue, takes the (unpointed) scroll of Isaiah, and shows that he is able to find his way around it and comment on it (Crossan in White, Crossan and Attridge 1998).
42 In Luke (23.34), Jesus says, 'Father, forgive them, for they know not what they do'. Compare this to the anguished 'My God, my God, why hast thou forsaken me?', in Matthew (27.46).
43 The concept of the 'divine man' (*theios aner*) was commonplace in Hellenistic philosophical thought and referred to a genius or superman figure who possessed extraordinary gifts and abilities, distinguished by his divine wisdom and power to perform miracles (Kingsbury 1983: 27). This concept may have passed into Luke from Mark, itself the product of one of the Hellenistic centres.
44 Thompson (2010: 327) goes as far as to suggest that Luke-Acts as a whole might be an apology for the Christian movement within the context of the Roman Empire and part of an attempt to persuade the authorities that Christians should be granted the same religious freedoms as Jews. See also White in Attridge et al. (1998).
45 The Muratorian Canon is the earliest known example of a New Testament canon list, dating from the late second century, which survives in a bad Latin translation of its original Greek. It is not believed to be an official church document.
46 Luke is actually mentioned in two letters commonly attributed to Paul but in fact written long after his death (Colossians and Timothy), which present him as a young devotee of Paul (Aslan 2014: 184).
47 See Thompson (2010: 328–9) for a summary of the various theories about the identity of Theophilus.
48 Bauckham (2017: 122–3) argues that 'eyewitnesses' and 'servants of the word' are describing a single category of source, and that given the latter phrase is also used to speak of the ministry of the Twelve in Acts 6.4, he must be referring to the disciples. Allen (2009: 325), on the other hand, interprets 'servants of the word' as second-generation preachers, which would add an additional layer of transmission.
49 This gospel has been considered a serious work of historiography, in the manner of Thucydides (Thompson 2010: 321) and indeed the invocation of Theophilus could serve as a marker of genre, since it was typical of the rhetoric of Hellenistic historiography (Bauckham 2017: 117).

50 The earliest source for the practice of the Eucharist is Paul's *First Epistle to the Corinthians* 11: 17–34 (*c.* 55 CE), in which he speaks of the rite as a celebration of a mandate established with Jesus at the Last Supper. The Acts of the Apostles 2.42 also mentions early Christians meeting for a ritual involving the 'breaking of bread'. Other accounts are found in Clement's First Epistle (*c.* 70 CE) and Justin Martyr's *First Apology* (*c.* 155 CE), Ignatius of Antioch, Tertullian and the *Apostolic Tradition* (*c.* 200 CE).

51 The first written account we get of the passion story actually comes in Paul (1 Corinthians 15), whose letters began some twenty years after the death of Jesus. Mark's gospel, which, as we have seen, was otherwise quite fragmented, presents the passion story in quite a structured coherent form, which supports the idea that it circulated independently. See Bauckham (2017: 183–201) for an in-depth analysis of Passion story in Mark.

52 The Jerusalem community continued to preach devotion to the Torah and respect for the Jewish law, which was incompatible with the new vision of Christianity championed by Paul (see Aslan 2014: 186–94). It was headed by Jesus's brother James, who seems to have been a prominent figure in first-century Palestine, mentioned by nonbiblical sources such as Josephus, Hegesippus and Clement. However, he was almost completely excised from the New Testament to be replaced by Peter and Paul. Aslan (Aslan 2014: 202) suggests that his identity as Jesus' brother, which would have been significant to the Jews, for whom legitimacy depended on kinship, became an obstacle to the imperial religion of Rome, particularly for those that advocated the perpetual virginity of his mother Mary.

53 Paul uses technical terms drawn from Jewish practice (*paradidōmi* [1 Cor. 11.2, 23], corresponding to Hebrew *māsar*, used for the handing-on of a tradition; and *paralambanō* [1 Cor. 15.1,3; Gal. 1.9; Col. 2.6; 1 Thess. 2.13; 4.1; 2 Thess. 3.6] corresponding to Hebrew *qibbēl*, referring to the receiving of a tradition) to refer to different kinds of tradition that he communicated to his churches when he founded them. Bauckham argues (2017: 264–5) that he would naturally have taken over the technical terminology (indicating actual possession of something) he was familiar with as Pharisaic teacher; the Greek terms, for their part, were used for formal transmission of tradition in the Hellenistic schools and would thus have been familiar to his gentile readers.

54 As well as the hypothetical Q and Gospel of Thomas, mentioned above, there were other gnostic gospels, such as those of Philip and Truth; various infancy gospels, some of which show Jesus performing miracles at a tender age; the gospel of Mary Magdalene, which presents her as one of the apostles; the Jewish Christian gospels of the Hebrews, Nazarenes and Ebionites; various Passion gospels, such as Peter, Bartholomew and Nicodemus; and others produced by individuals later pronounced to be heretics (such as the Gospel of Marcion, which rejects any connection with Judaism, or the Manichean gospel of Mani); and a whole series of epistles and other texts not counted as gospels.

55 For example, there were congregations that imagined the death of Christ as a martyrdom to justify 'a mixture of Jews and gentiles as equally acceptable in a new configuration of the people of God (or "Israel")', and others that were 'enclaves for the cultivation of spiritual enlightenment or knowledge (*gnosis*)' (Mack 1995).

56 André Lefevere's theory of constraints (1985; 1992) applies to all forms of rewriting, not only conventional interlingual translation. The main categories he uses are those of *poetics* (i.e. the literary norms operating in the culture of reception), *patronage*

(questions of ideology, economics and status affecting the translator/rewriter), *universe of discourse* (i.e. the knowledge, learning and customs of the receiving culture) and *natural language* (limitations of syntax, lexis etc.).

57 Toury (2012) refers briefly to constraints near the beginning of his famous article 'The Nature and Role of Norms in Translation' (1995: 53–69), mentioning 'the systemic differences between the *languages and textual traditions* involved in the act [of translation]' and 'the possibility and limitations of the *cognitive apparatus of the translator* as the necessary mediator' (1995: 60). He is, however, most interested in the *sociocultural constraints* operating in the target culture, which he develops into his full-flown theory of norms here and in the later edition of his book.

58 On the reliability of eyewitness testimony in criminal trials today, see Chew (2018).

59 It was precisely this problem that led oral testimony to be discounted in modern 'scientific'/empirical history as biased and unreliable. However, ancient historians valued oral testimony very highly – a perspective that is just now being recovered by proponents of oral history (Byskrog 2002: 19–25).

60 See Paul Ricoeur (2004: 55) on how the present affects the way the past is recalled in historiography (although Ricoeur does insist that the very fact that the truth is being sought serves to prevent exaggerated flights of fancy).

61 For more on the gospel genre debate, see Duling (2010: 300–1) and Thompson (2010: 324–8).

62 Clark (in Pagels et al. 1998) suggests that one of the criteria for inclusion as gospels may have been the presence of the Passion story, given that this was central to the identity of the Christian communities. On the development of the Christian canon, see Pagels et al. 1998; Mellowes 1998d; Mack 1995: 275–92.

63 Interestingly, it includes all four biblical gospels as well as the Acts of the Apostles, the Pauline Epistles and most of John's writings, and reflects the doctrines that would later become central to the institutionalized church. The main criterion used in the selection seems to have been a text's suitability for public reading during worship.

64 In 367, Bishop Athanasius of Alexandria produced a list of books that would later become the New Testament canon, and this was formally accepted at the Council of Rome (382), reaffirmed at the Synod of Hippo (393) and ratified at Carthage (397). Pope Damasus I's commissioning of the Latin Vulgate also contributed to the fixation of the Canon in the West.

65 For example, 'messiah' in Hebrew meant 'the anointed one' and in the scriptures alluded to the practice of pouring or smearing oil on someone charged with divine office (kings, priests, prophets etc.). At the time of the Roman occupation, calling oneself 'messiah' was tantamount to declaring war on Rome, and there were indeed a great many revolutionaries, before and after Jesus, that ostentatiously did so and were executed for sedition as a result. It was Paul of Tarsus, reimagining Jesus for a new Gentile audience, that translated 'messiah' into Greek as 'Christ' and in doing so, endowed it with the divine qualities that we understand today (Aslan 2014: 19, 188–9). Other key terms that were repurposed by the gospel writers included 'Kingdom of God' (Aslan 2014: 116–25), 'son of Man' (Aslan 2014: 168–9) and the phrase "Render unto Caesar the things that are Caesar's, and unto God the things that are God's" (Aslan 2014: 77).

66 Crucifixion was a common form of execution in antiquity, largely because it was cheap, and was conventionalized by Rome as a form of state punishment for (and deterrent against) political crimes such as treason, rebellion and sedition (Aslan 2014: 154–5). Those accused of such crimes were called *lestai* (bandits), which was the term specifically used about the men that were executed alongside Jesus;

this was then transmuted to *kakourgoi* ('evildoers') by Luke, who was clearly uncomfortable with the term (Aslan 2014: 18, 78–9, 156).
67 For example, the whole tale of Jesus' birth at Bethlehem seems to have been engineered to enable him to be born in the city of David, thereby fulfilling the prophecy of Mic. 5.2, while Matthew's account of the flight to Egypt fulfils the words of Hos. 11.1 (Aslan 2014: 29–33). Aslan points out that neither evangelist would have expected their immediate audience to understand these claims as historical fact; rather they would be understood as theological affirmations of Jesus's status as the anointed of God (Aslan 2014: 30, 33).
68 In the Gospel of John, which was produced after the others (possibly as late as 120 CE), Jesus has shed most of his worldly identity and become a manifestation of *logos*, the divine Word.
69 For example, scholars have tried to find a correlation between the Jerusalem council mentioned in Acts 15 and the encounter between Peter and Paul in Galatians 2 (Thompson 2010: 320).

References

Allen, O. Wesley Jr. (2009), 'Luke', in D. L. Petersen and G. R. O'Day (eds.), *Theological Bible Commentary*, 325–38, Westminster: John Knox Press.
Aslan, Reza (2014), *Zealot: The Life and Times of Jesus of Nazareth*, London: Westbourne Press.
Attridge, Harold, Hendrix, Holland Lee, Koester, Helmut, and White, L. Michael (1998), 'The Gospel of Luke: A Novel for Gentiles', *Frontline: From Jesus to Christ*, https://www.pbs.org/wgbh/pages/frontline/shows/religion/story/luke.html.
Aune, David E. (2010a), 'Form Criticism', in D. E. Aune (ed.), *The Blackwell Companion to the New Testament*, 140–55, Oxford: Wiley-Blackwell.
Aune, David E. (2010b), 'Literary Criticism', in D. E. Aune (ed.), *The Blackwell Companion to the New Testament*, 116–39, Oxford: Wiley-Blackwell.
Auvrayes-Assayas, Clara, Bernier, Christian, Cassin, Barbara, Paul, André, and Rosier-Catach, Irène (2014), 'To Translate', in B. Cassin (ed.), *The Dictionary of Untranslatables: A Philosophical Lexicon*, 1139–51, Princeton and Oxford: Princeton University Press.
Bauckham, Richard (2017), *Jesus and the Eyewitnesses: The Gospels as Eyewitness Testimony*, 2nd edn. Grand Rapids, MI: William B. Eerdmans Publishing Company.
Bassnett, Susan (1980), *Translation Studies*, London and New York: Methuen.
Bassnett, Susan and Johnston, David (eds.) (2019), *The Outward Turn in Translation Studies*. Special issue of *The Translator*, 25 (3).
Bennett, Karen (2018), 'Translation and the Desacralization of the Western World: From Performativity to Representation', in M. Baker (ed.), *Translation and the Production of Knowledge*. Special Issue of *Alif – Journal of Comparative Poetics*, 38: 91–120.
Bennett, Karen (2022), 'The Unsustainable Lightness of Meaning: Reflections on the Material Turn in Translation Studies and Its Intradisciplinary Implications', in G. Silva and M. Radicioni (eds.), *Recharting Territories: Intradisciplinarity in Translation Studies*, 49–74, Leuven: Leuven University Press.
Bennett, Karen (forthcoming), 'Standing on the Shoulders of Giants: Approaches to Knowledge Translation', in K. Marais and R. Meylaerts (eds.), *Routledge Handbook of Translation Theory*. London and New York: Routledge.

Blumczynski, Piotr (2017), *Ubiquitous Translation*, London and New York: Routledge.
Bryan, Christopher (1997), *A Preface to Mark: Notes on the Gospel in Its Literary and Cultural Settings*, New York: Oxford University Press.
Burkett, Delbert (2002), *An Introduction to the New Testament and the Origins of Christianity*, Cambridge: Cambridge University Press.
Byrskog, Samuel (2002), *Story as History – History as Story: The Gospel Tradition in the Context of Ancient Oral History*, Boston: Brill Academic Publishers.
Chew, Stephen L. (2018), 'Myth: Eyewitness Testimony Is the Best Kind of Testimony', in Association for Psychological Science, Myth: Eyewitness Testimony Is the Best Kind of Evidence – Association for Psychological Science – APS, https://www.psychologicalscience.org/uncategorized/myth-eyewitness-testimony-is-the-best-kind-of-evidence.html (accessed 30 August 2022).
Dewey, Joana (1994), 'The Gospel of Mark as Oral/Aural Event: Implications for Interpretation', in Elizabeth Struthers Malbon and Edgar V. McKnight (eds.), *The New Literary Criticism and the New Testament*, 145–63, Sheffield: Sheffield Academic.
Duling, Dennis C. (2010), 'The Gospel of Matthew', in D. E. Aune (ed.), *The Blackwell Companion to the New Testament*, 296–318, Oxford: Wiley-Blackwell.
Gentzler, Edwin (2017), *Translation and Rewriting in the Age of Post-Translation Studies*, London and New York: Routledge.
Gerhardsson, Birger (1961), *Memory and Manuscript: Oral Transmission and Written Transmission in Rabbinic Judaism and Early Christianity*, Lund: Gleerup.
Gundry, Robert H. (1994), *Matthew: A Commentary on His Handbook for a Mixed Church under Persecution*, 2nd edn, Grand Rapids: Eerdmans.
Hock, Ronald F. (2002), 'The *Chreia* in Primary and Secondary Education', in Jón Ma. Ásgeirsson and Nancy Van Deusen (eds.), *Alexander's Revenge: Hellenistic Culture through the Centuries*, 11–35, Reykjavik: University of Iceland Press.
Honoré, Anthony M. (1968), 'A Statistical Study of the Synoptic Problem', *Novum Testamentum*, 10 (2/3): 95–147.
Kelber, Werner H. and Byrskog, Samuel (eds.) (2009), *Jesus in Memory: Traditions in Oral and Scribal Perspectives*. Waco: Baylor University Press.
Kelly, Louis G. (1979), *The True Interpreter: A History of Translation Theory and Practice in the West*, New York: St Martins.
Kingsbury, Jack Dean (1983), *The Christology of Mark's Gospel*, Philadelphia: Fortress Press.
Kürzinger, Josef (1983), *Papias von Hierapolis und die Evangelien des Neuen Testaments*, Regensburg: Pustet.
Koester, Helmut (1990), *Ancient Christian Gospels: Their History and Development*, London and Philadelphia: SCM Press/Trinity Press International.
Koester, Helmut and White, L. Michael (1998), 'The Gospel of Matthew: Jesus as the New Moses', *Frontline: From Jesus to Christ*, https://www.pbs.org/wgbh/pages/frontline/shows/religion/story/matthew.html.
Lambert, José and van Gorp, Hendrik (1985), 'On Describing Translations', in T. Hermans (ed.), *The Manipulation of Literature: Studies in Literary Translation*, 42–53, London and Sydney: Croom Helm.
Le Cunff, Anne-Laure (2022), 'Memory Bias: How Selective Recall Can Impact Your Memories', *NESS Labs*, https://nesslabs.com/memory-bias (accessed 1 September 2022).
Lefevere, André (1985), 'Why Waste Our Time on Rewrites', in T. Hermans (ed.), *The Manipulation of Literature: Studies in Literary Translation*, 215–43, London and Sydney: Croom Helm.

Lefevere, André (1992), *Translation, Rewriting, and the Manipulation of Literary Fame*, London and New York: Routledge.
Mack, Burton L. (1993), *The Lost Gospel: The Book of Q & Christian Origins*, San Francisco: HarperSanFrancisco.
Mack, Burton L. (1995), *Who Wrote the New Testament? The Making of the Christian Myth*, San Francisco: HarperSan Francisco.
McGill, John (2020), 'The Connection between Language and Memory', https://languagedrops.com/blog/connection-between-language-and-memory (accessed 1 September 2022).
Mellowes, Marilyn (1998a), 'More about Q and the Gospel of Thomas', *Frontline: From Jesus to Christ*, https://www.pbs.org/wgbh/pages/frontline/shows/religion/story/qthomas.html.
Mellowes, Marilyn (1998b), 'The Gospel of Mark', *Frontline: From Jesus to Christ*, https://www.pbs.org/wgbh/pages/frontline/shows/religion/story/mmmark.html.
Mellowes, Marilyn (1998c), 'The Gospel of Matthew', *Frontline: From Jesus to Christ*, https://www.pbs.org/wgbh/pages/frontline/shows/religion/story/mmmatthew.html.
Mellowes, Marilyn (1998d), 'The Gospel of Luke', *Frontline: From Jesus to Christ*, https://www.pbs.org/wgbh/pages/frontline/shows/religion/story/mmluke.html.
Mellowes, Marilyn (1998e), 'The Emergence of the Canon', *Frontline: From Jesus to Christ*, The Story of the Storytellers – The Emergence of the Canon | From Jesus to Christ | FRONTLINE | PBS. https://www.pbs.org/wgbh/pages/frontline/shows/religion/story/.
Moeser, Marion C. (2002), 'The Anecdote in Mark, the Classical World and the Rabbis', in *Journal for the Study of the New Testament*, Supplement series 227, London: Sheffield Academic Press – Bloomsbury publishing.
Neyrey, Jerome S. J. (2010), 'Social-scientific Criticism', in D. E. Aune (ed.), *The Blackwell Companion to the New Testament*, 177–91, Oxford: Wiley-Blackwell.
Pagels, Elaine, White, L. Michael, Clark, Elizabeth, Attridge, Harold and Callahan, Allen D. (1998), 'Emergence of the Four Gospel Canon', *Frontline: From Jesus to Christ*, https://www.pbs.org/wgbh/pages/frontline/shows/religion/story/emergence.html.
Pawson, David, with Andy Peck (2007), *Unlocking the Bible*, Travelers Rest, South Carolina: True Potential Publishing.
Perrin, Norman (1969), *What Is Redaction Criticism?*, Philadelphia: Fortress Press.
Piper, Ronald A. (2010), 'Q: The Sayings Source', in D. E. Aune (ed.), *The Blackwell Companion to the New Testament*, 255–71, Oxford: Wiley-Blackwell.
Ricoeur, Paul (2004), *Memory, History, Forgetting*, translated by K. Blamey and D. Pellauer, Chicago: University of Chicago Press.
Saunders, Stanley P. (2009), 'Matthew', in D. L. Petersen and G. R. O'Day (eds.), *Theological Bible Commentary*, 293–310, Westminster: John Knox Press.
Schmidt, K. L. (1919), *Der Rahmen der Geshichte Jesu*, Berlin: Trowizsch.
Schröter, Jens (2010), 'The Gospel of Mark', in D. E. Aune (ed.), *The Blackwell Companion to the New Testament*, 272–95, Oxford: Wiley-Blackwell.
Smith, Ben C. (2022), 'The Healing of a Leper', *TextExcavation*, http://www.textexcavation.com/synhealleper.html (accessed 1 September 2022).
Steiner, George (1975), *After Babel: Aspects of Language and Translation*, London and New York: Oxford University Press.
Stierle, Karlheinz (1996), 'Translatio Studii and Renaissance: From Vertical to Horizontal Translation', in S. Budick and W. Iser (eds.), *The Translatability of Cultures: Figurations of the Space Between*, 55–67, Stanford, CA: Stanford University Press.
Thomas, Robert L. (1998), 'The Synoptic Gospels in the Ancient Church', in Thomas, Robert L. and Farnell, David F. (eds.), *The Jesus Crisis: The Inroads of Historical Criticism into Evangelical Scholarship*, 39–46, Grand Rapids, MI: Kregel Academic and Professional.

Thompson, Richard (2010), 'Luke-Acts: The Gospel of Luke and the Acts of the Apostles', in D. E. Aune (ed.), *The Blackwell Companion to the New Testament*, 319–43, Oxford: Wiley-Blackwell.

Toury, Gideon (2012), *Descriptive Translation Studies and Beyond*, rev edn, Amsterdam and Philadelphia: John Benjamins.

Vermeer, Hans (1989), 'Skopos and Commission in Translational Action', in Andrew Chesterman (ed. and trans.), *Readings in Translation Theory*, 173–200, Helsinki: Finnlectura.

White, L. Michael (1998), 'Kingdoms in Conflict', *Frontline: From Jesus to Christ*, https://www.pbs.org/wgbh/pages/frontline/shows/religion/first/kingdoms.html (accessed 21 August 2022).

White, L. Michael and Koester, Helmut (1998a), 'The Gospel of Mark: A Story of Secrecy and Misunderstanding', *Frontline: From Jesus to Christ*, https://www.pbs.org/wgbh/pages/frontline/shows/religion/story/mark.html.

White, L. Michael and Koester, Helmut (1998b), 'Importance of the Oral Tradition', *Frontline: From Jesus to Christ*, https://www.pbs.org/wgbh/pages/frontline/shows/religion/story/oral.html.

White, L. Michael and Koester, Helmut (1998c), 'The Gospel of Mark: A Story of Secrecy and Misunderstanding', *Frontline: From Jesus to Christ*, https://www.pbs.org/wgbh/pages/frontline/shows/religion/story/mark.html.

4

The historian's dilemma: Domestication or foreignizing?

Peter Burke

Introduction

In the last generation, a major turn in the study of culture has been the rise of the idea of 'cultural translation' (Bachmann-Medick 2012). Once confined to the relatively small circle of social and cultural anthropologists, the term is now commonplace in religious and of course in cultural studies. It has also come into use among cultural historians. This turn is scarcely surprising. Turning a text in one language into a text in a second is a special case of the mobility of items of culture from one place to another. Indeed, the English word 'translation' was once used to refer to any form of what we call 'transfer' or 'displacement', including the movement of bishops from one diocese to another.

As often happens when concepts move between disciplines, or more exactly when they are appropriated and employed by scholars in the second discipline, they bring with them not only fresh insights but also problems. In this chapter, I shall focus on one such problem. Historians may be described as translating the past for readers in the present, and in so doing they face analogous problems to translators between languages (Vidal Claramonte 2018).

The poet John Dryden, who translated Ovid and Virgil into English verse, once described translation as 'much like dancing on ropes with fettered legs'.[1] In China a similar image, 'dancing in chains', was employed to refer to poets of the Tang dynasty who tried to combine creativity with obedience to strict rules.[2] However, Dryden's vivid image of the difficulty of the enterprise has the advantage for our purposes of implying that the dancer must avoid falling either to the left or to the right. The need to navigate between two extremes was later elaborated into a theory of translation, notably by Friedrich Schleiermacher in the nineteenth century and Lawrence Venuti in the twentieth. They both distinguished between two opposite approaches to the task of the translator (Schleirmacher 1813: 49; see also Venuti 1995; Ajtony 2017).

One of these was taking the text to the reader, 'domesticating' it in the sense of making the text appear to have been written in the target language. For example, the translator Michael Hofmann recalled having been asked to produce a version of a German text 'as though it had been written in English yesterday' (Hofmann 1998: 67). The alternative to domestication is what Schleiermacher called 'taking the reader to the text', while Venuti christened it 'foreignizing', in other words emphasizing the 'alterity' of the text, its place in a culture different from that of the target audience. This second approach is close to the 'defamiliarization' (*ostranenie, Verfremdung*) advocated in the early twentieth century by the Russian critic Viktor Shklovsky and the German playwright Bertolt Brecht.

Unfortunately, something is 'lost in translation', whichever strategy is employed. In the case of domestication, what is lost, or at least greatly reduced, is the 'otherness' of the text, its place in the culture in which it was originally produced. The price of foreignizing, on the other hand, is a reduction of the text's intelligibility to its new readers. It is no wonder then that discussions of 'translatability' and 'untranslatability' remain central both to the study of world literature and to the new discipline of translation studies (Cassin 2004; Apter 2013: 31–44; Large 2018). However, an interest in these alternative strategies is not confined to studies of language and literature. In anthropology, religious studies and history, analogous problems have arisen and similar solutions have been discussed, as we shall see.

Translating texts

Translators between languages face this dilemma all the time. In a volume that focuses on the past it seems appropriate to take examples of translations from texts that were originally produced in a significantly earlier period. Nietzsche remarked that 'One can gauge the degree of historical sensibility an age possesses by the manner in which it translates texts'.[3] In different places and in different periods, there have been different cultures of translation, in the sense of different rules or conventions. In early modern Europe, for instance, it was commonplace for translators to leave out passages in the text they were translating without warning readers that they were doing so, and even, stranger still in late modern eyes, to insert passages of their own, again without warning (Burke 2007a). To be more exact, we should recognize that in a given period, historical sensibility is not homogeneous. A recent study of early modern translations of Tacitus notes instances of both domestication and foreignizing, in the first case converting ancient Roman currency into its sixteenth-century Spanish equivalent and in the second case retaining the original term *sesterces* (Martínez Bermejo 2010: 88).

As Umberto Eco (2003: 98–9) noted, domestication includes modernizing, while foreignizing includes archaizing. An unusual case of the latter comes from C. S. Lewis' history of sixteenth-century English literature. 'When I have quoted from neo-Latin authors', Lewis explained in his preface, 'I have tried to translate them into sixteenth-century English'. He made this decision to avoid giving the impression 'that the Latinists are somehow more enlightened, less remote, less limited by their age, than those who wrote English', thus reminding us of the effects of different strategies of translation on the reader's sense of the past, whether perceived as close or distant (Lewis 1954: v).

The translation of Homer in the last 500 years offers a series of vivid examples of the problems raised by both domestication and foreignizing. The *Odyssey*, for instance, was published in German translation in 1537, in French (in part) in 1547, in Spanish in 1550–6 and in Italian in 1581. In English, the version by George Chapman, which appeared between 1614 and 1616, itself became a classic. However, that did not prevent many other writers from attempting the same task, among them Thomas Hobbes (1675), Alexander Pope (1725), William Cowper (1791) Andrew Lang and Samuel Butcher (1879), William Morris (1887) and Émile Rieu (1946).

Some of the translators of the *Odyssey* chose the strategy of domestication. Pope's translation, for instance, was criticized by a rival translator, Cowper, for lacking what he called 'the air of antiquity' (Underwood 1998: 41). An extreme case of domestication was the Rieu translation, which sold over three million copies in the half-century following its publication. Rieu deliberately employed anachronistic phrases such as 'the meeting adjourned' and abandoned verse for prose as if Homer had written a novel instead of reciting an epic. Indeed, the classicist Adam Parry (1989: 42–4) criticized Rieu as 'the first to demonstrate beyond a doubt that Homer was really Anthony Trollope', as well as making Homeric heroes 'speak in the bantering, slightly ironic tones of the Common Room'.

On the other hand, Morris, like Lang and Butcher, introduced medieval or quasi-medieval archaisms into his translation of the *Odyssey* as a way of reminding readers of the poem's antiquity. In similar fashion, Francis Newman (1856: xvi) explained that his intention in translating the *Iliad* was 'to retain every peculiarity of the original ... *with the greater care the more foreign it may happen to be*'. Hence he chose to write in an archaic form of English, as close to Anglo-Saxon as was possible without becoming unintelligible to readers of his own day. It is worth emphasizing that this attempt at foreignizing did not make use of ancient Greek terms such as *basileus* for 'king'. Instead, it drew implicit analogies between Homer's archaic Greek and the archaic English of Chaucer and the Anglo-Saxon of *Beowulf*.

Originally transparent, translations become opaque over the years. Chapman's Homer now smells of the seventeenth century, Pope's of the eighteenth, Morris' of the nineteenth century and Rieu's of the mid-twentieth. In contrast, translations made in our own age seem timeless – but only to us. In this respect translations resemble forgeries, which also include what has been called a 'hidden clock', in the sense of revealing their date more clearly with the passing of time (Porębski: 143). A sense of anachronism has often aided the discovery of forgeries. In ancient Rome, the physician Galen had argued that a book *On the Nature of Man*, ascribed to Hippocrates, could not have been by him because it included technical terms that Hippocrates never used. In Song, Ming and Qing China, scholars such as Yao Jiheng (1647–c.1715) practised 'forgery detection' (*bianwei*). It was thanks to their sense of period style that they were able to detect forged texts and other artefacts (Grafton 1990: 20; Elman 2001: 103–4, 222, 238).

In Europe from the fifteenth century onwards, the argument from style became increasingly common in discussions of possible forgeries. The humanist Lorenzo Valla, for instance, had an acute consciousness of the way in which Latin had changed over the centuries. This consciousness helped him argue that the famous *Donation of Constantine* was a later forgery because it contained what he called 'linguistic barbarisms'. By this term Valla meant anachronistic phrases such as 'together with all our satraps' (*una cum omnibus satrapis nostris*). 'Whoever heard', he exclaimed, 'of satraps being named in deliberations of the Romans?' (Valla 2007: 66–7, 72–3, 76–7; see also Gaeta 1955: 77–126). In similar fashion, in the seventeenth century, the French scholar Isaac Casaubon demonstrated that the *Hermetic Corpus* of religious texts, previously dated to ancient Egyptian times, was actually produced after the time of Christ, since the style of the prose is a post-classical form of Greek, while Christian terms such as *homoousios* occur in the text (Yates 1964: 400; Grafton 1990: 89).

The general point that literary style reveals the period in which a given text was written was made with particular eloquence in another classic demonstration of forgery, this time the letters attributed to the ancient Greek tyrant Phalaris, unmasked by the eighteenth-century Cambridge scholar Richard Bentley. Once again, the late form of Greek used in the letters, its 'modernisms', gave the date away, since

> the Attic of the true Phalaris's age is not there represented, but a more recent idiom and style, that by the whole thread and colour of it betrays itself to be many centuries younger than he. Every living language, like the perspiring bodies of living creatures, is in perpetual motion and alteration; some words go off and become obsolete; others are taken in and by degrees grow into common use; or, the same word is inverted to a new sense and notion, which in tract of time makes as observable a change in the air and features of a language as age makes in the lines and mien of a face.
>
> (Bentley 1699: section xiii)

In other words, insensitivity to anachronism on the part of the forger leads to the detection of a forgery.

In similar fashion, in the case of faked paintings, the 'Vermeers' painted by Han Van Meegeren, for instance, which had once deceived the leading Vermeer specialist Abraham Bredius, now evoke the art of the early twentieth century. Indeed, it has been suggested that this very feature may have been part of the appeal of these unconscious 'translations' of Vermeer in the 1930s and 1940s (Bredius 1937; Kreuger 2007). Today, on the other hand, anachronisms in Van Meegeren's work that were virtually invisible at that time now spring to the eye.

Of particular interest to historians are cases in which classic texts require translation into a modern version of their original language because they have become more or less unintelligible as that language changed over the centuries. A well-known case is the translation into modern English of Geoffrey Chaucer's *Canterbury Tales* by the Oxford scholar Neville Coghill. In the introduction to his modern version, which was first published in 1951, Coghill noted that it was becoming increasingly difficult for non-specialists to read fourteenth-century English, which is considerably more distant from today's English than Dante's language from today's Italian. He rejected the practice of replacing obsolete words and phrases and retaining the rest of Chaucer's original text, since this compromise 'presents Chaucer's work as a conflict of styles, partly archaic and partly modern, a language that has never been spoken by anybody'.

Coghill therefore decided to treat the *Canterbury Tales* 'as any true translator would treat a classic in a foreign tongue', attempting to recapture Chaucer's conversational 'tone of voice' in the English of the 1950s. Unfortunately, this solution raises a new problem because the language of conversation changes, not only over the centuries but even over decades. Seventy years after the publication of Coghill's translation, some of his colloquial expressions, such as 'My hat!', have come to sound odd, if they are intelligible at all (Chaucer 1951: 16–17, 20). As we shall soon see, historians too face this problem.

In similar fashion to the *Canterbury Tales*, Montaigne's *Essays* have been translated into modern French three times since 1989. Another well-known case of modernization is that of the eleventh-century romance known as the 'Tale of Genji' (*Genji Monogatari*). *Genji* has become one of the classics of Japanese literature, but the text is written in a language 'further removed from modern Japanese than the language of Chaucer is from modern English' (Bowring 2003: 92). The romance has been translated (partially or completely) more than ninety times into modern Japanese, three times by the famous novelist Junichirō Tanizaki. Tanizaki's first translation, made in the late 1930s, was an expurgated one, omitting 'every reference to Genji's sexual liaisons with women who were, or would be, intimately involved with an emperor' (Emmerich 2013: 10, 342–3). This example, like that of some Western versions of the *Arabian Nights*, reminds us that expurgation has often been viewed as one of the tasks of the translator.

Movements of opposition to translations, whether for religious, aesthetic or political reasons, are of obvious interest to historians. Particularly well known is the long opposition of the Catholic Church to translations of the Bible into the vernacular, on the grounds that if lay people could read the text for themselves, the authority of the Church would be undermined and heresy would flourish (Fragnito 2005). In the Islamic world too there has long been a movement of opposition to translating the Koran from Arabic, the sacred language in which it was written (Zwemer 1915).

A rather different example comes once again from England, where a translation of Scripture that was first published in 1611 became accepted in the Anglican Church as the 'Authorized Version', otherwise known as the King James Bible because the translation was made in the reign of King James I. As in the case of Coghill's Chaucer, attempts have been made to modernize the language of this version, although the English of the early seventeenth century, however archaic it may sometimes sound, remains generally intelligible today. In this case, modernization has met with opposition for several different reasons: because the archaisms of the King James Bible are part of its charm, because they set the Bible apart from ordinary texts and because they belong to a cultural tradition, since what were once new coinages have passed into everyday English.

For this reason, when an emended text (known as the *Revised Version*) was produced in the 1880s, in order to incorporate the results of recent biblical scholarship, reverence for the language of the *Authorized Version* led the scholars working on the revision to imitate the English of the age of James I, thus 'producing the equivalent of mock-Jacobean architecture and "Ye Olde Tea Shoppe"' (Campbell 2010: 222; see also Nicolson 2011: 233). Indeed, the text has become part of the literary canon – along with Shakespeare, who still awaits his Coghill, although performances of his plays discreetly update the text in order to bring it closer to today's audience (but see Shakespeare 2011).

In the late twentieth century, cultural change led to further revisions. The editors of the *New Revised Standard Version* of 1989, responding to the challenge of feminism, decided to replace masculine by gender-neutral language, so that the word 'man' became 'person', while 'brothers' was turned into 'brothers and sisters' (Campbell 2010: 233). The NRSV, as it is generally known, is the version preferred by many Protestant churches in the United States and Canada. It has been agreed that this version will be updated regularly, a clear sign of the increasing distance between the *Authorized Version* and its readers. This example reminds us that the simple dichotomy between 'close' and 'distant' needs to be refined, since there are degrees of cultural distance as well as physical distance. The problem of translating Japanese texts and Japanese culture into English, for instance, is greater than the problem of translating Spanish texts and Spanish culture.

Translating religions, translating cultures

The problem of choosing between domestication and foreignizing is not confined to translators of texts. It has been experienced by missionaries and by anthropologists as well as by historians.

From the sixteenth century onwards, the expansion of Europe by trade and conquest was accompanied by the rise of Christian missions to China, Japan, India, Africa and the Americas. Missionaries confronted the problem of translation in both the literal and the metaphorical sense. At the literal level, they needed to translate texts and concepts from their own languages into those of the peoples they were trying to convert. A recurrent problem was that of translating the word 'God'. If missionaries used a local term (such as *tianzhu*, literally 'Lord of Heaven', in Chinese), their flock easily understood it, at the price of assimilating Christianity to the religious ideas of their own tradition. If, on the other hand, the missionaries employed a new term – Catholic missionaries often chose the Latin word 'Deus' – their flock might not be able to grasp it.

The linguistic problem was part of a larger challenge. By the sixteenth century, some Christian missionaries in South and East Asia had become aware of the need to separate the religious message from European customs in other words (those of the Jesuits) to 'accommodate' it to their audience in the region in which they were labouring (Bettray 1955; Rubiés 2005). In order to be taken seriously in their new environments, some Jesuits exchanged their black robes for the dress of an Indian holy man or a Chinese scholar. They argued that Chinese reverence for ancestors and the use of the sacred thread by Indian Brahmins were social rather than religious ideas and practices. For these reasons, we might describe early modern Jesuits such as Matteo Ricci in China and Roberto De' Nobili in India as free translators of Christianity.[4] So were their successors, Protestant as well as Catholic. In the China Inland Mission, for instance, founded in 1865, the missionaries wore Chinese robes, just as Ricci had done.

Thanks to these precedents, scholars in the field of religious studies have been relatively quick to employ the idea of cultural translation. In the 1980s, for example, Lamin Sanneh (2009), a professor of missions and world Christianity at Yale Divinity School, discussed not only the translation of the Bible into many languages but also its 'translatability', including the idea of Christianity as 'a translatable religion'. Historians of religion have taken up this idea (Ditchfield 2017). The concept of syncretism was given a new twist by the German Egyptologist Jan Assmann (1996: 25) in an essay on 'translating gods' in the ancient world in which he described the search for equivalents between the gods and goddesses of different peoples (Astarte, Aphrodite and Venus, for instance) as 'theological onomasiology'.[5]

Cultural distance has long been the concern of anthropologists. Indeed, overcoming it might be described as their raison d'être. Some of them have described their approach to this problem as 'cultural translation', a phrase that seems to have antedated the explicit comparison of cultures to texts. For example, in his famous ethnography of the Trobriand Islands, the Polish anthropologist Bronisław Malinowski (1922: 90) compared local objects of value to the British Crown Jewels, in order 'to show that this type of ownership is not entirely a fantastic South Sea custom, untranslatable into our ideas' (see also Geertz 1973).

It was a former student of Malinowski's, the British anthropologist Edward Evans-Pritchard (1951: 79, 81), who turned the metaphor of translation into a central concept in his discipline, writing about 'translation from one culture to another' and about the skill necessary 'to translate a foreign culture into the language of one's own'. Evans-Pritchard was a master who acquired a number of disciples, some of whom were attracted by this concept. Godfrey Lienhardt (1954: 97), for instance, suggested that 'The problem of describing to others how members of a remote tribe think … begins to appear largely as one of translation'. Malcolm Crick (1976: 164) described anthropology as 'an art of translation'. Thomas Beidelman (1971) edited a *Festschrift* for Evans-Pritchard under the title *The Translation of Culture*. Since that time, the idea of cultural translation may be said to have been domesticated in anthropology (Pálsson 1994).

In the case of cultures as in that of texts, attempts to translate encounter obstacles. Anthropologists face the practical problem of how to render the keywords used by the peoples being studied when these terms – *totem, tabu, mana, baraka* and so on – have no precise equivalents in the language of the public for whom they were writing. As Salman Rushdie (1983: 104) wrote in one of his novels, 'To unlock a society, look at its untranslatable words'. Awareness of what is known as the problem of untranslatability has led some anthropologists to reflect on the more general question of how to interpret one culture to another. In their turn, these reflections have influenced discussions of translation between languages. Umberto Eco (2003: 82), a polymath who was well acquainted with the work of anthropologists, defined translation as 'a shift, not between two languages, but between two cultures'.

Facing a similar problem to that confronted by earlier missionaries, Evans-Pritchard (1956: 1, 18) offered a compromise between translation and the refusal to translate. In his book on the religion of the Nuer, a people living in the Sudan, the first sentence reads as follows: 'The Nuer word we translate "God" is *kwoth*, "spirit". A few pages later, he wrote that the Nuer 'distinguish between *duer* and *gwac*', glossing these terms as 'fault' and 'mistake' but using the Nuer words without further translation in the rest of his book.

Translating the past

Historians have only recently become concerned with translation, including the idea that what they translate for readers, listeners and viewers in the present is not confined to specific documents but includes the past itself. Their new concern may be described as an example of translation between disciplines, since it was thanks to an interest in anthropology that some historians (myself included) became interested in the translation of cultures (Burke 2007b). However, this interest should not be limited, and indeed is no longer limited, to cases of encounters between cultures. Historians in general need to be concerned with the distance between the present and the past, viewing that past as a 'foreign country', in a famous phrase of the novelist L. P. Hartley (1953: 1; cf. Lowenthal 1985). In fact, the idea is older than this. In 1931, the historian Herbert Butterfield (1931: 66) wrote that 'Like the traveller', the historian 'describes an unknown country to us who cannot visit it'. More recently, a few historians, notably Mark Phillips (2013a-b), have made historical distance a major theme of their studies.

These historians may be 'rethinking' historical distance, but they are not, of course, the first to be aware of it. For example, a concern with the difference and the distance between the past and the present was present, to some degree, in ancient China. In the writings attributed to Chuang Tzu (Zhuangzi), for instance, the music master Chin (contradicting Confucius, who appealed to the examples of 'the Former Kings') claimed that 'our time and that of the Former Kings are as different as land from water; the empire of Chou over which they ruled [and today] are as different as boat from chariot' (Waley 1939: 19).

Whether or not this sense of the past as different and distant from the present can be found in the Middle Ages is a controversial question. Medieval writers such as refer to the 'chivalry' (*chevalerie*) of the ancient world. The problem is whether to explain these references as examples of the lack of a sense of anachronism (the traditional explanation) or as strategic anachronisms, designed to bring the past closer to readers, as has sometimes been suggested (Cormier 1974; Spiegel 1993: 104). The sense of the 'foreignness' of the past should be discussed not as a case of presence or absence but that of a difference in degree, sharper in the Renaissance than in the Middle Ages and sharper in the nineteenth century than in the Renaissance – though perhaps weaker today than in the twentieth century.

In the case of Renaissance Europe, in the effort to emulate ancient Greeks and Romans, artists, writers and thinkers became increasingly aware of their distance from their models (Burke 1969; 2001; 2013). The historian Francesco Guicciardini, for instance, remarked that it was a mistake to try to imitate the Romans. To do so, he wrote, would be to expect an ass to race like a horse (*Quanto si ingannano coloro che a ogni parola allegano e Romani! ... sarebbe volere che un asino facessi el corso di un cavallo*) (Guicciardini 1969: no. 110). Again, the French scholar François

Hotman (1567) studied Roman law but came to the conclusion that it was useless in the France of his day because it was the law of a past society with different customs, whereas 'the laws of a country should be accommodated to the state and form of government and not the government to the laws' (Kelley 1970: 109–11; Pocock 1987: 11–15, 22–5).

A sense of distance from the past extended, as we have seen in the case of Valla, to language. Historians writing in Latin were compelled to choose between anachronism on one side and inelegance – by classical standards – on the other. Leonardo Bruni, for instance, chose anachronism and described Lombardy as *Gallia Cisalpina*. In his history of Venice, Pietro Bembo called the Turkish galleys *biremes*, the spahis *equites*, the admiral of the Turkish fleet *prefectus classis Thraciae* and the sultan *Regem Thracium*. In the cases of Bruni and Bembo, we find what might be called anachronism in reverse, in other words using the language of the past to write about the present rather than the other way round.

On the other hand, Lorenzo Valla, writing the life of King Ferdinand I of Naples, preferred to call cannon *bombardae* (rather than *tormenta*, referring to ancient siege engines) and to call Muslims *Maomettani* (rather than Mauretani, the ancient inhabitants of North Africa). On account of these choices, Valla was criticized for inelegance by his rival Bartolomeo Fazio (1978), but delivered a withering reply to this critic on the grounds that 'a new thing requires a new word' (*nova res novum vocabulum flagitat*) (Valla 1981: 100, 106).

Awareness of historical distance might also be described as a sensitivity to anachronism. The word 'anachronism' came into use in several European languages only in the seventeenth century, though the idea is older. Anachronisms may be described as mistranslations of the past, projecting onto an earlier period – or more exactly, 'retrojecting', the ideas, assumptions, artefacts and practices of a later one.

Mistranslations of this kind are particularly visible in the case of costume. In what might be called the 'Roman soldier test', an examination of medieval images of the Resurrection, focusing on the soldiers guarding Christ's tomb, reveals them as wearing armour of the period in which they were painted. In this case at least we are in the presence of plain anachronism, rather than the strategic anachronism sometimes attributed to medieval writers, noted above. On the other hand, Renaissance images, notably paintings by Andrea Mantegna, increasingly represent Roman soldiers in the armour of their time (Burke 2001). Anachronism was already discussed (before the word was coined in the seventeenth century in Latin, French and English) in a sixteenth-century treatise on the errors of painters, criticizing painters for representing St Jerome in the red robes of a cardinal, since this form of clothing was unknown in Jerome's time (Gilio da Fabriano 1564).

The anachronistic reading of historical documents is extremely common, whether it is deliberate or unaware. A famous example is that of interpretations of Magna Carta over the centuries, in which a feudal document concerned with the rights of the barons became the foundation of English liberty via the translation of terms such as 'free man' (*liber homo*) that extended its reference beyond the nobility. For example, in 1628 Magna Carta was used to support the critique of Charles I by the Parliament for his attack on 'the liberties of thousands' (Thompson 1971). Because the text was read in an anachronistic manner over the centuries – whether conscious manipulation or what is known as 'creative misunderstanding' – it was always up to date.

Historians of their own culture face a particular temptation. It is all too easy to take for granted that certain words which are still current and perfectly intelligible have always carried the same meaning. In fact, these words are sometimes the equivalent of 'false friends' in two languages, similar words that have different meanings. When the anthropologist Hildred Geertz reviewed a book by the historian Keith Thomas (1971), *Religion and the Decline of Magic*, she pointed out that on some occasions he used the words 'religion' and 'magic' as they were used in early modern England, but on other occasions as they were used at the time he was writing. When studying people who hold beliefs that are alien to ours, she concluded, 'we need to know always when we are speaking in our own conceptual language and when we are speaking in theirs'. Geertz's observation (1975: 74) is an acute one, although it should be reformulated to take into account the fact that the words 'religion' and 'magic' often meant the same in the seventeenth century as they do today – though not always, thus making it all too easy for historians to slip between conceptual languages.

Anachronism has long been considered to be a mortal sin for historians. Already in the seventeenth century, the English scholar Sir Henry Spelman noted that 'the succeeding ages viewing the past by the present conceive the former to have been like to that they live in, and framing thereupon erroneous propositions, do likewise make thereon erroneous inferences and conclusions'. Eighteenth-century critics often faulted Shakespeare for mistakes such as showing Cleopatra playing billiards, long before that game had been invented (modern critics, on the other hand, are more inclined to emphasize the playwright's sensitivity to ancient Roman values such as Stoicism) (Spelman 1723: 57; Velz 1978). More generally, David Hume (1808: vol. 7, 204) remarked that it was 'unreasonable to judge of the measures embraced during one period by the maxims which prevail in another'. Translation has often been described as a kind of violence, forcing words and sentences in one language to fit into another (Samoyault 2020). In similar fashion, anachronism may be described as violence against the past.

Nevertheless, a comparison with the debate in the domain of translation between domesticators and foreignizers suggests a more nuanced approach to anachronism. Avoiding infidelity to the past, in other words avoiding anachronism, corresponds to foreignizing. It may be described as the 'default setting' for historians today. The problem is how to ensure that readers participate in this avoidance. One solution, perhaps the most important one, is to introduce readers to the concepts of a particular place, time and social groups that differ most from their own, 'honour' and 'shame', for instance, glossing them and explaining the contexts in which they were used as Evans-Pritchard did in the case of *kwoth*, *duer* and *gwac*. In so doing they are literally 'translating the past'.

However, a case may also be made and indeed has been made for the opposite strategy, domestication, an approach that makes it easier for readers who are not professional historians to understand the past (Loraux 1993; Dosse 2005; Burke 2006). For this reason, historians have often drawn parallels between institutions or ideas in the past and other institutions and ideas in the present. These parallels might be described as 'strategic' or 'productive' anachronisms, identified as such (Chakrabarty 2000: 243). They are introduced in order to help readers imagine the period that the historian is describing. Their function, in Macaulay's famous phrase, is 'to make the past present, to bring the distant near'.[6] Directors who stage Shakespeare in modern dress are pursuing a similar strategy. So did Malinowski when he made the reference to the 'Crown Jewels' quoted earlier, bringing the distant near in the case of space rather than time.

The English historian John Neale, in a little book about the religious wars in sixteenth-century France, published in 1943, remarked that 'I know no better way to secure an imaginative grasp of the situation than to reflect on the ideological movements of our own day', adding that Calvin's Geneva 'was in many ways like Moscow ... when the Soviet state dreamed of a world communist revolution' (Neale 1943: 22, 24, 32). I must confess that I made use of this analogy myself in 1967, translating Paolo Sarpi's description of the conflict between Venice and the Habsburgs as a *guerra occulta* by 'cold war' and comparing the smuggling out of Venice of Sarpi's anti-papal *History of the Council of Trent* and its publication in Protestant London to the publication abroad of works by Russian dissidents such as Boris Pasternak and Andrei Sinyavsky (Sarpi 1616: 132–3; Burke 1965: 426–7; Sarpi 1967: xl). The problem since the end of the Cold War is that these phrases have become as out of date as the expression 'My hat!', mentioned earlier, hindering rather than helping what Neale called the 'imaginative grasp' of sixteenth- and seventeenth-century conflicts.

What is to be done? It is obviously necessary to retranslate the past from time to time. As for the strategy to follow in so doing, a signpost to the way forward has been offered by the distinguished historian of late antiquity Peter Brown. Brown's study of the 'fall of Rome' in the West from 350 to 550 CE makes effective use of what might be called a counterpoint between what Hildred Geertz called 'our conceptual language' and 'theirs'. In this book, the author introduces his readers to some of the Latin keywords that, in Rushdie's phrase, 'unlock' a society but defy translation. They include *verecundus*, which 'summed up the quintessentially Roman virtue of knowing one's place'; *honestus*, 'heavy with a sense of ill-defined superiority'; and *otium*, which 'was not mere leisure. It implied engagement in intellectual pursuits'. This foreignization is in tune with remarks such as 'Ambrose was a lot less like us than we think' (Brown 2012: 44, 151, 156, 157, 164).

However, Brown combines this respect for the alien quality of the past with a regular use of strategic anachronisms. They include the 'minimal state', 'ultras', 'teach-ins', 'gentrification', 'counter-culture', 'fellow traveller', 'New Age', 'multinational company', 'belle époque' and even 'empire brat' (ibid., 4, 50, 72, 127, 156, 157, 158, 210, 389, 390). Words and phrases like these encourage readers to make comparisons, as Brown sometimes does at greater length, between early Christianity and early Buddhism, for instance, and even, in certain respects, between late Roman society and the British Navy in the time of Scott of the Antarctic (ibid., 25, 75–6). Sometimes past cultures are a great deal more like us than we think. Brown's book illustrates the value of what another ancient historian, Nicole Loraux, has called the value of 'a certain dose of anachronism' or a 'careful use of anachronism' (*une pratique contrôlée de l'anachronisme*), especially when writing about distant periods (Loraux 1993: 24, 28).

Combining opposite strategies in this way is one form of what has been called 'polyphonic history', in other words a story told from different points of view or, to continue with the aural metaphor, a story in which different voices can be heard: those of both sides (or many sides) in a conflict, for instance; those of the dominant and the dominated; those of men and women; and, not least, those of contemporaries and posterity (Burke 2010). Historians still walk the tightrope described by Dryden, trying to avoid the opposite dangers of infidelity to the past and unintelligibility in the present, but a concern with polyphony may help them keep their balance.

Notes

1   Dryden's preface to his translation of Ovid's *Epistles*, quoted in Aslanyan (2021: 7).
2   Willis Barnstone, 'An ABC of Translating Poetry', quoted in Bassnett (2014: 110).
3   Friedrich Nietzsche, *The Gay Science* (1882), quoted in Bassnett (2014: 84).
4   On Ricci and his colleagues, see Po-chia Hsia (2007); on De' Nobili, see Dahmen (1924).
5   Cf. Smith (2008).
6   Thomas Macaulay, 'Hallam's Constitutional History', quoted in Phillips (2013a: 1).

References

Ajtony, Zsuzsanna (2017), 'Taming the Stranger: Domestication vs Foreignization in Literary Translation', *Acta Universitatis Sapientiae, Philologica*, 9: 93–105.
Apter, Emily (2013), *Against World Literature: On the Politics of Untranslatability*, London: Verso.
Aslanyan, Anna (2021), *Dancing on Ropes: Translation and the Balance of History*, London: Profile Books.
Assmann, Jan (1996), 'Translating Gods: Religion as a Factor of Cultural (Un)translatability', in Sanford Budick and Wolfgang Iser (eds.), *The Translatability of Cultures*, 25–36, Stanford, CA: Stanford University Press.
Bachmann-Medick, Doris (2012), 'Translation: A Concept and Model for the Study of Culture', in Birgit Neumann and Ansgar Nunning (eds.), *Travelling Concepts for the Study of Culture*, 23–43, Berlin: De Gruyter.
Bassnett, Susan (2014), 'Translating across Time', in *Translation*, 81–103, Abingdon: Routledge.
Beidelman, Thomas O. (ed.) (1971) *The Translation of Culture: Essays to E. E. Evans-Pritchard*, London: Tavistock.
Bentley, Richard (1699), *A Dissertation upon the Letters of Phalaris*, London: Mortlock.
Bettray, Johannes 1955), *Die Akkomodationsmethode des Matteo Ricci in China*, Rome: Gregorian University.
Bourdieu, Pierre (2014), *On the State: Lectures at the Collège de France, 1989–1992*, 1st edn 2012, Cambridge: Polity Press.
Bowring, Richard (2003), *The Tale of Genji*, Cambridge: Cambridge University Press.
Bredius, Abraham (1937), 'A New Vermeer', *Burlington Magazine*, 71 (416): 210–11.
Brown, Peter (2012), *Through the Eye of a Needle: Wealth, the Fall of Rome, and the Making of Christianity in the West, 350–550 AD*, Princeton, NJ: Princeton University Press.

Burke, Peter (1965), 'The Great Unmasker: Paolo Sarpi, 1552–1623', *History Today*, 15 (6): 426–32.
Burke, Peter (1969), *The Renaissance Sense of the Past*, London: Edward Arnold.
Burke, Peter (2001), 'The Sense of Anachronism from Petrarch to Poussin', in Chris Humphrey and W. Mark Ormrod (eds.), *Time in the Medieval World*, 157–73, York: York Medieval Press.
Burke, Peter (2006), 'Triumphs and Poverties of Anachronism', *Scientia Poetica*, 10: 291–9.
Burke, Peter (2007a), 'Cultures of Translation in Early Modern Europe', in Peter Burke and Ronnie Po-Chia Hsia (eds.), *Cultural Translation in Early Modern Europe*, 7–38, Cambridge: Cambridge University Press.
Burke, Peter (2010), 'Cultural History as Polyphonic History', *Arbor* 186 (743): 479–86.
Burke, Peter (2013), 'A Short History of Distance', in Phillips (2013b): 21–33.
Burke, Peter and Po-Chia Hsia, Ronnie (eds.) (2007), *Cultural Translation in Early Modern Europe*, Cambridge: Cambridge University Press.
Butterfield, Herbert (1931), *The Whig Interpretation of History*, London: Bell.
Campbell, Gordon (2010), *Bible: The Story of the King James Version, 1611–2011*, Oxford: Oxford University Press.
Cassin, Barbara (ed.) (2004), *Vocabulaire européen des philosophies: dictionnaire des intraduisibles*, Paris: Seuil.
Chakrabarty, Dipesh (2000), *Provincializing Europe: Postcolonial Thought and Historical Difference*, Princeton, NJ: Princeton University Press.
Chaucer, Geoffrey (1951), *The Canterbury Tales*, translated by Nevill Coghill, Harmondsworth: Penguin Books.
Chrétien de Troyes (1974), *Cligès*, Paris: Champion.
Cormier, Raymond J. (1974), 'The Problem of Anachronism: Recent Scholarship on the French Medieval Romances of Antiquity', *Philological Quarterly*, 53 (2): 145–57.
Crick, Malcolm (1976), *Explorations in Language and Meaning*, London: Malaby Press.
Dahmen, Pierre (1924), *Un Jésuite Brahme*, Bruges: Beyert.
Ditchfield, Simon, Methuen, Charlotte and Spicer, Andrew (eds.) (2017), *Translating Christianity*, Cambridge: Cambridge University Press.
Dosse, François (2005), 'De l'usage raisonnée de l'anachronisme', *Espaces/Temps*, 87–88: 156–71.
Eco, Umberto (2003), *Mouse or Rat? Translation as Negotiation*, London: Weidenfeld and Nicolson.
Elman, Benjamin (2001), *From Philosophy to Philology: Intellectual and Social Aspects of Change in Late Imperial China*, 1st edn 1984, Los Angeles, CA: Asian-Pacific Institute.
Emmerich, Michael (2013), *The Tale of Genji: Translation, Canonization, and World Literature*, New York: Columbia University Press.
Evans-Pritchard, Edward (1951), *Social Anthropology*, London: Cohen and West.
Evans-Pritchard, Edward (1956), *Nuer Religion*, Oxford: Oxford University Press.
Fazio, Bartolomeo (1978), *Invective in Laurentium Vallam*, edited by Ennio Rao, Napoli: Società Editrice Napoletana.
Fragnito, Gigliola (2005), *Proibito capire: la Chiesa e il volgare nella prima età moderna*, Bologna: il Mulino.
Gaeta, Franco (1955), *Lorenzo Valla: filologia e storia nell'umanesimo italiano*, Napoli: Istituto per gli Studi Storici.
Geertz, Clifford (1973), *The Interpretation of Cultures*, New York: Basic Books.

Geertz, Hildred (1975), 'An Anthropology of Religion and Magic', *Journal of Interdisciplinary History*, 6 (1): 71–89.
Gilio da Fabriano (1564), *Dialogue on the Errors and Abuses of Painters*, edited and translated by Michael Bury, Lucina Byatt and Carol Richardson (2018), Los Angeles, CA: Getty Institute.
Grafton, Anthony (1990), *Forgers and Critics: Creativity and Duplicity in Western Scholarship*, Princeton, NJ: Princeton University Press.
Guicciardini, Francesco (1969), *Ricordi*, edited by Mario Farina, Torino: Loescher.
Hartley, Leslie P. (1953), *The Go-Between*, London: Hamish Hamilton.
Hofmann, Michael (1998), 'Confessions of a Translator', in Heide Ziegler (ed.), *The Translatability of Cultures*, 65–80, Stuttgart: Metzler.
Hotman, François (1567), *Anti-Tribonian*, edited by Howell Lloyd (2022), Leiden: Brill.
Hume, David (1808), *The History of England to the Revolution of 1688*, 10 vols. (1754–61), London: no publisher.
Kelley, Donald (1970), *Foundations of Modern Historical Scholarship: Language, Law and History in the French Renaissance*, New York: Columbia University Press.
Kreuger, Frederick H. (2007), *A New Vermeer: Life and Work of Han van Meegeren*, Rijswijk: Quantes.
Large, Duncan et al. (eds.) (2018), *Untranslatability*, London: Routledge.
Lewis, Clive S. (1954), *English Literature in the Sixteenth Century, Excluding Drama*, Oxford: Clarendon Press.
Lienhardt, Godfrey (1954), 'Modes of Thought', in Edward Evans-Pritchard (ed.), *The Institutions of Primitive Society*, 97–107, Oxford: Blackwell.
Loraux, Nicole (1993), 'Éloge de l'anachronisme en histoire', *Le Genre Humain*, 27 (1): 23–39.
Lowenthal, David (1985), *The Past Is a Foreign Country*, 2nd edn 2015, Cambridge: Cambridge University Press.
Malinowski, Bronisław (1922), *Argonauts of the Western Pacific*, London: Routledge and Kegan Paul.
Martínez Bermejo, Saúl (2010), *Translating Tacitus: The Reception of Tacitus's Works in the Vernacular Languages of Europe*, Pisa: Pisa University Press.
Neale, John (1943), *The Age of Catherine de' Medici*, London: Jonathan Cape.
Newman, Francis (1856), *The Iliad of Homer, Faithfully Translated into Unrhymed English Metre*, London: Walton and Maberly.
Nicolson, Adam (2011), *When God Spoke English: The Making of the King James Bible*, London: HarperCollins.
Pálsson, Gisli (ed.) (1994), *Beyond Boundaries: Understanding, Translation and Anthropological Discourse*, Oxford: Berg.
Parry, Adam (1989), 'What Can We Do to Homer?' in *The Language of Achilles*, 42–4, Oxford: Clarendon Press.
Phillips, Mark (2013a), *On Historical Distance*, New Haven, CN: Yale University Press.
Phillips, Mark, Caine, Barbara and Thomas, Julia Adeney (eds.) (2013b), *Rethinking Historical Distance*, Basingstoke: Palgrave Macmillan.
Pocock, John (1987), *The Ancient Constitution and the Feudal Law*, 1st edn 1957, Cambridge: Cambridge University Press.
Porębski, Mieczysław (1977), 'Attribuzione', in *Enciclopedia Einaudi*, vol. 2, 137–53, Torino: Einaudi.
Ronnie, Po-chia Hsia (2007), 'The Catholic Mission and Translations in China, 1583–1700', in Peter Burke and Ronnie Po-chia Hsia (eds.), *Cultural Translation in Early Modern Europe*, 39–51, Cambridge: Cambridge University Press.

Rubiès, Joan-Pau (2005), 'The Concept of Cultural Dialogue and the Jesuit Method of Accommodation', *Archivum Historicum Societatis Jesu*, 74 (147): 237–80.
Rushdie, Salman (1983), *Shame*, London: Jonathan Cape.
Samoyault, Tiphaine (2020), *Traduction et violence*, Paris: Seuil.
Sanneh, Lamin (1989), *Translating the Message: The Missionary Impact on Culture*, 2nd edn 2009, Maryknoll, NY: Orbis Books.
Sanneh, Lamin (2009), *Translating the Message: The Missionary Impact on Culture*. Maryknoll: Orbis Books.
Sarpi, Paolo (1616), 'Aggionta agl'Historia degli Uscochi', in Gaetano and Luisa Cozzi (eds.) (1965), *La Repubblica di Venezia, la Casa d'Austria e gli Uscocchi*, Bari: Laterza.
Sarpi, Paolo (1967), *History of Benefices and Selections from the History of the Council of Trent*, edited and translated by Peter Burke, New York: Washington Square Press.
Schleiermacher, Friedrich (1813), 'On the Different Methods of Translating' (*'Über die verschiedenen Methoden des Übersetzens'*), in Lawrence Venuti (ed.), *The Translation Studies Reader*, 3rd edn 2012, 43–63, London: Routledge.
Shakespeare, William (2011), *William Shakespeare's Othello Retold in Plain and Simple English*, Buchanan NY: BookCaps Study Guides.
Smith, Mark (2008), *God in Translation: Deities in Cross-Cultural Discourse in the Biblical World*, Tübingen: Mohr Siebeck.
Spelman, Henry (1723), 'Reliquiae Spelmannianae', in *English Works*, London: Browne, Mears and Clay.
Spiegel, Gabrielle (1993), *Romancing the Past: The Rise of Vernacular Prose Historiography in Thirteenth-Century France*, Berkeley: University of California Press.
Thomas, Keith (1971), *Religion and the Decline of Magic: Studies in Popular Beliefs in Sixteenth- and Seventeenth-Century England*, London: Weidenfeld and Nicolson.
Thompson, Faith (1948), *Magna Carta. Its Role in The Making of the English Constitution 1300–1629*, Minneapolis: University of Minnesota Press.
Underwood, Simeon (1998), *English Translators of Homer from George Chapman to Christopher Logue*, Plymouth: Northcote House.
Valla, Lorenzo (1981), *Recriminationes in Facium* and *Antidotum in Facium*, edited by Mariangela Regoliosi, Padova: Antènore.
Valla, Lorenzo (2007), *De falso credito Constantini Donatio/On the Donation of Constantine*, edited and translated by Glynn Bowersock, Cambridge MA: Harvard University Press.
Velz, John W. (1978), 'The Ancient World in Shakespeare: Authenticity or Anachronism?', *Shakespeare Survey*, 31: 1–12.
Venuti, Lawrence (1995), *The Translator's Invisibility*, 2nd edn 2008, Abingdon: Routledge.
Vidal Claramonte, Carmen África (2018), 'El historiador como traductor', in *La traducción y la (s) historia (s)*, 77–107, Granada: Editorial Comares.
Waley, Arthur (1939), *Three Ways of Thought in Ancient China*, new edn 1956, New York: Doubleday.
Yates, Frances (1964), *Giordano Bruno and the Hermetic Tradition*, London: Routledge.
Zwemer, Samuel (1915), 'Translations of the Koran', *The Moslem World*, 5: 244–61.

5

'*Chance*' in Max Weber's later writings

Keith Tribe

In his 1932 essay *Legalität und Legitimität* Carl Schmitt observed:

> The word *Chance* is here left untranslated. It belongs to ways of thinking and talking quite typical of a liberal age of free competition and expectation [Engl.], and captures the mixture of luck and determinacy, freedom and calculability, arbitrariness and liability characteristic of the era. Other words of the same kind are, for example: ideology, risk, also 'ought' together with all its 'related terms', likewise all possible types of 'validity'. Words like these are best left untranslated, so that the stamp of their intellectual heritage remains visible. In Max Weber's sociology '*Chance*' occurs especially frequently.[1]
>
> (Schmitt [1932] 1980: 30)

This frequency in Weber's use of the lexeme '*Chance*' can easily be confirmed by leafing through the first three chapters of *Wirtschaft und Gesellschaft*; and during 1919–20, when these chapters were written, Schmitt had attended Weber's lectures and a Saturday seminar that Weber ran for junior colleagues (Hübinger 2009: 50).[2] However, his decision to leave the term untranslated was not because he wished to highlight its significance; rather, because he believed that it denoted a diffuse intellectual heritage of which he was sceptical. Three years later Alexander von Schelting reviewed Weber's conceptions of causality, determinacy and '*Zufall*' without even once using the word '*Chance*' (von Schelting 1934: 312–20).[3] And so it more or less remained in Weber commentary for the next forty-five years, until Ralf Dahrendorf noted this lack of attention but chided Weber for being 'naïve and unreflective' in his usage (Dahrendorf 1979: 62).[4] More recently Kari Palonen (1999: 535–538; 2011)[5] has emphasized the importance of '*Chance*' in Weber's political writing; while Luca Mori (2016) has written a whole book dedicated to the topic. But we have had to wait until 2022 for an elaboration of the argument that recognition of the significance of '*Chance*' in Weber's writing implies a major revision to our understanding of his work (Strand, Lizardo 2022).

Faculty of History and Archaeology, Tartu University. Work on this essay was supported by Estonian Research Council grant PRG 318.

My aim in the following is not primarily directed to the implications of Weber's use of '*Chance*', as with Strand and Lizardo but, rather, to identify shifts in the meaning of '*Chance*' in the later nineteenth century, so that we might better understand how Weber drew on these changes in his understanding of causality. '*Chance*' is of course a term possessing many nuances – opportunity, coincidence and probability among others[6] – and Weber's usage implies 'probabilistic opportunity', or simply 'probability'. Exploring these nuances is rendered more difficult in the German language given the absence of any serious philological investigation of the term. None of the major historical sources – Zincke, Zedler, Grimm – include '*Chance*' as a headword, while the entry by Johannes Winckelmann in the *Historisches Wörterbuch der Philosophie* simply outlines the probabilistic context to Weber's usage without any consideration of when or why this Anglo-French loan word became part of German usage, nor how it shifted its meaning in the later nineteenth century.[7]

But if '*Chance*' is indeed a key concept for Weber, why has its significance been neglected for so long? This can at least be easily explained. The emergence of Max Weber as a leading social theorist was fostered chiefly from the United States in the 1940s; through the translations of Hans Gerth and C. Wright Mills, Edward Shils and Talcott Parsons, Weber became an outrider for the rising dominance of the American social sciences. Max Weber was transformed in their hands into a 'modern sociologist' and repatriated in this guise to German academia; this much was clear at the 1964 centenary meeting in Heidelberg, where in their different ways Herbert Marcuse and Jürgen Habermas presented garbled versions of an American Max Weber.[8]

Central to this construct of Max Weber as a sociologist was Talcott Parsons' translation[9] of the three chapters plus a fragment of Weber's text *Wirtschaft und Gesellschaft* completed before his death in June 1920. This translation was published in 1947 under the title *The Theory of Social and Economic Organization* by Oxford University Press, New York.[10] In 1968 Gunther Roth and Claus Wittich brought out a 'complete' version of *Economy and Society*, a compendium of existing translations that included the original section from 1919–20, to which was added drafts that Weber had last worked on in 1913, ordered according to the fourth German edition of 1956 which did not itself correspond directly to the version published in 1922.[11] Although Roth and Wittich did revise Parsons' original translation, the minor changes they made did not involve the central point here: that in translating Weber's text Parsons simply eliminated '*Chance*'. The lexeme which so plainly litters the pages of the German text[12] is no longer visible in English; it is replaced by periphrasis or the direct substitution of 'advantage' or 'expectation'.

The tenth definitional paragraph of *Economy and Society* Ch. 1 (Weber 2019: 123–4; 1947: 139–49; 1968: 43–4) includes the lexeme *Chance(n)* twelve times. Neither Parsons' version nor the lightly revised version of Roth and Wittich contain it at all. Here is my translation of the beginning of the second part of this definitional paragraph:

> A closed social relationship can secure its monopolised *Chancen* to participants in a number of ways.
>
> (Weber, 2019: 123)[13]

According to Parsons:

> There are various ways in which it is possible for a closed social relationship to guarantee its monopolized advantages to the parties.
> (Weber 1947: 140)[14]

Elsewhere Parsons uses 'probability':

> §16. **Power** can be defined as every *Chance*, within a social relationship, of enforcing one's own will even against resistance, whatever the basis for this *Chance* might be.
> (Weber 2019: 134)

And in Parsons:

> 'Power' (Macht) is the probability that one actor within a social relationship will be in a position to carry out his own will despite resistance, regardless of the basis on which this probability rests.
> (Weber 1947: 152)[15]

These examples could be multiplied, but the general point is a simple one: a concept that has in recent years been increasingly seen as central to Weber's analysis of social action and organization has been invisible to generations of Anglophone readers of Weber, while few German readers have understood the implications of Weber's relentlessly consistent use of language.[16]

'*Chance*' first appears as an organizing concept in the course of Weber's 1913 'Essay on Categories', assuming a central position only in the last writings of 1919–20. In late May 1919 Weber had returned from Versailles to Munich, where on 24 June he began lecturing in a late summer semester on 'Die allgemeinsten Kategorien der Gesellschaftswissenschaft' (Weber 2012: 647, 655). This repeated material he had delivered in Vienna the previous year, and by late September the material had been recast as *Wirtschaft und Gesellschaft* Ch. 1.[17] Drawing on the 1913 essay, the rigour and consistency of his usage and exposition here clearly benefited from having since lectured on the topic twice, and the conceptual framework that he deployed in the following two chapters built on this initial systematization. These three chapters, together with the fragment of a fourth, were then published in March 1921 as the initial instalment of a much larger work to which Marianne Weber then added drafts dating from 1913 and earlier to form the work published in 1922 as *Wirtschaft und Gesellschaft*. As already suggested, there is a long and tangled history for this 'book', but for present purposes it is important to recognize that the material that follows on from the initial instalment published in March 1921 lacks the consistent analytical framework developed by 1919–20. The 1922 text has 817 pages; the first instalment has 180. To understand what Weber was doing in 1919–20 we need to set aside everything after p. 180;[18] this all predates what Weber began to call 'my sociology' in November 1913, but of which he had still not written one line in February 1915.[19]

To understand where Weber's use of '*Chance*' came from we need to start with his critique of a lecture Eduard Meyer had given to some colleagues in Halle during June 1902 (Weber 1906; cited here according to Weber 1982: 215–90). Meyer here disputed the idea that there could be any kind of 'historical method' that might lend structure to past events, that it was illegitimate to transfer the kind of regularity (*Gesetzmäßigkeit*) typical of scientific study to the infinite variety of the singular which was the historical past. Meyer's target was the popular writing of Karl Lamprecht, and his concern was to re-assert the role of free will and the chance event ('*Zufall*'). '*Zufall*' and necessity, he maintained, are linked to cause and effect: that a cause can be treated as necessary only in the context of a definite causal chain (Meyer 1902: 17–18). History, he argued, was not a matter of laws but of singular events whose significance was known only through their effects, hence retrospectively; historical research therefore works from effect to cause (Meyer 1902: 39–40).

Meyer's 1902 lecture could be seen as a formulaic takedown of a historian whose popular readership made him an easy target; raising the question of why, four years later, Weber would build a lengthy argument about historical causality on this rather elementary foundation. Why, for example, did he not take up the related, but far more substantive, work of Emile Durkheim, whose 1897 book on suicide, as a social phenomenon that manifested itself in singular actions, speaks to much the same issue that Meyer raised, albeit with a solid argument and an extensive empirical foundation? Most probably the answer is that he had never heard of Durkheim's work – was unfamiliar with the *Année Sociologique* and contemporary international social science journals – and that he was more familiar with American than with European developments in the social sciences.[20] Plus, of course, that it is only the assumption that Weber was 'a sociologist' that might raise the question of his relationship to Durkheim.

Weber began his critique of Meyer by stating his general intention: to address new work on the logic of the cultural sciences, beginning with purely historical problems and then moving on to distinguish the social from the natural sciences. Here, he said, discussion still presumed that history was a discipline dedicated purely to the collection of material that might serve as building blocks for genuine scientific work. It was unfortunate, he went on, that historians still understood their work to be qualitatively distinct from 'scientific' studies, since they believed that concepts and rules had no part to play in historical studies. He then states his initial question: what is 'historical' work from a logical perspective? (Weber 1982: 216–17).

Meyer's scepticism about the value of methodological studies, that a historian could only be trained through practice, not through method, was something with which Weber agreed – it was as little use for practical work as a knowledge of anatomy is in learning how to walk. What methodology could do for historical studies was help it ward off 'philosophically-embellished dilettantism' and so enable it to focus on the 'identification and solution of **substantive** problems' that were the real business of scientific study (Weber 1982: 217).

He then reproduces Meyer's three-point summary of the methodological perspective on historical work that his lecture argues against. Weber notes that he will in the following omit all those parts of Meyer's text that deal with Lamprecht in particular, so that he can reorganize Meyer's argument, making his critique more accessible. He then moves directly to Meyer's account of free will and '*Zufall*' in history, opening with a tortuous paragraph that begins as follows:

> As regards the discussion of '*Zufall*' (pp. 17ff.), E. M. naturally understands this concept not as objective 'absence of cause' ('absolute' '*Zufall*' in a metaphysical sense), nor as subjective; rather as the absolute impossibility of knowing the causal conditions ('absolute' '*Zufall*' in the epistemological sense*) necessarily arising anew for every single instance (as for example in throwing dice); but as a 'relative' '*Zufall*' in the sense of a logical relationship between causal complexes conceived separately; and so on the whole, using a formulation that is naturally not universally 'correct', in the manner that this concept is still accepted today as mostly founded upon Windelband's early text on formal logic, despite some advances in detail.

The asterisk here marks a footnote:

> This '*Zufall*' is the basis of so-called games of chance ('*Zufalls*'-Spielen), for instance with dice or lotteries. Constitutive of the possibility of a 'calculation of probability' (*Wahrscheinlichkeitsrechnung*) in the strict sense of the word is the absolute obscurity of the relationship between particular parts of the specific conditions determining the concrete outcome and the outcome itself.
> (Weber 1982: 219)

Hence Weber approaches Meyer's conventional contrast of '*Zufall*' and necessity in historical explanation in terms of a probabilistic causality. And having established this, it is now obvious that here Weber is already talking about "*Chance*", although in this essay he almost always uses the lexeme '*Zufall*'.[21] Consequently he continues onward, parsing Meyer's usage, whereas this analogy with games of chance is his own, and as I will show, very important for any understanding of '*Chance*'.

As is evident from my brief summary of Meyer's lecture, his approach to causality was retrospective, seeking a proximate cause for a subsequent event. But Weber's introduction of probabilistic reasoning implies assessing likely outcomes of present actions, hence a prospective causality. Meyer only touches on this in the context of free will – that while I might will something, that is an inadequate cause for a future event. Weber rejects this polarity of free will and determinism in favour of probabilistic reasoning – that, for example, even talking about what the weather will be like tomorrow involves judgements of probability of varying degrees of accuracy. As he goes on to point out, free will is not an absolute matter and as such this is reflected in the practices of conviction and sentencing in criminal courts.

Weber's critique is roughly twice as long as the original lecture, and he continues onwards picking to pieces Meyer's simple points, dragging in Goethe, his letters to Charlotte von Stein, Marx's *Capital* – for someone who so resolutely maintained the emptiness of methodological argument he devotes a remarkable number of pages to this. Meyer's lecture is in two main halves: the first critique, the second a positive evaluation of historical work and the investigation of facts. Weber's critique also has a second part, with a subheading 'Objective Possibility and Adequate Causation in a

Causal Historical Perspective', roughly one-third of his essay. Here, at last, we move away from the bludgeoning of Meyer, the conditionality of causal elements for any given outcome is clearly stated and given the name of 'objective possibility' (Weber 1982: 269). A new figure is introduced: Johannes von Kries.

Kries was a physiological psychologist whose publications mainly dealt with reflex action, blood flow and vision. In 1886 he had published *Die Principien der Wahrscheinlichkeitsrechnung*, a comprehensive survey of the subject that included as a final chapter a history of probability theory (von Kries 1886). The book appeared at a time of major shifts in the understanding of probability and inferential reasoning, the transformation of 'statistics' as whole populations of data into the manipulation of data on a probabilistic basis. As Ian Hacking (1990: 1 and 3) summarizes, twentieth-century physics would put an end to determinism – causality became qualified, past events would no longer determine precisely the occurrence of future events. He describes this as the 'erosion of determinism'. For social phenomena, this took the form of replacing the manipulation of whole populations of data with the use of samples that could provide a (probabilistic) certainty about the population as a whole.

There were, however, substantial barriers to an acceptance that social statistics might exhibit regularities that defied immediate explanation. Early notions of probability were based on random, equiprobable events generated by throwing dice or drawing black or white balls from an urn. Given the binary option of a male or a female birth, it had seemed a short step to confirming the equiprobability of a male or female birth, but it turned out from the records that more males were born than females and that this observation was stable over many years. The phenomenon and its stability were explained in terms of natural theology, or the harmony of nature (Hacking 1975: 170), Süssmilch arguing that this birth differential, associated with the differential mortality rates of boys and girls, led to a perfect balance between the sexes by the time of marriage, thus facilitating population increase as a human goal.

The mathematical means for investigating these regularities of social life had long been available, but were thought inapplicable to social data. By the mid-eighteenth century astronomers and navigators had struck an arithmetic mean among a small number of measurements that were treated as equivalent since they had been recorded by the same observer under similar conditions. By the 1820s the method of least squares had been developed for reduction, together with the binomial distribution of observations (Stigler 1986: 12–16). Adolphe Quetelet, a young Belgian astronomer trained in Paris in the early 1820s, linked his interest in astronomy to social statistics, extending a belief in the natural order of the planets to that of the animate world – initially of plant and animal life, then of the human species. Here he was able to derive a statistical law relating natality and mortality to times of the year, subscribing to the view that any phenomenon in the natural or human world that could be enumerated could be shown to conform to the domain of mathematical probability (Porter 1986: 45). But Quetelet was shocked when in 1827 French government statistics revealed that the various forms of criminal activity varied little from year to year, commenting on 'the frightening regularity with which the same crimes are committed' (Porter 1986: 49). No one could think of a divine end that would be served by this. *L'homme moyenne*, the analytical tool with which his name is associated, was predicated on the idea that statistical regularities could be identified for large populations but not for any one individual, for whom no probabilistic calculation was possible. He almost never employed mathematical techniques in his empirical work on social statistics, compiling but not analysing masses of social data. As Porter notes, the 'science of social physics' that he promoted was 'an extravagant system of metaphors and similes linking the social domain to the theories and even the mathematics of physics and astronomy' (Porter 1986: 46).

Nonetheless, the proposition that large populations of social data were subject to law-like behaviour was transferred into physics by James Clerk Maxwell, seeking to make sense of molecular motion in gases (Porter 1986: 111). Probabilistic calculation was developed in astronomy as a means for the removal of error; taken up by statisticians, it became a method for the determination of homogeneity and law-like behaviour in a given population; adopted by physicists in the 1870s, it developed into a technique for the removal of uncertainty. Then, rather than this new physics directly relaunching a reformed social physics, via Galton's work on heredity and the development of statistical technique by Edgeworth, Pearson and Yule, statistics was transformed from the assembly and tabulation of numerical information to systems for understanding relationships between numbers (Stigler 1986: 326ff).

However, as the techniques of probabilistic reasoning became more elaborated, these were restricted to fields in which precise ascriptions of numerical probability could be made. Kries suspected that there were many fields to which probabilistic reasoning might be applied but where precise mathematical statements of probabilities could not be made. Furthermore, there were problems with the way in which equiprobability had been classically stated by Laplace in terms of being 'equally undecided' about a certain number of cases: that uncertainty was epistemic, not objective. Kries criticized an example introduced by Poisson of two cards found on a table, arguing that knowledge of the (objective) rules according to which they had originally been dealt altered our (subjective) assessment of the probability of a (second) red or black; in this case, Kries suggested, no calculation of a numerical probability was possible (Zabell 2016: 135). 'Degrees of belief' could not be numerically calculated, but while we might be ignorant of initial conditions that vary from one moment to the next, we might have knowledge of the (objective) non-contingent elements of the process by which any one factor was realized. '*Chance*' then becomes a property of the initial conditions, and to deal with this, Kries introduced the concept of *Spielraum*, of latitude, tolerance, clearance, range, what Maynard Keynes in his *Treatise on Probability* called a 'field' (Keynes 1952: 88).[22] This directed attention to the construction of the possibility set: not to the work of applying the probability calculus to a given set of events, but to the definition of a suitable set of events (Fioretti 2001: 246).

As will become evident, Weber's direct use of Kries in 1906 is limited to the applications for decision-making in legal process and forensic psychology, and he does not directly address the central concept of *Spielraum*. For our purposes, Fioretti usefully summarizes Kries in a manner that aligns his work more closely with the arguments of Eduard Meyer that had prompted Weber's lengthy response:

> Von Kries viewed probability as a logical relation based on analogy: by drawing analogies between the present and the past, an individual is able to say that a certain course of events is more or less 'probable'. However, the reliability of an

> analogy depends on the similarity between the past cases and the present one: strictly speaking, situations are almost never the same, and analogies are almost never perfect. Consequently, probabilities cannot be expressed numerically.
>
> (Fioretti 2001: 247)

Kries developed his argument about *Spielräume* using the simple examples repeatedly encountered in the literature: that when tossing a coin we have a (subjective) expectation of the outcome while at the same time attributing to this an (objective) necessity (Kries 1886: 160). On the other hand, we cannot think of a law-like regularity governing the constancy of dead letters in a postal system from one year to the next, since there appears to be no connection at all between those who fail to address their letters correctly and those who do (Kries 1886: 161–2). Nonetheless, we invoke the general regularity of all events – 'the law of large numbers' (Kries 1886: 164) – in explaining this, despite the fact that we have no (objective) explanation for the relationship between properly and improperly addressed letters. Our expectation has an indefinite basis. It is in fact the same with a game of roulette; although we expect there to be an equal likelihood of a ball landing or red or black, we do not have an explanation for it falling on either red or black in any one instance. Moving beyond the repertoire of cases commonly encountered in the literature, Kries considered the outcomes of therapeutic treatment. If in giving cold baths to patients suffering from pneumonia fewer on average died than the remainder not given such treatment, the first treatment consequently being viewed as positive, the justification for this conclusion

> rested at least in part on the fact that this assumption regarding the factually observed events corresponded to a much greater *Spielraum* in real behaviour than in the opposite assumption, which explained the phenomenon as coincidence ('*Zufall*').
>
> (Kries 1886: 175)

Here again, Kries points to the fact that, while we could derive a numerical probability from such a therapeutic experiment that would confirm its utility, we would be as little aware of the causal connection in any one instance as with the fall of dice or the spinning of a roulette wheel. Instead, the idea of 'adequate causation' converted one particular objective causal condition into a subjective expectation.[23]

Weber spends three pages of the second part of his 1906 essay summarizing the argument so far, and then shifts gear: that these problems of historical logic have been addressed neither by historians nor by historical methodologists, but specialists in quite different domains. This is the theory of the 'so-called "objective possibility"', deriving from the work of von Kries, and applied to criminological work by others.[24] He formulates the specific problem here as follows:

> under what circumstances might one claim that someone has 'occasioned' (*verursacht*) through their action a particular external outcome is a pure question of causality – moreover, one obviously of the same logical structure as the question of historical causality.
>
> (Weber 1982: 270)

For the historian the question of causality involves assigning substantive outcomes to substantive causes, not attribution to abstract law-like regularities. For the legal specialist, there is the additional issue of whether the objective, causal imputation of the outcome of the action of an individual is also sufficient to characterize that individual's subjective guilt. He then restates the problem:

> how is the imputation of a substantive 'outcome' to one single 'cause' in principle at all possible and achievable given that in actuality there is an infinity of causal elements that determine the coming into being of an individual 'event', and that really, for the creation of the outcome in its substantive form, simply all of the individual causal elements were indispensable?
>
> (Weber 1982: 271)

Posed in this way it is evident how closely Weber is following Kries, but here we are interested primarily in how this borrowing from Kries relates to Weber's understanding of '*Chance*'. Summarizing, it can be said that Weber here moves beyond the standard tropes of historical causality as articulated by Meyer, in which singular events 'cause' particular outcomes and which, pushed to its extreme, can support arguments to the effect that in the absence of this single cause, that particular event would never have subsequently occurred. A present event is determined by the existence of an anterior cause, but we cannot predict future outcomes since there are so many current conditions and which of these will be causal of future outcomes can only be known in retrospect. Shifting the argument into a probabilistic framework undermines the unilinearity of this understanding of historical determination, separating objective processes from initial conditions and assigning likelihoods to potential outcomes that in turn form the basis for subjective expectations. Towards the end of the essay Weber directly raises the issue of probability in a framework clearly derived from Kries, and runs through the familiar arguments regarding the throwing of dice and the drawing of balls from urns. Here for the first time he refers to '*Chancen*' – of throwing a particular number in a game with dice, where the way in which the dice are thrown has no impact upon the equiprobability of the outcome – the distinction of objective and subjective probabilities that Kries had emphasized.

Weber did not again directly address these issues of probability and causality, of determining conditions and outcomes, until 1913, in his essay on categories published in the autumn of that year (Weber 1913; cited here as in Weber 1982: 427–74). This opens, like *Economy and Society* Ch. 1, with a discussion of the regularities of human action, the emphasis being on the interpretive understanding of this action and its rationality, not on the causality of the action. In a discussion of inheritance and the degree to which this might lead to sociologically relevant qualities and motivations that might bring about a striving for 'particular kinds of social power or the '*Chance*' of gaining such power' (Weber 1982: 431) – hence dropping the term into the exposition almost casually, as though this had already been established as governing the relationship between action and outcome.

The second section of the essay follows close on this, and moves away from the issue of interpretive understanding to the causality of the action that is to be so understood. But the provisional nature of this exposition can be read out of the fact that the paragraph with which this section opens stretches over nearly three and a half pages. As I emphasized in my 'Introduction' to *Economy and Society*, its first chapter is the fourth version of this original draft, and so has an expositional rigour not always evident in the following two chapters. The third chapter is based on the draft printed as the last part of the 1922 edition, and so benefits from a process of revision. By contrast, the second chapter is the first draft of something that Weber had never before set down and is characterized by a progressively loose structure that reflects this. So far as I am aware, no systematic comparison of the structure of the 1913 essay with Ch.1 of *Economy and Society* has been made, but these clues to the way in which Weber is, as it were, in 1913 'writing out loud' are very important for understanding the development of his ideas. In 1913 there is a tendency for Weber to try and say everything at once, but this itself provides insights into the development of his conceptual framework.

Once Weber begins to develop the relationship between motivation and causal explanation, the term '*Chance*' appears again – the highly variable degree of '*Chance*' that we might in the individual instance assume that subjectively meaningful motivational connections exist (Weber 1982: 437). And so towards the close of the essay, '*Chance*' appears with increasing frequency, moderating causal relationships and the motivation for action. This will all become rationalized in 1919, and '*Chance*' will assume a central position in Weber's sociology, a means of connecting causes to outcomes without assuming, as with Eduard Meyer, that 'free will' and 'determination' are clashing alternatives, and positing an open future in which action and expectation are closely linked.

Quite how provisional Weber's arguments in 1913 are can be demonstrated with respect to another central concept of *Economy and Society*: that of *Verband*. By 1919 this had become a generic building block of social order, the sense that social action was not merely individual action but action within organizational frameworks that generated social action. In 1919, a *Verband* came with a 'staff', rulership and legitimacy – it was an organizational form of varying degrees of formality and with diverse objectives, but with the means to plan for and execute those objectives and to which legitimacy was ascribed. Towards the end of the 1913 essay the new concept of *Verband* makes an appearance (Weber 1982: 448, 450, 466, 472), but as an organizational form devoid of personnel (*Stab*), of any rulership that might facilitate the regular execution of its functions; nor is it associated with the idea that the exercise of rulership is dependent on a belief in the legitimacy of decision-making. It has not yet gained the content that would in 1919 make it the central concept of social organization.

And so it is also with '*Chance*'. By opening up the wider implications of Weber's introduction of Kries into his 1906 essay, it is possible to see how Weber was able to move on from historical causality to an assessment of the likely outcomes of present action. At that time his reference to Kries involved only the paper he had written in 1888, extending arguments about probability exposed in his book of 1886. This book had been reviewed the same year by Wilhelm Lexis (1886), who had made explicit the linkage between Kries' arguments and the contemporary development of statistics. Lexis had been a colleague of Kries at Freiburg from 1876 to 1884, when he had moved to Breslau, and then to Göttingen. But Kries was still in Freiburg when Max Weber arrived in the autumn of 1894 as the replacement for Eugen von Philippovich, who had in turn previously replaced Lexis in the chair of political economy. We might then presume that even if Weber had been unfamiliar with recent developments in the theory of probability in the mid-1890s, his move to Freiburg would have brought him into contact with Kries.

Perhaps it is coincidental that in 1908, when Weber reviewed Brentano's lecture on the history of the economic theory of value delivered that February, he ignored more or less all of what Brentano had to say bar one very short section towards the end. Here Brentano (1908: 66) began discussing Bernoulli's argument that a ducat of pleasure was worth more to a poor than to a rich person, noting how this idea had first been demonstrated in Germany with Steinheil's work on increments of light, and then generalized by Ernst Heinrich Weber through small changes in weight that we sense, lengths of line that we see and tones that we hear. This then in turn formed the point of departure for Fechner's work, *Elemente der Psychophysik* (1860), which showed that in all areas of physical sensation the same rule for the dependence of stimulation held good, as Bernoulli had argued with money and pleasure. Brentano notes that Fechner renamed this Bernoulli Law the Weber Law, that a perceptible increase in stimulation is proportional to the existing stimulation, and called it the basic psychophysical law. The connection to Bernoulli and Lange that Weber makes in his review can be found in Brentano, but the way that Weber's entire review of Brentano's substantial lecture is directed just to these two pages suggests that he was here reminded, as in 1906, of the work on sensation and physiology of his former Freiburg colleague, Johannes von Kries (Weber [1908] 1982: 387–9).

Notes

1   The footnote 1 is to the section heading, 'Legality and the Equal Chance of Gaining Political Power', implying a probabilistic understanding of the term.
2   He also attended the lectures on social and economic history that Weber gave in Winter Semester 1919–20 (Mehring 2009: 118).
3   Part 4 Section 8 '"Objektive Möglichkeit," "adäquate Verursachung" und '*Zufall*'".
4   Andreas Anter (2014) lists a number of earlier sources that touch on this usage; his book was first published in 1995 and contains the first detailed argument for the centrality of '*Chance*' in Max Weber's writing (pp. 88–95).
5   Fritz Ringer (2002; 2006) also discussed the influence of von Kries on Weber's conception of causality (discussed below), but without linking this to Weber's later use of '*Chance*'.
6   I briefly discuss this in the Translation Appendix to Weber (2019: 464–5).
7   Winckelmann (1971). Menzel's *Literatur-Blatt* Nr. 116 (12 November 1830) p. 464 compares two contemporary German-English dictionaries with respect to their entries on '*Chance*'; the *Oxford English Dictionary* cites usage from Middle English

8   of the early fourteenth century, also the presence in Old French of *cheance*, which is presumably where Middle English usage came from.
8   By contrast, Wolfgang Mommsen's Weber was always 'German', from the time of his *Max Weber und die deutsche Politik*, J. C. B. Mohr (Paul Siebeck), Tübingen 1959.
9   As I explain in my 'Introduction' to Weber (2019: 28–34), Parsons worked from draft translations of the first two chapters by Alexander Henderson, who was credited as a joint translator. No copies of Henderson's drafts seem to have survived, and so for present purposes Parsons is treated as sole translator.
10 Although originally commissioned and published by William Hodge and Co., London 1947.
11 The complex history of this text both in German and English is not directly relevant here, and is summarized in my 'Introduction' to Weber (2019: 1–2 and 33–6).
12 Dahrendorf (1979: 62) writes of the 'more than one hundred places' where the lexeme occurs in *Wirtschaft und Gesellschaft* Part One – 'Life Chances'.
13 I italicize '*Chance*', plural *Chancen*, throughout my translation to draw attention to the consistent and repetitive use of this lexeme.
14 Roth and Wittich is identical (Weber 1968: 44).
15 Roth and Wittich is identical (Weber 1968: 53).
16 Dahrendorf's discussion is predicated on a belief that Weber's usage always has a definite meaning, but not an entirely consistent one; and that as such, his meaning is different from the English meaning of '*chance*' (Dahrendorf 1979: 64). He construes Weber's meaning not in terms of causality, but sociology, understood as 'an understanding of structures ("certain facts and events") which make a determinate behaviour regularly probable' (Dahrendorf 1979: 65).
17 The chapter was sent to his publisher on 25 September 1919 (Weber 2012: 789).
18 With the caveat that pp. 603–817, a 'Part III' entitled 'Types of Rulership' is in fact the draft material for what became Part I Ch. 3, entitled 'The Types of Rulership'. In her editorial introduction to this 'Third Part', separately published as *Max Weber Gesamtausgabe* I/22.4 *Wirtschaft und Gesellschaft. Herrschaft*, Edith Hanke drew on this material to trace among other things the late development of Weber's conceptions of legitimation, charisma and rulership; it is important to bear in mind that this last section of the book published in 1922 *predates* Part I Ch. 3 by more than six years. See my account of Hanke's editorial work in Tribe (2017), with a summary in my 'Introduction' to Weber (2019: 47–8).
19 'Wie soll denn nur daran *gedacht* werden, daß ich *jetzt* auch nur eine Zeile meiner "Soziologie" druckfertig stelle, korrigiere etc.' Max Weber to Paul Siebeck, 21 February 1915 (Weber 2008: 21).
20 Both the range of and gaps in Weber's acquaintance with contemporary international economic writing are clear from his Freiburg and Heidelberg lectures during the later 1890s.
21 Which is why I have left '*Zufall*' untranslated in both Meyer and Weber. I discuss later the point where Weber introduces '*Chance*' in the 1906 essay.
22 Keynes originally drafted this in 1907 as a dissertation in support of his (unsuccessful) application for a King's College Fellowship; it was published in 1921, the 'Preface' being dated 1 May 1920 (Skidelsky 1983: 182–3).
23 See the discussion by Heidelberger (2015), although Heidelberger begins from John Stuart Mill and seeks to link his discussion to Weber's conception of *Verstehen*.
24 Weber is here referring to Kries (1888).

References

Anter, Andreas (2014), *Max Weber's Theory of the Modern State. Origins, Structure and Significance*, Basingstoke: Palgrave Macmillan.

Brentano, Lujo (1908), 'Die Entwickelung der Wertlehre', *Sitzungsberichte der Königliche Bayerisch Akademie der Wissenschaften. Philosophisch-philologische und historische Klasse*: 1–84.

Dahrendorf, Ralf (1979), 'Max Weber's Concept of "Chance"', in his *Life Chances. Approaches to Social and Political Theory*, 62–74, London: Weidenfeld and Nicolson.

Fioretti, Guido (2001), 'Von Kries and the Other 'German Logicians': Non-numerical Probabilities before Keynes', *Economics and Philosophy*, 17 (2): 245–73.

Hacking, Ian (1975), *The Emergence of Probability. A Philosophical Study of Early Ideas about Probability, Induction and Statistical Inference*, Cambridge: Cambridge University Press.

Hacking, Ian (1990), *The Taming of Chance*, Cambridge: Cambridge University Press.

Hanke, Edith (2005), 'Introduction', in Max Weber (ed.), *Wirtschaft und Gesellschaft. Herrschaft (Max Weber Gesamtausgabe I/22.4)*, Tübingen: Mohr Siebeck.

Heidelberger, Michael (2015), 'From Mill via von Kries to Max Weber: Causality, Explanation and Understanding', *Max Weber Studies*, 15 (1): 13–45.

Hübinger, Gangolf (2009), 'Editorische Bericht', in Max Weber (ed.), *Allgemeine Staatslehre und Politik (Staatssoziologie). Unvollendet. Mit-und Nachschriften 1920 (Max Weber Gesamtausgabe, III/7)*, Tübingen: Mohr Siebeck.

Keynes, John Maynard (1952), *A Treatise on Probability*, London: Macmillan.

Kries, Johannes von (1886), *Die Principien der Wahrscheinlichkeitsrechnung. Eine logische Untersuchung*, Freiburg: J. C. B. Mohr (Paul Siebeck).

Kries, Johannes von (1888), 'Ueber den Begriff der objectiven Möglichkeit und einige Anwendungen desselben', *Vierteljahresschrift für wissenschaftliche Philosophie*, 12: 179–240.

Lexis, Wilhelm (1886), 'Über die Wahrscheinlichkeitsrechnung und deren Anwendung auf die Statistik', *Jahrbücher für Nationalökonomie und Statistik*, N. F. 13: 433–50.

Mehring, Reinhard (2009), *Carl Schmitt. Aufstieg und Fall. Eine Biographie*, Munich: C. H. Beck.

Meyer, Eduard (1902), *Zur Theorie und Methodik der Geschichte. Geschichtsphilosophische Untersuchungen*, Halle: Verlag Max Niemeyer.

Mommsen, Wolfgang (1959), *Max Weber und die deutsche Politik*, Tübingen: J. C. B. Mohr (Paul Siebeck).

Mori, Luca (2016), *Chance. Max Weber e la filosofia politica*, Pisa: Edizioni ETS.

Palonen, Kari (1999), 'Max Weber's Re-conceptualization of Freedom', *Political Theory*, 27 (4): 523–44.

Palonen, Kari (2011), 'The State as a '*Chance*' Concept: Max Weber's De-substantiation and Neutralisation of the Concept', *Max Weber Studies*, 11 (1): 99–117.

Porter, Theodore M. (1986), *The Rise of Statistical Thinking 1820–1900*, Princeton, NJ: Princeton University Press.

Ringer, Fritz (2002), 'Max Weber on Causal Analysis, Interpretation, and Comparison', *History and Theory*, 41 (2): 163–78.

Ringer, Fritz (2006), 'Comparison and Causal Explanation', *Comparative Education*, 42 (3): 363–76.

Schelting, Alexander von (1934), *Max Webers Wissenschaftslehre. Das logische Problem der historischen Kulturerkenntnis. Die Grenzen der Soziologie des Wissens*, Tübingen: J. C. B. Mohr (Paul Siebeck).

Schmitt, Carl ([1932] 1980), *Legalität und Legitimität*, 3rd edn, Berlin: Duncker und Humblot.

Skidelsky, Robert (1983), *John Maynard Keynes. Hopes Betrayed 1883–1920*, London: Macmillan.

Stigler, Stephen M. (1986), *The History of Statistics. The Measurement of Uncertainty before 1900*, Cambridge, MA: Harvard University Press.

Strand, Michael and Omar Lizardo (2022), 'Chance, Orientation, and Interpretation: Max Weber's Neglected Probabilism and the Future of Social Theory', *Sociological Theory*, 40 (2): 124–50.

Tribe, Keith (2017), 'Review Essay: Wirtschaft und Gesellschaft', *Max Weber Studies*, 17 (2): 289–94.

Weber, Max (1906), 'Kritische Studien auf dem Gebiet der kulturwissenschaftlichen Logik', *Archiv für Sozialwissenschaft und Sozialpolitik*, 22 (1): 143–207; cited as in Weber (1982).

Weber, Max (1908), 'Die Grenznutzenlehre und das "psychophysische Grundgesetz"', *Archiv für Sozialwissenschaft und Sozialpolitik*, 27 (2): 546–58; cited as in Weber (1982).

Weber, Max (1913), 'Über einige Kategorien der verstehenden Soziologie', *Logos*, 4 (3): 253–94; cited as in Weber (1982).

Weber, Max (1947), *The Theory of Social and Economic Organization*, New York: Free Press.

Weber, Max (1968), *Economy and Society. An Outline of Interpretive Sociology*, vol. I, edited by Gunther Roth and Claus Wittich, New York: Bedminster Press.

Weber, Max (1982), *Gesammelte Aufsätze zu Wissenschaftslehre*, 5th edn, Tübingen: J. C. B. Mohr (Paul Siebeck).

Weber, Max (2008), *Briefe 1915–1917 (Max Weber Gesamtausgabe*, II/9), Tübingen: Mohr Siebeck.

Weber, Max (2012), *Briefe 1918–1920 (Max Weber Gesamtausgabe*, II/10.2), Tübingen: Mohr Siebeck.

Weber, Max (2019), *Economy and Society. A New Translation*, translated by Keith Tribe, Cambridge, MA: Harvard University Press.

Winckelmann, Johannes (1971), 'Chance', *Historisches Wörterbuch der Philosophie*, 1: 979–80.

Zabell, Sandy (2016), 'Johannes von Kries's 'Principien': A Brief Guide for the Perplexed', *Journal for the General Philosophy of Science*, 47 (1): 131–50.

6

'We politicians': Translation, rhetoric and conceptual change

Kari Palonen

6.1. Introduction[1]

Politician is a type of person that has always been viewed with suspicion, frequently even by members of parliament. Scholars since Max Weber have largely agreed that parliamentary and democratic politics can hardly dispense with the professional politician. Most West European parliamentarians today accept the public and academic practice of being treated as politicians, and, since the late twentieth century, they have been increasingly willing to speak of themselves as politicians. In this chapter, I shall discuss this change as a neutralizing translation practice.

In *Reason and Rhetoric of the Philosophy of Hobbes*, Quentin Skinner (1996: 135–61; see also Skinner 1974) discusses the translation of concepts as being a rhetorical redescription by means of paradiastolic normative judgement, which involves depreciating virtues, extenuating vices or a neutralizing of both. His point is that successful rhetorical moves tend to avoid direct confrontations between affirmation and denial, and instead make recourse to indirect strategies and tactics. Skinner (1996, chapter 4) distinguishes between renaming, the revising of a range of applications, the modifying of the weight of a concept and the re-evaluating of virtues in comparison to neighbouring vices. These moves can be understood as styles of conceptual translation that have different political implications. I shall use these Skinnerian tools to analyse the judgements made about politicians in the parliamentary plenary debates of particular European countries and languages.

Who are regarded as politicians, what do they do and how are they judged? I refer to the existing literature as background, but my main point is to analyse the conceptual transformation involved as a translation (in the sense of Koselleck 1986; see also Palonen 2012a) of the use of 'politicians' in parliamentary debates.

To speak of politicians in this manner runs the risk of anachronistic projection and pejorative labelling. Many examples from past debates illustrate how even members of parliament have shared the popular contempt for politicians or, in line of Carl Schmitt's footnote (1932/1963: 27), applied the term to others rather than to themselves. To carry out a paradiastolic rehabilitation against such tendencies requires a special effort (see discussion in Palonen 2012a).

The first stage consists of replacing the advisors to princes of the ancient and early modern period with the parliamentary politicians of eighteenth-century Britain. This is followed by a discussion of different conceptions of the professionalization of politics, and a discussion on the Francophone distinction between *hommes politiques* and *politiciens*. The final section deals with the arrival and the momentum of 'we politicians' as a speech act. Both the recent forms of professionalization and 'we politicians' neutralize the ideal type of politician. In a previous study (Palonen 2012b), I found that the denunciations of politicians tend to be repeated from time to time and from country to country. There, I also discussed the *laudatio* of politicians in different genres of writing. In parliamentary debates, when members are facing their peers, such panegyrics would be either unnecessary or naïve. Neutralization of the popular contempt is a more appropriate response.

European languages inherited the vocabulary of politics from ancient Greece (see Meier 1980). Max Weber speaks of ancient Greek politicians in his account of the historical types of politicians:[2]

> Dem Okzident eigentümlich ist aber, was uns näher angeht: das politische Führertum in der Gestalt zuerst des freien 'Demagogen', der auf dem Boden des nur dem Abendland, vor allem der mittelländischen Kultur, eigenen Stadtstaates, und dann des parlamentarischen 'Parteiführers', der auf dem Boden des ebenfalls nur im Abendland bodenständigen Verfassungsstaates gewachsen ist.
>
> (Weber 1919 [1994]: 38)

As a classically educated scholar, Weber would have known that the ancient actors could not have used such language. Neither *polités* nor *politikós* participated in the disputes of the *ekklesia* and other *polis* institutions. Mogens Herman Hansen comments on the vocabulary: 'Etymologically, of course, "politician" is via the Latin *politicus*, derived from the Greek adjective *politikos*. It is worth noting, however, that the meaning of *politikos* is "statesman" and "not politician". It is used by philosophers in a complimentary sense about a true political leader' (Hansen 1983: 36).

Nonetheless, *polités* and *politikós* lie behind our speaking on politicians. Hansen notes: 'In the wider sense, "politician" denotes all politically active citizens, i.e. in Athens all citizens who attended the ekklesia … "Politician" in this sense would be a good translation of *ho politeuomenos* in its wider meaning, and it squares well with the Greek concept of active citizen' (ibid., 35). The tension between the citizen as a political actor and the politician as one intensely dedicated to 'politics' is still highly relevant. Weber's view on Greek demagogues as the first professional politicians corresponds to Hansen's comment in a footnote: '*Dēmagōgós* means "leader of the people", sometimes in a positive sense … sometimes in a neutral sense' (Hansen 1983, 46). The active *polites* refers to Weber's 'Gelegenheits politiker', the occasional politician, which 'we all' are when acting politically (Weber 1919: 41).

Emma Claussen's recent study, *Politics and 'Politiques' in the Sixteenth-Century France* (2021), contains a thorough discussion of the discipline 'la politique', the adjective 'politique' and 'les politiques' as actors. Following the shifts from the early sixteenth-century post-Aristotelian respect for 'les politiques' to the ambiguous uses in the sixteenth century in the French civil war with the Huguenots and the accession of Henri de Navarre to the throne in 1594, Claussen identifies both the rhetorical view of the defenders and the anti-rhetorical polemics of the detractors in speaking of 'les politiques'. She regards the party of 'les Politiques' in France as an ex post facto construct (as do Turchetti 2012 and Papenheim 2017). The sixteenth-century French debates applied paradiastolic moves of devaluation and revaluation of 'les politiques', whereas neutralization was out of the question.

Claussen's conclusions are in line with the early modern practices in various languages. The acceptance of 'politicians' reflects the period of mixed government when the monarch was advised by courtiers, lawyers, assembly members and others. The rhetorical defences of writers in that period include classical virtues, such as wisdom and prudence, and vices, such as being tricky or cunning. For example, James Harrington (1656 [1992]: 9) in *The Commonwealth of Oceana* defended Machiavelli as 'the only politician of the modern age', that is, as a writer on politics.

Republican authors such as Harrington appreciated the politician, but in the post-Westphalian German duchies, *Politikus* was widely depreciated or ridiculed (see Palonen 2006 and Zimmermann et al. 2007).

As William Selinger (2019) discusses in detail, most cabinet ministers in eighteenth-century Britain were chosen among the members of parliament, contrary to Montesquieu's doctrine of separation of powers. In addition, the British parliament beginning in 1741 claimed the power to dismiss the government on the grounds of political expediency (Turkka 2007), which enabled speaking of both ministers and front-bench parliamentarians as politicians. However, before the reforms of 1832 and 1867, the British parliament was based on selection rather than election (Kislansky 1986), which restricted the range of politicians to the 'ministrable' front benches. Nonetheless, membership in either House of Parliament had become a necessary condition for being called a politician.

How was this attested in the British parliamentary debates? In the Hansard documentation (UK), available from 1803 onwards, French Laurence applied the term 'politician' (in the singular) as something well known:

> What ... was the cry of unpopularity, even if it attached to a particular course of policy, to weigh with the mind of an enlightened statesman, to urge him to the abandonment of that course, against the conviction of his own judgment. The idea was too ridiculous to be entertained. No sound politician could support it. That popularity was highly desirable, was an indisputable proposition, because it was, independently of other considerations, a powerful instrument for a politician to work with.
>
> (UK: 14 December 1803)

Laurence equates 'enlightened statesman' with 'sound politician', while acknowledging that 'popularity' is 'a powerful instrument for a politician', for whom parliamentary representation and support from the electorate already mattered. In a later speech on the Petition of Ireland Laurence argued: 'Surely there is no serious Christian of the present age who will approve the existence of such religious intolerance, nor any wise politician who will wish for the continuance of so pregnant a source of discontent in our navies and armies' (UK: 14 May 1805). 'Wise' and 'sound' are classical epithets for advisors. Terms such as 'wise', 'sound' and 'politic' were now applied to ministers and parliamentarians. 'Innovating ideologists' connect to already existing vocabularies (Skinner 1974), and here this is used to facilitate the acceptance of politicians.

William Windham also used 'politicians' as a well-known term when he referred to the opinion of 'Mr. Pitt, Mr. Burke, and Mr. Fox, the most distinguished politicians that had adorned any country' (UK: 26 June 1807). Dennis Browne hinted at 'alarms, which have been both mentioned and propagated by some apparently great politicians' and that '[t]he good sense and liberality of the people have prevailed against the misapplied zeal of the bigot, and the interested speculation of the miserable politician' (UK: 26 June 1807). Here politicians were appreciated or denounced according to the quality of their deeds.

6.2. The forms of professionalization

Democratization, parliamentarization and bureaucratization were major changes in the politics of the nineteenth century. All had implications for the standing and the reputation of politicians (see Steinmetz 2019).

6.2.1 Party patronage

An attempt to combine democratization with de-bureaucratization was the spoils system, which has been practised in the United States since the presidency of Andrew Jackson (1829–37). It initiated a new paradigm for politicians. The system was based on party patronage, replacing appointment based on merit by elected officials with appointment based on which party had won elections. The system was limited by the Civil Service Reform in the 1880s, but partisan nominations to offices have remained a perennial topic in the criticism of politicians (for a defence of the spoils system, see interview with George W. Plunkitt in Plunkitt of Tammany Hall, 1905/48).

Fears of the spoils system spreading to Europe were common after the democratization of suffrage (see Palonen 2012b, chapter 2). James Bryce in *The American Commonwealth* made a distinction between the British (and European) usage of 'politicians' from the US usage:

> In England it usually denotes those who are actively occupied in administering or legislating, or discussing administration and legislation. That is to say, it includes ministers of the Crown, members of Parliament (though some in the House of Commons and the majority in the House of Lords care little about politics), a few leading journalists, and a small number of miscellaneous persons … trying to influence the public. … The former, whom we may call the inner-circle men, are professional politicians in this sense, and in this sense only, that politics is the

main though seldom the sole business of their lives. But at present extremely few of them make anything by it in the way of money.

(Bryce 1888/1914: 731)

The 'inner circle' of politicians was larger in the United States. Bryce distinguished between politicians living for politics and living off politics (see also Weber 1919).

In America we discover a palpable inducement to undertake the dull and toilsome work of election politics. It is the inducement of places in the public service. To make them attractive they must be paid. They are paid, nearly all of them, memberships of Congress and other federal places, state places (including memberships of state legislatures), city and county places. Politics has now become a gainful profession, like advocacy, stockbroking, the dry goods trade or the getting up of companies (Bryce 1888/1914, 735).

Bryce indicated three conceptual shifts in the US understanding of politicians: (1) Their range was multiplied to include candidates for a huge number of offices, both elected and appointed by the election winners; (2) the 'work' of politics means in America the winning of nominations and elections' (ibid., 734), as winning candidates, appointed officers and partisan functionaries have much less to do with the content and direction of politics than do European ministers and parliamentarians; and (3) finally, the 'professionalism' of politicians came to mark no longer an honoured status, but simply a paid position similar to those of the representatives, elected officials and party functionaries.

US type of politician has shaped the public image of politicians in Europe, including the contemptuous view and devaluation of them as second-rate political hacks. Experienced parliamentarians were challenged when the success of their parties and not their own parliamentary performance became the criterion for candidature (for Britain see Ostrogorski 1903/1912). It is worth taking a closer look at what has been said about politicians in European parliamentary debates.

6.2.2 Payment of members

The professionalization of politicians was debated before the First World War especially in the German and British parliaments. Though parliamentarism was abhorred in Bismarckian Germany, male suffrage was adopted in the Reichstag, while a census or plutocratic suffrage prevailed in the federal states. In Britain, the parliamentary responsibility of the government had been accepted in the mid-1830s, but the reform of suffrage and redistribution of seats between constituencies proceeded cautiously. The arguments for and against the payment of members and the professionalization of politics were quite different between the two countries (see also Palonen 2012b, chapter 3).

Chancellor Otto von Bismarck declared afterwards that the 1867 decision to elect the Reichstag through the manhood suffrage had a counterpart in the non-paid membership. He opposed the payment of members in order to keep the Reichstag powers limited. After paying lip-service to dedicated members, Bismarck expressed a vision combining representation on a broad popular basis with the role of the Reichstag representatives restricted to mediating information about the people in their different classes and professions as well as their mood (*Stimmung*) to the government (GE: 19 April 1871). He argued against prolonged sittings (*lang gedehnte Parlamentssitzungen*), lifelong membership (*Lebensberuf*) and the favour accorded to eloquent members in debate (GE: 5 May 1881; on Bismarck's anti-rhetorical stance see Goldberg 1998).

Even if the Reichstag did not have power to elect and dismiss the government, the need for new legislation grew and Reichstag representatives were at the core of political debates. The Social Democrats paid a fee to their Reichstag members, and journalists such as the Liberal Eugen Richter secured their living by reporting from the Reichstag. Ignaz Auer (SPD) openly supported a debating parliament and the turning of elected representative into professional politicians who make 'das Parlamentieren, das Diplomatieren und Politiktreiben als Volksvertreter sich zum Berufe' (GE: 26 November 1884). The Reichstag voted repeatedly in favour of modest payments for members. This gained the support of the federal Bundesrat only in 1906, thus affirming a certain degree of professionalization of parliamentarians (see Palonen 2012b, 55–61).

In Britain the success of the parliament led to an expansion of its agenda, and loopholes in the rules of debate were 'misused' in an obstruction campaign by Irish members around 1880. To prevent a paralysis of parliament, governments introduced procedural reforms aimed at limiting the speaking occasions and the length of speeches that could be given (Redlich 1905; Palonen 2014). Critics foresaw in this a danger of growing governmental power which could render the parliament into a simple ratifying assembly for government motions. The Newcastle Radical Joseph Cowen sketched a nightmare scenario of a powerless parliament:

> If we are merely to vote as we are told – which is the motto of the Caucus – why are we sent here? It is a great waste of power, of health, of time, and of temper. Instead of 600, 60, or, indeed, 6 would suffice. All that is wanted is a body of experts to whom the decisions taken in the different constituencies might be sent ... The work of legislation might be greatly simplified by such a course of procedure. Government shrinks from such a result; but it is the logical, inevitable, and irresistible outcome of their course of action.
>
> (UK: 10 November 1882)

With this reductio ad absurdum, Cowen defends a parliament with wide, elected membership, and regular and thorough debates on the items on the agenda according to procedural rules. For him, the parliamentarian represents the quintessential politician. Westminster preserved the idea of a deliberative parliament as a point of reference when debating the payment of members. Fears that the procedural reforms on parliamentary time would disempower parliament have not been realized (see Campion 1929; Evans 2017).

In the Commons, Rowland Blenderhassett (Irish Party) warned against the US type of professional politician: 'The most perfect electoral machinery, the most complete and elaborate political organization, will be necessary to reach and to wield the new masses of voters. The professional politician, the skilled electioneer, the accomplished and unscrupulous wire-puller will be all-powerful' (UK: 4 March 1879). Samuel Smith (Lib) feared that 'to supplant the voluntary with the professional politician' would lead to 'abuse' and 'corruption' (UK: 29 March 1889). George Curzon (Cons) defended parliamentarians of independent means and ventured that the respect for MPs in Britain persisted because nobody could gain financially from membership (UK: 29 March 1889). Austen Chamberlain (Cons) warned of 'the new and undesirable type of professional politician' (UK: 10 August 1911) but declared being himself 'in one sense, a professional politician. I have given up practically the whole of my life to politics' (UK: 21 March 1907; see also UK: 16 May 1911). For him, dedication to parliament and investing the time it demanded were the marks of professionalism: functionaries and party-appointed officials were at best second-rate politicians.

The paradiastolic alteration of the normative tone neutralizes its object, whether a concept or an actor, and leaves open a range of evaluative possibilities in actual cases. In academic discourse, Max Weber's *Parlament* pamphlet from 1918 neutralized the figure of the professional parliamentarian. What he says on the *Berufsparlamentarier* has a wider significance for the polity:

> Der Berufsparlamentarier ist ein Mann, der das Reichstagsmandat ausübt nicht als gelegentliche Nebenpflicht, sondern – ausgerüstet mit eigenem Arbeitsbüro und -personal und mit allen Informationsmitteln – als Hauptinhalt seiner Lebensarbeit. Man mag diese Figur lieben oder hassen, sie ist rein technisch unentbehrlich, und sie ist daher schon heute vorhanden.
>
> (Weber 1918: 244)[3]

For Weber, the professional parliamentarian is already there, liked or not by the public and regardless of the wishes of the members themselves. An efficiently debating and controlling parliament presupposes professional politicians as members with offices and staff. Economically independent members were already rare in Weber's time. The new problem was about how to enable living for politics among those who were living off politics in parliament. The neutralization of professional politicians justified for Weber the treating of all properly paid parliamentarians as professional politicians.

In the parliamentary debates after the First World War, suspicions towards professional politicians persisted. In the German-language speeches of the Swiss parliament, polemics against *Berufspolitiker* were particularly common. The Social Democrat Johannes Huber saw the danger that political affairs would be conducted by *Berufspolitiker* and no farmer, entrepreneur (*Gewerbetreibender*) or persons from the free professions would be included, but only secretaries, journalists and government officials (*Regierungsräte*). What he called *Berufspolitiker* referred to groups who were available to the membership in parliament on a continual basis, as opposed to the ancient Roman Cincinnatus' ideal of returning to the farm when the mission was completed (SWI: 5 January 1921).

In Westminster, Charles Fenwick (Lib) said the following in the 1911 payment debate, in a sense close to Weber's views: 'The professional politician is a living entity at this moment many of them, who occupy seats on the Front Opposition and Front

Treasury Benches ... are professional politicians' (UK: 10 August 1911). After the First World War, the willingness of political leaders to call themselves professional politicians increased. The Conservative leader Andrew Bonar Law admitted that '[p]eople ... like myself are more or less professional politicians' (UK: 4 March 1921). Ramsay Macdonald as the prime minister of the national government declared: 'We are politicians who are legislators', and in contrast to law professors, we politicians can change 'certain of our most cherished constitutional principles' (UK: 18 October 1932). He thus connects parliamentary sovereignty to the leadership of politicians.

The shift reached even backbenchers. Frank Kingsley Griffith (Lib) declared: 'We are all professional politicians in one sense. No one has levelled any accusation against those whose political job is their only job, and to whom it is their whole life' (UK: 23 January 1930). David Graham Pole (Lab) agreed: 'I am not afraid of being called a professional politician ... if anyone is going to stand for Parliament, he ought to make Parliament his first job and be ready to give his time to the job' (UK: ibid.). George Buchanan (Independent Labour) illustrated ad hominem how it was possible live on the modest payment provided for MPs: 'I only have my income as a Member of Parliament' and 'I have lived on my £400, and lived not badly' (UK: ibid.). These members did not praise their dedication to politics but recognized that they were expected to do politics by facing a growing number of issues in a professional way. The professional politician has here become neutralized in its normative tone.

After the Second World War, several members recognized politics to be the point of sitting in parliament. Frank Pakenham (Lab) addressed Patrick Berkely Moynihan: 'I must ask the noble Lord to remember that when he joins us on these Benches he is a politician; he belongs to this fraternity which he is so anxious to discredit' (UK: Lords, 28 October 1948). To Walter Fischer's (Cons) declaration, 'I am not a professional politician like the hon. Lady and others', Jennie Lee (Lab) responded, 'I suggest that when Members of this House do not respect their status and their profession as Members of this House, they are not fit to sit in this Chamber' (UK: 27 October 1949). Herbert Morrison (Lab) also said on some adversaries that they do not deserve to be called politicians (UK: 28 May 1946 and UK: 27 November 1948).

Around 1970, several Conservative MPs also identified themselves as professional politicians. Harry Legge-Bourge understood that 'the more we [may] become professional politicians, and may become so because of the pressure and burden of work in the House' (UK: 19 November 1968). The frontbencher Quintin Hogg praised parliamentarians as debaters over military experts, 'because ... we are professional politicians who are known to have a double dose of original sin, and for all our faults, are more sensitive to nuances than professional soldiers are' (UK: 9 April 1970).

After the new beginning of parliamentary politics in West Germany, parliaments and politicians long remained suspect in the media and among academics (see Ullrich 2009). In the early Bundestag debates, several members distanced themselves from being a *Berufspolitiker* (e.g. Max Becker, FDP, GEdb: 17 July 1952; Fritz Becker, Deutsche Partei, GEdb: 26 May 1954). Nonetheless, Hans-Joachim v. Merkatz (Deutsche Partei) regarded the contempt (*Diffamierung*) for professional politicians as posing a danger for democracy (GEdb: 22 September 1950), while *Bundestagspräsident*

Eugen Gerstenmaier (CDU) recognized that payment of members enabled them to be independent of outside financial influence (GEdb: 18 April 1958).

At the end of the 1960s, the parties took the initiative for a reform of the Bundestag procedure that would strengthen the powers of the Bundestag and improve the status of individual members (see Recker 2018). Hans Apel (SPD) was a vocal advocate in favour of recognizing the Bundestag members as professional politicians: he proposed that membership in the Bundestag demanded the interest of the entire person (*den ganzen Mann*) and the will to be a professional politician (*den Berufspolitiker zu wollen*) with staff and other resources (GEdb: 27 March 1969). During a social-liberal government, *Bundestagspräsidentin* Anne-Marie Renger (SPD) argued that members should be professional politicians for their entire parliamentary term, as taking a seat in the Bundestag poses a risk for their career: realization of the free mandate depends on providing remuneration and resources for Bundestag members (GEdb: 18 June 1973).

The *Diätenurteil* of the *Bundesverfassungsgericht* from 1975 judged Bundestag membership to be a full-time activity, that is, that remuneration-receiving professional politicians without other professions can be expected to be the rule and others the exception. After that, no major debates on the professional politician have arisen. The debate has shifted instead towards the duty to report members' extra-parliamentary incomes. The neutralization of the figure of professional politician has also been widely accepted among the members of the Bundestag.

Weber was afraid that the party apparatus would take the place of parliamentarians in political leadership. However, since the Second World War full-time members with staff and other resources have gained the upper hand. Jens Borchert (2003: 27) rightly emphasizes how the paid parliamentary mandate has become again a precondition for being party leader or a minister. For major parties, the professional parliamentarian is a major indicator of the well-working of democratic parliamentary polities.

The neutralization of the professional politician marks a point in history where becoming a member of parliament is neither an honour nor a sign of a selection to an elite, and where members no longer need to worry about popular contempt. The elected members have learnt to accept that they are both treated and expected to act as politicians, and that their power in parliament depends on their willingness to act as politicians.

6.3. The Francophone dichotomy: *hommes politiques* versus *politiciens*

Renaming is for Skinner one paradiastolic way of altering the normative colour. An interesting practice of renaming politicians lies in the French distinction between *l'homme politique* (in the all-male Third Republic and in Belgium) and *politicien*, adopted from the US practice in the 1860s (on the dictionaries, see Zimmermann et al. 2007: 151–3). After about 1880, the French Third Republic was a parliamentary regime in which plenary debates played a major role (Roussellier, 1997, speaks of un *parlement d'éloquence*), but contempt for *politiciens* and their *politique politicienne*, or politician-style politics, remained widespread.

Affirming the parliamentary paradigm, former prime minister Louis Barthou wrote: 'Le Politique exercer or il veut exercer son action dans le Parlement ou dans le Gouvernement' (Barthou 1923: 14), but '[l]e politicien et le Politique sont des choses différentes, comme sont choses différentes la politique et l'intrigue' (Barthou 1923: 105–6). The term 'intrigue' connects the *politiciens* to the pre-parliamentary figure of cunning and tricky persons.

In the Third Republic, *politicien* remained mostly a pejorative term, as in a speech by Henri Joseph Dugue de la Fauconnière (Union des droites): 'il s'agit d'opter entre deux politiques: la politique des politiciens et la politique du pays' (FR: 10 June 1886). The politics of *politiciens* is seen to consist of petty intrigues against the raison d'état.

The syndicalist-style stereotype of a proletarian MP denying being a *politicien* is visible in a speech by Jacques Lauche (Parti socialiste), who claimed to be unable of lying: 'pour être un politicien avisé, il faut savoir mentir, je ne serai jamais ce politicien' (FR: 23 November 1911). In contrast, Alexandre Bracke (Parti socialiste) asserts, 'Entre le politicien et l'homme nous n'acceptons le partage' (FR: 28 Novembre 1917; for a critique of the anti-political left, see also Jean Jaurès, Parti socialiste, FR: 30 October 1903).

The common contempt for *politiciens* was explicitly questioned in a debate in which Paul Beauregard, a centrist (Groupe progressiste) professor of economics, contrasted science with the noisy politics of politicians: 'tant que quelque politicien ne vient pas de requiller des bruits' (FR: 31 Janvier 1902). Marius Devèze (Union socialiste) asked him from the floor:

> M. Devèze. Qu'est-ce que un politicien?
> M. Paul Beauregard. Ce n'est pas très difficile de savoir.
> M. Devèze. Un politicien est un homme qui fait de la politique. Vous êtes donc un politicien. Vous avez abandonné votre chaire pour venir à la Chambre.
> M. Paul Beauregard. Je ne parlerai donc pas des hommes, mais des circonstances amènant du necessité de parler quelque peu des principes.
> (FR: 31 Janvier 1902)[4]

Beauregard, an academic notable in parliament, distances himself from *politique politicienne*. Devèze, however, assumes that everyone who acts politically is a *politicien*; that is, every elected member of parliament should understand oneself as a politician. Beauregard sees himself as being above the daily politicking of *politiciens*, whereas Devèze wants to neutralize the term and to consider all elected parliamentarians as *politiciens*. This view is shared by Alexandre Zevaès (socialiste independent): 'Ceux que vous appelez les politiciens dependent du suffrage universel' (FR: 15 January 1909), whereas in the first parliament after the Great War, the former Socialist Florentin Levasseur declared: 'Nous sommes des législateurs et nous ne sommes pas des politicians' (FR: 21 January 1921).

In the Belgian Chambre, the distinction between *hommes politiques* and *politiciens* was also disputed already before the First World War.

> M. Helleputte, ministre des chemins de fer, postes et télégraphes. – Je suis un homme politique et non pas un politicien.

M. Furnémont. – Vous vous trompez, vous êtes un homme d'Etat. (Nouveaux rires sur les mimes hues.)

M. Lemonnier. – Quand on est votre adversaire, on est un politicien, et quand on est un ami, on est un homme politique.

(BE: 12 April 1910)[5]

The Catholic minister Joris Helleputte's declaration received two interjections from the floor. The Socialist Léon Furnément parodied him, using the honourable title of *homme d'État*, which hardly few parliamentarians would dare apply to themselves. Liberal Maurice Lemonnier's reply then ridicules the making of a distinction between the term.

An ironic use of the conceptual pair was repeated forty years later, when the Socialist Gaston Baccus commented on a letter from General Terlinden against those whom he 'nomme, avec un mépris non déguisé, "les politiciens"'. Baccus was also casting an ironic aspersion upon 'M. Scheyven, qui, comme chacun le sait, n'est pas un politicien, mais un homme politique' (BE: 30 January 1950). Both Terlinden and Scheyven show their contempt for les *politiciens*; the latter claims to be un homme politique.

Although the pejorative tone remains strong in the French and Belgian debates, the term *politicien* is frequently used of political adversaries in a slightly neutralizing way. The Belgian examples and French MP Charles Eugène Lacotte (non-inscrit) ('Messieurs, le débat est devenu purement politique, je pourrais même dire purement politicien', FR: 21 Janvier 1921) apply the common rhetorical tools of irony, parody and ridicule. The rhetorical distancing of the speaker is also achieved by disputing the legitimacy of the distinction between *hommes politiques* and *politiciens*.

In the French Fourth Republic (1946–58), *politicien* continued to be mostly a pejorative term and the Communists (PCF) were responsible for most of the fierce polemics against it. Jacques Duclos, the number two of the party, in his diatribe against *politiciens*, instrumentalizes the Assemblée nationale for his anti-parliamentary polemic by opposing party militants in parliament to career politicians: 'Nos élus ne font pas carrière politicienne; ils restent des militants au service du peuple' (FRd: 19 November 1948). A declaration of the agrarian right faction (Groupe paysan) was equally militant against les *politiciens professionnels* (FRd: 30 December 1953).

My selective searches debates of the French Fifth Republic indicate that, at least for the Gaullist period (1958–69), even the derogatory use of *politicien* disappears from the debates, as if the word itself had become a part of unparliamentary language. In later scholarly discourse, the word seems to be completely outdated. 'Politicien. Le terme a été progressivement evincé du marche linguistique pour raisons politiques et scientifiques. Et au fond, il avait trop servi. Du coup le terme "professionel de la politique" s'est imposée' (Damamme 1999: 60). My guess is that this French *Sonderweg* is connected to the de-parliamentarizing turn of the Fifth Republic.

In the 1960s and 1970s, the French-speaking Swiss parliamentarians did not, however, have problems with addressing each other and referring to themselves as *politiciens*. For example, the Liberal François Jeanneret contested the intervention of politicians into labour market relations: 'les politiciens n'ont pas pour tâche de régir dans le détail les relations des employés et des salariés' (SWI: 13 March 1963). The

Radical-democrat Carlo Speziali spoke of himself in the following way: 'Mais je suis un politicien et préfère terminer par des considérations politiques' (SWI: 19 March 1976).

6.4. The parliamentary 'we'

As a final step in analysing the paradiastolic neutralization of the (professional) politician, I turn to the parliamentary uses of 'we politicians'. The expression assumes that the parliamentary mandate, as such, renders members politicians, without denying that members of local assemblies, party activists and functionaries might also be politicians. The point lies in the shared identity of parliamentarians as politicians, across party lines and other divides.

'We politicians' allows different rhetorical uses regarding the quality and range of the parliamentary 'we' among the members. The parliamentary 'we' can be inclusive or exclusive, the latter situating the speaking member and her/his party outside the parliamentary 'we'. Its normative colour is neutral, enabling different relationships to be implied towards the voters.

I looked for 'we politicians', the nominative first-person plural that emphasizes the shared professional identity of political actors in the plenary debates. I extended the search to parliaments in: Britain and Ireland; France and (French) Belgium; (West) Germany, Austria and Switzerland; and Sweden and Norway.

6.4.1 A history of regularization

The profile of the uses of 'we politicians' is by and large similar in these parliaments. The first examples are occasional uses, then the usage increases and finally there is a regularization of the uses. I have focused on the early examples and on the period of increasing momentum, whereas the regularized uses are too frequent for my approach.

'We politicians' in the British parliament was used 4 times before 1914, 22 times from 1914 to 1944, and 21 times from 1945 to 1959. Taking the decades to be the unit, I found 35 'hits' for 1960–9, 41 for 1970–9, then a slight decline: 59 for 1980–99, then a new expansion: 201 for 2000–2019. Compared to Westminster, the numbers in the (West) German Bundestag are low in the early years (4 for 1949–65), begin to grow with the CDU–SPD grand coalition (9 for 1965–9) and the social-liberal coalition (67 for 1969–83), and remain at the higher level after that, without showing any definite profile according to coalition.

A similar trend with increasing momentum and regularization of usage can also be discerned in other parliaments. In Britain, the momentum for 'we politicians' can be noted already in the years 1927–30. A rather simultaneous momentum for 'we politicians' can be dated to the 1960s in four countries: West Germany, Austria, Sweden and Norway, which I studied together as a group. In Ireland, Belgium and Switzerland, there is no clear momentum, and Gaullist France seems to be an exception, avoiding any usage of 'politicians' at all.

According to the digital search, the earliest use of the formula can be found in the Belgian Chambre, when the Catholic Eugène Verhaegen disputed that *nous hommes politiques* follows a heart like ours and instead he emphasized our duty (BE: 24 January 1859). Here 'hommes politiques' with the ethos of the duty refers more to an older layer of *homines politici*, that is, to persons passionate about politics, than it does to 'we politicians'.

The Liberal Jules Guillery regarded street demonstrations that were staged for 'us politicians' as detrimental to freedom: 'parce que nous, hommes politiques, nous comprenons qu'elles ne peuvent servir la cause de la liberté' (BE: 29 November 1871). He seems to restrict politics proper to the elected parliamentary representatives, as does Jules Bara, Liberal Minister of Justice, who polemized against accusations made against mandated politicians on private grounds (BE: 24 November 1882; see also the Liberal Paul Hymans on the priority of *hommes politiques* over associations, BE: 5 June 1905). Reflecting on responses to a strike, the Socialist Samuel Donnay regarded militant critics of it as bad *politiciens* and neutralizes the term by applying it to others, as he says they are commonly called: 'Quant à nous, politiciens, comme on nous a appelés pendant ces événements, ce conflit nous a également donné à réfléchir' (BE: 7 February 1911).

The earliest Westminster user of the parliamentary 'we' was, according to Hansard, Wilfrid Lawson (Lib), who used it to emphasize the contrast between opinions inside and outside parliament: 'Whatever we politicians may think sitting here in the calm and security of this House, that is not the opinion out-of-doors' (UK: 17 May 1876). He exercises self-criticism in deference to the popular opinion. Hugh Cecil (Cons) argues in a similar tone: 'We politicians have so often said that all sorts of great issues are involved that the people have begun to think that politics is an unreal occupation in which people use a great deal of language to which they attach very little importance' (UK: 12 March 1913).

In the 1920s and 1930s, there were few mentions of 'we politicians' in the parliaments of Austria, Ireland, Norway and Switzerland, and none in the Belgian Chambre or the French, German or Swedish parliaments. Patrick James Hogan, Irish Minister of Agriculture (Fine Gael), was critical of politicians: 'I mean we politicians have got to get on it, the inferiority complex. We ought to realise that the farmer is very much more important than we are' (IR: 6 June 1929). A counterposition was taken by Alf Mjoen (Arbeiderdemokraterne) in the Norwegian Stortinget, who insisted that, despite lacking popularity, 'we politicians' bear the burden of ruling: 'Vi politikere er ikke sa svært populære. ... Der er nu endgang så med dem som styrer' (NO: 31 January 1933).

6.4.2 The Westminster momentum in 1927–30

In the British House of Commons, the parliamentary 'we' gained momentum in the years 1927–30 towards a neutralization of 'politician'. Ramsay Macdonald (Lab) used the term as follows: 'Of course we politicians can fight as much as we like about our varying political opinions, but ... we should have uniformity of public administration' (UK: 1 March 1927). He insisted on a strict division between partisan politics and non-partisan administration at the local level, on the grounds of the equal treatment of citizens. Carlyon Bellairs (Cons) shares Macdonald's view on separating politics from administration but thinks that many Lords 'have not taken part in politics' and are better administrators, and he asserts: 'We politicians are outsiders when we come to govern the great Departments' (UK: 11 July 1928). Henry Graham White (Lib) supports 'an inquiry ... should be carried out free from any political preoccupation with an open mind, and especially should it be free from the political bias from which we politicians find it so difficult to dissociate ourselves' (UK: 4 April 1930). Frederick Macquisten (Cons), in contrast, deplores politicians' loss of powers: 'We politicians here are mere corks on the water for Government officials' (UK: 31 October 1930).

An actively policy-oriented view was represented by Cecil Wilson (Lab), who asked: 'What can we do, we politicians in the House of Commons, to help forward the improvement of trade and industry in this country?' (UK: 19 December 1927). David Kirkwood (Independent Labour) rejected a reduction in wages in Britain and opposes 'amongst my colleagues those who say ... that we politicians should leave it to the trade unions and the employers' (UK: 25 June 1930). Henry Snell (Lab) regarded the government's appointment policy as better than the church's and concludes: 'We politicians have at least as high a moral standard as ecclesiastics' (UK: 13 June 1928). His formula thus disputes the popular view on the immorality of politicians. Samuel Rosbotham's (Lab) statement that 'we politicians were apt to forget, but I do not think that we ought to forget seeing that we represent the people of the country' (UK: 12 November 1930) shows that, for Rosbotham, being a parliamentary representative suffices for the definition of being a politician.

These different speech acts take for granted that House of Commons members are politicians. By their speeches, they form a parliamentary 'we', neutral in tone.

6.4.3 The 1960s momentum in four parliaments

The relative simultaneity of the momentum of talking about 'we politicians' was prevalent in the 1960s in West Germany, Austria, Sweden and Norway independently of the different political constellations. It marks a routinization of parliamentary government, including a strengthening of the resources of parties and MPs, while challenging the post-war continuities in the government constellations, which were different in each of the countries.

The president of the Austrian Nationalrat, Alfred Maleta (ÖVP), while contesting the popular view that 'we politicians' are narrowly self-interested and stupid disputants, admitted that 'we politicians' might be in our doings *betriebsblind* (AU: 27 April 1965). Viktor Kleiner (SPÖ) accepted that 'we politicians' must be transparent and occasionally dressed down (*bis aufs Hemd ausgezogen*) (AU: 8 June 1966). In the Norwegian Stortinget, Olaf Watnebryn (*Arbeiderpartiet*) noted that 'we politicians' must accept that we can be played out of the game (*hengt ut*), but we are also able to withstand much criticism (NO: 9 April 1964). Helmut Schmidt, the SPD parliamentary leader in the Bundestag, parodied the politician-bashing of economics journalists: 'wir Politiker uns in den Niederungen befinden' (GEdb: 8 November 1967). Being subjected to criticism is an obvious occasion for using a parliamentary 'we'.

As in the British practice, a self-criticism by *politicians* was part of many 'we politician' speeches. One variety involved *politicians* limiting their own intervening in business and administration. In the Bundestag, Hans-Georg Emde (FDP) disputed whether 'we politicians' do have a mandate to decide on the burdens (*Belastungen*) of the people indefinitely (GEdb: 16 April 1964). The Swedish Social Democrat Per Edvin Sköld thought that 'we politicians' tend to overestimate the significance of our doings (SWE: 10 January 1965) and his party-fellow, Finance Minister Gunnar Sträng, warned that 'we politicians' should avoid giving people false visions of swift improvements (SWE: 22 February 1967).

In Austria, the Proporz system of dividing posts between the conservative ÖVP and social democratic SPÖ was criticized by supporters of the new ÖVP majority government beginning in 1966. Matthias Krempl spoke of the *Politikerklausel* that 'we politicians' now accept creating a *sachlich* space, operating with 'economic necessities' instead of distributing benefits between the parties (AU: 16 December 1966). Hermann Withalm demanded that 'we politicians' must rationalize political decision-making in order to bear the responsibility entrusted by the people (AU: 27 October 1967). Walter Suppan required that 'we politicians' must reduce our privileges (AU: 2 December 1970). These demands combined economic liberalism with the dismantling (*Abbau*) of bipartisan appointments.

Another *topos* regarding 'we politicians' involves their attaining office in popular elections. Its passive variant emphasizes the dependence of politicians on voters; the active version emphasizes the parliamentarians' responsibility for decision-making. In the Austrian Nationalrat, Friedrich Peter of the nationalist FPÖ declared, 'We politicians must orient ourselves to the voters' (AU: 2 December 1970), while Herbert Kohlmeier (ÖVP) demanded that 'we politicians' should be consistent in order to be taken seriously by the Austrian population' (AU: 10 December 1970). Hertha Firnberg (SPÖ) saw that Austrian women regarded female politicians (*Politikerinnen*) of all parties as no longer trustworthy (AU: 14 December 1968). In the Swedish Riksdag, Axel Georg Pettersson (Centre) thought that, to be credible, 'we politicians' must take seriously the public talk about equality and reforms (SWE: 12 November 1969). In the Norwegian Storting, Gunnar Garbo (Venstre) judged that overcoming the reluctance towards development aid depended on how 'we politicians' present the topic (NO: 17 December 1962).

Others argued that the people need the guidance of politicians. In the Bundestag, Johann Baptist Gradl (CSU) maintained that 'we politicians' should present the situation, the ways and the difficulties to the people (*dem Volk*) by keeping in mind that they rarely possess such political virtues (*Tugenden*) as patience and persistence, and that they need encouragement and trust (DEdb: 14 March 1968). In the Riksdag, Ingrid Sundberg (Högern) asserted that changes in the environment are not produced unless 'we politicians ... guide (styra) them' (SWE: 14 November 1968).

Several Swedish Liberals (Folkpartiet) submitted that 'we politicians' have a responsibility (*ansvar*) to overcome popular prejudices regarding development aid (Olle Dahlen, SWE: 17 April 1967) and environmental questions (Sören Norrby, SWE: 11 May 1967). Party leader Sven Wedén thought idealism and enthusiasm were not enough, as 'we politicians' have a duty to obtain practical results (SWE: 16 May 1968), while Bo Skårman admitted that 'we politicians' are in part responsible for the bad conditions (*misförhållandena*) and their removal (SWE: 9 February 1969). These members were more open to new items on the political agenda than the ruling Social Democrats but lacked the latter's belief in 'the people'.

In the Bundestag several members discussed *Politikberatung*, the relation of scholarly advice to parliamentary decision-making. Heinz Frehsee (SPD) looked to science (*Wissenschaft*) to help politicians identify prospective developments (DEdb: 27 June 1962), and Käte Strobel (SPD) relied on social scientists (*Sozialforschern*) to help politicians with their knowledge (*Erkenntnis*) over the state of affairs (DEdb: 24 April 1963). Walter Hammersen (FDP) was critical of areal planning (*Raumplanung*), and called on 'we politicians' to be 'manly enough' (*Manns genug*) to defend the constitutional rights and freedoms (DEdb: 4 December 1963). Kurt Schober (CDU) stated even more openly that 'we politicians' should not let our decision-making powers slip out of our hands (*nicht die Entscheidung darüber aus der Hand nehmen lassen*) (DEdb: 7 February 1968).

In the Nationalrat, Michael Luptowits (SPÖ) saw the day approaching when 'we politicians' could only say 'yes' (*ja*) to what science and technology presuppose (*vorsetzen*) (AU: 17 June 1966). He also thought that poets and writers have a deeper knowledge of social life than do 'we politicians' (AU: 29 November 1966). In line with this pessimistic vision, he insisted that 'we politicians' should not leave university politics to executives and specialist commissions (AU: 24 April 1968).

The use of 'we politicians' in discussions of the 1960s added new *topoi*, for example, relating to scientific knowledge, to the earlier British ones. The parliamentary 'we' addressed the collegiality and mutual respect between parliamentary members. It allowed different views on such issues as the range of action of politicians (which economic liberals wanted to reduce), optimistic and pessimistic views on the powers of politicians, and the government-versus-opposition divide. British Labour members used the 'we politicians' formula more willingly than did the Conservatives, whereas in continental parliaments, no such clear division was to be found. Unlike in the context of professionalization, there was no need to insist on politics as the main occupation of parliamentarians: the rhetoric of a parliamentary 'we' tacitly assumed it.

6.5. The rhetoric of translation

Paradiastolic redescription is a commonly used tool for judging political action. In this chapter, I have used this rhetorical scheme for illustrating the rather complex history of the *politician*. The examples from different parliaments provide, in Koselleck's (1972) sense, both indicators and factors for the modification of the normative colour of politicians, who have been a notorious target of contempt and lamentation through commonplaces frequently repeated across time and place.

In a previous study (Palonen 2012b), I discussed the apologetics of politicians and their different rhetorical devices in the twentieth century. Here, I have focused on neutralization as a major change in the speech of politicians in twentieth-century parliamentary debates as a rhetoric of modesty. The emphatic form 'We, the politicians' is inapplicable to parliamentary debates. The growing acceptance of professionalization and increased use of 'we politicians' in the second half of the twentieth century are signs of agreeing to use politician as a neutral denomination. This corresponds to the growing awareness what parliamentarians do and can do, independently of their party affiliation or national traditions.

Although the reputation of *politicians* in popular opinion, in the media and in parts of academia is as bad as ever, this is perhaps a sign of the Weberian insight that *politicians* are an indispensable part of parliamentary and democratic polities. When members of parliament across countries have identified themselves with *politicians*, they have responded to the public expectations as well as reflected upon their own experiences. Declarations of not being a professional *politician* or accusing others of being one still exist, but they are marginal in parliaments.

Speaking of an inclusive parliamentary 'we' reflects the character of the parliament as a thoroughly political site of action, which largely transcends the dividing lines between members and parties and exemplifies the parliamentary way acting politically with a common agenda and specific procedures and conventions. The parliamentary language of politicians is largely independent of their 'natural' languages. While parliamentarians do have opposing purposes for their actions, it is precisely this political dissent, this agreeing to disagree, that underlies and informs the use of the parliamentary 'we'.

To summarize in formal terms the conceptual changes: the ancient Greeks' ambivalent vocabulary has been applied in modern languages. In early modern use, the terms describing writers on politics as laudable were confronted with terms condemning, but *politic* described a person, or *Politikus*, who combined both. The decisive move towards regarding parliamentarians and ministers as politicians retained a link to the older ideals, and it was rather easy to reactivate the old condemnations when talking about the intrigues of second-rate politicians focussed narrowly on their own electoral success. In the French, the dualism resulted in two words: *homme politique* and *politicien*.

Early debates on the payment of parliamentarians concerned the opposition between a dedicated living for and an instrumental living off politics, as well as the frequently opposing demands of parliamentary performance versus adapting to voters' opinions. With the growing agenda and workload for parliaments, the distinction between living for and living off politics lost its cogency: 'doing politics' became the main justification for membership in parliament. Full-time membership became the rule and, with the ability of the formula 'we politicians' to transcend party lines as well as the government-versus-opposition divide, a parliamentary 'we' was formed and later regularized. However, in France the neutralization of the term *politicien* failed. With the exception of the populists, European parliamentarians today willingly understand themselves as politicians.

Notes

1 **Parliamentary records:**
   AU: Austria, *Stenographische Protokolle, Nationalrat – Plenarsitzungen*, https://www.parlament.gv.at/PAKT/STPROT/
   BE: Belgium, Belgian Chamber or Representaties, *Proceedings of the plenary sessions*. https://sites.google.com/site/bplenum/proceedings
   FR: France, III République, *Journal officiel de la République française. Débats parlementaires. Chambre des deputes*, https://gallica.bnf.fr/ark:/12148/cb328020951/date.

FRd:	*Débats parlementaires de IV République et constituantes*, Assemblée nationale, http://4e.republique.jo-an.fr
GE:	Germany, *Verhandlungen des Deutschen Reichstags, Reichstagsprotokolle*, https://www.reichstag-abgeordnetendatenbank.de/volltext.html
GEdb:	Deutscher Bundestag, *Drucksachen und Plenarprotokolle des Deutschen Bundestags*, https://dip.bundestag.de
IR:	Ireland, The Houses of Oreachtas, *Dail debates*, https://www.oireachtas.ie/en/debates/find/?debateType=dail
NO:	Norway, *Statsmaktene. Digitale søknader fra regering, stortinget og domstolerna*, https://www.nb.no/statsmaktene/search.statsmaktene?lang=no
SWE:	Sweden, Sveriges Riksdag, *Protokoll*, https://www.riksdagen.se/sv/dokument-lagar/?doktyp=prot
SWI:	Switzerland, Bundesversammlung, *Amtliches Bulletin, Protokolle, Findmittel*, https://www.amtsdruckschriften.bar.admin.ch/setLanguage.do?lang=DE&currWebPage=searchHome
UK:	United Kingdom, UK Parliament, *Hansard*, https://hansard.parliament.uk/search.

2   'In the Western world, however, we find something quite specific which concerns us more directly, namely *political* leadership, first in the figure of the free "demagogue", who grew from the soil of the city-state, a unique creation of the Mediterranean culture in particular, and then in the figure of parliamentary "party leader" who also sprung from the soil of the constitutional state, another institution indigenous only to the West' (Weber 1994: 313).

3   'The professional member of parliament is a man who exercises his mandate in the Reichstag, not as an occasional or subsidiary duty, but as the main content of his life's work, equipped with his own office and staff and with every means of information. One may love or hate this figure, but he is indispensable in purely technical terms and is *already there with us* today' (Weber 1994: 190).

4   M. Devèze: Who is a *politicien*?
    M. Beauregard: It is not so difficult to know.
    M. Devèze: A *politicien* is a man who pursues politics. Hence you are a *politicien*. You have abandoned your academic chair for membership in the Chamber.
    M. Beauregard: I don't speak of men, but of the conditions that make it necessity to talk about principles.

(trans. KP)

5   M. Helleputte: Minister of railways, post and telegraph – I am a homme politique, not a politicien.
    M. Furnemont: You are mistaken, you are a Statesman. (laughs, mimic crying)
    M. Lemonnier: Who is an adversary, is a politicien; who is a friend, is a homme politique.

(trans. KP)

References

Barthou, Louis (1923), *Le Politique*, Paris: Hachette.
Borchert, Jens (2003), *Die Professionalisierung der Politik*, Frankfurt/M: Campus.
Bryce, James (1888/1914/1995), *The American Commonwealth* I–II, Indianapolis: Liberty Press.

Campion, G. F. M. (1929), *Introduction to the Procedure of the House of Commons*, London: Allen & Co.
Claussen, Emma (2021), *Politics and 'Politiques' in Sixteenth-Century France. A Conceptual History*, Cambridge: Cambridge University Press.
Damamme, Dominique (1999), 'Professionnel de la politique, un métier peu avouable', in Michel Offerle (ed.). *La profession politique xixe-xxe siècles*, 37–66, Paris: Belin.
Diätenurteil (1975), BVerfGe 40, 296, *Abgeordnetendiäten*. https://www.servat.unibe.ch/dfr/bv040296.html.
Evans, Paul (ed.) (2017), *Essays in the History of the Parliamentary Procedure*, London: Bloomsbury.
Goldberg, Hans-Peter (1998), *Bismarck und seine Gegner. Politische Rhetorik im kaiserlichen Reichstag*, Düsseldorf: Droste.
Hansen, Mogens Herman (1983), *The Athenian 'Politicians', 403–322 BC*, Institute of Advanced Study, https://grbs.library.duke.edu/article/viewFile/6001/5201.
Harrington, James (1656 [1992]), *The Commonwealth of Oceana*, edited by J. G. A. Pocock, Cambridge: Cambridge University Press.
Kislansky, Mark (1986 [2009]), *Parliamentary Selection*, Cambridge: Cambridge University Press.
Koselleck, Reinhart (1972), 'Einleitung', in *Geschichtliche Grundbegriffe* Bd. I, xiii–xxvii, Stuttgart: Klett.
Koselleck, Reinhart (1979), *Vergangene Zukunft*, Frankfurt/M: Suhrkamp.
Koselleck, Reinhart (1986), 'Sozialgeschichte und Begrifffsgeschichte', in Wolfgang Schieder and Volker Sellin (eds.), *Sozialgeschichte in Deutschland*, vol. 1, 89–109, Göttingen: Vandenhoek und Ruprecht.
Meier, Christian (1980), *Die Entstehung des Politischen bei den Griechen*, Frankfurt/M: Suhrkamp.
Ostrogorski, Moisei (1903/1912 [1993]), *La démocratie et les partis* politiques, Paris: Calmann-Lévy.
Palonen, Kari (2006), *The Struggle with Time. A Conceptual History of 'politics' as an Activity*, Münster: LIT.
Palonen, Kari (2012a), 'Reinhart Koselleck on Anachronism, Translation and Conceptual Change', in Martin J. Burke and Melvin Richter (eds.), *Why Concepts Matter*, 73–92, Leiden: Brill.
Palonen, Kari (2012b), *Rhetorik des Unbeliebten. Lobreden auf Politiker im Zeitalter der Demokratie*, Baden-Baden: Nomos.
Palonen, Kari (2014), *The Politics of Parliamentary Procedure. The Formation of the Westminster Procedure as a Parliamentary Ideal Type*, Leverkusen: Budrich.
Papenheim, Martin (2017), 'Politique', *Handbuch politisch-sozialer Grundbegriffe in Frankreich 1680–1820*, vol. 21, 9–86.
Plunkitt of Tammany Hall (1905 [1948]), *A Series of Very Plain Talks on Very Practical Politics. Delivered by the Ex-Senator George Washington Plunkitt, the Tammany Philosopher, from his Rostrum – the New York County Court House-Bootblank Stand – and Recorded by William L. Riorden*, New York: Knopf.
Recker, Marie-Luise (2018), *Parlamentarismus in der Bundesrepublik* Deutschland. *Der Deutsche Bundestag 1949–1969*, Düsseldorf: Droste.
Redlich, Josef (1905), *Recht und Technik des Englischen Parlamentarismus*, Leipzig: Duncker & Humblot.
Roussellier, Nicolas (1997), *Le parlement de l'éloquence*, Paris: Presses de Sciences-po.
Schmitt, Carl (1932/1963 [1979]), *Der Begriff des Politischen*, Berlin: Duncker & Humblot.

Selinger, William (2019), *Parliamentarism from Burke to Weber*, Cambridge: Cambridge University Press.
Skinner, Quentin (1974), 'Some Problems in the Analysis of Political Thought and Action', *Political Theory*, 2: 277–303.
Skinner, Quentin (1996), *Reason and Rhetoric in the Philosophy of Hobbes*, Cambridge: Cambridge University Press.
Steinmetz, Willibald (2019), *Europa im 19. Jahrhundert*, Frankfurt/M: Fischer.
Turchetti, Mario (2012), 'Bodin as the Self-translator of His Republique', in Martin Burke and Melvin Richter (eds.), *Why Concepts Matter?*, 109–18, Leiden: Brill.
Turkka, Tapani (2007), *The Origins of Parliamentarism. A Study on the Sandys' Motion*, Baden-Baden: Nomos.
Ullrich, Sebastian (2009), *Der Weimar Komplex*, Göttingen: Wallstein.
Weber, Max (1918 [1988]), 'Parlament und Regierung im neugeordneten Deutschland', in Wolfgang J. Mommsen (ed.), *Max-Weber-Studienausgabe* 1/15, 202–302, Tübingen: Mohr.
Weber, Max (1919 [1994]), 'Politik als Beruf', in Wolfgang Schluchter und Wolfgang J. Mommsen (eds.), *Max-Weber-Studienausgabe* 1/17, 35–88, Tübingen: Mohr.
Weber, Max (1994), *Political Writings*, edited by Peter Lassman and Donald Speirs, Cambridge: Cambridge University Press.
Zimmermann, Isolde, Johannes Wagemann and Philipp Sprick (2007), 'Von edlen Staatsmännern und eitlen Kannegiessern: Der 'Politiker' in deutschen, englischen und französischen Lexika des 18. bis 20. Jahrhunderts', in Willibald Steinmetz (ed.), *'Politik'. Situationen eines Wortgebrauchs*, 134–61, Frankfurt/M: Campus.

7

Translated history and historical time: Transtemporal understandings of Greek and Roman concepts

Alexandra Lianeri

7.1. On the concept of translating the past[1]

The function of the historian, writes Peter Burke, is 'to mediate, like a translator, between past and present. This function involves rethinking and rewriting history in every generation' (2012: 171). In what sense do historians translate the past? How does the idea of translation correspond to the mediation of conceptual and spatiotemporal borders that is specific to historical understanding? The act of translating is an essential and vital dimension of historiographical discourse, as Burke suggests. Yet it is only recently that historians began discussing the methodological implications of the concept of translating the past.

No doubt the study of translations has long entered empirical historical research, wherein a profusion of works is devoted to exploring how translations have played a key role in mediating cultural interaction, constructing forms of identity and otherness, and establishing routes and politics of dealing with borders and border-crossing practices. In the field of research into antiquity, translation has claimed a privileged position in investigations of antiquity's reception and cultural history. The scope of this study is breath-taking and has ranged from theorizing the ancient classics as tentatively constituted and contingent upon translation, through tracking cultural rewritings of authors, texts or genres, to the study of translating Greek and Roman cultures as a whole (see for example Martindale 1993; Hardwick 2000; Lianeri and Zajko 2008; Refini 2020).

While these studies have substantiated our understanding of translation *in* history, reflection on the operation of translation in present scholarly writings about the (ancient) past seems to be more limited. This is more evidently true for historians than for literary and cultural scholars, for whom the task of interpreting ancient literatures generates a strong translational dimension and thereby a 'double vision' or plural vision between past and present, setting aside older questions of 'capturing the original' or 'veiling difference', as Simon Goldhill put it (2022). But the messy 'conference of tongues' that is translation, as Theo Hermans phrased it (2014), does not easily fit within the conventional positing of the historical discipline as empiricist, objectivist or premised on the distinction between subject and object of research. As opposed at once to the idea of rigorous transposition of sources and the aspiration of historiographical narratives claiming to represent the past, translation destabilizes key assumptions of historiographical research. This includes modern notions of historical time as neutral, irreversible and moving one way, but also the entire range of temporalizing conceptions of the past, present and future as empty frames delimiting the object of historical research. Moreover, reflection on translation challenges metanarrative premises of temporal continuity or discontinuity, connectivity and disjunction, inviting us instead to ask more about transtemporal arrangements bringing together past, present and future.

In this chapter, I explore a structure of historical understanding that is shaped in and through translation, argue for the comprehension of this structure as temporalized, and seek to ground the transtemporal dimension of translating in examples related to the historical understanding of Greek and Roman concepts. My interest is in binding the translational dimension of historical understanding to recent debates on rethinking modern legacies of historical time (Tamm and Olivier 2019) and enquiring about 'sediments of time' (Koselleck 2018) and transtemporal entanglements through which the 'borders between present, past and future' are negotiated (Lorenz and Bevernage 2013).

The starting point of this discussion is David Armitage's notion of transtemporal history: a method of historical enquiry that intends 'to stress elements of linkage and comparison across time' – still, a method which remains opposed to a merely unifying transhistorical perspective, and 'is time-bound not timeless' (2012: 498). The consideration of the transtemporal in terms of the time-bound, and vice versa, I argue, is the provocation which the notion of translating the past may illuminate. Engaging with translation accentuates specific mediations, confrontations, and politics of time, through which the transtemporal perspectives of Reinhardt Koselleck's long-term history of concepts, but also of big history, deep time or the cultural *longue durée*, may be approached. By the same token, the notion of translating the past may denaturalize metanarratives of historical distance and proximity as unquestioned features of our relation to time (Phillips 2013), highlighting their mediated constitution in a thick historical present. Translated history is transtemporal not only in the sense that it expands our scope of study but also because it requires us to transform historiography's own self-image, in order for the latter to recognize itself anew in the relational operation of translating.

Translating the past builds bridges. Yet it does not bridge an assumed space of the past over the gap or border that separates it from the space of the present and future. It bridges temporal sensibilities: the sense of coming afterwards and having to catch up with the past; the sense of a double or even plural conceptual vision in relation to the events, practices and languages of the past; the sense of encountering (visions of) the past in the present; the sense of being driven towards the future or, conversely, being deprived of a future because of the weight of the past; and the sense of anachronistic presences that thicken present time by remaining at odds with what is conceived as 'belonging' to it. Translated history stresses the temporal relatedness and excess of concepts and metanarratives of historical understanding: first as a certain convergence and confrontation of past, present and future concepts; and second, as the indecisiveness of the borders of historiographical temporalities, a merging of assertions of continuity with the kind of self-interrupting disjunction indicating that, around translation, there is at once conceptual surplus and loss, and thus an entangled and messed time.

From the viewpoint of translating the past into Western historical thought, Greek and Roman concepts are not external to categories of understanding but, also, internal to them: a field wherein the past is at once contingent upon translations acting upon it, and actively present in these translations, constantly contesting and transforming them. In this domain of translation, pasts, presents, and futures are mutable and contestable; hence the focus of scholarly analysis is on the transformations and adaptations through which transtemporal survival takes form as well as the temporal divisions redrawn through movement. By the same token, such translations are especially opened to new occupations of history, or new determinations of what Jacques Rancière described as the 'distribution of the sensible' about past, present and future: a historical sensibility that defines, redefines or makes contestable what is visible and audible in the past in view of particular historico-political and, as Rancière stresses, aesthetico-political regimes (2013).

Translated history seeks to account for transtemporal relationality as the source of some kind of semantic flooding and dissipating thickness of concepts. By focusing on such translation into historiographical languages I am seeking to make sense of: (a) the thick time of conceptuality in and through which historical understanding is performed; (b) the distribution and redistribution of borders of time that establish antiquity's distance or proximity; and (c) the construction of historical sensibilities involving distributions and transformations of the sensible in a moving present, that is sensibilities that map out the availability and circulation of certain dimensions of the ancient past, modalities of unequal relations to it, and routes through which historical understanding becomes a scene of deciding and – in Michel Foucault's vocabulary – disciplining what constitutes past and present.

To attempt to elaborate on this temporality I focus on three major aspects of translated (conceptual) history, which I will approach by engaging with theoretical debates and examples of intellectual history, in which notions of translation and non-translation frame historical understanding. The first I shall identify as the aporetic temporality of concepts through which we translate the past, which I discuss in Section 7.2 on 'Translation's Aporia'. By this I mean a time involving movement between source and translated text, language or historical present, which is simultaneously not movement, a transtemporal passage that also constitutes time's merging, messiness, interruption, recalibration or suspension. In Section 7.3, I discuss two aspects of translation pertaining to historiographical metanarratives, wherein the evoked transparency of historiographical languages is saturated by modes of translating the past. These are the temporal thickness of historiographical concepts produced by translation and the contestability of borders between present and past (and thereby subject and object) of historical understanding – in other words, the idea that such borders are tentatively shaped by plural and conflicting modalities of translation mediating their manifestation. In 7.3.1 I discuss the semantic and temporal thickness of historiographical categories by expanding on the tensions of the premise of (non) translation in Arthur Lovejoy's history of ideas, which transform the operation of historical understanding beyond the field's evoked universalism. In 7.3.2, I examine the temporality of (un)translatability at work in the paradigm of contextualist intellectual history formulated by the Cambridge school of political thought with a focus on Quentin Skinner and J. G. A. Pocock. Here the idea of historiographical contextualism will give way to the claim that all diachronic translations, and especially translations of the Greek and Roman pasts, may generate a self-critical anachronism but also to the question of whether historicist anachronism is dense enough as a reading that brings the past against the present without foregrounding what is critical about the temporality of that translation.

Both the notion of thick conceptuality and that of fluid and contestable temporal borders build implicitly on Koselleck's conceptual history and theory of time. The last section thematizes these two notions in the context of *Begriffsgeschichte* and concludes by foregrounding a third aspect of translated history centred on the temporal politics of translating the past. Such translation, I suggest, emphasizes a non-paradigmatic relation between past, present and future agency, a transtemporal shaping of historical sensibilities that are actively engaged in defining and reconfiguring 'models of speech or actions but also regimes of sensible intensity', as Rancière puts it. 'They define variations of sensible intensities, perceptions, and the abilities of bodies' – including human bodies, social bodies, political bodies, bodies of thinking and making, as well as geographical and temporal ones (Rancière 2013: 35).

7.2. Translation's aporia: An impossible time-passing

The idea of linking historical understanding to translation is not new but owes much to the hermeneutical reflection on understanding – from Friedrich Schleiermacher, through Martin Heidegger and Hans-Georg Gadamer, to Paul Ricoeur – which approached translation as paradigm of interpretation, often in terms of the distinction between understanding (*Verstehen*) and explanation (*Erklären*). While remaining indebted to this line of thought, in this chapter I focus on the transtemporal qualities of the notion of historians translating the past. This orientation builds on Zoltán Boldizsár Simon's attempt to delink historical understanding from both hermeneutical and narrative modes of comprehending the past, in order to rethink its constitution in terms of 'temporal configurations between past, present, and future', stressing that these temporalities are multiple and historical in multiple ways (2022: 5, 8). Can the binding of historical understanding to translation illuminate the plural and interconnecting forms of past, present and future, and the temporally polymorphous density of historiographical narratives of Greek and Roman concepts?

There are, of course, as many answers to this question as there are notions of history and translation. And the latter are no less difficult to delimit than the former. The category of translation has been variously deployed to denote modes of transference, appropriation or untranslatability, and to set the scope of translating in between texts, authors, languages, cultures or epochs. What is more, translation has gone by many different names, each of which is linked to distinct conceptual and methodological approaches: adaptation, paraphrase, metaphrasis, imitation, rewriting, assumed translation, pseudo-translation and so on (cf. Baker and Saldanha 2020). We cannot attribute to translation a simple definition or essence, which would be valid in all places and times, and which could be introduced into debates about historical understanding. Indeed, translation theorists suggest it might even be more helpful to 'think of translation not so much as a category in its own right, but rather as a set of textual practices with which the writer and the reader collude … It is time to free ourselves from the constraints that the term "translation" has placed upon us', Susan Bassnett asserts, 'and recognise that we have immense problems pinning down a term that continues to elude us' (1998: 39). Not only is the theoretical question 'what is translation?' deeply challenging to answer but the historical questions of 'Who is Doing What For/Against Whom and Why?', as André Lefevere (1996) phrases them, are just as elusive and complex.

Still, holding on to the idea of translating the past may not require us to produce a transhistorical definition, but rather to elaborate on a differential concept of translation, which nonetheless breaks through the limits of the historical discipline and may offer reflexive insights about its vocabularies, methods and premises. My point of departure, therefore, is not a rigidly framed notion but a quest for theorizing the shifting actuality of translating as fundamentally aporetic, insofar as translations bear the paradoxical promise of a movement that is at once made and suspended, performed and disrupted, accomplished and destructed.

For all their differences, the above-mentioned terms and concepts of translation pertain, in one way or another, to this aporia. Since the myth of Babel, which George Steiner made paradigmatic for Western translation theory in *After Babel* (1992), notions of translation evoke an idea of border or division, which needs to be confronted and mediated: translation as exposition and performance of border-negotiation and border-crossing or passage, even if this means passing across the internal borders of a language or idiom. At the same time, translation stresses the peculiar nature of this movement, which is intertwined with the repetitive rhythm that Burke attributes to historical scholarship: no translation can ever achieve full identity with a prior text or cultural work. Rather, translations always differ from their source, even when their writing takes the form of transferring the original work itself; think, for instance, of Jorge Luis Borges's fictional character Pierre Menard, whose verbatim 'translation' of *Don Quixote* was both a transposition and still a new version of Cervantes' novel (cf. Arrojo 2018; Gambier and Doorslaer 2009). Likewise, as Neville Morley has aptly argued, the refusal to translate Greek and Roman terms in contemporary historiography transforms them by creating 'a particular image of antiquity: the distinctive combination of (imagined) ancient and (concealed) modern, of translatability and untranslatability, that constitutes the classical' (Morley 2008: 132, 144).

The passing or crossing that translation performs seems then to converge with the aporetic movement that Jacques Derrida tracks in the idea of crossing the ultimate border, the end of one's life:

> Who has ever done it and who can testify to it? The 'I enter', crossing the threshold, this 'I pass' (*perao*) puts us on the path, if may say, of the aporos or of the aporia: the

difficult or the impracticable, here the impossible, passage, the refused, denied, or prohibited passage, indeed the nonpassage, which can in fact be something else, the event of a coming or of a future advent [*événement de venue ou d'avenir*], which no longer has the form of the movement that consists in passing, traversing, or transiting.

(Derrida 1993: 8)

Crossing the threshold of death is an impossible passing, a movement performed in and through the impossibility of moving; or, as Derrida (1993: 10) puts it in an idiomatic, untranslatable, phrase, '*Il y va d'un certain pas*'.

This paradoxical movement resonates with Walter Benjamin's essay 'Task of the Translator', which attributes to translation a complex transtemporal dimension involving important parallels with Benjamin's philosophy of history. What concerns us here is the role of translating in establishing a work's transtemporal survival, which echoes the claim that the pastness of what is now gone and no longer present demands the dynamic recognition of it by the present: 'For every image of the past that is not recognized by the present as one of its own threatens to disappear irretrievably' (1968: 255, thesis v). For Benjamin *Übersetzung*, translation, is linked to *Überleben* through the same logic of binding pastness and present sensibility: 'a translation issues from the original', he writes, 'not so much from its life as from its afterlife' (1968: 71). The term *Überleben*, variously translated as afterlife, survival or revival, marks the interconnection of cultural trajectories in the present.

Still, this present is no longer a moment that is set in a continuous timeline oriented towards an endpoint – the future; neither is it part of successive, mutually unrelated times. The crossing performed by translation, as Antoine Berman notes commenting on Benjamin, confronts both linear and historicist temporalities with a complex time of surviving and waiting, a temporal grid of anticipation, postponement, repetition and return. The prefix *über-* brings into Benjamin's use of *Überleben* a whole thread of German thought, from Romanticism through to Heidegger, which expands translation as survival beyond denoting a mere state of continuation of or disjunction from the past. Benjamin's notion accentuates a paradoxical act of moving and waiting, insofar as 'translation's default consists of the fact that it does not deliver where it is supposed to (and could) deliver. This default', Berman explains, 'is inherent in translation. The location of defaults can vary, but they always exist. Re-translation highlights them but is not free of them'. This aporetic failure of translators to live up to their immanent, self-defining task raises two major questions for Berman, to which I return from the viewpoint of history's self-positing: first, why does this defaulting structure exist; and second, why it has been historically transformed to a 'fault', a deformation attributed to translations or translators. (Berman 2018: 89, 96. 96n.15)

What can this peculiar time of translating – marked at once by living on, ongoingness, movement and survival, but also crisis, belatedness, pause and even repetition as countertemporality – mean for historiographical discourse? Can translation's equivocal time offer some insights into the equivocity of the notion of the historical that Heidegger identified as both past and present, for instance in the form of tradition or historical knowledge? (1996: 341-370, section v.) How may we identify the paradoxical convergence of the past's presence and absence in the case of understanding/translating concepts of antiquity without losing sight either of historical disjunctions and difference or of the ways in which such concepts have already shaped the vocabularies of historical thinking? Can we trace in translation a temporal heterogeneity and plurality of historical understanding, the (non)crossing of borders between past, present and future, which simultaneously constitutes these borders?

We may begin to grasp this aporetic temporality by briefly discussing Koselleck's example of etymological translation at work in concepts derived from Latin and Greek vocabularies. If one uses a term such as 'bourgeoisie' (*Bürgertum*), Koselleck observes, he is denoting a modern social formation originating in the French and the Industrial Revolutions. On the other hand, 'whoever speaks of "civil society" (*bürgerliche Gesellschaft*) may come to the same finding but proceeds on the shaky ground of a millennial tradition. *Bürgerliche Gesellschaft*, *société civile* or civil society are etymologically translations from the Latin. They refer to the Roman *societas civilis* which, for its part, had its terminological model in the *koinōnia politikē* of the Greeks' (2002: 208).

Koselleck draws attention to an aggregation of meanings and references that the concept of 'civil society' inscribes – potentially – in the present. I will come back to this potential and its dependence on present contesting action over historical sensibilities. Here, we may observe that Koselleck's recourse to translating sets aside the understanding of concepts as a finished product, displaying those meanings of their past that are preserved in a given present and those that are lost and obsolete. 'Civil society', in his argument, attests to a temporally dense and moving concept, wherein the present neither merely terminates the past nor continues an already foreclosed timeline moving towards a future endpoint. Rather translation marks this past as both finite and still active, absent and present in forms that are not directly perceptible or visible in either domain. Such a present is dense and overdetermined by multiple temporalities, setting it against conventional forms of periodization, as Helge Jordheim argued about Koselleck's theory of time (2012). For this reason, it is also a present that politicizes time, as translational choices open or close the potential for a normative concept such as 'civil society' and a normative sensibility of the classical to be legitimized, idealized, disciplined or, conversely, relativized, expanded or even exploded.

This feature, for Koselleck, is not incidental but essential to conceptuality, generating a concept's inherent tensions and ambiguity, which makes it contestable and therefore impossible to reduce to a stable definition: 'a concept unites within itself a *plenitude of meaning*. Hence, a concept can possess clarity, but must be ambiguous' (2004: 85, my italics). However, it is heightened in concepts produced by a history of translations that are heavily involved in the cultural politics of Western modernity, such as those going back to the Greek and Roman pasts. The contestability of the concept of 'civil society', for instance, is made visible when we recognize that Aristotle's or Cicero's considerations of it is 'in no way entirely outdated', as Koselleck notes; for contained in the concept's etymological translation 'are the earlier conceptions of a free political self-organization that cannot be erased from the European experience' (2002: 208).

In the neighbourhood of the present, translation still moves us to a temporal plane beyond where we are supposed to be, both spatially and temporally. For instance, Fania Oz-Salzberger's *Translating the Enlightenment* explores the translation of Scottish civic discourse into eighteenth-century Germany in terms of a contestation over the nature of the concept of civil society that pluralizes its definitions and cultural contexts (1995). The transtemporal dimension of this translation, I suggest, may offer some key insights into the configuration of conceptuality and of temporalities of ancient concepts such as *societas civilis*/civil society, the *politikon*/'political', *respublica*/'republic', *historia*/'history' and so on. These concepts are at once set in the past and interwoven into the fabric of modern and contemporary languages through transtemporal trajectories, wherein the aporetic (non)movement of translation is performed.

This transtemporal domain is not confined to the history of Greek and Roman concepts. Yet in the context of modern historical thinking, which has been shaped by the West's conceptual engagement with antiquity, but also by the translation encounters of the European repertoire with vocabularies and idioms on a global level (Cf. for example Chakrabarty 2000; Liu 1999), the case of Greek and Roman concepts offers privileged access to the question of the transtemporal and the operations of translation at work in the historiographical present. As opposed to assumptions of unchanging transhistorical concepts associated with traditional classicism, but also to those forms of historicism in which past and present are either intertwined moments in a processual temporality (Cf. Simon 2019) or, as we shall see, distinct and mutually untranslatable frames, translation foregrounds the transtemporal dimension of historical understanding as a site of tensions generated by antiquity's simultaneous absence and survival, loss and movement into the present. It is therefore a domain that is shaped and interrupted by different conceptual meanings and times, and as such remains unfinished and contestable, premised on the need for rewriting and retranslation.

By the same token, translating the Greek and Roman pasts highlights what we may call border-temporality of ancient concepts, which intervenes in the shaping and distribution of present historical sensibilities. This is a temporality centred on the interconnecting and undecidable contours of concepts across different historical times and languages, which brings a thick time of historical understanding into an excessive, even flooding, configuration of conceptuality. Recognizing a translational structure in the modes of making sense of these concepts informs, in turn, an understanding of translated history, which establishes the historian's dense and mutable conceptual plane, and thereby exemplifies a heterogeneous time of historical understanding, wherein the intertwining of the past's finitude and survival takes form.

7.3. Transtemporal (non-)translation and historical understanding

In exploring Western philosophy's aspiration to translingual conceptual unity, John Sallis takes as his starting point what he calls the 'dream of non-translation': a premise of conveyance of meaning, which he traces back to Leibniz's 1677 configuration of a 'language or universal characteristic', aimed at bringing 'into proper order' all concepts and things (2002: 9). Yet the analysis of this dream suggests its own dissolution and asserts a forceful return of translation. 'What would it mean not to translate?', Sallis asks. 'What would it mean to begin thinking beyond all translation?' If thinking consists in speaking to oneself, as Plato and Kant have argued, it is already thinking in language; hence, 'it will never have outstripped such translation … In other words, for thinking to begin beyond such translation would mean its collapse into a muteness that could mean nothing at all' (2002: 9, 14, 1–2).

In the fields of intellectual and cultural history, the dream of non-translation is not one. It includes at once assertions of direct understanding of the past and considerations of its radical difference and untranslatability, appeals to transhistorical, unmediated concepts and configurations of historical disjunction. Still these metanarrative claims and premises are all saturated by the aporetic temporality of translating. Engaging with the immense scope of this dream in historiography will involve two steps. The first will consist in exploring the internal tensions of it: how the assertion of non-translation as a condition of historical understanding is captured in advance by the logic it would seek to move beyond, so that its very aspiration to evade translating would illuminate its failure. In other words, I will track interruptions of the dream manifested in the translational structure of historiographical concepts. The second step will shift our attention to the temporality of translating that emerges out of this analysis. Here I approach translation as both premise and medium of historical understanding, in order to rethink historiographical zones of transtemporal ongoingness and connectivity, and recast translation as an alternative way of talking about historical time and the relation between past and present.

7.3.1 (Non-)translation and the thickness of historiographical concepts in and through Lovejoy's *History of Ideas*

A distinct configuration of the idea of non-translation in intellectual history can be tracked in the domain of history of ideas, especially in its classical formulation by Arthur Lovejoy. Lovejoy's idealizing and reifying approach to 'unit ideas' has been extensively criticized by Quentin Skinner, John Dunn and the wider Cambridge School, as well as by social and cultural historians, from Robert Darnton to Michel Foucault, so it will not concern us here at any length (McMahon and Moyn 2014). My interest is in a more focused examination of Lovejoy's methodological claims from the viewpoint of translation, which seeks to capture their interruption by acts of translating and discuss the idea of the transtemporal in terms of the tensions that the dream of (non-)translating entails in this framework. I examine how Lovejoy's history of ideas aspired to broaden the temporal perspective of historical study by evoking translation as key to the movement of ideas but also presupposed a condition of non-translation in order to establish a subject-object distinction as an a priori premise in the field. Displacing this premise will allow me to build on the border-crossing potential of this paradigm, in order to foreground a semantic and temporal thickness of ideas or concepts of historical understanding, mediated by translation.

A vital claim of the history of ideas is that historians need to constantly expand the limits of their object: 'The more you press in towards the heart of a narrowly bounded historical problem', Lovejoy (1948: 6) argued, 'the more likely you are to encounter in the problem itself a pressure which drives you outward beyond those bounds'. This contention was first focused on disciplinary boundaries and the need to establish an interdisciplinary understanding of ideas. 'Any unit-idea which the historian … isolates', Lovejoy (1964: 15) wrote, 'he next seeks to trace through more than one ultimately, indeed, through all – of the provinces of history in which it figures in any important degree, whether those provinces are called philosophy, science, literature, art, religion, or politics'. The history of ideas also questioned spatiotemporal borders, for instance, 'by countries, races or languages' (1964: 18–19), which were recognized as porous and permeable by translation. Lovejoy frequently illustrated this border-crossing with cases of reception and translation of ancient works. Milton's *Paradise Lost*, for example, he argued (Lovejoy 1948: 4–5), manifests a conceptual richness that cannot be adequately understood without considering its conversation with antiquity: for instance, at the moment when Milton's Adam quotes Aristotle in translation. More radically Lovejoy tracked the hybrid roots of an incipient eighteenth-century Romanticism in appropriations of (neo-)classical as well as Chinese legacies, variously transmitted by rewritings and translations (Lovejoy 1948: 99–135).

Such references served to exemplify Lovejoy's crucial premise that 'ideas are the most migratory things in the world' (1940:4). But the implications of this premise were ambivalent. The idea of travelling concepts was criticized for advancing an undiscriminating assumption of conceptual continuity of 'unit-ideas' across different contexts (Dunn 1980: 13–28 as well as Skinner's criticism discussed in this section). On the other hand, this criticism tended to ignore, first, that the notion of travelling concepts does not have to entail conceptual unity, as studies of reception indicate, and second, how the idea of the 'unit-idea' not only encouraged interdisciplinary research but also directed attention away from what was to be recognized – several decades later – as intellectual history's methodological nationalism (Conrad 2016) and sanctification of borders between past and present.

Accounting for translation allowed Lovejoy to identify variation and transformation in the articulation of 'unit-ideas'. For instance, he quotes Herder's *Ideen* arguing that the influence of the passing of time on thought is 'undeniable. Seek no, or attempt, an *Iliad*, try to write as Aeschylus, Sophocles and Plato did; it is impossible' (Lovejoy 1948: 168). Moreover, acknowledgement of variety inscribed conflict in the notion of 'ideas' itself. So, on the one hand, Lovejoy considered unit-ideas as universalizable, autonomous entities, 'the primary and persistent or recurrent dynamic units' (Lovejoy 1964: 7); yet, on the other, he sought to account for the diverse 'manifestations' of these ideas moving and circulating through translation (Lovejoy 1948: 19, 103, 105, 135).

He addressed this tension by positing a realm of non-translation in the domain of historiographical vocabularies, wherein translating became, paradoxically, a one-way process: from the abstraction of unit-ideas to their varied articulations in historical actuality. In the *Great Chain of Being*, for example, he envisioned this translational operation by evoking a Platonic vision of 'translation of all the ideal possibilities into actuality' (Lovejoy 1964: 50). Commenting on Leibniz's engagement with the Platonic legacy of relating the world of essences to existence, he also spoke of 'essences conceived as materials for translation into existence' (Lovejoy 1964: 170). When translation is tracked by Lovejoy in the object of historiography or the movement from essences to actuality, it attests to the multitudinous articulation of ideas. However, insofar as the act of translating that links unit-ideas to actuality is seen as moving one way, from the former to the latter, it also ensures that both the contours of historiographical categories (unit-ideas) and the contours of borders that separate these categories from the language of historical actors remain unchallenged.

Lovejoy's hypothesis of the transhistorical required this dream. Seen from its perspective, the unit-ideas are revealed to the historian in the supposedly plain and manifest existence of the factual. Their configuration is premised on the condition of no mediation or translation:

> In the whole series of creeds and movements going under the one name, and in each of them separately – Lovejoy writes – it is needful to go behind the superficial appearance of the singleness and identity, to crack the shell which holds the mass together, if we are to see the real units, the effective working ideas, which in any given case are present.
> (Lovejoy 1964: 6)

Like a kernel that we simply encounter once the shell is removed, unit-ideas become apparent beyond translation and as such beyond historical transformation and time.

Yet, even if these ideas are posited as transhistorical and timeless, their articulation as historiographical categories cannot be. If the task of the historian is to include the totality of manifested elements in each idea, as Lovejoy insists, this task would be founded on the mediating action of these elements, which would bring translation back into the very structure of historiographical concepts. As he writes, 'the translation of supersensible possibilities into sensible realities' involves an accumulative configuration of unit ideas, as it entails 'an increase, not a loss, of value'. This means, for instance, that 'the very essence' of an idea such as 'the good consists in the maximal actualization of variety' (Lovejoy 1964: 98–9). The method for delimiting unit ideas, insofar as it is dependent on the multiplicity of empirical phenomena – in other words, it requires the accumulation of all concrete articulations in the 'unit-idea' – is translational. Hence in the concluding remarks of the *Great Chain of Being* Lovejoy writes that these phenomena cannot ultimately be reduced to partial translations but need to be recognized as the domain in which the totality of the history of ideas unfolds in its diversity:

> The world of concrete existence, then, is no impartial transcript of the realm of essence; and it is no translation of pure logic into temporal terms – such terms being themselves, indeed, the negation of pure logic. It has the character and the range of content and of diversity which it happens to have.
> (Lovejoy 1964: 332)

The paradox of ideas that are both divided and derived from historical languages delimits here the domain of historiographical categories. The world of conceptual existence is mutable; yet in its diversity it mediates any representation of unit-ideas that is possible. By rejecting the vision of translated historical existence as inferior copy of ideas, translation reclaims a key role in the field from which it was excluded. The configuration of historiographical concepts needs – ultimately – to rely upon the specificity of idioms and upon the interactivity and migration of language diversities.

Exploring the dream of (non)translation as a site of tensions in Lovejoy's hypothesis suggests that translation is the very domain in and through which the transtemporal aspirations of his vision of intellectual history could be formulated. But this recognition entails the recasting of the paradigm's self-image of the historical: the evoked transtemporal dimension of unit-ideas becomes translational. The categories through which it is possible to track the transtemporal diversity of 'ideas' are produced by translating past configurations and lines of translation into the present. This translational structure heightens the density of historiographical concepts, which are no longer unified, but ever expanding and pluralized, and therefore internally conflicting and contestable, as they rewrite the vast domain of mixing and interacting languages constituting the object of historical understanding.

7.3.2 Untranslatability and anachronistic understanding

Skinner and the other historians of the Cambridge school shifted the object of intellectual history from ideas to language uses or discourses formulated in response to contextually specific problems and questions. Drawing on R. G. Collingwood's notion of *Verstehen* and L. Wittgenstein's 'meaning-is-use' theory, Skinner (1988: 56) challenged histories of ideas for effacing the contingency of intellectual history, insofar as 'there *is* no determinate idea to which various writers contributed, but only a variety of statements made with the words by a variety of different agents with a variety of intentions'. This is why, he explained, the project of studying a body of works in order to extract from them some 'timeless elements' is methodologically mistaken. It interprets what historical actors intended to say and do, that is to say, the questions they have set for themselves in their particular situation and the ways they responded to those questions, by reducing them to the critic's assumptions and expectations about what they must have said – a move that implicitly affirms the canonicity and transhistorical meaning of those assumptions (Skinner 1988).

The finite character of ideas moved the research focus of the Cambridge school towards contextually specific meaning, with an emphasis on the primacy of linguistic contexts. From this perspective, language was understood as framed by discursive conventions and conceptual uses which were taken to express specific intentions, both individual (authorial) and collective. Skinner treated these intentions as intersubjective and manifested in specific discursive forms, language games, paradigms or ideologies (Tully 1988). But he was also acutely observant of dissonance and variation in an author or a corpus, challenging the presumption of coherence as producing 'a history of thoughts which no one ever actually succeeded in thinking, at a level of coherence which no one ever actually attained' (Skinner 1988: 40).

Translation rarely entered Skinner's writings as theoretical category, even though his vision of contextualism offers a rich repertoire for such theorizing, as is attested by translation theories that built on Skinner's thought (Cf. Hermans 2022; Palonen 2014). A key reason for this absence is methodological. Skinner's rigid contextualism, at least in his early writings (Cf. Richter 1995: 124–42), could not accommodate an idea of translation as medium for the transmission of texts beyond their time; for it was precisely this transtemporal movement that he considered as reifying and ahistorical. 'Any statement – he insisted – is inescapably the embodiment of a particular intention, on a particular occasion, addressed to the solution of a particular problem, and thus specific to its situation in a way that it can only be naive to try to transcend.' Or, as he put it in different terms, drawing on Collingwood, 'there simply are no perennial problems in philosophy: there are only individual answers to individual questions, with as many different answers as there are questions, and as many different questions as there are questioners' (Skinner 1988: 65).

The absence of reflection on translation attested to the autonomy of (political) languages and language uses from earlier or subsequent ones. More strongly, Skinner conceptualized – though never termed as such – a relation of untranslatability among discourses, insofar as he rejected an operation of translation enabling transtemporal historical survival. For instance, he posited a realm of untranslatability between a modern liberal concept of democracy and the uses of the concept in past political languages, as in the Leveller movement and ideology, criticizing the anachronism that such rendition entails (Skinner 1988: 47). Likewise, in discussing the concept *virtù* deployed by Machiavelli and his contemporaries, he offers a Latin but not a modern equivalent: 'Machiavelli's pivotal concept of *virtù* (*virtus* in Latin) cannot be translated into modern English by any single word or manageable series of periphrases' (Skinner 1981: vi). The issue is not linguistic but historiographical, Skinner explained: 'Seeking a translation for this term, historians have generally begun by observing that, even in Machiavelli's writings, persons of courage and prudence are often described as *virtuosi*. This leads to the conclusion that Machiavelli "sometimes uses virtù in a traditional Christian sense"' (Skinner 2002: 48). However, Skinner writes, Machiavelli's use of *virtù* confronts us with a much wider variety of meanings emerging from a great diversity of uses that translation effaces (Skinner 2002: 48).

Setting aside Skinner's intentionalist theory of meaning (formulated in a time which had just begun criticizing the Romantic notion of the author, for example with Roland Barthes' 1967 *La mort de l'auteur*), we must reaffirm the vital contribution of the Cambridge school to a version of intellectual history that allows us to understand past languages and cultural practices, including translation, in terms that remain irreducible to a conceptual world outside the perspective of historical actors that produced them. It is worth noting here that the discipline of translation studies was also founded in the 1970s on basis of the same contention: that the mediating force of translation 'changes everything', in Lawrence Venuti's formulation (2013), and thus translations need to be set within the background of norms, conventions and ideological priorities of the culture and society which produces them, rather some dehistoricizing ideal of faithfulness or transfer across times and cultures (Toury 2012). By positing this premise in intellectual history, Skinner made it possible to explore links between past discourses and their historical situation without assimilating them to the present, but also to recognize these discourses as modes of thinking and understanding before they came to be the object of historiographical investigation.

The implications of Skinner's assumption of untranslatability were drawn for historians by Bernard Williams, who was himself in dialogue with both Collingwood and the Cambridge school. Williams spoke against approaches to the history of philosophy that immediately translate, for instance, a Greek expression as 'moral obligation' and then deploy this translation to claim that Aristotle, or whoever it was who used it, had an inadequate theory of moral obligation. 'The point of reading philosophers of the past – Williams wrote (2006: 344) – is to find in them something different from the present.' Likewise, Skinner, whose later writings focused systematically on the ongoing political significance of past thinkers, provided key examples of this difference and its potential to challenge the present. His 1997 inaugural lecture as Regius professor of history at the University of Cambridge, published with the title *Liberty before Liberalism*, tracked a neo-Roman theory of freedom developed by early modern Britain's encounter with antiquity. Skinner (1998) explored this encounter in order to provide alternatives to contemporary notions of freedom associated with liberal thought, socialism and human rights. Other historians and political theorists linked to the Cambridge school, from Moses Finley through Dunn to Paul Cartledge, approached the democracy of the ancients, particularly of Athens, in order to emphasize difference, once *dēmokratia* was cast 'in their own terms ... examining what they were trying to do, how they went about it, the extent to which they succeeded or failed, and why' (Finley 1983: 84; 1985), and in doing so sought a critical and reflexive perspective on modern liberal democracy (Dunn 1992; Cartledge 2016).

Still, the untranslatability of the past posited by contextualist histories was imbued with a paradox, grasped from the outset by Dunn. 'The problem of interpretation – Dunn wrote – is always the problem of closing the context. What closes the context in actuality is the intention (and much more broadly, the experiences) of the speaker.' But this closure, for Dunn, involves tension: 'The problem for the historian is always that his experience also drastically closes the context of utterance' (Dunn 2002: 27). Skinner also recognized this aporetic premise of contextualism, noting that 'my almost paradoxical contention is that the various transformations we can hope to chart will not strictly speaking be changes in concepts at all. They will be transformations in the applications of the terms by which our concepts are expressed' (Skinner 2002: 179).

From this perspective, Skinner occasionally sought to resolve this paradox by recognizing some kind of translation in contextualist intellectual history. Considering how a person (A) of a particular time and place (*t2*) is trying to understand an utterance by a speaker (S) at a different time and place (*t1*) makes it

> indispensable that A should be capable of performing some act of translation of the concepts and conventions employed by S at t1 into terms which are familiar at t2 to A himself, not to mention others to whom A at t2 may wish to communicate his understanding.
>
> (Skinner 1970: 136)

This claim joins a debate on untranslatability going back to the modern configuration of the concept in German Romantic thinkers, such as Wilhelm von Humboldt and Friedrich Schleiermacher (Cassin 2019; Hermans 2019). In her consideration of 'untranslatables' Barbara Cassin returns to Humboldt's 'Introduction to the *Agamemnon* of Aeschylus', where the translator considers the untranslatability of the tragedy in order to point out that it is Humboldt who also translates the text. The paradox is resolved through translation's – and historiography's – role in negotiating the boundaries between past and present: the untranslatable therefore, Cassin concludes, is 'not what one does not translate, but what one never ceases to (not) translate' (Cassin 2018: 15; Cassin et al. 2014).

There is a crucial temporal dimension in this consideration of untranslatability, which will be clarified in the last section. At this point I want to move on to a theorist of the Cambridge school who reflected on translation by linking it directly to historical time, namely Pocock. Advancing a distinct type of contextualism, which was both centred on a discursive present and oriented towards the *longue durée*, Pocock set the paradox of untranslatability at the heart of intellectual history (cf. Lianeri 2014). Like Skinner, he stressed the need for the historian to 'present the text as it bore meaning in the mind of the author or his contemporary reader', also considering language as context of meaning. His interest, however, was ultimately in long-term historiographical narratives tracing difference as well as encounters and relations among discourses. In Iain Hampsher-Monk's words, Pocock set 'political languages in time' by 'constructing narratives in the history of political thought' and kept to the fore changes and developments in the tradition of ideas chosen for investigation (Hampsher-Monk 1984: 90).

Translation entered this framework as what we may term – appropriating Fredric Jameson's term – a vanishing mediator of narratives of discourses. It was theorized as medium in which cultural tradition and movement took form; yet it was effaced as premise in terms of which Pocock sustained both the temporality of context-bound discourses and his long-term narratives of cross-border relations among these discourses. In other words, Pocock ascribed – and largely restricted – translation to the object of history, considering its role first as index of difference in the domain of this object, and, second, as connecting force across diverse discourses and times.

Translation's attestation of difference was identified when Pocock considered the long-term history of discourses in terms of succession, tracing the

> constant adaptation, translation, and reperformance ... in a succession of contexts by a succession of agents, and second, and under closer inspection, that of the innovations and modifications performed in as many distinguishable idioms as originally were compounded to form the text and subsequently formed the succession of language contexts in which the text was interpreted.
>
> (1985: 21)

This was to make translation a central dimension of the history of discourses: 'The history of discourse now becomes visible as one of *traditio* in the sense of transmission and, still more, translation', Pocock observed (1985: 20). But this new position entailed a specific conception of cross-border translation which was reduced to appropriation and adaptation to the target context. This translation, he said, 'is of the kind which Petrarch imagined between himself and Cicero or Livy – "from you, in your age, in your world, to me, in mine"' entailing 'an element of translation, and necessarily of *traduttore traditore*' (Pocock1972: 7).

However, if the premise of timelessness entails the absence of temporal succession, it does not follow from this that the specificity of historical temporality is to be reduced to a succession of discourses, with each step of this timeline being separated from others by impenetrable borders. That is to say that such a temporality does not arise from some neutral comparison of discourses but depends upon the premise of untranslatability as principle of differentiation and narrative connection in the form of succession.

While Pocock himself tracks translation disjunctions in the domain of research objects, untranslatability constitutes an unacknowledged theoretical premise, on which his vision of contextualism is contingent. Insofar as recognizing untranslatability depends on an unfinished operation of (non)translation, the historian's identification of mutually untranslatable concepts or works is mediated by their translation into the present, and indeed a translation which makes it possible to perceive difference. This translation sustains, in turn, Pocock's metanarrative premise of the history of discourses as a whole. Let me clarify this with an example. Both Pocock and Skinner have set Aristotle, Polybius, Cicero and Machiavelli within a much broader republican language, which, as Elena Fasano Guarini (1990: 18) notes, they build around the concepts of *virtú* and *vivere civile* as a tradition of border-crossing encounters 'in which *The Prince* and the *Discourses* represent an important turning point', attesting to the distance between classical and modern uses. In order for the concepts of *virtú* and *vivere civile* to frame a narrative of the history of republicanisms, ancient and modern, they need to be translated into the categories through which historians make sense of the transformations of the language of republicanism in a long-term perspective. But the logic of this master narrative is ultimately formed in translation, or, indeed, in several translations. To connect past articulations of virtue and civil life to a succession of non-converging discourses, one needs to translate them into a temporalizing discourse that foregrounds disjunction and difference.

Once this translation operation is recognized, however, it reveals a tension, since the historiographical renderings of these concepts claim an access to past languages that sets them apart from the forces and contingency of historical actors-translators. Moreover, this modality of translation may be linked methodologically to Pocock's setting of the temporal scope of intellectual history in the *moyenne durée*. It is the premise of untranslatability that allows Pocock to affirm that intellectual history is only 'interested in acts performed and the contexts in and upon which they were performed. *Moyenne durée* enters with, but is not confined to, the language context; in the *longue durée* [the historian] is interested only in so far as it gets verbalized, and thus enters the *moyenne durée*' (Pocock 1987: 22). In certain threads of the field, as in the history of mentalities, Pocock goes on, the historian may find himself dealing with deeper levels of continuity, 'but he supposes there to be a depth at which structures are not cognised, employed in rhetoric, or discussed in theory. At this depth there is *longue durée* but nothing more, and he does not go down there ... At depths where no self-propelling organisms swim, he is not sure there is any history' (Pocock 1987). In other words, the historian pursues the appropriating translations across discourses; that is to say, the historian tracks what Venuti (1995) has called domesticating translations, considering the limits of the target culture as the limits of interpretive context. But in order to distinguish between the domesticating act from the original, Pocock is required to perform a foreignizing translation (Cf. Venuti 1995), which is itself as much embedded in its present as the translations produced by historical actors.

However, alongside the temporality of the *moyenne durée*, Pocock (2009: 84) elaborated on a kind of cross-border, transtemporal survival, which he approached through the category of 'diachronous' or 'diachronic translation'. Discussed sporadically, this category has not received much theoretical attention. Yet its formulation, I argue, condenses some key tensions in Pocock's thought, whose discussion offers important insights into historical understanding and the notion of translating the past.

Diachronic translation is immediately associated by Pocock with the movement of certain texts beyond their time. In considering this survival, he recognizes a disruption of the unity of discourses and the very division between past and present. 'There are texts – he writes – which outlive the author and the language world which "he" knew, so that the acts of utterance which they perform are translated into systems of discourse inconsonant with those in which they were performed by the author' (Pocock 2009: 84). Pocock remained hesitant regarding the domain and modalities of this disruption: whether it takes form as survival of concepts or texts or whether it may ultimately be recognized as movement at all. As he wrote:

> The phenomenon of diachronous translation – as it may be termed – is one of the most recalcitrant for the historian to deal with; yet this is probably the point at which 'he' is most likely to feel justified in decomposing the texts into 'ideas' and claiming that 'ideas' have a 'history'.
>
> (Pocock 2009: 84)

Diachronic translation is provocative because it challenges the idea that meaning is context-specific in a radical sense, and this challenge becomes highlighted in the domain of conceptual history or history of ideas.

Pocock's empirical historiographical work intensified these tensions. In the *Machiavellian Moment*, for instance, he traced both the translation of ancient writers, such as Aristotle, Cicero and Polybius, and the distinct conceptual routes through which Greek and Roman considerations of *politeia* and the *respublica* were reconfigured as 'republican' tradition: 'I here presume that the revival of the republican ideal by civic humanists posed the problem of a society, in which the political nature of man as described by Aristotle was to receive its fulfillment, seeking to exist in the framework of a Christian time-scheme which denied the possibility of any secular fulfillment' (Pocock 2003: vii).

When Pocock describes the object of this survival as the cross-temporal articulation of difference, he reduces translation to a medium defining the temporal and language-borders of a story of succession that may not accommodate the transtemporal. Yet, this contention is diffused when he analyses translation as a field mediating transition and connectedness through and across difference. This is the case when he notes the role of translations in mediating the rewriting of ancient republican thought by civic humanists, exploring, for example, the key role of Latin translations of Aristotle by Renaissance scholarship in configurations of political concepts, such as virtue, but also reconfigurations of the republican past as such (Pocock 2003: 89).

Accordingly, when Pocock expands his theoretical reflection to include diachronous translation as methodological category, he gains some important insights into transtemporal relations and translated history. The first is that the time of successive discourses is no longer a neutral framing alongside which certain past works or concepts may cross borders and enter new contexts. A new mode of contextualizing enters this image to transform and complicate it, that is, translation time. As Pocock writes in his essay 'Texts as Events', first published in 1987, 'a most interesting category of texts surviving in language matrices that modify the actions performed with them but that they continue to modify through their surviving capacity to act in themselves as matrices for action' (Pocock 2009: 116). Texts that move across time, texts that survive as matrices of action, are texts in translation. Recognizing these translations as contexts of discursive and practical action, we are invited to approach this action in terms of the aporia of translation, the paradox of movement that is not movement across time. This means that categories formulated in these contexts do not fit squarely within an autonomous present – that is, a present that is separated from the past. Rather, translation casts this present as an idiom of transtemporal relationality, something ongoing, which is not separated from the past, but saturated by the effects of other times that overdetermine its borders rendering the present constantly at odds with itself.

This transtemporal perspective makes room for a notion of translation that is no longer domesticating or appropriating, but, as Pocock writes, anachronistic in the sense that it involves connections across linguistic/temporal borders. Indeed,

> The most interesting acts of translation are anachronistic. They are performed by readers who live in times during which the matrices, idioms and language games have been modified, so that texts that are still current and still acting as the matrices for action are no longer limited to the performance of the illocutions they performed at first publication, and perhaps are no longer capable of performing those illocutions.
>
> (Pocock 2009)

The impossibility of transtemporal interaction, that is to say, the premise of translation's radical alignment with the receiving language, as we saw, functioned as demarcation of Pocock's setting of the history of discourses in *moyenne durée*. Anachronistic translation, on the other hand, transforms at once the scope and temporality of historical narrative. Not only is this concept central to the temporal expansion of the history of discourses in the *longue durée*. Anachronistic translation further requires the elaboration of temporalities that move beyond the idea of disjunction and succession in time. The category builds a case for a converging articulation of concepts and experience in an ongoing moment, which may retrospectively be recognized as belonging to a language or era, but which, in the frame of its making, marked the fluidity and overdetermination of borders among past, present and future, including the borders through which historians separate their time from that of their object.

7.4. Conceptual history and temporal sensibilities of translating the past

The concept of 'translating the past' came to be paramount in Koselleck's theorization of conceptual history (Burke and Richter 2012; Palonen 2003; Richter 2005; Richter 2012; Lianeri 2014). As Kari Palonen succinctly puts it, Koselleck proclaimed translation's omnipresence. In his writings, translations are not only a medium for negotiating change in the domain of the historian's object but also a method in conceptual history. Acts of translating render conceptual changes from past to the present intelligible but also foreground the inevitable use of contemporary language in historiographical accounts of such changes (Palonen 2003). Indeed, Koselleck argued explicitly that 'The history of concepts may be reconstructed through studying the reception, or more radically, the translation of concepts first used in the past, but then pressed into service by later generations' (Koselleck 1996: 62).

This strong thesis captures some dimensions of historical understanding that we have begun to identify by way of translation's negating intrusion into other paradigms, and which we addressed as especially pertinent to the history of Greek and Roman concepts. The first is that translation needs to be recognized as a vital and essential structure of historiographical categories aspiring to mediate the long-term trajectories of conceptual pasts. The methodological consequence of this premise is that such categories exceed conventional delimitations of their meaning and timeline. This is to join Koselleck's consideration of a concept's condensation of meaning we discussed in the first section. But it is also to converse with recent attempts to globalize conceptual history, which strongly emphasize how world-ranging processes of transmission and transformation of concepts hinge on translation practices (Pernau and Sachsenmaier 2016).

In this context, the notion of translated structures of historiographical concepts may offer some insights into the problem of diachronic translatability of global conceptual history. The aspiration to write a border-crossing, global history of concepts derived from Western vocabularies, such as 'civil society' as Willbald Steinmetz observes, generates 'a particularly great danger of writing the history of non-Western countries primarily in terms of a deficit'. This is especially the case for the vocabulary of scholarship, law and many other areas drawn from the Greek and Latin traditions, whose history 'had a certain standardizing effect in European history' for which 'there has been no equivalent … in the older, pre-colonial history of the non-Western countries'. Steinmetz finds a way out of this difficulty in the routes through which many of these concepts 'that have been conveyed through Western languages since the nineteenth century form a veneer, as it were, of common vocabulary, which could ameliorate the problem of translatability in the long term' (Steinmetz 2016: 356–7).

We may push this critique a step further. We may consider first how translating the object of historical enquiry into the languages of historiography may restore some internal diversity of concepts such as 'civil society', 'history' or 'democracy', which will in turn make them useable as tools for investigating practices, languages and subjectivities, wherein such categories have been recognized as absent. This translation resonates with Marcel Detienne's quest for 'comparing the incomparable', a manifesto against the dangers of incommensurability aimed at 'constructing comparables' in the ancient world, beyond the Eurocentric timelines and languages of historiography (Detienne 2008). But it also stresses that such a construction of comparables is not to be reduced to a semantic accumulation, a mere expansion of the meanings of historiographical categories. Rather, it needs to address the temporality of historical sensibilities produced by them: the conceptual borders and divisions that determine what is visible and invisible, translatable and untranslatable, in the domain of the past, and how this realm of pastness may be affirmed or challenged by new translations.

The second dimension of historical understanding, which we examined through Skinner's and Pocock's notion of historiographical (un)translatability, was the overdetermination of historical borders and the disturbing gesture of untimely pasts entering the present. We can now link this notion to Koselleck's category of plural times, whose actuality depends on different modalities of translating. Koselleck's theory of historical time never lost sight of historical specificity, with translation foregrounding processes of decontextualization and re-contextualization, though which concepts cross borders by way of transformation:

> Concepts can become outdated because the contexts within which they were constituted no longer exist. Thus, although concepts age, they have no autonomous history of their own. The concept of *politeia* cannot be separated from the practice of citizenship in the Greek poleis; the concept of *res publica* in Cicero depends upon the political order of republican Rome in the first century. Methodologically, I hold that such epistemological purism is required for any adequate analysis of how language may be matched to the contexts within which it functions. To that extent, a rigorous historicism registering the non-convertibility of what is articulated by language is the precondition of every conceptual analysis.
>
> (Koselleck 1996: 62)

This marks a site of convergence between conceptual history and the contextualist historical perspective of the Cambridge school (Cf. Richter 1990; Palonen 2014). Still, Koselleck's hypothesis moved beyond contextualism to include a transtemporal dimension. As he noted, '*Begriffsgeschichte* does not end there', since every reading and reception by later generations of past concepts transform the entire spectrum of meanings associated with the concept. As the original contexts of concepts change, 'so, too, do the original or subsequent meanings carried by concepts' (Koselleck 1996: 62–3).

This is a complex temporality which inscribes into the problematic of translating the past major epistemological aporias about historical time, and particularly the aporia of conceptualizing the conjunction of synchrony and diachrony. I am referring to the challenge that theorist of history Eelco Runia described as the impossibility of relating continuity and discontinuity in a 'temporal, vertical' sense: 'To understand continuity and discontinuity requires being able "to walk around" the events in question—but as soon as we start to look backwards, the second dimension needed for approaching events from different angles somehow gets lost' (Runia 2014: 59).

Koselleck recourse to translation foregrounds a field in which he links synchrony and diachrony in terms that make the history of concepts possible (Cf. Lianeri 2014). 'At all times – he writes in the introduction to the *Geschichtliche Grundbegriffe* – the diversity of historical experience – past and present – has been captured by concepts in different languages and in their translations' (Koselleck 2011: 7). It is the notion of translation that allows Koselleck to contend that synchrony and diachrony are closely interwoven, and yet remain irreducible to one another:

> Synchrony and diachrony cannot be separated empirically. The conditions and determinants that, in a temporal gradation of various depths, reach from the "past" into the present intervene in particular events just as agents "simultaneously" act on the basis of their respective outlines of the future. Any synchrony is eo ipso at the same time diachronic. In actu, all temporal dimensions are always intertwined, and it would contradict experience to define the "present" as, for instance, one of those moments that accumulate from the past into the future or, conversely, that slip as intangible points of transition from the future into the past.
>
> (Koselleck 2002: 30)

By focusing merely on synchrony, 'history deteriorates into a pure space of consciousness in which all temporal dimensions are contained at once'. Conversely 'if we focus on diachrony, the active presence of human beings would, historically speaking, have no space of action' (Koselleck 2002: 60). As Jordheim (2012: 61) observes, this temporal merging is inscribed in the temporal density of concepts as specific moments in history (*Zustand*) that also unveil a 'diachronic movement', expressing at once the past, present and future. My claim is that concept's unveiling of multiple times in a specific historical present may be conceptualized as translated history.

Translation provides conceptual history with a field wherein an impossible passing is actualized in terms that challenge not only reifying claims to universality but also appeals to some genuine encounter with the past's alterity either in traditions of 'Verstehen' (Dilthey), 'reenactment' (Collingwood) and 'tradition' (Gadamer) or in contemporary evocations of the past's presence (for a critical overview, see Ghosh and Kleinberg 2013) including the quest to 'rescue' forgotten past voices and lives from 'the enormous condescension of posterity', as E. P. Thompson put it (1963: 12). While such rescuing remains a central historiographical task, this is a task that is itself actualized in translation, in and through which all forms of anachronism and proximity are performed. In this respect, evoking translation addresses the problem of the past's presence, pointed out by Ethan Kleinberg (2013), which is inevitably mediated as 'presence in absentia'.

Allow me to close by adding a third dimension of historiographical understanding that emerges from the concept of translating the past, which I will approach by way of reflecting on a tension in Koselleck's hypothesis. Despite affirming translation's methodological omnipresence, Koselleck also conceptualized fields of non-translation. One of them was marked by the affinity of present analytical categories with the domain of conceptual history after the *Sattelzeit*, with 1900 demarcating a realm outside the aporias of translating and, indeed, the very need to translate. As he writes in the introduction to the *Geschichtliche Grundbegriffe*:

> The heuristic presupposition guiding the research presented in this work is that since the middle of the eighteenth century a profound change has occurred in the meaning of the classical topics (topoi) of political discourse. Old words have taken on new meanings, which for us *do not require translation*. What is posited is the emergence of a threshold period (*Sattelzeit*) in which the past was gradually transformed into the present.
>
> (Koselleck 2011: 9)

In the contemporary historical domain, whose limits were established around 1900, concepts remain translatable to the present, while the historian's engagement with previous periods requires 'a retranslation (*Rückübersetzung*) of the vanished content of words into our current language' (Koselleck 2011: 17).

As with Lovejoy, Skinner and Pocock, the domain of non-translation in Koselleck's thought posits the borders of the historical and historiographical present. As such it maps an index not just to specific conceptualities that prevailed in this particular time but to the politics of transtemporal translation that established these borders. However, the domain of non-translation also marks a potential scene for retranslation and future historical understandings – what Burke terms as constant rethinking and rewriting of the past. Historiographical translations of the Greek and Roman concepts may play a major role in this scene of rewriting. But such an enterprise, as we saw, cannot only take the form of self-expansion and accumulation of past meanings, even when these are formulated as anachronistic presences outside borders the present. It further needs to explore points wherein concepts of antiquity make it possible for the distribution of the sensible to be disturbed. Such a disturbance would involve the past as 'presence in absentia' (Kleinberg 2013) or 'spectacle' (Rancière 2014: 59). It would thus require a translation of the past whose (im)possibility disrupts (present) time, generates time and challenges historical perspectives and sensibilities of the contemporary world.

Note

1   I am grateful to Peter Burke and Lorna Hardwick for their insightful comments on this chapter and to Luigi Alonzi for illuminating discussions on the topic. Ethan Kleinberg's critical questions regarding a previous article on translation and historiography (Lianeri 2014) continued to pose challenges to which this piece attempted to respond.

References

Armitage, David (2012), 'What's the Big Idea? Intellectual History and the *Longue Durée*', *History of European Ideas*, 38 (4): 493–507.
Arrojo, Rosemary (2018), *Fictional Translators: Rethinking Translation through Literature*, Milton Park, OX and New York: Routledge.
Baker, Mona and Gabriela Saldanha (eds.) (2020), *Routledge Encyclopedia of Translation Studies*, London: Routledge.
Bassnett, Susan (1998), 'When Is a Translation Not a Translation?', in André Lefevere and Susan Bassnett (eds.), *Constructing Cultures: Essays on Literary Translation*, 25–40, Clevedon, Philadelphia: Multilingual Matters.
Benjamin, Walter (1968), *Illuminations*, edited by H. Arendt, translated by H. Zorn, New York: Schocken Books.
Berman, Antoine, Isabelle Berman and Valentina Sommella (2018), *The Age of Translation: A Commentary on Walter Benjamin's 'The Task of the Translator'*, translated by C. Wright, London: Routledge.
Burke, Martin J. and Malvin Richter (eds.) (2012), *Why Concepts Matter: Translating Social and Political Thought*, Leiden: Brill.
Burke, Peter (2012), 'An Intellectual Self-Portrait, or the History of a Historian', in Alun Muslow (ed.), *Authoring the Past: Writing and Rethinking History*, 171–82, Abingdon, Oxon and New York: Routledge.
Cartledge, Paul (2016), *Democracy: A Life*, Oxford: Oxford University Press.
Cassin, Barbara (2018), 'Humboldt, Translation and the Dictionary of Untranslatables', in Duncan Large, Motoko Akashi and Wanda Józwikowska (eds.), *Untranslatability: Interdisciplinary Perspectives*, 13–26, New York: Routledge.
Cassin, Barbara (2019), 'Humboldt, Translation and the Dictionary of Untranslatables', in Duncan Large, Motoko Akashi and Wanda Józwikowska (eds.), *Untranslatability: Interdisciplinary Perspectives*, 13–26, New York: Routledge.
Cassin, Barbara et al. (eds.) (2014), *Dictionary of Untranslatables: A Philosophical Lexicon*, Princeton: Princeton University Press.
Chakrabarty, Dipesh (2000), *Provincializing Europe: Postcolonial Thought and Historical Difference*, Princeton, NJ: Princeton University Press.
Conrad, Sebastian (2016), *What Is Global History?*, Princeton: Princeton University Press.
Derrida, Jacques (1993), *Aporias: Dying-Awaiting (One Another at) the 'Limits of Truth' (Mourir–s'attendre Aux 'Limites de La Vérité')*, Stanford, CA: Stanford University Press.
Detienne, Marcel (2008), *Comparing the Incomparable*, Cultural memory in the present, translated by J. Lloyd, Stanford, CA: Stanford University Press.
Dunn, John (2002 [1980]), *Political Obligation in Its Historical Context: Essays in Political Theory*, Cambridge: Cambridge University Press.
Dunn, John (ed.) (1992), *Democracy: The Unfinished Journey, 508 BC to AD 1993*, Oxford: Oxford University Press.
Fasano Guarini, Elena (1990), 'Machiavelli and the Crisis of the Italian Republics', in G. Bock, Quentin Skinner and Maurizio Viroli (eds.), *Machiavelli and Republicanism*, 17–40, Cambridge: Cambridge University Press.
Finley, Moses I. (1983), *Politics in the Ancient World*, The Wiles lectures, Cambridge: Cambridge University Press.
Finley, Moses I. (1985), *Democracy Ancient and Modern*, 2nd edn, London: Hogarth Press.

Gambier, Yves and Luc van Doorslaer (2009), *The Metalanguage of Translation*, Amsterdam: John Benjamins Pub. Co.
Ghosh, Ranjan and Ethan Kleinberg (eds.) (2013), *Presence: Philosophy, History, and Cultural Theory for the Twenty-First Century*, Ithaca: Cornell University Press.
Goldhill, Simon (2022), *What Is a Jewish Classicist? Essays on the Personal Voice and Disciplinary Politics*, New York: Bloomsbury Academic.
Hampsher-Monk, Iain (1984), 'Political Languages in Time – The Work of J. G. A. Pocock', *British Journal of Political Science*, 14 (1): 89–116.
Hardwick, Lorna (2000), *Translating Words, Translating Cultures*, London: Duckworth.
Heidegger, Martin (1996), *Being and Time*, SUNY, translated by Joan Stambaugh, Albany, NY: State University of New York Press.
Hermans, Theo (2014 [2007]), *The Conference of the Tongues*, Manchester: St. Jerome Pub.
Hermans, Theo (2019), 'Untranslatability, Entanglement and Understanding', in Duncan Large, Motoko Akashi and Wanda Józwikowska (eds.), *Untranslatability: Interdisciplinary Perspectives*, New York: Routledge.
Hermans, Theo (2022), *Translation and History: A Textbook*, London: Routledge.
Jordheim, Helge (2012), 'Against Periodization: Koselleck's Theory of Multiple Temporalities', *History and Theory*, 51 (2): 151–71.
Kleinberg, Ethan (2013), 'Presence in Absentia', in Ranjan Ghosh and Ethan Kleinberg (eds.), *Presence: Philosophy, History, and Cultural Theory for the Twenty-First Century*, 8–25, Ithaca: Cornell University Press.
Koselleck, Reinhart (1996), 'A Response to Comments on the Geschichtliche Grundbegriffe', in Hartmut Lehmann and Melvin Richter (eds.), *The Meaning of Historical Terms and Concepts: New Studies on Begriffsgeschichte*, 59–70, Washington, DC: German Historical Institute.
Koselleck, Reinhart (2002), *The Practice of Conceptual History: Timing History, Spacing Concepts*, translated by Todd S. Presner, Stanford, CA: Stanford University Press.
Koselleck, Reinhart (2004), *Futures Past: On the Semantics of Historical Time*, translated by Keith Tribe, New York: Columbia University Press.
Koselleck, Reinhart (2011), 'Introduction and Prefaces to the *Geschichtliche Grundbegriffe* [*Basic Concepts in History: A Historical Dictionary of Political and Social Language in Germany*]', *Contributions to the History of Concepts*, translated by Melvin Richter, 6 (1): 1–37.
Koselleck, Reinhart (2018), *Sediments of Time: On Possible Histories*, Cultural memory in the present, translated by Stephan L. Hoffmann and Sean Franzel, Stanford, CA: Stanford University Press.
Lefevere, André (1996), 'Translation: Who Is Doing What For/Against Whom and Why?', in Marilyn G. Rose (ed.), *Translation Horizons beyond the Boundaries of Translation Spectrum [Translation Perspectives IX]*, 45–58, Binghampton: State University of New York.
Lianeri, Alexandra (2014), 'A Regime of Untranslatables: Temporalities of Translation and Conceptual History', *History and Theory*, 53 (4): 473–97.
Lianeri, Alexandra and Vanda Zajko (2008), *Translation and the Classic: Identity as Change in the History of Culture*, Oxford: Oxford University Press.
Liu, Lydia H. (ed.) (1999), *Tokens of Exchange: The Problem of Translation in Global Circulations*, Post-contemporary Interventions, Durham, NC: Duke University Press.
Lorenz, Chris and Berber Bevernage (eds.) (2013), *Breaking Up Time: Negotiating the Borders between Present, Past and Future*, Göttingen: Vandenhoeck & Ruprecht.
Lovejoy, Arthur O. (1940), 'Reflections on the History of Ideas', *Journal of the History of Ideas*, 1 (1): 3–23.
Lovejoy, Arthur O. (1948), *Essays in the History of Ideas*, Baltimore: Johns Hopkins.

Lovejoy, Arthur O. (1964), *The Great Chain of Being: A Study of the History of an Idea*, The William James lectures, Cambridge, MA: Harvard University Press.
Martindale, Charles (1993), *Redeeming the Text: Latin Poetry and the Hermeneutics of Reception*, Cambridge: Cambridge University Press.
McMahon, Darrin M. and Samuel Moyn (eds.) (2014), *Rethinking Modern European Intellectual History*, Oxford: Oxford University Press.
Morley, Neville (2008), '"Das Altertum Das Sich Nicht Übersetzen Lässt". Translation and Untranslatability in Ancient History', in Alexandra Lianeri and Vanda Zajko (eds.), *Translation and the Classic: Identity as Change in the History of Culture*, 128–47, Oxford: Oxford University Press.
Oz-Salzberger, Fania (1995), *Translating the Enlightenment: Scottish Civic Discourse in Eighteenth-Century Germany*, Oxford: Oxford University Press.
Palonen, Kari (2003), 'Translation, Politics and Conceptual Change', *Redescriptions: Political Thought, Conceptual History and Feminist Theory*, 7 (1): 15–35.
Palonen, Kari (2014), *Politics and Conceptual Histories: Rhetorical and Temporal Perspectives*, Baden-Baden, Germany: Nomos, Bloomsbury.
Pernau, Margrit and Dominic Sachsenmaier (eds.) (2016), *Global Conceptual History: A Reader*, London: Bloomsbury Academic.
Phillips, Mark (2013), *On Historical Distance*, New Haven: Yale University Press.
Pocock, John G. A. (1972), *Politics, Language and Time: Essays on Political Thought and History*, London: Methuen.
Pocock, John G. A. (1985), *Virtue, Commerce, and History: Essays on Political Thought and History, Chiefly in the Eighteenth Century*, Ideas in context, Cambridge: Cambridge University Press.
Pocock, John G. A. (1987), 'The Concept of a Language and the *métier d'historien*: Some Considerations on Practice', in Anthony Pagden (ed.), *The Languages of Political Theory in Early-Modern Europe*, 19–40, Cambridge: Cambridge University Press.
Pocock, John G. A. (2003), *The Machiavellian Moment: Florentine Political Thought and the Atlantic Republican Tradition*, Princeton, NJ: Princeton University Press.
Pocock, John G. A. (2009), *Political Thought and History: Essays on Theory and Method*, Cambridge: Cambridge University Press.
Rancière, Jacques (2013), *The Politics of Aesthetics: The Distribution of the Sensible*, translated by G. Rockhill, London: Bloomsbury Academic.
Rancière, Jacques (2014), *The Politics of Aesthetics: The Distribution of the Sensible*, translated by G. Rockhill, London: Bloomsbury.
Refini, Eugenio (2020), *The Vernacular Aristotle: Translation as Reception in Medieval and Renaissance Italy*, Cambridge: Cambridge University Press.
Richter, Melvin (1990), 'Reconstructing the History of Political Languages: Pocock, Skinner, and the Geschichtliche Grundbegriffe', *History and Theory*, 29 (1): 38–70.
Richter, Melvin (1995), *The History of Political and Social Concepts: A Critical Introduction*, New York: Oxford University Press.
Richter, Melvin (2005), 'More Than a Two-Way Traffic: Analyzing, Translating, and Comparing Political Concepts from Other Cultures', *Contributions to the History of Concepts*, 1 (1): 7–20.
Richter, Melvin (2012), 'Introduction: Translation, the History of Concepts and the History of Political Thought', in Martin J. Burke and Martin Richter (eds.), *Why Concepts Matter: Translating Social and Political Thought*, 1–40, Leiden: Brill.
Runia, Eelco (2014), *Moved by the Past: Discontinuity and Historical Mutation*, New York: Columbia University Press.

Sallis, John (2002), *On Translation*, Studies in Continental Thought, Bloomington: Indiana University Press.
Simon, Zoltán Boldizsár (2019), 'The Transformation of Historical Time: Processual and Evental Temporalities', in Marek Tamm and Laurent Olivier (eds.), *Rethinking Historical Time: New Approaches to Presentism*, 71–84, London: Bloomsbury Academic.
Simon, Zoltán Boldizsár (2022), 'Historical Understanding Today', in Zoltán Boldizsár Simon and Lars Deile (eds.), *Historical Understanding Today: Past, Present and Future*, London: Bloomsbury Academic.
Skinner, Quentin (1970), 'Conventions and the Understanding of Speech Acts', *The Philosophical Quarterly*, 20 (79): 118.
Skinner, Quentin (1981), *Machiavelli*, New York: Hill and Wang.
Skinner, Quentin (1988), 'Meaning and Understanding in the History of Ideas', in James Tully (ed.), *Meaning and Context: Quentin Skinner and His Critics*, 29–67, Princeton, NJ: Princeton University Press.
Skinner, Quentin (1998), *Liberty before Liberalism*, Cambridge: Cambridge University Press.
Skinner, Quentin (2002), *Visions of Politics*, vol. 1, Cambridge: Cambridge University Press.
Steiner, George (1992), *After Babel: Aspects of Language and Translation*, Oxford: Oxford University Press.
Steinmetz, Willibald (2016), 'Forty Years of Conceptual History – The State of the Art', in Magrit Pernau and Dominic Sachsenmaier (eds.), *Global Conceptual History: A Reader*, 339–66, London: Bloomsbury Academic.
Tamm, Marek and Laurent Olivier (eds.) (2019), *Rethinking Historical Time: New Approaches to Presentism*, London: Bloomsbury Academic.
Thompson, Edward P. (1963), *The Making of the English Working Class*, New York: Pantheon Books.
Toury, Gideon (2012), *Descriptive Translation Studies and Beyond*, Amsterdam: John Benjamins Pub. Co.
Tully, James (1988), 'The Pen Is a Mighty Sword: Quentin Skinner's Analysis of Politics', in James Tully (ed.), *Meaning and Context: Quentin Skinner and His Critics*, 7–25, Princeton, NJ: Princeton University Press.
Venuti, Lawrence (1995), *The Translator's Invisibility: A History of Translation*, London: Routledge.
Venuti, Lawrence (2013), *Translation Changes Everything: Theory and Practice*, London: Routledge.
Williams, Bernard (2006), *The Sense of the Past: Essays in the History of Philosophy*, edited by Myles Burnyeat, Princeton, NJ: Princeton University Press.

8

'Just ask the stones': Eco-translation, natural history and geomedia

Karin Littau

Novalis' theory of translation (published in 1798) is brief but expansive. It amounts to a few notes that sketch three kinds of translation: 'grammatical', 'transformative', 'mythic'.[1] This is a schema that applies to '[n]ot just books, everything can be translated in those three ways' (*Nicht bloss Bücher, alles kann auf diese drei Arten übersetzt werden*) (1987: 337). The idea that every-*thing* involves translation might be understood in the context of an arising global modernity around 1800 where translation becomes central to intercultural exchange.[2] Equally, however, it resonates with the then emerging concept of deep time and in salient respects anticipates Ursula Le Guin's concept of *geolinguistics* (1974) and Michael Cronin's *geotranslation* (2022). As a student of mining engineering Friedrich von Hardenberg, alias Novalis, was confronted first-hand with traces of deep time and earth's ancient history. The means by which the earth recorded that history – which might be called *geomedia*, that is, the rock strata and fossil records of now extinct animals – had provided material evidence that the planet was older than humanity by millions of years, thus putting geological and oryctognostic thinking at odds with the Bible's Mosaic timeline. In Novalis' lifetime *geohistory* had 'burst the limits of time'[3] and opened a chasm between an unimaginably long natural history and a relatively short human history, a chasm whose aftershocks echo in an epistemic rift between nature and culture. While Novalis' contemporary Henrich Steffens addressed this chasm by insisting that 'history itself had to become nature through and through if it hoped to assert itself as history in the context of nature, that is, in all aspects of its existence' (1908: 176–7 translation mine), Novalis treats this chasm as a translation issue. As I will show in this chapter, Novalis' 'speculative theory' of translation[4] seeks to bridge, in highly imaginative ways, the false dichotomy between nature and culture, pointing to a *natureculture* and a *medianature*[5] continuum that speaks to our present ecological concerns.

8.1. A prehistory of eco-translation

The rift that would see geology and history emerge as different disciplines over the nineteenth century, or, more pointedly put, that would recast planets and persons as located in distinct genres of time, has gained renewed attention in our own time as the extent of human-induced changes in the physical processes of the earth is becoming increasingly legible. If humans are geological agents responsible for global warming and species extinction, this means, as Dipesh Chakrabarty explains, that the 'geological now of the Anthropocene has become entangled with the now of human history', thus collapsing 'the distinction between human and natural histories' (2009: 212, 207). Key concerns for those in the environmental humanities have therefore revolved around how human history might be reconnected with earth history and how the 'convergence between geology, archaeology and history', as Chakrabarty puts it, might be usefully deployed in this regard and with view to a new historiography (219); or, how incommensurable temporal scales – acceleration and slowness, catastrophic tipping points and gradualism – and what Amitav Gosh (2016) calls their 'derangement' might be realigned and made into a global concern.

Novalis' writing on geology and mining, precisely because it addresses the entanglement between natural and human history, is pertinent to these issues, but so is his thinking on translation. While his 'mineral' fictions have made him a key figure of the pre-Anthropocene in literary studies, even a proto-petrocultural thinker (Groves 2020: 17–35), his translation theory has been often been overlooked, including as a potential antecedent of Anthropocene translation studies. 'The human alone does not speak – the universe *speaks* too – everything speaks – infinite languages' (*Der Mensch spricht nicht allein – auch das Universum spricht – alles spricht – unendliche Sprachen*), writes Novalis in 1798/9 (2007: 24, translation modified; 1993: §143). Two interrelated points follow from this claim: first, nature itself speaks, a stone speaks, mountains speak, plants speak and animals speak; in short, the inhuman and the non-human speak *too*, even though the human may not understand or even discern all the infinite languages – mineral, vegetable, animal – that the universe speaks.[6] Second, therefore, *among* the languages that the universe speaks are human languages. A further and interrelated point is articulated in Novalis' philosophical essay-poem *The Novices of Sais* (written between 1798 and 1799 and set in the ancient Egyptian city of Sais), where nature communicates in a cipher language of strange signs and hieroglyphs that are discernible 'everywhere', inviting decipherment. Nature communicates, he writes,

> in wings, eggshells, clouds and snow, in crystals and in stone formations, on ice-covered waters, on the inside and outside of mountains, of plants, beasts and men, in the lights of heaven, on scored disks of pitch or glass or in iron filings round a magnet, and in strange conjunctures of chance […]. In them we suspect a key to magic writing, even a grammar […].

(*auf Flügeln, Eierschalen, in Wolken, im Schnee, in Kristallen und in Steinbildungen, auf gefrierenden Wassern, im Innern und Äußern der Gebirge, der Pflanzen, der Tiere, der Menschen, in den Lichtern des Himmels, auf berührten und gestrichenen Scheiben von Pech und Glas, in den Feilspänen um den Magnet her, und sonderbaren Konjunkturen des Zufalls […]. In ihnen ahnet man den Schlüssel dieser Wunderschrift, die Sprachlehre derselben […]*).

(2005: 3; 1987: 95)[7]

In other words, translation is everywhere. Hence Novalis' is not just a thinking of translation but a translatory thinking,[8] revealing the translations among which thought itself figures: it expands translation into the realm of the mythic, the inorganic, the non-human, into deep time and, as we shall see, into the medial, and thus re-envelops thought within the world from which it emerges. Accordingly, Novalis' arch-romanticist claim prefigures solutions for which our contemporaries still plead.

If forms of communication are not limited to human language as Novalis suggests at the cusp of the nineteenth century and as new (eco)materialists emphasize in our own age, a reorientation of our thought-world is prerequisite and an expanded notion of translation[9] is called for, and with it a greater emphasis on the materialities of translation (Littau 2016). What is translated is not necessarily a natural language or text, and not necessarily spoken by Anthropos, written by human hand or intended for and thus accessible by *Homo sapiens*. Here, the candidates for translation or, for that matter, for history need not be the products of the invention of writing,[10] or stem from the medium of the book or its predecessor book forms, but might well be objects, or marks and traces on earth's surfaces. If so, we need to ask a new set of questions about translation and its material substrates, and focus neither primarily on verbal translation[11] nor on so-called 'artificial' or human-made media technologies as I have done elsewhere (Littau 2011), but also on elemental media, including geomedia, as I intend to do here.[12]

To this end, the aim in this chapter is to travel part of the way in company with Michael Cronin's ground-breaking work on eco-translation and historicize what he calls geo- and terra-centric translation narratives (2017; 2022) by going back to Novalis and the Jena romantics. Whereas Cronin develops an ethics of eco-translation, which applies anthropocenic and ecocritical concerns to translation studies, my aim is to develop a natural history of translation from which an eco-politics of translation may justly be derived. In other words, this chapter excavates an evolutionary history of translation, whereby translation developed out of earth's history. Here, eco-translational theory is not applied to the earth; translation itself emerges from the earth. As is demonstrable in nature-philosophical writings around 1800, culture is not at odds with nature but issues from and in it, which confronts us with a hierarchy which may well turn out to be non-reversible: 'without nature to produce human animals there can be neither culture nor politics, whereas without culture and politics there still can be nature' (Littau 2006: 12; see also 2017: 99). Given the copious writings by the Jena circle on nature, nature's language and translation, I will confine my present attention to Novalis' novel *Heinrich von Ofterdingen* (1802; 1987), translated as *Henry von Ofterdingen* (1992), with the occasional detour to his friend Ludwig Tieck's story *Der Runenberg* (1804; 1985), published in English as *The Rune Mountain* (2012) – two works which, set in mountains, caverns and mines, tell stone stories/histories (*Gesteingeschichten*) and give the lithic a voice. Through these works can be unearthed not only a prehistory of eco-translation but also an eco-translation prior to history.

8.2. Translating animal, vegetable and mineral languages

Novalis' untimely death at the age of twenty-eight meant that *Heinrich von Ofterdingen* (written 1799–1800) was never finished. It was posthumously published under the editorship of Friedrich Schlegel and Ludwig Tieck; and notes by both Tieck and Novalis exist that indicate how its second part might have been completed. It is a

Bildungsroman that mixes medieval road novel, fairy story and epic poetry, comprising several tales, each of which contributes to Heinrich becoming a poet. The novel is populated, as is Tieck's *The Rune Mountain*, by strangers (*Fremde*) who travel from one region or country to another, or from cultivated landscapes to deep forests and rugged mountain terrains and visit caverns/mines. Set in the Middle Ages, it recounts young Heinrich leaving his father's hometown of Eisenach in the north-east of modern-day Germany to travel south with his mother to her parental city of Augsburg. On his journey, which he undertakes in the company of merchants, he encounters war-drunk crusaders, the displaced and captive Saracen Zulima who speaks in broken German, a peripatetic and wise old miner, a learned hermit in a cave and the accomplished poet Klingsohr – each encounter occasioning a tale that he is told of other lands, some near, others far or foreign, or imagined.

Attention is drawn not only to his human companions' different languages and dialects but also to the languages of 'creatures' (*Kreaturen*), each of which 'clearly expressed its inner nature [...] in its own peculiar vernacular' (*ihre innere Natur [...] in einer eigentümlichen Mundart vernehmlich aussprach*) (1992: 77; 1987: 191). Such passages not only highlight the correlation between the language of nature and natural language but also make it clear that there is not one language of nature but many, just as there are diverse natural languages. As Kate Rigby puts it, '[t]he idea that language extends beyond the human plays an important role in German romantic thought and literature in the guise of the topos of "natural language" or the "language of nature" (*Natursprache*)' – an idea, she says, that makes *Natursprache* a precursor of biosemiotic theories of communication (2015: 33). That nature speaks to humans is not the preserve of fiction, or the stuff of fairy tales, or an anthropomorphic gesture. For instance, in a lecture from 1793 by the natural historian Karl Friedrich Kielmeyer, who Georges Cuvier famously sought out to be his teacher, 'I [NATURE]' gives a monologue that addresses humankind directly about their 'path of development' as a living species:

> the history of your race [*Geschlechts*] has permitted you to see only a small element of this path [...] Whether one day I will let your species too (like individuals) be replaced by another newer species [*Gattung*] – you need no information on that matter for now.
>
> (2021: 4–67)

I Nature can see more than we can and knows more about our species' history than we do. Novalis, who was familiar with Kielmeyer's ideas, similarly opens up a space for nature's auto-presentation in his writing.

Right at the beginning of *Heinrich von Ofterdingen* we are introduced to the languages of nature when Heinrich muses: 'Once I heard tell of the days of old, how animals and trees and cliffs talked with people then' (*Ich hörte einst von alten Zeiten reden; wie da die Tiere und Bäume und Felsen mit den Menschen gesprochen hätten*) (1992: 15; 1987: 130–1). This erstwhile communion with nature appears now lost. Alex Goodbody reads this passage as Heinrich's memory of a common *Ursprache* no longer shared (1984: 97); conversely, it might be read as a utopian panlingualism reminiscent of a golden age,[13] which Heinrich senses might be about to resume: 'I feel just as though they [animals and trees and cliffs] might start any moment now and I could tell by their looks what they wanted to say to me' (*Mir ist gerade so, als wollten sie allaugenblicklich anfangen, und als könnte ich es ihnen ansehen, was sie mir sagen wollten*) (1992: 15; 1987: 131). Although his sense perception is finely attuned to visual signs and body language, understanding verbal language is not without obstacles given limited linguistic abilities, as Heinrich acknowledges in the next sentence: 'There must be many words I do not know; if I knew more, I could grasp everything much better' (*Es muß noch viel Worte geben, die ich nicht weiß: wußte ich mehr, so könnte ich viel besser alles begreifen*) (1992: 15; 1987: 131). Novalis' thinking entails the acquisition of language skills which, as Reinhard Babel has pointed out, are requisite for any translator (Babel 2015: 76). Core therefore to communication with nature (animal, plant or stone) is the necessity of translation, if existence is to be meaningful in the cosmos. The implied ecocritical relevance is made explicit by Alice Kuzniar when she writes that what 'we find in Novalis [is] an intense desire to comprehend the diverse languages of nature combined with a keen consciousness of the inaccessibility of these languages if man does not try to escape the confines of his familiar, anthrocentric worldview' (2003: 435).

Indeed, we would be mistaken were we to assume that nature only talks to humans and that humankind is always the addressee or at the centre of nature's communications; rather, plants and animals also speak among themselves. According to Novalis' notes, he planned for the second part of the novel to have 'flowers and animals talk about humankind, religion, nature and sciences' (*Gespräche der Blumen und Tiere über Menschen, Religion, Natur und Wissenschaften*) (1987: 285).[14] This in effect not only creates a human-free communicative space but also decentres human forms of communication. Novalis gives all material forms (organic and otherwise) a voice so that they may interact, even 'intra-act'.[15] If anything, a more pronounced speaking platform is given to plants and stones than to animals, thus evading at least in part what Manuel De Landa so presciently called 'organic chauvinism' in the mid-1990s.[16] 'Just ask the stones, you'll be astonished when you hear them talk' (*Frage nur die Steine, du wirst erstaunen, wenn du sie reden hörst*) (2012: 70, translation modified; 1985: 203), says Christian in *The Rune Mountain* to his father, who prefers to speak with plants and deeply distrusts mountains and his son's lithic obsession, be this with sparkling gemstones or humble pebbles. For Christian, however, the 'once magnificent worlds of rocks' (*vormaliger herrlicher Steinwelten*), because of their primordiality, can tell us a great deal about earth's historicity and its geotrauma of being shaped and reshaped by long processes of upheaval, erosion, accretion and sedimentation, of which short-lived plants have no knowledge, or of which latecomers such as humans have little understanding. 'Whether anyone has ever understood the stones', Novalis writes in *The Novices of Sais*, 'I do not know [...] so rare [is] an understanding of the stone world' (2005: 91).

Neither Tieck nor Novalis privilege entities that are animate, living and lively over those that are inanimate, non-living, and inert – a binary bias towards the biological (humans, animals, plants) over and above the geological (rocks, stones, mountains). Rather, if the earth itself, as Dennis Mahoney suggests, is 'a living creature'[17] that communicates, or more pointedly still, if the earth – this mighty rock – is an animate thing that speaks in the ur-language of things, then, to borrow Jeffrey Cohen's words, 'lithic existence' is not 'a blank materiality, a thing unthought so that thoughtful things may flourish in their self-awareness' (2015: 50). Rocks and stones do not depend on 'thoughtful things' like humans but have multiple existences and historicities that precede humans and their history. Moreover earth is an animate, living creature, not because it is an organic entity, a Gaia figure,[18] but because it is creative, creating itself by turning heat into stone, and transforming rocks into sediments, etc. with little prospect of a beginning or end.[19] Put differently, if rocks and stones speak and inscribe their histories in geomedia, they are endowed with what Jane Bennett calls 'the vitality of matter'[20] that gives them and, by extension, all of nature agency and a function that is never just background or man's workshop.[21]

While it is the case that Novalis' speaking animals, plants and rocks appear at once arcane and queer, his romanticism is pertinent to ecocriticism, because it imagines an 'entangledness' (*Verbundenseyn*) (Novalis 2003: §48, my translation) of humans-and-nature. And, although Novalis did not articulate his notion of mythic translation with reference to translating animal, vegetable and mineral languages, it lends itself to such a reading, not least because mythic translation embraces an 'ideal' that may not exist in reality or, as he says, for which 'there exists still no complete pattern'.[22] Closer to our own moment in history and in a similar vein, Ursula Le Guin's speculative fiction imagines communicative possibilities with nature that too involve translation.[23] In her 1974 short story 'The Author of the Acacia Seeds and Other Extracts from the Journal of Therolinguistics', Le Guin addresses 'the difficulty of translation' of non-human languages (1974: 217), such as Ant, Penguin or Dolphin, which might involve translating 'script written almost entirely in wings, neck, and air' (217) or 'kinetic' text forms (218). As one of the story's characters, the President of the Learned Society, complains: while much had been done in the field of therolinguistics, by contrast, phytolinguistics and geolinguistics were under-researched. Although mid-twentieth-century scientists and artists, the President continues, had once mocked the idea that 'Dolphin would ever be comprehensible' (222), the phytolinguists of the future will find it just as ludicrous that there was ever a time when we 'couldn't even read Eggplant' (222). Moreover, the 'first geolinguist' after them will 'smile at our ignorance' when digging beneath the 'newly deciphered lyrics of the lichen on the north face of Pike's Peak', because what the geolinguist will discover there is 'the still less communicative, still more passive, wholly atemporal, cold, volcanic poetry of the rocks: each one a word spoken, how long ago, by the earth itself, in the immense solitude, the immenser community, of space' (222). Her science fiction story thus picks up on the biocentric bias that still persists into the future. While Le Guin's story makes translation – and literary translation especially – an important aspect of the *arts of living on this planet*,[24] it is her emphasis on geolinguistics that interests me, precisely because stone is primal matter – the ground, so to speak as we shall see, in which translation first emerges.

Le Guin's and Novalis' approaches to translation also resonate with those in contemporary translation studies that have sought to expand translation into the new and innovative realms of the post-human and/or non-lingual. When Cronin advances the notion of 'terratranslation' that would extend to 'multiversal translation between species' (2022: 11) and the notion of 'geotranslation' that would seek 'to interpret non-written material remains from the past that extend indefinitely beyond recorded human history' (7), he does so for pressing ethical reasons.

> The biosphere can typically be threatened by climate change, exponential human population growth, biotic impoverishment, reduction of biodiversity or renewable resource depletion, to name but a few factors. In the case of the tradosphere, the principal danger comes from the collapse of translation systems that allow humans to interact in a viable and sustainable way with other sentient and non-sentient beings on the planet.
>
> (Cronin 2017: 71)

With the concept of the 'tradosphere' as 'the sum of all translation systems on the planet', Cronin seeks to draw our attention to the interconnectedness between humans and non-humans, which has now become so out of kilter, and the need therefore for 'a viable theory of translation for the coming times' (2017: 72). Similarly, Hedwig Fraunhofer's proposal for including 'plant translation' in translation studies to foster 'communication with the natural world' is motivated by a sense that 'the Anthropocene [is] the result of mistranslation' (2022: 49), in effect, a 'translation failure that is now threatening an entire planet' (42). Both Cronin and Fraunhofer are thus concerned with the role that translation and/or translation studies might play at this moment in earth's evolutionary history, namely the Anthropocene. Relatedly, Kobus Marais' theory of 'biosemiotic translation' (2019: 54) lends itself to ecocritical concerns as Cronin has shown (2022: 4). Additionally, by adopting a Peircean model, Marais widens the scope of translation by including sign-based communication, such as non-verbal communication between human and non-human animals, and chemical communication between Acacia trees (2019: 50). When he argues, drawing on Peirce, that '[t]he chemist who analyses the stone and the paleontologist who studies the fossil of the fish are both fulfilling a translation function, creating an interpretant from a material representamen' (111), it is clear that translation exceeds and unsettles its traditional remit of interlingual translation as 'translation proper' in Roman Jakobson's sense (1966: 233). This translation function, however, could not be fulfilled were it not for the material base of the stone on which the code is inscribed. As the medialogist Régis Debray once said, 'the code is thus not everything' because it depends on and is inseparable from its 'material embodiment' (1996: 74). Where, that is, there is embodiment occurs, something *is* embodied that had not been, or: matter becomes medium.

8.3. Translating the hieroglyphs of nature

The geologists who examined stone and the palaeontologists who examined fossils around 1800 too were translators, and overtly so, since they cast themselves in the role of would-be Champollions of nature's hieroglyphic and/or runic inscriptions. The romantic fascination with hieroglyphs cannot be underestimated especially in the period between the Rosetta Stone's discovery in 1799, its colonial transplantation from Egypt to the British Museum (which itself is a form of translation) and its decipherment by Jean-François Champollion in 1822. Champollion worked from an inked lithographic copy that had been taken of the carved inscriptions – a printing process which allowed the message on the stone to be circulated among scholars (Allan 2016: 46–7). I mention this lithographic method because it goes to the heart of the argument of this section of the chapter, namely that earth's materials become the media for writing and for translation.

Before the Rosetta Stone was moved to its place of exhibition, the floor of the museum had to be strengthened given its sheer weight. Since then, the stele with its chiselled hieroglyphic markings – standing for puzzle, a lost language (even a lost *Ursprache*) and the possibilities of translation across place and time – has been a magnet of fascination. Even after Champollion's translation, the hieroglyphic imagination continued to cast hieroglyphics as a *Wunderschrift* (wonder script) and a *Rätselschrift* (enigma script) that would, once unlocked, 'yield undreamed-of information' of lost pasts or buried memories, as Freud famously put it in 1896 when he compared the work of the psychoanalyst to the archaeologist (1953–74: 192). As I am writing this, the British Museum has just opened a major exhibition, entitled *Hieroglyphs. Unlocking Ancient Egypt* (13 October 2022–19 February 2023) to commemorate the 200-year anniversary of the hieroglyphs' decipherment by Champollion.

Not quite script and not quite image, but an intermedial mesh of both, hieroglyphs came to represent, as the Egyptologist Jan Assmann and the media historian Aleida Assmann have pointed out, a *Dingschrift* (thing-script) (A. and J. Assmann 2003: 20) – 'an alphabet of things, and not of words', as Sir Thomas Browne had remarked in the seventeenth century (qtd. J. and A. Assmann 2003: 22). Supposedly, their markings stood in a direct relation to the world of things, referring neither to concepts nor to sounds – an assumption that Champollion proved wrong. Even before the Romantics, hieroglyphs came to be regarded as a writing system that did not just transcribe a particular language, but 'nature itself' (Assmann 2003: 272). It was precisely this association with *Naturschrift* (script of nature) that made hieroglyphs into the prototype of the romantic artwork per se (Assmann 2003: 274). For, the opportunity to decipher and grasp their meaning would be 'nothing less than an attempt to regain a true relationship with nature' (Schaber 1973: 38) – hence, Novalis' allusion in *Novices of Sais* to hieroglyphs as a *Chiffernschrift* (a cipher script) of nature's strange signs. What *Chiffernschrift* as *Naturschrift* opens up is the possibility of nature's auto-presentation, or what Antje Pfannkuchen so aptly has referred to as the 'self-writing of nature' (2015: 140).

Nature here is not just conjured up by the artist's imagination; nature is the artist, whose foreign signs the human artist transcribes and translates. As the nature philosopher Friedrich Wilhelm Joseph von Schelling put it succinctly in 1803:

> Nature for us is an ancient author, who wrote in hieroglyphs, and whose leaves are colossal, as the Artist says in Goethe. Even those who want to investigate nature only empirically need to know nature's *language* so that utterances now extinct may become intelligible. The same is true of philology in the higher sense of the term. The earth is a book made up of fragments and rhapsodies from very different

ages. Each mineral is a real philological problem. In geology we still await the genius who will analyse the earth and show its composition as [the philologist Friedrich August] Wolf analysed Homer.

(*Die Natur ist für uns ein uralter Autor, der in Hieroglyphen geschrieben hat, dessen Blätter kolossal sind, wie der Künstler bei Goethe sagt. Eben derjenige, der die Natur bloß auf dem empirischen Wege erforschen will, bedarf gleichsam am meisten* Sprach-Kenntniß *von ihr, um die für ihn ausgestorbene Rede zu verstehen. Im höheren Sinn der Philologie ist dasselbe wahr. Die Erde ist ein Buch, das aus Bruchstücken und Rhapsodien sehr verschiedener Zeiten zusammengesetzt ist. Jedes Mineral ist ein wahres philologisches Problem. In der Geologie wird der Wolf noch erwartet, der die Erde ebenso wie den Homer zerlegt und ihre Zusammensetzung zeigt.*)

(1966: 40, translation modified; 1856–61: 246–7)

Schelling brings together two related motifs, both of which echo those of his contemporaries, including Novalis: one is the trope of the hieroglyphs of nature, the other of the book of nature with immensely large pages. Depicting stone with hieroglyphic markings, or with runic-like markings, and drawing attention to its 'typographic characters', as the Scottish geologist James Hutton did in his book *Theory of the Earth* (1795: 106), or casting nature in medial terms as Schelling does, and as Charles Lyell will do some decades later, and subsequently also adopted by Charles Darwin, was commonplace in this period.[25] Earth was variously described as a book,

James Hutton, *Theory of the Earth, With Proofs and Illustrations*, In Four Parts, Vol. I, Plate II (Edinburgh: William Creech, 1795).

a library or archive, or an ancient monument. Lyell famously described the study of earth in terms of 'the alphabet and grammar of geology' (1997: 356), and Darwin referred to 'the geological record' as having been 'written in a changing dialect' and of earth consisting of a 'volume', with missing chapters, and pages of just a few lines each (2008: 229). Changing dialect means that earth has changed and transformed, and therefore has a historicity, something previous ages had overlooked, because they saw earth's staticness not as slow history but as nature's constancy.

Although contemporary critics almost exclusively refer to Lyell's and Darwin's descriptions of earth in terms of metaphors of reading, strictly speaking they are metaphors of translation,[26] or perhaps not mere metaphors at all. After all, are books and their precursor book forms not made of earthy things such as stones, plants and animals? Do the stone tablet, the papyrus roll or the parchment codex not also belong to earth's materials? And are processes that go into printing not also based on earth's minerals and metals? Is the book, including its precursor and modern versions, not made of non-human things like clay, papyrus reed, animal skin, flax, wood pulp, silicon, lithium, and so on, harvested, prepared or extracted from earth? Or relatedly, how have these non-human materials been physically transplanted around the globe, when, where, to what effect; that is, how have natures been translated, as Alan Bewell (2017) asks, in the context of colonialist, environmental legacies? And in turn, how have natures in translation, say the importation of this or that plant, changed not just landscapes or whole ecosystems, as Bewell shows, but also the materials for bookish production at the microlevel – a natural history produced not just on paper but as paper? Is the history of written text not therefore also a history of intersections of culture and nature, of meaning and medium, inviting us to combine book history, nature's materialities and the environmental humanities, as Joshua Calhoun (2020) has done for early modern studies by scrutinizing the material nature of the page? In a nutshell, is the history of media not literally a translation of nature and as such also a natural history of and as media?

8.4. Natural histories of translation and media

In a recent essay on the profound implications of the material/medial turn for translation studies, Karen Bennett makes this concluding remark: 'it may now be time to consider the even more audacious integration of the natural world as falling within the remit of translation' (2022: 69). One way in which to approach this task is to take the requisite steps towards a geomedia history of translation. The point here is that pursuing translation into the terrains of natural history must also turn into a natural history of media, or perhaps, into a history of the geomedia that exhibits the first act of translation, the first act of *setting something onto something else*, to take the composite word in German for translation – *Übersetzung* – literally: a setting down of one upon another, that is, a *deposition* legible in a script articulated by and as stratification. *Übersetzung* thus invites a conception of translation as adding layers to works in the cultural record. Moreover, the stratification model of translation would entail that we open the book of nature to pay attention not only to what is there written but to what it is written upon. In so doing, we find that even the attempt to separate human from natural history will have been written, primordially, in stone. Put differently, a medium *will have been first* only *once* something has been placed upon it, once an *Über-setzung* has taken place. This entails a reciprocal relation: one cannot record without a medium, and *it will be* the recording that makes the medium into the medium it thereby becomes. Rock, that is, would not be a medium unless and until something (a script of jewels, a chiselled text, a cave painting, the heat and pressure differentials revealing stratification, etc.) is recorded on it, and there would not be a recording without the rock that could become a medium. And that is why there is an eco-translation prior to history: a primordial *Übersetzung*, so to speak, is an account of the *first emergence of recording media*. Translation *always also* takes place physically.

The earth is the first recording medium when it translates heat to stone, transforms stone to sand and so on and so forth. It records its multi-layered histories in stones and fossils, inside mountains, on bedrock and in rock faces. This is why the mineralogist and the miner are privileged figures in Novalis' and Tieck's respective stories: these figures have first-hand knowledge of earth's work and workings, its stratigraphic translations from one material form into another, and thus witness the autobiography the earth wrote in jewels and deposited deep in its colossal strata over unimaginable scales of time. When Heinrich and his companions, led by the wise old miner, first enter the cavern, the spectre of Georges Cuvier looms large:

> what engaged the attention of all particularly was the countless number of bones and teeth which covered the floor. Many were preserved; others had marks of integration, and those that stuck out of the wall here and there appeared to be petrified. Most of them were of unusual size and strength. The old miner was delighted by these vestiges of a primeval age; only the farmers felt a bit eery, for they regarded them as clear traces of near-by beasts of prey, however convincingly the old miner showed that the bones were indications of inconceivable antiquity [...].

> *(was die Aufmerksamkeit Aller vorzüglich beschäftigte, war die unzählige Menge von Knochen und Zähnen, die den Boden bedeckten. Viele waren völlig erhalten, an andern sah man Spuren der Verwesung, und die, welche aus den Wänden hin und wieder hervorragten, schienen steinartig geworden zu sein. Die meisten waren von unmöglicher Größe und Stärke. Der Alter freute sich über die Überbleibsel einer uralten Zeit; nur die den Bauern war nicht wohl dabei zumute, den sie hielten sie für deutliche Spuren naher Raubtiere, so überzeugend ihnen auch der Alte die Zeichen eines undenklichen Altertums daran aufwies [...].)*
>
> (1992: 78; 1987: 192)

That no human fossils had ever been found, as Cuvier's paleontological work had made clear, despite Johann Jakob Scheuchzer famously mistaking a fossilized salamander for a human skeleton,[27] was archival evidence of a history before, and without, humans. Thus, the descent into the cavern/mine is synonymous with the discovery of earth's historicity. Novalis' miner looks to the mine for knowledge about this prehistoric world but also for wisdom. He rejects what we would now call resource extractivism and sees the subterranean world of mines as 'hidden treasure chambers of nature' (*verborgenen Schatzkammern der Natur*) (1992: 66; 1987: 180) and wonderous landscapes with trees laden with ruby fruits that grow out of crystal soil (see 1992: 88; 1987: 202). This magic of mining[28] chars in the present-day context of the Anthropocene, even when the miner makes it clear that this underground world is not to be abused for profit but should be cherished for what it offers for the common good of all. Before I return to this issue, I want to stay with the idea that the mine is a source of knowledge about earth's history (which too is a form of extractivism) and a place to marvel earth's artistry.[29]

Heinrich too senses earth's tumultuous history when he enters the cavern and wonders about the vibrant world deep below: 'might it be possible that beneath our feet a world of its own is stirring with tremendous life?' (*wäre es möglich, daß unter unsern Füßen eine eigene Welt in einem ungeheuren Leben sich bewegte*) (1987: 192–3, my translation). But this is not a world untouched by humans since they also find fresh footprints that belong to the hermit who has made the cavern his home. The mine is thus a transition zone between the traces of natural history and the imprints of human history, a 'latent Anthropocene' to borrow Jason Groves' term (2020: 3). That the cavern contains both human footprints and fossils of extinct animals, each representing traces from different times and of differing durations, is indicative of the multi-layeredness of history, what Reinhart Koselleck calls 'the simultaneity of the nonsimultaneous' in history (2018: 45).[30] In salient respects the novel lays some of the groundwork for understanding Koselleck's geological metaphor for history (*Geschichte*) as 'sediments [or strata or layers] of time' (*Zeit-schichten*), where 'time' (*Zeit*) and 'strata' (*Schichten*) are moulded together to make history (*Geschichte*) – terms which in German hark back to 'rock strata' (*Gesteinsschichten*).[31] Novalis literalizes this, especially in Heinrich's cavern scene: he tells stories/hi*stories* (*Geschichten*) about rocks (*Gestein*).

Indeed, human history is addressed head on through the figure of the hermit, Count of Hohenzollern, who is introduced to us as a scholar of history books. Our first encounter with this figure is as a reader of a large book laid out on a stone slab, surrounded by other books scattered on the ground, as if emerging from the soil itself. What ensues is a lengthy exchange with the miner about the interrelations between natural and human history. That the hermit studies human history inside a cavern, which is the locus of earth history, suggests that human history is embedded in earth's history.[32] This is an important inversion, neither is 'human history a recapitulation of the *whole* history of the earth' to borrow Nicholas Rupke's words (1990: 256) nor is human history the core or centre of history per se; that, rather, is the earth. Human history is repositioned as part of a larger non-human history. In other words, human history is *of* earth history, a smaller part of a larger whole. The same is true of media history. If earth itself is a storage and recording medium, then the presence in the cavern of the medium of the book, which too is a storage and recording medium, is a medium-within-medium.

Heinrich is fascinated by the hermit's books and 'leafed through them with endless joy' (*blätterte mit unendlicher Lust umher*) (1992: 90; 1987: 204). We are told that each was 'large and beautifully illuminated' (*großen schöngemalten Schriften*) (1992: 90; 1987: 204), thus drawing attention to a materiality these works share with the medieval codex. One book takes his interest especially. It is written in a language Heinrich does not understand but contains pictures which appear to depict scenes from his life. He thus recognizes himself in the book, reading the very book he is holding. The book, which is also a book-within-the-book, is not finished and its last pages remain obscure. That this book contains images in sequence which add up to a story anticipates the mid-nineteenth-century, proto-cinematic flip book (whereby successive drawings and later photographs are rapidly flipped by the thumb to create the illusion of motion), which had its forerunner in medieval miniatures, as researchers at the University of Heidelberg discovered when they digitally scanned pages from the Stuttgart codex from around 1470 of the *Sigenot* epic and found that the illuminations had been sequentially arranged with such frame by frame precision, along the principle of the storyboard or even the flip book, that when scrolling through the pages on the computer screen, the images could be watched like an animated 'film'.[33] Alice Kuzniar (1999: 219) does not pick up on this particular media-historical point but makes a larger one about '[t]echnologization of appearances', 'accelerated vision' and movementation in Novalis, when she points to the numerous references to signs, figures and images that appear to be mobile and mobilized by variegated light sources from sparkling stones to flickering flamelets to projected beans.[34] Heinrich's book is thus already a medial *Übersetzung*, comprised as it is of medial layers that contain traces of both written and optical media technologies.

Something similar occurs in Tieck's story, when Christian is handed a book – or rather, a stone tablet – from a cavern in the Rune Mountain by the *Waldweib* (forest woman). The tablet comes from a mountain, and therefore from earth, and is made of stone which is earth's primal matter. Moreover, it comes from the Rune Mountain, the name of which references an ancient writing system (Gasperi 2015: 420), which suggests that the mountain and, by extension, nature write in runes. The story thus foregrounds stone as an ancient recording medium both in the geological and archaeological sense. Inlaid with sparkling stones, rubies and diamonds, '[t]he tablet appeared to form a fantastical, incomprehensible figure with its various colours and lines' (*Die Tafel schien eine wunderliche unverständliche Figur mit ihren unterschiedlichen Farben und Linien zu bilden*) (2012: 61, translation modified; 1985: 192). It variously blinds and soothes Christian's eyes with its colourful shimmer, but its cryptic design conveys no clear message other than lore for him and repulsion for his father.

> My son, my heart shudders when I look at the contours of these stones and, pondering, sense the meaning of this strange syntax; see how coldly it sparkles, what gruesome looks these stones give [...]. Throw away this inscription [...]
>
> (*Mein Sohn, mir schaudert recht im Herzen, wenn ich die Lineamente dieser Steine betrachte und ahnend den Sinn dieser Wortfügung errate; sieh her, wie kalt sie funkeln, welche grausame Blicke sie von sich geben [...]. Wirf diese Schrift weg [...]*)
> (2012: 72, translation modified; 1985: 204)

On the one hand, lingual translation is evoked by reference to hieroglyphic discourse and the task to translate nature's strange signs into a comprehensible human language; here 'concretized' in the stone tablet, as Carlos Gasperi points out, 'by way of petrification into a language of magical stones' (2015: 420). On the other hand, the 'magic tablet' (*magische Tafel*) (2012: 72; 1985: 204) evokes the media technology of the magic lantern with its phantasmagoric projections. For, the capacity of the stone tablet to generate shimmering images suggests that affordances specific to the magic lantern have been translated – or transmediated – into the stone tablet, thus inserting an additional medial layer into the stone. The stone tablet contains at least two medialities, perhaps even prefiguring, as Groves notes, the touch-screen tablet device (2020: 260).

As we have seen, the earth is overtly described as a book by geologists in this period; Heinrich encounters books deep inside the earth and Christian receives a book of sorts that too comes from inside the earth. Translation is omnipresent here as both reading and recording, and thus as irreducibly both semantic and medial. That is, translation is omnipresent both as readings of a record and as recordings of these readings: the book and the stone tablet bear the traces of strange figures (suggestive of hieroglyphs and/or runes) that invite translation; the same figures sometimes also appear to be in motion, and thus point to intermedial translation. On the one hand, storage devices such as stone tablets, books, flip books, magic lantern slides manifestly belong to the world of culture, as do their modes of inscription. On the other hand, these objects also belong to nature, are *of* nature. Nature as book (Schelling, Lyell, Darwin) is turned into the book in nature (Novalis, Tieck). Why else would the hermit's books be strewn over the ground, the uppermost stratum of the earth, or Tieck's tablet be bejewelled, made of the mountain's stone? Each book scene is an image of geomediation and therefore of the natural history of culture. Novalis' and Tieck's fictions do not make nature into culture but make culture an integral part of nature. Put differently, human history is integrated into earth history, what Donna Haraway (2003) would call *natureculture*, and media history is integrated into earth history, what Jussi Parikka (2011) calls *medianature*.

8.5. Geomedia and translation

Among Novalis' notes for a romantic encyclopaedia, he includes this: 'PHYSICAL HISTORY: Enquiry into the question whether or not nature has essentially changed with the growth of culture?' (*PHYSIK[ALISCHE] GESCH[ICHTE]: Untersuchung der Frage ob sich nicht die Natur mit wachsender Kultur wesentlich geändert hat*) (2007: 8, translation modified; 1993: §54). In this note Novalis foreshadows the implications of his own profession, namely that of a mining engineer, and the effect that mining has had on the environment since the late eighteenth century, which is the date often given to the beginnings of the Anthropocene – although it could be dated earlier, starting with colonialization, plantations and intense farming, or perhaps even extending the timeline as far back as humans' first use of fire. The magic of mining that we encountered in the figure of the old miner is alien to us in the context of our fossil-fuelled modernity that now threatens the entire planet. While it is tempting to 'recover from Novalis's subterranean sages an ecophilosophical ethos' that could direct us to 'an alternative way of thinking and doing (or desisting from) mining' than that which prevails in our profit-driven model of intense resource extractivism (Rigby 2017: 112), it is just as important to expose the descent into the mine as a descent to the dark side of ecology, as Groves has suggested (2020: 22). What is brought back to the surface, into the light of day so to speak, is not just an enlightened sense of the inorganic liveliness of nature that stirs below our feet. The descent into the mine also brings to the surface, in the sense of making visible, a hidden complicity with environmental devastation and what Heather Sullivan calls 'dirty nature' from which, she says, Novalis and his contemporaries tended to look away (2011: 121). While, that is, they importantly refocus our attention on the grounds of our history in the earth's, they tended not to see that, if rock layers revealed awe-inspiring vistas of deep time, the mechanism of this revelation augurs and accelerates end-times for all life.

Their ecocritical deficit notwithstanding, however, Novalis and Tieck irrevocably recast the earth as a medium that makes legible the transformations and traumas in and between its stony layers. If so, when does media history begin? Indeed, what is the difference between 'natural' and 'artificial' media? Media theory has addressed these questions and drawn attention to the imprints and inscriptions of human history in the geologic record in distinct ways. John Durham Peters' work, for instance, has expanded the study of media into geological, deep time, arguing that earth as a repository of readable data too is a medium (2003; 2016) and that media therefore encompass not just technical but also elemental media. This is a reorientation, he argues, which is 'fully relevant in a time when our most pervasive surrounding environment is technological and nature [...] is drenched with human manipulation' (2016: 2). Like Peters' entangling of geology and media, Parikka too has made a 'return to earth',[35] focusing on mines and mining especially. It is from the depth of the mine that we can excavate the prehistory of media and examine the materialities of media: 'the depths of mines', Parikka says, are 'essential places for the emergence of technical media culture' (2014: 6). Our media technologies come out of mines, they come out of the earth, but they also go back into the earth as toxic substances, and thus become part of earth's history in the future. We only need to think of the lithium that powers the battery of the computer. Its extraction in inhumane and so is its waste disposal. 'Media are *of* nature, and return *to* nature', writes Parikka (2011), which is why extraction and waste disposal are inextricably linked. Paradoxically, this is also why the computer is 'millions, even billions of years old' (Parikka 2015: back cover) and why dumping its components will seep contaminants into bodies now[36] and into the deep future. Here, too, the distinction between artificial, technological, human-made media and natural media is not as clear-cut as we might think.

The inscriptions of human history in the geologic record – plastiglomerates for instance – leave their marks and scars on earth when plastic amalgamates with stone. This too is *Über-setzung*: plastic is *über-setzt*, set *upon* stone. Throughout earth's long history geomediation has made such acts of translation visible in/on stone. If so, when does translation history start? This question prompts us to dig more deeply into the *raw* and *crude* materialities of translation. From a book- and media-historical perspective, for instance, we might consider how raw materials – such as stone or nature's other non-human plant- or animal-based materials – have shaped or are shaping writing and translation.[37] Or, nudging the issue closer to the environmental humanities, Michael

Cronin's work has indicated new paths for thinking about translation ecocritically, including taking into account resource extractivism and exuberance in terms of just how much energy high-tech networked translation saps and burns (2017: 6). When viewed through the lens of the energy humanities, we would have to rethink, as Patricia Yaeger (2011) and Imre Szeman (2011) have suggested for the field of literary studies, how we might frame our historical inquiries. To apply their thinking to translation studies: what would happen if we framed our historical inquiries of translation not according to centuries (the eighteenth century, nineteenth century, twentieth century) or periods (the Enlightenment) or movements (Romanticism, realism, post/modernism), but in relation to 'Wood, Tallow, Coal, Whale Oil, Gasoline, Atomic Power, and Other Energy Sources' (Yaeger 2011: 5), precisely those things that have made our media and cultural products possible in the first place? In what units of time or according to what spatial coordinates (regional, national, continental, planetary) would we then organize our studies? To ask about the material conditions of translation and how these changed and are changing in tandem with specific energy sources would require a shift from cultural to natural history.

Such an approach might even shed light on why George Steiner posits translation as a form of 'open-cast min[ing]' in *After Babel* (1975/1998: 314), a metaphor which has vexed translation scholars.[38] Yet, if we follow through the chain of associations of Steiner's four-pointed hermeneutic model for translation – trust, extraction, appropriation, reparation – and seize on wordings such as 'the shell smashed and the vital layers stripped', 'materially thinner', 'empty scar in the landscape', 'despoliation', 'importation', 'consumed', 'energies and resources', 'piston-stroke', 'disequilibrium throughout the system by taking away', 'violent transport', 'economic', 'compensation', 'conservation' (1998: 314–19) in the order in which they appear in his text, a pattern emerges that is expressive of what Yaeger calls an 'energy unconscious' (2011: 306): a hydrocarbon culture which not only motors cars, drives economies, oils the modern war machine but oozes into all aspects of our un/conscious lives. The acknowledgement page in *After Babel* is signed off by Steiner and dated October 1973, the same month that OPEC declared their intent to cut oil production, the culminative act of a bubbling oil crisis in that year. Am I extracting too much meaning here? Through a petrocultural lens, the 'shell' is more likely to be the fossil of plankton once buried by sediments and cooked by heat and pressure, and now the source for oil, than the 'eggshell' that Brian O'Keeffe (2021: 218) sees in Steiner's choice of words; and the 'metaphorics of consumption' (O'Keeffe 2021: 226) less about feeding stomachs and more about oil addiction; which is to say that all the talk of extraction, energy, resources, economics and finally reparation do make sense in the context of drilling for oil, digging up fossil fuels, plundering of earth, and colonialism. So, when Steiner says that 'words have […] their concavities and force of tectonic suggestion' (1998: 308), we should perhaps take this literally. And here we are back in mining territory and with Novalis to give the last word to the miner, who translates into human language, one can assume, what the rocks told him: 'nature has no desire to be the exclusive possession of any single individual' (*Die Natur will nicht der ausschließliche Besitz eines einzigen sein*) (1992: 70, translation modified; 1987: 184).

Notes

1. According to Novalis: '[g]rammatical translations are translations in the ordinary sense' (*[g]rammatische Übersetzungen sind Übersetzungen im gewöhnlichen Sinn*) and '[t]ransforming translations, if they are to be authentic, are of the highest poetic spirit [...] The true translator of this kind must in effect be an artist' (*Zu den veränderten Übersetzungen gehört, wenn sie echt sein sollen, der höchste, poetische Geist [...] Der wahre Übersetzer dieser Art muß in der Tat der Künstler selbst sein*); by contrast, 'mythic translations are translations of the highest style [...] They do not give us the actual work of art, but its ideal. There exists, I believe, still no complete pattern of this' (*Mythische Übersetzungen sind Übersetzungen im höchsten Stil. [...] Sie geben uns nicht das wirkliche Kunstwerk, sondern das Ideal derselben. Noch existiert, wie ich glaube kein ganzes Muster derselben*) (1987: 337, my translation).
2. Intercultural exchange is tinged with German nationalism in Novalis (2014: 212).
3. Rudwick (2005: 506) uses this phrase after Georges Cuvier.
4. This phrase is by Berman (1992: 103–22), who explores Novalis' translation theory in relation to natural languages, whereas I explore it in relation to the languages of nature.
5. For 'natureculture', see Haraway (2003); for the reworking of this term into 'mediaculture', see Parikka (2011).
6. That nature speaks is also a theme in Shelley's poem 'Mont Blanc' (1816): 'Thou hast a voice, great mountain [...] not understood / By all'.
7. For a fascinating take on the significance of Novalis' reference to 'scored disks of pitch or glass' in relation to 'sound-figures' and '*nature-writing* by way of electricity', see Pfannkuchen (2021).
8. The Jena romantics' entire understanding of literature, as Huyssen has shown, is '*übersetzerisch*' (translatory) (1969: 145).
9. There has been a noticeable increase in publications over the past decade that have expanded the remit of translations studies; see Bassnett and Johnston (2019) who call this an 'outward turn'.
10. On this point and on the expansion of the discipline of history into deep time, see Tamm (2019: 4–5).
11. That translation is not necessarily lingual or textual, but variously semiotic, multimodal, visual, performative, sensory, experiential, speculative, medial and material, has gained traction in translation studies of late; see for instance, Cronin (2017), Marais (2019), Weissbrod and Kohn (2019).
12. I am taking my cue here from Peters, who has explored geology as an inquiry into media (2003). Elsewhere, he makes an elegant case why media studies might wish to switch focus from *media as environments* to *environments as media*, and thus expand to include elemental media, see Peters (2016: 3).
13. The golden age, Novalis says elsewhere, is a time when words would 'plasticise' (*plastisieren*) and 'musicalize' (*musizieren*) (1987: 437, my translation) – a formulation that is as relevant to multimodal translation as to the intermedial relations between art forms.
14. Additionally, his notes suggest that he was planning to have Heinrich transform into 'Flower – Animal – Stone – Star' at the end of the novel, following, he says, Jakob Böhme's thinking (Novalis 1987: 283).
15. 'Intra-action' is Karen Barad's alternative term for interaction, through which 'agency' can be understood 'as not an inherent property of an individual or human

to be exercised, but as a dynamism of forces', as Whitney Stark explains, 'in which all designated "things" are constantly exchanging and diffracting, influencing and working inseparably' (online at: https://newmaterialism.eu/almanac/i/intra-action.html).

16   See interview with De Landa, given at the 1996 *VirtualFutures* conference at the University of Warwick, where De Landa ushered in a 'geological turn' that arguably gave rise to the new materialism; see also De Landa's book (1997), where he explains that 'organic chauvinism' has led us 'to underestimate' not just 'the vitality of processes of self-organisation' but also the dependency relation of both 'living creatures and their inorganic counterparts [...] on intense flows of energy and materials' (1997: 103–4). Insofar as earth is self-organizing, it is productive, producing itself.

17   Although Mahoney makes this point in relation to *Henry von Ofterdingen*, it is just as applicable to *The Rune Mountain* (1992: 119).

18   For a critique of the biologism inherent in the Gaia figure, see De Landa (1996).

19   The geologist James Hutton famously made this point (also picked up by Charles Lyell) in his *Theory of the Earth*: 'The result, therefore, of this physical inquiry is, that we find no vestige of a beginning, – no prospect of an end' (1795: 200).

20   As Bennett explains, 'Why advocate the vitality of matter? Because my hunch is that the image of dead or throroughly instrumentalized matter feeds human hubris and our earth-destroying fantasies of conquest and consumption' (2010: ix).

21   The idea that earth is man's workshop, that is, that earth is 'put on the rack' to give up its secrets or treasures, is Francis Bacon's.

22   See endnote 1.

23   Le Guin and Novalis share a conviction of the importance of translation: for Le Guin 'the act of writing is itself translating' (1989: 112), and for Novalis 'all poetry is translation' (2014: 213).

24   Le Guin presented sections from her short story at the 2014 conference *Arts of Living on a Damaged Planet*, the proceedings of which are in Tsing et al. eds. (2017).

25   On Cuvier, see Outram (1984: 141–60); on Lyell and Darwin, see Beer (1996: 95–114) and Peters (2003).

26   Mehne (2008) makes this mistake, despite citing evidence which points to metaphors of translation rather than reading.

27   Scheuchzer had ascribed to the fossil the name *Homo Diluvii Testis* (The Human Witness of the Flood, 1726), see Rudwick (2005: 500).

28   As Ziolkowski notes, 'the figure of the miner and the image of the mine helps distinguish German Romantic literature not only from German literature of the ages preceding and following, but also [...] from contemporary English Romantic literature' (1990: 19), where mines were associated with coal around 1800 rather than silver and gold given that industrialization happened much earlier in Britain than in Germany (25). See also Weiler (2020), who discusses the contradictions between Novalis' role as a saline mine assessor, weighing up profitability, and his poetic work.

29   The miner 'takes delight in their pecular structure and their strange origin and habitat than in their possession' (*freut er sich mehr über ihre wunderlichen Bildungen, und die Seltsamkeiten ihrer Herkunft und ihrer Wohnungen, als über ihren alles verheißenden Besitz*) (1992: 69; 1987: 183).

30   Koselleck's concept of 'the simultaneity of the nonsimultaneous' lends itself to the Anthropocene, where through acceleration and compaction present-day human footprints are becoming rapidly legible in the deepest and oldest layers of the earth.

31 I am drawing on an explanation of Koselleck's geological metaphor by his translators, Hoffmann and Franzel (2018: xiv).
32 Rigby draws a similar conclusion (2017: 123).
33 See Cod. Pal. germ. 67, especially 15v-20r at the University Library of Heidelberg, online at (in scroll mode): https://digi.ub.uni-heidelberg.de/diglit/cpg67/0042/scroll; for additional details, see Karin Wehn and Ingo Linde, 'Daumenkino', Telepolis, 18th August 2005, online at: https://www.telepolis.de/features/Daumenkino-3402298.html. On the late medieval/early modern flick book as a optically primitive precursor of the nineteenth-century proto-cinematic flip book, see Gunning (2004: 31–2).
34 This is especially the case in the Klingsohr fairy tale section of the novel: 'Then the high stained-glassed windows of the palace began to brighten from within, and their figures moved. Their movements grew more lively, the stronger the reddish light became, which began to light up the streets' (*Da fingen die hohen bunten Fenster des Palastes an von innen und heraus helle zu werden, und ihre Figuren bewegten sich. Sie bewegten sich lebhafter, je stärker das rötliche Licht ward, das die Gassen zu erleuchten began*) (1992: 120; 1987: 232). Kuzniar hazards that if 'one were to project Novalis' tale onto screen', it would be akin to the 'digitally rapid flow of flashing images in a video game' (1999: 220). Alternatively, if projected against a cloth screen, the 'reddish light' play, framed as it is by a window, is already recognizable in the pre-cinematic technology of the shadow play; as are the faint and glaring lights, the 'beam of light' (Novalis 1992: 133) and the 'flamelets' (134) that are visible through cracks in the rock or through cracks in door frames.
35 On these two trajectories in media studies, respectively represented by Peters and Parikka and representing 'a return to earth', see Harris et al. (2018: 4).
36 See the film documentary *Terra Blight* (2012), online at: http://www.terrablight.com.
37 In a fascinating analysis of Simonides stone poetry, the classical translator and poet Anne Carson demonstrates how 'the physical facts of the stone and the stylistic facts of the language' go hand in hand (1999: 111).
38 As Robinson puts it, 'For example, I read "The simile is that of the open-cast mine left an empty scar in the landscape" and think: *um, really?*' (2021: 128).

References

Allan, Michael (2016), *In the Shadow of World Literature: Sites of Reading in Colonial Egypt*, Princeton, NJ: Princeton University Press.
Assmann, Aleida (2003), 'Alte und neue Vorrausetzungen der Hieroglyphen-Faszination', in Aleida and J. Assmann (eds.), *Hieroglyphen. Stationen einer abendländischen Grammatologie*, 261–80, Bonn: Wilhelm Fink Verlag.
Assmann, Aleida and Jan Assmann (2003), 'Einleitung: altägyptische Ursprünge abendländischer Grammatologie', in Aleida and J. Assmann (eds.), *Hieroglyphen. Stationen einer abendländischen Grammatologie*, 9–25, Bonn: Wilhelm Fink Verlag.
Babel, Reinhard (2015), *Translationsfiktionen. Zur Hermeneutik, Poetik und Ethik des Übersetzens*, Bielefeld: Transcript Verlag.
Bassnett, Susan and David Johnston (eds.) (2019), *The Outward Turn*, Special Issue of *The Translator* 25.
Beer, Gillian (1996), *Open Fields. Science in Cultural Encounter*, Oxford: Oxford University Press.

Bennett, Jane (2010), *Vibrant Matter. A Political Ecology of Things*, Durham, NC: Duke University Press.
Bennett, Karen (2022), 'The Unsustainable Lightness of Meaning: Reflections on the Material Turn in Translation Studies and Its Intradisciplinary Implications', in Gisele Silva and Maura Radicioni (eds.), *Recharting Territories: Intradisciplinarity in Translation Studies*, 49–73, Leuven: Leuven University Press.
Berman, Antoine (1992), 'The Speculative Theory of Translation', in *The Experience of the Foreign. Culture and Translation in Romantic Germany*, translated by S. Heyvaert, 103–20, New York: State University of New York Press.
Bewell, Alan (2017), *Natures in Translation. Romanticism and Colonial Natural History*, Baltimore: Johns Hopkins University Press.
Calhoun, Joshua (2020), *The Nature of the Page: Poetry, Papermaking, and the Ecology of Texts in Renaissance England*, Philadelphia: University of Pennsylvania Press.
Carson, Anne (1999), *Economy of the Lost*, Princeton, NJ: Princeton University Press.
Chakrabarty, Dipesh (2009), 'The Climate of History: Four Theses', *Critical Inquiry*, 35 (2): 197–222.
Cohen, J. Jeffrey (2015), *Stone. An Ecology of the Inhuman*, Minneapolis: University of Minnesota Press.
Cronin, Michael (2017), *Eco-translation*, London: Routledge.
Cronin, Michael (2022), 'Translation, Ecology and Deep Time', in Pamela Beattie, Simona Bertacco and Tatjana Soldat-Jaffe (eds.), *Time, Space, Matter in Translation*, 4–18, London: Routledge.
Darwin, Charles (2008), *On the Origins of Species*, edited and introduced by Gillian Beer, Oxford: Oxford World's Classics.
Debray, Régis (1996), *Media Manifestos*, translated by Eric Rauth, London: Verso.
De Landa, Manuel (1996), 'An Interview with Manuel De Landa with Konrad Becker and Miss M. at *VirtualFutures*, Warwick 96', http://future-nonstop.org/c/bad189cc715b73b2e88626a072d17a64.
De Landa, Manuel (1997), *A Thousand Years of Non-Linear History*, New York: Zone Books.
Fraunhofer, Hedwig (2022), 'Translating Plants. A Starting Point', in Pamela Beattie, Simona Bertacco and Tatjana Soldat-Jaffe (eds.), *Time, Space, Matter in Translation*, 39–52, London: Routledge.
Freud, Sigmund (1953–74), 'The Aetiology of Hysteria [1896]', in James Strachey (ed.), *The Standard Edition*, vol. III, 189–221, London: Hogarth Press.
Gasperi, Carlos (2015), 'On the Language of Nature in Ludwig Tieck's *Der Runenberg*', *Monatshefte*, 107 (3): 405–30.
Goodbody, Alex (1984), *Natursprache: Ein dichtungstheoretisches Konzept der Romantik und seine Wiederaufnahme in der modernen Naturlyrik*, Neumünster: Wachholtz.
Gosh, Amitav (2016), *The Great Derangement: Climate Change and the Unthinkable*, Chicago: University of Chicago Press.
Groves, Jason (2020), *The Geological Unconscious: German Literature and the Mineral Imaginary*, New York: Fordham University Press.
Gunning, Tom (2004), 'Flickers: On Cinema's Power of Evil', in Murray Pomerance (ed.), *Bad: Infamy, Darkness, Evil, and Slime on Screen*, 21–37, New York: State University of New York Press.
Haraway, Donna (2003), *The Companion Species Manifesto: Dogs, People, and Significant Otherness*, Chicago: Prickly Paradigm Press.

Harris, Paul A., Richard Turner and A. J. Nocek (2018), 'Introduction: Rock Records', *Rock Record*, Special Issue of *SubStance*, 47 (2): 3–7.
Hoffmann, Stefan-Ludwig and Sean Franzel (2018), 'Introduction: Translating Koselleck', in Reinhart Koselleck (ed.), *Sediments of Time. On Possible Histories*, ix–xxxi, Stanford: Stanford University Press.
Hutton, James (1795), 'Theory of the Earth, With Proofs and Illustrations', in *Four Parts*, vol. I, Edinburgh: William Creech.
Huyssen, Andreas (1969), *Die Frühromantische Konzeption von Übersetzung und Aneignung. Studien zur frühromantischen Utopie einer deutschen Weltliteratur*, Zürich: Atlantis Verlag.
Jakobson, Roman (1966), 'On Linguistic Aspects of Translation', in Reuben A. Brower (ed.), *On Translation*, 232–9, New York: Oxford University Press.
Kielmeyer, Karl Friedrich (2021), 'On the Relations between Organic Forces in the Series of Different Organisations, and on the Laws and Consequences of These Relations', in Lydia Azadpour and Daniel Whistler (eds.), *Kielmeyer, and the Organic World*, 29–50, London: Bloomsbury.
Koselleck, Reinhart (2018), *Sediments of Time. On Possible Histories*, translated and introduced by Stefan-Ludwig Hoffmann and Sean Franzel, Stanford: Stanford University Press.
Kuzniar, Alice (1999), '"The Crystal Revenge": The Hypertrophy of the Visual in Novalis and Tieck', *Germanic Review*, 74 (3): 214–28.
Kuzniar, Alice (2003), 'A Higher Language: Novalis on Communion with Animals', *The German Quarterly*, 76 (4): 426–42.
Le Guin, Ursula K. (1974), 'The Author of the Acacia Seeds and Other Extracts from the Journal of Therolinguistics', in Terry Carr (ed.), *Fellowships of the Stars. Nine Science Fiction Stories*, 213–22, New York: Simon and Schuster.
Le Guin, Ursula K. (1989), 'Reciprocity of Prose and Poetry [1983]', in *Dancing at the Edge of the World: Thoughts on Words, Women, Places*, 104–14, New York: Grove Press.
Littau, Karin (2006), *Theories of Reading. Books Bodies and Bibliomania*, Cambridge: Polity.
Littau, Karin (2011), 'First Steps towards a Media History of Translation', *Translation Studies*, 4 (3): 261–81.
Littau, Karin (2016), 'Translation and the Materialities of Communication', *Translation Studies*, 9 (1): 82–113.
Littau, Karin (2017), 'Response by Littau to the Responses to 'Translation and the Materialities of Communication', *Translation Studies*, 10 (1): 97–101.
Lyell, Charles (1997), *Principles of Geology*, edited by James Secord, London: Penguin.
Mahoney, Dennis (1992), 'Human History as Natural History', in *The Novices of Sais and Heinrich von Ofterdingen*', *Historical Reflections/Réflexions Historiques*, 18 (3): 111–24.
Mehne, Philipp (2008), 'Reading Nature: Emerson, Cuvier, Lyell, Goethe and the Intricacies of a Much-Quoted Trope', *Comparative American Studies*, 6 (2): 103–22.
Marais, Kobus (2019), *A (Bio)Semiotic Theory of Translation. The Emergence of Social-Cultural Reality*, London: Routledge.
Novalis (1987), *Novalis Werke*, edited by Gerhard Schulz, München: Beck.
Novalis (1992), *Henry von Ofterdingen*, translated by Palmer Hilty, Prospect Heights, IL: Waveland Press.
Novalis (1993), *Das Allgemeine Brouillon. Materialien zur Enzyklopädistik*, introduced by Hans-Joachim Mähl, Hamburg: Felix Meiner Verlag.

Novalis (2003), *Fichte Studies*, translated by Jane Kneller, Cambridge: Cambridge University Press.
Novalis (2005), *The Novices of Sais*, translated by Ralph Manheim, Brooklyn, NY: Archipelago Books.
Novalis (2007), *Notes for a Romantic Encyclopaedia. Das Allgemeine Brouillon*, translated and edited by David W. Wood. Albany: State University of New York Press.
Novalis (2014), 'From a Letter to A. W. Schlegel [30 November 1797]', translated by Douglas Robinson, in Robinson (ed.), *Western Translation Theory. From Herodotus to Nietzsche*, 212, London: Routledge.
O'Keeffe, Brian (2021), 'George Steiner's Metaphors for Translation: A Critical Commentary', in Marco Agnetta, Larisa Cercel and Brian O'Keeffe (eds.), *Yearbook of Translational Hermeneutics*, 1: 209–42.
Outram, Dorinda (1984), *Georges Cuvier. Vocation, Science and Authority in Post-revolutionary France*, Manchester: Manchester University Press.
Parikka, Jussi (ed.) (2011), *Medianatures. The Materiality of Information Technology and Electronic Waste*, Ann Arbor, MI: Open Humanities Press, https://livingbooksaboutlife.org/pdfs/bookarchive/Medianatures.pdf.
Parikka, Jussi (2014), *Anthrobscence*, Minneapolis: University of Minnesota Press.
Parikka, Jussi (2015), *A Geology of Media*, Minneapolis: University of Minnesota Press.
Pfannkuchen, Antje (2015), 'Rewriting Romanticism, Again and Again', *German Studies Review*, 38 (1): 138–40.
Pfannkuchen, Antje (2021), 'Image, Language, Science: Hieroglyphs and the Romantic Quest for Primordial Truth', in Kirsten Belgum, Vance Byrd and John D. Benjamin (eds.), *Before Photography. German Visual Culture in the Nineteenth Century*, 243–66, Berlin, Boston: De Gruyter.
Peters, John Durham (2003), 'Space, Time, and Communication Theory', *Canadian Journal of Communication*, 28: 397–411.
Peters, John Durham (2016), *The Marvelous Clouds: Towards a Philosophy of Elemental Media*, Chicago: The University of Chicago Press.
Rigby, Kate (2015), 'Art, Nature, and the Poesy of Plants in the *Goethezeit*: A Biosemiotic Perspective', in Adrian Daub and Elizabeth Krimmer (eds.), *Goethe Yearbook 22*, 23–44, Rochester, NY: Camden House.
Rigby, Kate (2017), '"Mines aren't really like that": German Romantic Undergrounds Revisited', in Caroline Schaumann and Heather I. Sullivan (eds.), *German Ecocriticism in the Anthropocene*, 111–28, New York: Palgrave Macmillan.
Robinson, Douglas (2021), 'George Steiner's Hermeneutic Motion and the Ontology, Ethics, and Epistemology of Translation', in Marco Agnetta, Larisa Cercel and Brian O'Keeffe (eds.), *Yearbook of Translational Hermeneutics*, vol. 1, 103–38, Journal of the Research Center, Hermeneutics and Creativity, University of Leipzig.
Rudwick, Martin (2005), *Bursting the Limits. The Reconstruction of Geohistory in the Age of Revolution*, Chicago: Chicago University Press.
Rupke, Nicholas (1990), 'Caves, Fossils and the History of the Earth', in Andrew Cunningham and Nicholas Jardine (eds.), *Romanticism and the Sciences*, 241–59, Cambridge: Cambridge University Press.
Schaber, Steven C. (1973), 'Novalis's Theory of the Work of Art as Hieroglyph', *The German Review*, 48 (1): 35–43.
Schelling, F. W. J. (1856–61), 'Vorlesungen über die Methode des akademischen Studiums', in K. F. A. Schelling (ed.), *Schelling's Sämmtliche Werke*, XIV vols. V, 229–374, Stuttgart and Augsburg: J.G. Cotta Verlag.

Schelling, F. W. J. (1966), *On University Studies*, translated by E.S. Morgan (ed.) (introduced by) Norbert Guterman, Athens: Ohio University Press.

Steffens, Henrich (1908), *Lebenserinnerungen aus dem Kreis der Romantik*, edited by Friedrich Gundelfinger, 176–7, Jena: Eugen Diederichs.

Steiner, George (1998), *After Babel* [1975], 3rd edn, Oxford: Oxford University Press.

Sullivan, Heather (2011), 'Dirty Nature: Ecocriticism and Tales of Extraction – Mining and Solar Power – in Goethe, Hoffmann, Verne, and Eschbach', *Colloquia Germanica*, 44 (2): 111–31.

Szeman, Imre (2011), 'Literature and Energy Futures', *PMLA*, 126 (2): 323–5.

Tamm, Marek (2019), 'Introduction: A Framework for Debating New Approaches to History', in M. Tamm and Peter Burke (eds.), *Debating New Approaches to History*, 1–20, London: Bloomsbury.

Tieck, Ludwig (1985), 'Der Runenberg', in Manfred Frank (ed.), *Schriften in zwölf Bänden, Band 6. Phantasus*, 184–209, Frankfurt am Main: Suhrkamp.

Tieck, Ludwig (2012), 'The Rune Mountain', in Peter Wortsman (ed. and trans.), *Tales of the German Imagination from the Brothers Grimm to Ingeborg Bachmann*, 54–75, London: Penguin.

Tsing, Anna, Heather Swanson, Elaine Gan and Nils Bubandt (eds.) (2017), *Arts of Living on a Damaged Planet. Ghosts and Monsters of the Anthropocene*, Minneapolis: University of Minnesota Press.

Weiler, Christina (2020), 'The Metaphysical Machinery of Mining in Novalis's Works', in Michael Demson and Christopher R. Clason (eds.), *Romantic Automata. Exhibits, Figures, and Organisms*, 204–220, Lewisburg: Bucknell University Press.

Weissbrod, Rachel and Ayelet Kohn (2019), *Translating the Visual. A Multimodal Perspective*, New York: Routledge.

Yaeger, Patricia (2011), 'Editor's Column: Literature in the Ages of Wood, Tallow, Coal, Whale Oil, Gasoline, Atomic Power, and Other Energy Sources', *PMLA*, 126 (2): 305–10.

Ziolkowski, Theodore (1990), *German Romanticism and Its Institutions*, Princeton: Princeton University Press.

9

The historian as translator of the past

Luigi Alonzi

9.1. History as contemporary history

In 1893 Benedetto Croce published an article entitled *La storia ridotta sotto il concetto generale dell'arte* (*History Treated as Subsumed by the Concept of Art*). He was twenty-seven years old, and had only recently begun his active intellectual life in Naples, concerning himself especially with monuments and local events (the *storia patria*). It seems that just before delivering to the printer one of his manuscript demonstrating that history was a science, Croce had decided to write the above-mentioned essay endorsing exactly the opposite thesis: that history was not to be considered a science but an art, since it was founded on the intuition of the historian. In his 1936 lectures on the 'idea of history' Robin Collingwood was very positive about Croce's text, arguing that

> by denying that history was a science at all, [Croce] cut himself at one blow loose from naturalism, and set his face towards an idea of history as something radically different from nature. We have seen that the problem of philosophy everywhere in the late nineteenth century was the problem of liberating itself from the tyranny of natural science; the boldness of Croce's move was therefore exactly what the situation demanded. It was the clean cut which he made in 1893 between the idea of history and the idea of science that enabled him to develop the conception of history so much further than any philosopher of his generation.
>
> (Collingwood 2006: 193)

Though still a young man, Croce had thought carefully about the conception of history as conceived by *Historismus*, insisting on the need for the historian to relive the past ('rivivere il passato', the German *Erlebnis*), since historiography was not a natural science but an art aiming at the re-actualization of the past, uniting the individual with the universal (as Vico had taught). German philosophers by contrast thought that

---

I wish to thank Karen Bennett, Peter Burke, Hephzibah Israel, Alexandra Lianeri and Keith Tribe for their support and comments.

historiography was to be placed within the concept of science, distinguishing between natural and human sciences, that is, *Naturwissenschaften und Kulturwissenschaften* or *Geisteswissenchaften*, Collingwood noting that 'Croce's early theory already marks an advance on the German view which it so much resembles'. According to Collingwood, the definition of the intuition provided by Benedetto Croce was not yet satisfactory and would be completed with the *Logic*, published in 1909, and to which he later returned in order to specify what he called the *Logic of Questions and Answers*. The example of Croce's new methodological and philosophical position given by Collingwood deserves attention:

> I open a history book at random and read the following sentence: 'It must not be forgotten that monarchs such as Louis XI and Ferdinand the Catholic, notwithstanding their crimes, completed the national work of making France and Spain two great and powerful nations'. This sentence implies that the writer and reader understand the terms 'crime', 'nation', 'powerful', and so forth, and understand them in the same sense: it implies that the writer and reader possess in common a certain system of ethical and political ideas. The sentence, as an historical judgment, assumes that these ideas are coherent and logically defensible; that is, it presupposes an ethical and political philosophy. It is through the medium of this ethical and political philosophy that we grasp the historical reality of Louis XI; and conversely, it is because we find the concepts of this philosophy realized in Louis XI that we grasp what those concepts are.
>
> (Collingwood 2006: 195–6)

Most likely in writing this passage, Collingwood, who begun his correspondence with the Neapolitan philosopher in 1912 (Vigorelli 1991), implicitly took account of the text published by Croce in 1915, examined below. He understood perfectly the problem that had brought Croce to elaborate the concept of history as contemporary history. However, Collingwood placed this concept in a semantic and lexical perspective that Croce had not. A fundamental turning point in Croce's intellectual trajectory was the lecture 'Storia, cronaca e false storie' ('History, Chronicle and False Histories') delivered on 3 November 1912, at the Pontaniana Academy in Naples (Croce 1912). This speech provoked a broad reaction, including one from the Italian literary critic Renato Serra. His rebuttal of Croce has been used by Carlo Ginzburg to support his criticisms of the historiographical stance taken by Hayden White. And this has itself led discussion in a particular direction, given the interest of Ginzburg in the relationship between historical events and historical narratives, often oversimplifying the Crocean discourse and overshadowing the core of his theory.[1]

In the years following the speech at the Pontaniana Academy, Croce further developed the concept of 'history as contemporary history' and the corresponding idea of the identity between history and philosophy, leading him to decline the invitation to write a book on the 'philosophy of history' from the German publisher Paul Siebeck. As documented by the correspondence with Fritz Medicus (Piccardi 2002), Croce no longer considered a book on the 'philosophy of history' feasible. It was from this perspective that his book on the theory and history of historiography emerged, published at first in German by Siebeck in 1915, and then in Italian in 1917.

The first chapter of the book reproduced the lecture delivered at the Pontaniana Academy, hinting also at the controversy it had caused. Croce responded by emphasizing his new idea of history, an idea that was soon acknowledged by Carl Schmitt, among others:

> That all historical knowledge is knowledge of the present, that such knowledge obtains its light and intensity from the present and in the most profound sense only serves the present, because all spirit is only spirit of the present, has been said by many since Hegel, best of all by Benedetto Croce.
> (Schmitt 2007: 80)

This statement by Carl Schmitt can be found in the opening of the chapter on 'Das Zeitalter der Neutralisirung und Entpolitisierung', a lecture first published in 1929, then in 1932 reprinted in *Der Begriff des Politischen*; Schmitt does, however, seem to have underestimated Croce's innovation. Collingwood did not. By emphasizing how Crocean philosophy superseded existing German philosophy, he contributed to the dissemination of the concept of history as contemporary history in the English-speaking world; furthermore, Collingwood translated Croce's *Autobiography* into English, from which he later took inspiration for his own autobiography.[2]

Jaume Aurell related the autobiographies of Croce and Collingwood to their philosophical and historical approach, emphasizing that an opposition to mere antiquarianism in the reconstruction of the past was

> precisely the central point of Croce (and Collingwood's) philosophy of history [...] Connected to his affirmation that all history is contemporary history, Croce argues that history is seen mainly through the eyes of the present and in relation to its problems. As a consequence, historians do not conceive of the past as a distant object to be admired (*antiquarianism*) but as an adjacent reality that shapes and continues to influence one's personal and collective life (*presentism*).
> (Aurell 2009: 220)

Aurell relates this conception with the problem of anachronism but did not take into consideration all the necessary hermeneutic consequences. Furthermore, the term 'presentism', as interpreted in the light of recent historiography, could be misleading. It is important to note that historians have focused their attention on the political-ideological and cultural aspects of the concept of history as contemporary history, the past being continually reconstructed and open to new interpretation (re-enacted) on the basis of the changing interests of historians; for the only past issues that are really interesting to us are those that still have meaning for us. As we will see, it is even more important to grasp the cognitive and linguistic implications of the concept of history as contemporary history, since the past is not only continually re-enacted by historians but also re-actualized through present language.

This does not imply the subordination of the past to the exigencies of the present, and, equally, it does not imply the nullification of the past and its dissolution into the present. The problem Croce and Collingwood faced was, at least initially – later the dictatorships would open other perspectives, both morally and politically –

a philosophical and hermeneutic problem. As Collingwood noted, 'All history is contemporary history: not in the ordinary sense of the word, where contemporary history means the history of the comparatively recent past, but in the strict sense. The consciousness of one's own activity as one actually performs it. History is thus self-knowledge of the living mind' (Collingwood 2006: 202–3; see also Johnson 2012; Connelly 2016).

In the light of the concept of history as contemporary history, the old idea of *historia magistra vitae* appears deceptive. According to Croce, it was not the past that illuminates the present; on the contrary, historians make it possible for the past to speak to the present. While philosophers living in the first half of the twentieth century paid attention to the way historical concepts came to be thought about, focusing on how the individual mind connected with the flow of thoughts linking the present to the past, attention will be given here to the empirical-cognitive process linking the mind of the historian to the current objects speaking of the past to that historian. In other words, we will focus on the empirical and cognitive aspects of the concept of history as contemporary history, pointing out that historians are in fact concerned solely with an object in the currently existing past, forming our only access to the past; in this case, history as narration of the past can be considered 'contemporary history' because the objects through which the past exists and can still live are our contemporaries.

9.2. Translating meanings and discourses

Before encountering a concept or finding a meaning, the eyes and brain of historians encounter a sign, in many cases a concrete written/printed word. This does not provide any explicit meaning or immediate conceptual reference, besides the meaning or concept related to this word that he/she had already in his/her mind. To grasp the meaning of a word and to outline the conceptual content of a word in different times and places, historians must indeed firstly reconstruct the unique linguistic contexts in which such a word was used and, as far as possible, delineate the history of this word, seeking to clarify its different meanings and conceptual references through time. In 1969 Quentin Skinner made a reasoned and perceptive attack on the history of concepts, meanings and 'unit ideas', continuing on to develop and refine it. Following the linguistic theories developed mainly by Ludwig Wittgenstein and John Austin, he maintained that the purpose of the historian should be 'to grasp not merely what people are saying but also what they are *doing in* saying it', since 'the study of what someone says can never be a sufficient guide to understanding what was meant' (Skinner 2002a: 82).

One of the main controversial objectives of the arguments put forward in that article was the methodological approach practised by historians such as Arthur Lovejoy, who went in search of 'perennial' ideas and ended up committing the unforgivable sin of anachronism; according to Skinner, the works of these historians were invalidated by three types of mythology (the mythology of doctrines, the mythology of coherence and the mythology of prolepsis), which together would have not enabled historians to understand what the ancient writers were doing using certain words, since these words were interpreted through the lens of preconceived paradigms. Many of the criticisms raised by Skinner regarding this historiographical practice are certainly acceptable, and in particular his call to carefully analyse different linguistic contexts is exemplary; however, his methodological approach to the study of words has left some central issues unresolved.

Significantly, in criticizing the traditional approach to the history of ideas, Skinner often appealed to the authority of Collingwood, aligning himself with Collingwood's assertion that 'there are no perennial problem in philosophy', and thereby implying that his own historiographical approach was sufficient to put the analysis of words and texts on the right path. Furthermore, in the article's closing remarks, while pointing out that the 'philosophical, even moral, value' of studying history lies in the heightened awareness of the individuality of historical phenomena, Skinner argued that 'there is a tendency (sometimes explicitly urged, as by Hegel, as a mode of proceeding) to suppose that the best, and not merely escapable, vantage point from which to survey the ideas of the past must be that of our present situation, because it is by definition the most highly evolved' (Skinner 2002a: 88). This is exactly the point. Curiously enough, here Skinner makes reference to Hegel and not to Croce, whose precedence in the development of this point had been acknowledged by Carl Schmitt. As already noted, the inescapable question of the continuity of patterns of thoughts reconstructed by historians from the perspective of the present is not merely a moral question but, first and foremost, an epistemological question, related to the inescapable necessity of translating past words with present usage.

Several years later, replying to some of his critics, Skinner (1988) felt himself obliged to respond to this very question; in particular, he referred extensively to the remarks made by Martin Hollis about the relations between rationality and the translatability of concepts as a basic assumption of the work of anthropologists. Hollis (1970a; 1970b) emphasized the fact that this relation was to be considered not a hypothesis but a necessary condition for the understanding of other languages and cultures. Hollis's point made it possible for Skinner to clarify himself:

> Hollis's main contention is that, if we cannot 'pair' the terms used by alien people with 'counterparts' in our own language, then we cannot embark on the task of translating their utterances [...] For Hollis, as for many other philosophers of social science, translatability is thus taken to be a condition of intelligibility, with the result that the main issue is held to be that of establishing how translation was possible.
>
> (Skinner 1988: 46)

Equally clear is Skinner's position on this subject:

> But even in the form in which Hollis and others have defended it – as a thesis about the need to be able to pair basic terms of alien languages with equivalents in our own – the claim that intelligibility presupposes translatability is surely mistaken.
>
> (Skinner 1988: 46)

This time, without citing Collingwood but surely having him in mind, Skinner maintained that he was not seeking to re-enact or to re-create the experiences or beliefs of past or alien people, but to

> recover the concepts they possessed, the distinction they drew and the chain of reasoning they followed in their attempts to make sense of their world. What I cannot see is why this should be thought to require us to map their distinctions and the terms they used for expressing them on to the very different distinctions and expressions we happen to use ourselves. Historical understanding is a product of learning to follow what Ian Hacking [(1982: 59–61)] has called different styles of reasoning; it is not necessarily a matter of being able to translate those style into a familiar ones.
>
> (Skinner 1988: 47)

Once again, Skinner's argument returns to the same *vulnus*, refusing to draw all the necessary epistemological and linguistic consequences from the concept of history as contemporary history. It is not so much a question of acknowledging the inescapable vagueness of translation or of considering different styles of reasoning but rather of putting the question of translatability at the centre of the historical work, relating it to the concept of history as contemporary history. Indeed, not only are historians obliged to use the language in its current meaning in order to be understood by contemporaries but they also only have at their disposal this language in seeking to understand past or alien cultures; this means that they are obliged to 'translate' past and alien concepts. Furthermore, this happens not only at the conceptual level but also, with different implications, at the linguistic level.

Very often our vocabulary is made up of words that have been used for hundred years, and in this case historians have to 'translate' these words; they are obliged to retrace the different meanings of the same word. Of course, historians also encounter a 'moral question' when they judge past events and alien cultures, but this has nothing to do with the epistemological problem of historical knowledge; this problem is not even related to the question of truth and rationality. Rather, it is a question of recognizing that in historical knowledge and in the knowledge of other cultures, we are necessarily linked to our own language and to our own system of values, with all that this entails on the epistemological level. Certainly, we can use periphrasis to explain alien or past words, but this periphrasis is composed of 'our' words; failure to recognize this problem leads into a vicious circle. Take, for instance, the case of the word 'economy'. For a long time this word had a meaning very similar to our word-concept 'order/administration', but any time we use the word 'economy' it is inevitable that the current meanings of this word comes to mind. As a consequence, when confronted with the different meanings of the word 'economy' in different times and places, we are obliged in the first instance to compare those meanings with our current meaning (Tribe 2015; Alonzi 2022).

In replying to his critics, Skinner did not take into consideration the important *Introduction* by John Pocock to *Virtue, Commerce, and History*, published a few years earlier in 1985. Skinner rarely refers directly to Pocock's works in support of his thesis;

nor does he do so in another article republished in *Visions of Politics*, where Skinner links Collingwood's logic of question and answer to Austin's theory of speech acts (Skinner 2002b: 115-16). Pocock's *Introduction* represented a profound and acute review of Skinner's approach to historical method, often insisting on the unresolved questions raised above by recalling the Collingwoodian perspective. Pocock subjected the idea that the meaning of an utterance derives mainly from the intention of the author to detailed criticism, decisively shifting the historiographical perspective from agency to language, from linguistic action to discourse analysis, from sentences to idioms and modes of speech.

Pocock emphasizes the complexity of discourse analysis and the necessity of including in it not only authorial intention but also reader reaction, and indeed the interaction between different authors. He continued to point out the importance of the language of the historian studying these languages, along with the languages of historical actors:

> The problem of interpretation recurs in a more pressing form when we consider that the historian studies languages in order to read them, but not to speak or write them. His own writing will not be constructed in a pastiche of the various idioms they interpret, but rather in language he has devised in order to describe and explicate the workings of these idioms. If in Collingwoodian terminology he has learned to 'rethink the thoughts' of others, the language in which he reiterates their utterances will not be that used by them, but his own.
>
> (Pocock 1985: 10)

Exactly this same problem and perspective has been noted by Peter Burke when studying the 'fabrication of Louis XIV', stating: 'What interests me in historical writing is above all the task of mediating between two cultures, the past and the present, of setting up a dialogue between the two systems of concepts, of translating from one language into the other' (Burke 1992: 6). Evoking the conceptualization used by Collingwood to explain the Crocean concept of history as contemporary history, he argued:

> For example, should one speak of the 'policy' of a medieval king? The word does not occur in medieval texts. It was not necessary, since a medieval king did not have to convince voters to elect him by presenting them with a programme for future action. A policy in the sense of some principles or strategies underlying everyday political action, from doing justice to extending his realm, he may have had, but a policy in the modern sense of programme is an anachronistic concept.
>
> Again, can a historian speak of 'propaganda' for Louis XIV? In its political sense, the term was coined in the late eighteenth century in order to compare techniques of religious conversion as practised by the Catholic Church and its institutions 'for the propagation of the faith' (*de propaganda fide*). On the other hand, writers and artists in the service of Louis not only glorified the king in general but justified particular actions such as the expulsion of Protestants from France in 1685. I would therefore argue that to speak of 'propaganda' for Louis is

culturally appropriate even if it is technically anachronistic. It is a free translation but not an unfaithful one.

(Burke 2007: 7–8)

As we shall see, anachronism is the crux (and the cross) of any discourse on 'translating history', on relating the historical approach to the method and theory of translation. On the other hand, the recourse by Burke to a term-concept like 'unfaithful' is symptomatic: is the reconstruction-translation of the past a matter of faith? There is no doubt that by evoking the concept of faith we are entering into a semantic space extremely fertile, important for history and translation as well as for history as translation. The English term 'faith' refers to trust in someone's ability or knowledge; the Latin term 'fides', which should be literally translated into Italian with the theological sense of 'fede' (as in the above-mentioned *Congregazione de Propaganda Fide* or, more generally, as faith in some divinity), can in different contexts also be conceptually translated as 'fedeltà', just as with the English term 'fidelity', on the bases of different contexts. This ambiguity is in part both poetic and meaningful. In the sixteenth century the French translator Étienne Dolet wrote that *fides* 'emerges in proportion to the translator's self-detachment from the servitude of word and clause'. Referring also to this conceptualization, Andrea Rizzi, Birgit Lang and Anthony Pym founded the entire structure of translation history on the concept of 'trust', intended as the key to understand the work of historians and translators.

> We submit that *translation* – by which we mean a spoken or written text-based interlingual transfer – is not possible without trust.
>
> By examining theories and practices of trust from sociological, philosophical, and historical studies, and with reference to interdisciplinarity, we outline a methodology that enables us to approach translation history and intercultural mediation from three discrete, concurrent perspectives on trust and translation: the interpersonal, the institutional, and the regime-enacted [...]
>
> We need detailed, empirical study to appreciate the specific ways in which trust is produced through cultural and linguistic mediation. Specifically with reference to translation and interpreting, by 'trust' we mean not only who was *entrusted* to produce the texts we can access and study today, but also how *trustworthy* the authors of these texts were considered to be by their contemporaries.

(Rizzi 2019: 11)

The German scholar Christiane Nord (2007) referred to a similar concept using the term 'loyalty', moving within the same semantic space. Evidently, the concepts of 'trust', 'fidelity' and 'loyalty' can be related both to the relationships between historians and archival sources and to the relationships between translator and source text; as well as between historians/translators and historical actors, clients, patrons, readers or audiences. We are confronted here with very complex relationships. Indeed, not only historians/translators and historical actors have different analytical categories for interpreting reality but they have different languages that are not simple and transparent media for meanings. Language always has a historical weight, steeped in usages and conventions that condition the linguistic action performed by authors/writers, both as historians/translators and as historical actors. The analysis of the historical weight of language, that is, of historically layered languages, implies study of the transmission of languages/idioms or, more precisely, as lucidly stated by Pocock, the translations of languages/idioms over time:

> The history of discourse now becomes visible as one of *traditio* in the sense of transmission and, still more, translation. Texts composed of *langues* and *paroles*, of stable languages structures and speech acts and innovations that modify them, are transmitted and reiterated, first by nonidentical actors in shared identical contexts, and then by actors in historically discrete contexts.
>
> (Pocock 1985: 20–1)

Pocock reiterates this point later, but in this case too he does not seem to give sufficient consideration to the fact that the work of the historian is an integral part of the constantly renewed *traditio* of texts, intended as a continued work of transmission, that is, the translation/interpretation of texts. Once again, the Italian language has here a poetic and meaningful implication, since the verb *tradire* also refers to the possibility to 'be unfaithful', recalling mind the semantic space formed by terms such as 'faith', 'fidelity', 'loyalty', 'trust'; we can add 'reliability', emphasizing that this quality is entirely based on the ability of the historian/translator to use the correct language and to choose proper words. However, in order to do this historians and translators should be aware that their language is not only linked to discrete cultural contexts but also completely imbricated in the flow of time; as an example, Pocock considers the language of the historian not as a language but as a paralanguage or metalanguage, as if the historian might be placed metaphorically in a control tower, uninvolved in the flow of historical events and, especially, without imbrication in the language through which these events are described. It is at this level that historians take part in the work of translation and can as such be considered to be cultural translators, as translators of cultures from the past to the present. In fact, the historian 'translates' words that are expression of cultures between past and present. We might speak of meeting, hybridization, cross-fertilization between past and present, but at the same time it has to be noted that this encounter does not occur between equal partners, especially when we refer to the work of the historian as a cultural translator. Signifiers of the past represent a constraint to be reckoned with; the final outcome of this encounter between past and present is always expressed in terms of the latter, that is, with the language of the historian.

If it is true that the historian must take into consideration the languages and meanings of the past (this is what the work involves), it is also true that the past must necessarily be mediated by the historian; even when we read the primary sources, the paratext and the context formed by our contemporaneity prevent those sources from being read in their immediacy. In her paper 'Archival Dea(r)th: Tracing the Afterlives of Translation Memory', Hephzibah Israel (*forthcoming*) made a distinction between the 'excavationist historian', who prioritizes 'fact' and 'authenticity' as the foundations on which the past can be recounted accurately and reliably, and the 'refractive historian', who is aware that the archive, in each of its cultural and material expressions, supports a predominant interpretation of the past. Nowadays, we are more and more conscious of the fact that the professionalization of historians, the building of nation-states and the structuration of archives and archival museums powerfully contributed to the ordering of modern space(s) and time(s) at the end of the nineteenth century (Steglich 2021).[4]

The transmission of sources, of which the historian is part and parcel, is founded on a permanent process of selection and memorialization which is never neutral, but which is the outcome of choices reflected in material structures and single representations; the same can be said for objects and musealization processes, as particularly shown by Ruth Phillips (2011; see also Phillips 2020; Coombes 2020), with considerations revolving around issues of identity, decolonization and indigenization that foreshadowed the problems raised by the 'cancel culture' in the Canadian incandescent context. By the same token, it can be added that the world around us is also a great archive and the 'remains' through which we study history are literally what remains from the past, the objects through which we re-construct the past. These objects are not randomly dispersed objects in the world (buildings, statues, mausoleums, but also trees, stones and rivers) but often reproduce an order, an 'archivization' of the world, which imply a synchronization of different temporalities (Huyssen 2003). In this context, also proper archives and museums must be framed, the places consciously chosen by men/women and by institutions to preserve what they think important, what according to them should constitute the memory to be handed down.

Most importantly, we should become used to thinking of words as objects, which retain layers of meaning accumulated over time. Even when we do not notice it, these meanings are encrusted somewhere in the words, and historians/translators often revive some of these layers of meaning by bringing them to the fore and passing them down to posterity, thus building a renewed memory of the past. In this sense, our language is also an 'archive of words and meanings'; the point to be particularly kept in mind is that words, like objects from the past, are all present. Historians and translators, or better historians as translators, must relocate these words/objects of the present in the past; in this way they construct 'possible' stories/histories. It is like a circle that starts from the present, enters the past and returns to the present, all the while with a view to the future; in this circle we mix meanings of the present with meanings of the past in order to pass them on in the future (Alonzi, *forthcoming* a).

9.3. Anachronism, history and semantics

An excellent approach to these issues is represented by Kari Palonen's article devoted to 'Reinhart Koselleck on Translation, Anachronism, and Conceptual Change'. Palonen (2012) notes that the main issue at stake in Koselleck's historiographical reflection on conceptual change was linked to the intertwined problems of translation and anachronism.

> Two distinct conclusions can be drawn from the Koselleckian formula. The first one concerns what is denied by the formula, namely an imaginary limit situation

of the simultaneous interpretation, for which there is no need for conceptual history. The ideal of simultaneity refers to the possibility that the translatable and the translated appear in the exact same present, *Gegenwart*, or perhaps more exactly in rhetorical terms, in the same audience. The second conclusion is that the linguistic transfers over time always require translation, even within the same language, and conceptual history is an indispensable tool of such an intertemporal translation. The point is that in order to avoid the pitfall of anachronism, we must engage in conceptual history when speaking about the past to a present audience.

(Palonen 2012: 73)

In his theoretical construction Koselleck referred principally to Rudolf Eucken and Max Weber, the last of whom had attained the elaboration of the well-known concept, and analytical tool, of *Idealtypus*; the recent edition of Max Weber's (2019) *Economy and Society* by Keith Tribe, which provides a thorough description and explanation of the work, shows how profoundly Weber was committed to a restless job of definition of abstract concepts.[5]

Like Weber, who did this work at the highest level, many social scientists in the first quarter of the twentieth century felt it was their primary duty to create an appropriate scientific language that could also be applied to the study of history. In this, Rudolf Eucken can be considered a pioneer. In 1879 he had published a *Geschichte der Philosophischen Terminologie. Im Umriss dargestellt* (*Outline of the History of Philosophical Terminology*), in which he invited scholars to carefully study philosophical language in order to construct a scientific terminology enduring over time and, indeed, independent of words and ideas, independent from geographical and historical circumstances (i.e. from natural languages). Curiously enough, Eucken believed that the construction of this new scientific language by philosophy and social sciences should be done by American scholars, who had 'proved themselves by their work in other fields to be the peers of the scholars of the Old World' (Eucken 1986: 515); Eucken's project[6] was instead largely developed through the volumes of the *Geschichtliche Grundbegriffe*, and it is not by chance that Koselleck explicitly refers to the *Geschichte der Philosophischen Terminologie* as an example 'for all the humanities and the social sciences' in one of his most important essays on the subject devoted to 'Sozialgeschichte und Begriffsgeschichte' (Koselleck 1986).[7]

Koselleck extensively revised Otto Brunner's constitutional history, arguing that 'a description of constitutional history in terms bound to the language of sources turns mute if the past concepts themselves are not translated or redescribed for the present. Otherwise, it remains a representation of the text in the old sources in a one to one relation'.[8] As emphasized by Palonen, the criticisms raised by Koselleck of Brunner's approach to the study of historical concepts pointed out that 'it is not enough to avoid anachronism when translating from the present to the past, but this procedure also requires a complementary re-translation from the past to the present. The historian not only engage in a dialogue with the past through her sources, but is also required to connect this dialogue to the debate in her own contemporary context' (Palonen 2012: 81).

In sum, the conceptual and intellectual historian must perform a double act of translation:

> The key heuristic tool in Koselleck's critique of Brunner lies in the demand for a 'translation' between the present and the past and viceversa. Both forms of this type of translation occur within the same language [...]
>
> It would be easy to speak of a metaphorical extension of the ordinary meaning of translation to the conceptual transfer over time within the same language. In Koselleck's case, labelling the use of translation in this context as a metaphor would, however, be misleading. It would be missing the central role that Koselleck attributes to the translation as the very procedure through which concepts can be rendered commensurable with each other over time and thus become potential objects of historiography. It is in this sense that both his critique of Brunner and his thesis of the *Sattelzeit* become more intelligible, and we can refer to all translations as the inter-contextual transfer of concepts, irrespective of whether or not the sources and scholars share a common language.
>
> (Palonen 2012: 81)

Indeed, in order to do her/his job correctly the historian need to perform a *Rückübersetzung*, that is, 'an act of retranslation [requiring] an explication of past concepts in a manner that can be rendered commensurable with the present-day debates'. This is not an easy job, however, for words and concepts are historically layered, and moreover between the eighteenth and nineteenth century a *Sattelzeit* (Saddle Period) in the historical process had occurred, making it difficult to reconstruct the relationship between present words and past concepts, as Koselleck had emphasized in *Vergangene Zukunft* (Palonen 2012: 82; see Koselleck 1979; 1985; 2004). To avoid confusion between present language and past concepts, Koselleck came up with a solution that Palonen defines as paradoxical: 'the historicization of the study of concepts requires the identification of analytical categories, as they represent the only possible means of carrying out a re-translation of older sources to the language of present scholarship' (Palonen 2012: 83).

In other words, in order to carry out her/his work correctly, the historian would have to resort to a sort of 'meta-language', which calls to mind Eucken's scientific terminology and Weber's *Idealtypus*. Koselleck referred here also to Hans-Georg Gadamer (1971) and Eugenio Coseriu (1974), as well as to Pocock's 'Introduction' to *Virtue, Commerce, and History*, where (as mentioned earlier) a similar statement had been made. According to Koselleck, the economy of the language adopted by the historian has to distinguish between source-bound concepts (*quellebegrundete Begriffe*) and scholarly categories of knowledge (*wissenschaftliche Erkenntnisskategorien*), not only to avoid the problem of anachronism but also to avoid being 'captured with a fatal relativism'. The distinction between historical concepts and analytical categories represents, therefore, the principal task for the intellectual historian, who must translate the former with the latter (and vice versa), making readers aware of the differences between them.

It is in discussing this crucial issue that Kari Palonen introduces some fundamental questions about Reinhart Koselleck's approach:

> The question thus remains whether such a strict distinction can always be made, or whether it itself should be modified and historicized. In other words, the analytical categories may at some point, to use Koselleck's expression, be moved from the metahistorical to the historical level in the course of the research process or the borderlines between the usages may otherwise be ambiguous.
>
> In Koselleck's own vocabulary, the main 'hypotheses' for the interpretation of conceptual change in the *Geschichtliche Grundbegriffe* – democratization, temporalization, ideologizability, and politicization – serve as analytical categories. The question is really the extent to which he manages to retain the categories independently of the histories of democracy, time, ideology, and politics, when all of them refer to key concepts that were subject to change during the *Sattelzeit* period. Is it not anachronistic to speak, for example, of democratization and politicization without giving any consideration at all to the conceptual changes which have taken place in the concept of democracy and politics, as both of them are discussed in the *GG*? Following Koselleck's critique to Brunner, we can also ask whether by choosing to focus on these specific hypotheses he has failed to historicize them, instead blindly accepting some of the everyday or academic usages of the formative period of the lexicon as metahistorical categories.
>
> By recognizing both the heuristic role of the distinction between historical concepts and analytical categories and the fatal consequences of blurring its borders, the question I would like to focus on is how we should make this distinction. How can we choose analytical categories that are both beneficial in the historical analysis of concepts and separate from the concepts themselves?
>
> (Palonen 2012: 84)

The answer to these questions provided by Kari Palonen in the following pages, based on his previous works (Palonen 1985; 1990; 2014), is arranged on two levels of different importance. Firstly, he reiterates the need for historians 'to clearly make the distinction between the two types of conceptual use'. Secondly (and most importantly) he observes that 'categories cannot be used for the study of periods or sources in which the categories themselves are immediately a part of the conceptual controversy'. This second statement calls into question the whole theoretical edifice construed from Eucken and Weber up to Koselleck, and the very possibility of using abstract analytical categories in the study of history (not only in the case indicated by Palonen). Furthermore, this last issue should not be confused with the use of a metalanguage in the study of historical concepts, which remains one of the main critical point of conceptual history. It deserves notice that, while considering possible, indeed indispensable, the use of a metalanguage in the study of the same historical context, that is, in studying the same language, Koselleck considered the existence of a metalanguage for the study of concepts and ideas expressed in different languages implausible.

In a well-known article devoted to the 'Three *bürgerliche* Worlds' represented by Germany, France and England, he flatly stated:

A comparative analysis of the facts related to the concept can thus only be methodologically verifiable when unintegratable linguistic differentiations are also reflected. Thus, in addition to a social-historical metatheory that enables international comparisons, there also really needs to be a metalanguage that mediates the differences. But there is no such metalanguage. The *Gesellschaft der Bürger* in the nineteenth century was not only a society in transition; it can also only be analyzed and recognised when it is translated inter-linguistically and diachronically.

(Koselleck 2002: 2017)

Some years later, interviewed by Javier Fernández Sebastián and Juan Francisco Fuentes, Koselleck substantially confirmed this belief:

A metalanguage would be necessary. This seems clear to me. We need a language capable of incorporating historical and social differences reflected in language. These three experiences we just talked about (France, England, and Germany) create three different worlds [...] It is a passionate subject and I understand that it would be very interesting to get into it, but it is truly very challenging.

(Sebastian and Fuentes 2006: 111–12; see also Müller 2014; Steinmetz 2017; Cananau 2019; Heiskanen 2021)

In fact, the concept of a metalanguage, distinctly defined by Roman Jakobson (1985) as a linguistic problem, was never thoroughly elaborated as a historiographical method either by Pocock or by Koselleck; its possible use in the study of history really lies at the heart of the task of the historian as a translator, involving a consideration of the problem of anachronism to which new answers can be given in the light of recent work in the study of semantics, cognitive linguistics and materiality. First of all, on a semantic basis, we must return to a fundamental distinction already made by Reinhart Koselleck, though later substantially neglected: the distinction between semasiology and onomasiology. It should be noted that Koselleck invoked this analytical tool in debate with John Pocock on the differences between conceptual history and intellectual history:

With this assertion I reenter the minefield of questions posed by Professor Pocock. As my previous comments indicate, I dealt with the issues he raises already long ago. In our method, concepts are treated as more than meanings of term that can be unambiguously defined. Rather political and social concepts are produced by a longterm semiotic process, which encompasses manifold and contradictory experiences. Such process may evoke complex, conflicting reactions and expectations. Obviously, a political and social concept with many facets derived from its past uses cannot be reduced to a simple basic idea. Its manifold extralinguistic content can be clarified only by alternating two types of

analysis: semasiological (the study of all meaning of a term, word or concept) and onomasiological (the study of all names or terms for the same thing or concept).
(Koselleck 1996: 64; see also Palonen 1997: 50)

The semasiological and onomasiological approaches had been separately developed since the nineteenth century to deals with linguistic issues; what has rarely been noticed is that these two linguistic approaches provide a fundamental analytical tool to deal with the central problem raised by Eucken, Weber and finally Koselleck, whose reference to it has been often overlooked. The distinction between semasiology and onomasiology deals with the problem of anachronism in the study of language as well, and when used in historical research, it involves a range of epistemological, methodological and cognitive aspects which deserve due attention. In this case, it is not possible to follow the different paths opened by semasiological and onomasiological research in recent years, some of which devoted to the study of lexical and conceptual change (Zgusta 1990; Geeraerts 2002; Janda 2003; Vázquez González 2006; Geeraerts 2010; Winters 2010; Glynn 2015; Stolova 2015).

9.4. Conclusion

In some respects, the idea put forward here of history as a translation of the past aims at resolving and unifying two potentially conflicting and unresolved problems in Koselleck's work: the relation between his concept of time(s) and his 'theory' of language. A recent collection of Koselleck's essays (2018) recalls the key expression 'sediments of time', otherwise translated as 'layers of time' (*Zeitschichten*), linked to the well-known expression 'the simultaneity of the non-simultaneous' (*die Gleichzeitigkeit des Ungleichzeitigkeit*), otherwise translated as 'the contemporaneous of the non-contemporaneous'. The introduction to *Zeitschichten* by Sean Franzel and Stefan-Ludwig Hoffmann sharpens the need to answer this fundamental question, left unresolved by Koselleck. In recent years, Helge Jordheim (2007; 2012; 2017) has returned to this conceptual issue time and again. In relation to *Zeitschichten*, he has synthetically retraced the formation of the notion of 'stratigraphy' from the Danish anatomist and geologist Nicolaus Steno (Niels Stensen) up to Fernand Braudel, Krysztof Pomian and Reinhart Koselleck (Jordheim 2022a). Leaving aside the possible contribution that this perspective can make to the debate on the Anthropocene, on which Jordheim concentrates, we are here especially interested in the possible use of the notion of 'stratigraphy' or 'sediments of time' as a metaphor useful, in general, in the study of history.

Chris Lorenz (2022) has brusquely stated that 'Koselleck's idea concerning *Zeitschichten* in history is little more than a seductive metaphor': that Koselleck selected this geological metaphor without any great reflection, and was not well-acquainted with the complex ontological and epistemological implications of the notion. Taking inspiration from George Kubler and Hans-Jörg Rheinberger, the American historian John Zammito sought to clarify the meaning of the geological metaphor used by Koselleck, suggesting that it was aimed to avert the idea of a *Zeitgeist*, conceived as a total time (as in the concepts of *paradigm* and *episteme*). Indeed, this metaphor was intended to promote the concept of a multi-layered time evoking the notions of '*rhizomic* connections' and '*mosaic*', and as such is considered to be a 'useful conceptualization of the "patchy" nature of the coordination of practices, events, and cultures in a given historical moment' (Zammito 2015: 213). More recently, Zammito (2021) has reiterated that *Zeitschichten* 'is Koselleck's most important theoretical metaphor', while pointing out that 'Koselleck's theory of "sediments of time" aims at the *enablement* of historical practice, but that practice must find its disciplinary rigor in the acknowledgment of incompleteness, mutability, plurality'.

Above all, 'Koselleck insisted that historical practice cannot be reduced to hermeneutics – the analysis of texts or the language of texts – even if hermeneutics remains an indispensable element in historical practice' (ibid., 402–3). Hence, Koselleck was well aware that between the 'reality of the past' and the 'linguistic articulation of the past', there is always a hiatus, but he explicitly rejected covering that empty space with the rhetorical or hermeneutic blankets weaved by Hayden White and Hans-Georg Gadamer. It was the task of the historian to solve this 'epistemological aporia' through the concept of 'sediments of time', reconstructing stratum by stratum the different layers which connected the past with the present (Zammito 2004). It is just at this level, according to Frank Ankersmit (2021), that Koselleck's theoretical approach appears problematic, and that his ontology of time(s) seems to come into conflict with his historical epistemology and methodology. After recalling that the analysis of time requires the use of spatial metaphors and that this usage cannot be placed at the same level of epistemological statements about truth, Ankermsit explains that 'Koselleck's layers of time are layers *cutting vertically through* geological time instead of following how the layers are ordered. Only in *this* way can they be said to connect different times (or layers) together and to effect this "simultaneousness of the nonsimultaneous" that fascinated Koselleck so much' (ibid., 43).

In this context, of utmost importance for the idea of history as translation of the past is Koselleck's observation that concepts too must be studied in the light of the metaphor of 'layers of time': 'Jeder Begriff, so scheint es, hat viele Zeitschichten' (Koselleck 2000: 15) – something tangentially indicated by different authors, but never properly developed. Almost inadvertently, in a note referring to the problem of periodization, Ankersmit criticized Palonen's (2004: 241–4) interpretation of Koselleck's idea of history as translation of the past, also examined by Alexandra Lianeri (2014), arguing that 'we translate *words*, not *meanings*, even though meaning will be our guide in the translation of words; however, meanings are unquestionably at stake in Koselleck's conceptual history' (Ankersmit 2021: 47). Helge Jordheim too, discussing the problem of periodization in Koselleck's theoretical approach to time, connects it opportunely to the analysis of language and concepts:

> Indeed, it would be possible to claim that Koselleck's successful reworking of some of the paradoxical consequences of the linguistic turn starts with his entirely pragmatic and contextual distinction between 'word' and 'concept'. Both words and concepts might have several meanings, but whereas the meaning of a word can be determined with reference to the context, concepts are by definition ambiguous.
>
> (Jordheim 2012: 163)

Furthermore, not only Jordheim points out that language/concepts and reality have different temporalities, causing the 'simultaneousness of the nonsimultaneous', but concepts themselves have their own internal temporal structure (intralinguistic time). Following from this, the most important aspect of Koselleck's approach is to be found in the intertwining of diachronic and synchronic analysis of words and concepts, expressed in the formula of the 'synchronicity of the non-synchronous'. In the words of Jordheim:

> even if history appears to be frozen at a particular moment, in a *Zustand*, which is analyzed synchronically, there will always be a diachronic movement through the synchronic moment that manifest itself in the instances of nonsynchronicity, in the *Ungleichzeitigkeiten*, which can be analyzed, or remains in the semantics of *Zeitschichten*, which can be excavated, one temporal layer beneath the other.
>
> (ibid., 170)

But it is just at the level of the relationship between language and concepts that Koselleck's theoretical approach encounters one of its main 'aporie', since his 'theory' in this context does not fit with the central metaphor of *Zeitschichten* and does not provide a suitable solution for the important concept of the 'simultaneity of the non-simultaneous'. As said, the problem with this 'aporia', and with the entire conceptual history conceived by Koselleck, is that he tries to cope with this methodological and epistemological issue by invoking the possibility of identifying a meta-language capable of interpreting/translating events, words and concepts. Supposing that this meta-language could ever be found, it would be devastating for the idea of the temporality of concepts and language, contrasting also with other important aspects of Koselleck's theoretical approach, first of all with the distinction between semasiology and onomasiology. In the study of history there is no metalanguage (*pace* Pocock and Koselleck)! Or at least an agreement should be found on what is meant by metalanguage; we can certainly use an *idealtypus*, but it is not a metalanguage; it is a tool used to compare, formed in a specific spatial and temporal context.

Every term the historian uses is at the same time a word and a concept, and every term the historian finds in texts can/must be considered as a word (semasiology) and compared to a concept (onomasiology); it is not possible to use terms such as 'politics', 'democracy' or 'constitution' as abstract concepts, without taking into account that they are also concrete historical concepts/words. This consideration, outlined by Palonen (2012) in the conclusion of his essay, is substantially contained in the distinction between semasiology and onomasiology made by Koselleck, without, however, drawing from it all the necessary consequences. When we emphasize that the study of concepts should be accompanied and intertwined with the study of words, we are fundamentally recalling attention to the inescapable fact that language has a material/cognitive structure that cannot be obliterated. In this structural framework lies the unavoidable necessity for the historian to translate past words/concepts into present language, which has (most likely) the function attributed by Koselleck to metalanguage; indeed, our present language constitutes the only 'measure' through which it is possible to interpret the past, and it is the methodological tool that allows historians to make comparisons with past words and concepts.

This is the fundamental reason why the linguistic and conceptual analysis of texts and events must be strictly intertwined with a complex analysis of time in history and translation (Wakabayashy 2019; History and Theory 2021; Hartog 2022); it is not by chance that, in studying the function of analogy and allegory in history, Peter Burke has related this issue to the problem of anachronism, observing that

> the historian may be viewed as a kind of translator, turning the language of the past, especially its key concepts, into the language of the present, in search of what translators often call 'equivalent effect'. Like translators between languages, historians face a dilemma. They have to make a difficult choice between faithfulness to the past, which means avoiding anachronism, and intelligibility in the present, which involves using anachronism strategically.
>
> (Burke 2019: 9)

As argued by Neville Morely:

> historians have proved resistant to any ideas, such as those raised by translation theory, that threaten to undermine belief in their direct, unmediated access to and knowledge of a 'real' past [...] In so far as historians engage at all with questions of language, their primary concern is always the fear of 'anachronism', of understanding antiquity in terms of concepts that are excessively modern.
>
> (Morley 2008: 128)

Unavoidably, whenever a historian writes she/he resets time through translating past terms into present language, moving herself/himself into a complex time, defined by Alexandra Lianeri as 'a time of suspension indicating a condition of waiting, the quest for interpretation and the possibility of future translations' (Lianeri 2014: 477); in fact, the translation of the past can be interpreted as a form of anachronism that synchronizes for a moment the different temporalities of words and concepts through a present language that can be conceived, in Heideggerian terms, as a continuous *Stilllegung* of concepts that run straight toward the future (Alonzi, *forthcoming* b).

Notes

1   For a recent survey of this debate and its consequences, see Charles L. Levitt IV (2017), who outlines the difficult relationships many intellectuals and Italian historians had with the legacy of Benedetto Croce, a difficulty – it could be added – that even today affect the international image of Croce.

2   As regards Croce's concept of autobiography not completely convincing is Myra E. Moss (2013); see also Myra E. Moss (1999).

3   In the note attached to this passage, Jan van der Dussen argues, 'The section on Croce was written in 1936 and not subsequently amplified to take account of his

    La Storia come Pensiero e come Azione: Bari 1938 [English translation, *History as the Story of Liberty* (London 1941)]'.
4   On archival sources, history and translation, see the recent interesting inquiry performed by Rachel Kaufman (2021).
5   See the important Introduction by Keith Tribe, where due attention is given to the context and to the paratext into which Weber's work was placed.
6   This project is summarized and translated from Professor Eucken's manuscript by Thomas J. McCormack, in *The Monist*, 6 (4), 1986, 497–515, although this rendering leaves much to be desired.
7   This article has been translated as 'Social History and *Begriffsgeschichte*' (Koselleck 1988). Another (not well conceived) translation is also available (Koselleck 1989).
8   Revised translation from Palonen (2012: 80), citing Reinhart Koselleck, 'Begriffsgeschichtliche Probleme der Verfassungsgeschichtsschreibung', *Der Staat*, 6, 1983: 13; see also Koselleck (2010).

References

Alonzi, Luigi (2022), *'Economy' in European History. Words, Contexts and Change over Time*, London: Bloomsbury.
Alonzi, Luigi (*forthcoming* a), 'Language – History – Presence'.
Alonzi, Luigi (*forthcoming* b), 'History as Translation/Anachronism as Synchronism'.
Ankersmit, Frank R. (2021), 'Koselleck on "Histories" versus "History"; or Historical Ontology versus Historical Epistemology', *History and Theory*, 60 (4): 36–58.
Aurell, Jaume (2009), 'Benedetto Croce and Robin Collingwood: Historiographic and Humanistic Approaches to the Self and the World', *Prose Studies*, 31 (3): 214–26.
Burke, Peter (1992), *The Fabrication of Louis XIV*, New Haven and London: Yale University Press.
Burke, Peter (2007), 'Cultures of Translation in Early Modern Europe', in Peter Burke and Ronnie Po-chia Hsia (eds.), *Cultural Translation in Early Modern Europe*, 7–38, Cambridge: Cambridge University Press.
Burke, Peter (2019), 'Analogy, Allegory, and Anachronism', in Andreas Leutzsch (ed.), *Historical Parallels, Commemorations and Icons*, 12–35, London: Routledge.
Cananau, Iulian (2019), 'Toward a Comparatist Horizon in Conceptual History', *History of European Ideas*, 45 (1): 117–20.
Collingwood, Robin George (2006), *The Idea of History. Revised Edition with Lectures 1926–28*, edited with and introduction by Jan van der Dussen, Oxford: Oxford University Press.
Connelly, James, Peter Johnson and Stephen Leach (2016), *R. G. Collingwood. A Research Companion*, London: Bloomsbury.
Coombes, Annie E. and Ruth B. Phillips (eds.) (2020), *Museum Transformations: Decolonization and Democratization*, 1st edn 2015, Chichester, UK: Wiley Blackwell.
Coseriu, Eugenio (1974), *Synchronie, Diachronie, und Geschichte: Das Problem des Sprachwandel*, Münich: Fink.
Croce, Benedetto (1893), 'La storia ridotta sotto il concetto generale dell'arte', *Atti dell'Accademia Pontaniana*, 23: 1–29.
Croce, Benedetto (1912), *Storia, cronaca e false storie: memoria letta all'Accademia Pontaniana nella tornata del 3 novembre 1912 dal socio Benedetto Croce*, [Napoli]: R. Stabilimento tipografico Francesco Giannini & figli.

Croce, Benedetto (1938), *La Storia come Pensiero e come Azione*, Bari: Laterza.
Eucken, Rudolf (1986), 'Philosophical Terminology and Its History. Espository and Appellatory', *The Monist*, 6 (4): 497–515.
Fernández Sebastián, Javier and Juan Francisco Fuentes (2006), 'Conceptual History, Memory and Identity: An Interview with Reinhart Koselleck', *Contributions to the History of Concepts*, 2 (1): 99–127.
Gadamer, Hans-Georg (1971), *Die Begriffsgeschichte und die Sprache der Philosophie*, Opladen: Westdt. Verlag.
Geeraerts, Dirk (2002), 'The Scope of Diachronic Onomasiology', in Vilmos Ágel, Andreas Gardt, Ulrike Hass-Zumkehr, A. Gard, Thorsten Roelcke (red.) (eds.), *Das Wort. Seine strukturelle and kulturelle Dimension. Festschrift für Oskar Reichmann zum 65. Geburtstag*, 29–44, Tübingen: Niemeyer.
Geeraerts, Dirk (2010), *Theories of Lexical Semantics*, Oxford: Oxford University Press.
Glynn, Dylan (2015), 'Semasiology and Onomasiology: Empirical Questions between Meaning, Naming and Context', in *Change of Paradigms – New Paradoxes. Recontextualizing Language and Linguistics*, 47–79, Berlin: Mouton de Gruyter.
Hacking, Ian (1982), 'Language, Truth, and Reason', in Martin Hollis and Steven Lukes (eds.), *Rationality and Relativism*, 48–66, Cambridge MA: MIT Press.
Hartog, François (2022), *Chronos. The West Confronts Time*, 1st edn., 2019, New York: Columbia University Press.
Heiskanen, Jaakko (2021), 'Found in Translation: The Global Constitution of the Modern International Order', *International Theory*, 13 (2): 231–59.
History and Theory (2021), 60 (3): 'The Eight History and Theory Lecture'.
Hollis, Martin (1970a), 'The Limits of Irrationality', in Bryan R. Wilson (ed.), *Rationality*, 214–20, Oxford: Basil Blackwell.
Hollis, Martin (1970b), 'Reason and Ritual', in Bryan R. Wilson (ed.), *Rationality*, 221–39, Oxford: Basil Blackwell.
Huyssen, Andreas (2003), *Present Pasts. Urban Palimpsests and the Politics of Memory*, Stanford: Stanford University Press.
Israel, Hephzibah (*forthcoming*), 'Archival dea(r)th: tracing the afterlives of translation memory'
Jakobson, Roman (1985), 'Metalanguage as a Linguistic Problem', in S. Rudy (ed.), *Selected Writing*, vol. VII, 113–21, Paris: Mouton.
Janda, Richard D. and Brian D. Joseph (2003), 'On Language, Change, and Language Change – Or, of History, Linguistics, and Historical Linguistics', in Richard D. Janda and Brian D. Joseph (eds.), *The Handbook of Historical Linguistics*, 1–180, Malden Oxford Melbourne Berlin: Blackwell Publishing, 2003.
Johnson, Peter (2012), *Collingwood's the Idea of History. A Reader's Guide*, London: Bloomsbury.
Jordheim, Helge (2007), 'Thinking in Convergences – Koselleck on Language, History and Time', *Ideas in History*, 2 (3): 65–90.
Jordheim, Helge (2012), 'Against Periodization: Koselleck's Theory of Multiple Temporalities', *History and Theory*, 51 (2): 151–71.
Jordheim, Helge (2014), 'Introduction: Multiple Times and the Work of Synchronization', *History and Theory*, 53 (4): 498–518.
Jordheim, Helge (2017), 'In the Layer Cake of Time: Thoughts on a Stratigraphical Model of Intellectual History', in D. Timothy Goering (ed.), *Ideengeschichte heute: Traditionen und Perspektiven*, 195–214, Bielefeld: Transcript.
Jordheim, Helge (2022a), 'Stratigraphies of Time and History: Beyond the Outrages upon Humanity's Self-Love', in Anders Ekström and Staffan Bergwik (eds.), *Times of*

History, Times of Nature. Temporalization and the Limits of Modern Knowledge, 19–44, New York – Oxford: Berghahn.
Kaufman, Rachel (2021), 'Translating History', *Rethinking History*, 25 (1): 21–30.
Koselleck, Reinhart (1979), *Vergangene Zukunft. Zur Semantic geschichtlicher Zeiten*, Frankfurt am Main: Shurkampf.
Koselleck, Reinhart (1985), *Futures Past. On the Semantics of Historical Time*, translated and with an introduction by Keith Tribe, Cambridge, MA: MIT Press.
Koselleck, Reinhart (1986), 'Sozialgeschichte und Begriffsgeschichte', in Wolfgang Schieder and Volker Sellin (eds.), *Sozialgeschichte in Deutschland*, 89–109, Göttingen: Vandenhoeck und Ruprecht.
Koselleck, Reinhart (1988), 'Social History and *Begriffsgeschichte*', in Iain Hampsher-Monk, Karin Tilmans and Frank van Vree (eds.), *History of Concepts: Comparative Perspectives*, 23–35, Amsterdam: Amsterdam University Press.
Koselleck, Reinhart (1989), 'Social History and Conceptual History', *International Journal of Politics, Culture, and Society*, 2 (3): 308–25.
Koselleck, Reinhart (1996), 'A Response to Comments on the *Geschichtliche Grundbegriffe*', in H. Lehmann and M. Richter (eds.), *The Meaning of Historical Terms and Concepts. New Studies on Begriffsgeschichte*, 59–70, New York: German Historical Institute.
Koselleck, Reinhart (2000), *Zeitschichten: Studien zur Historik (mit eine beitrag von Hans-Georg Gadamer)*, Frankfurt: Schurkampf verlag.
Koselleck, Reinhart (2002), 'Three 'bürgerliche' Worlds? Preliminary Theoretical-Historical Remarks on the Comparative Semantics of Civil Society in Germany, England and France', in *The Practice of Conceptual History: Timing Histories, Spacing Concepts*, 208–17, translated by Todd Samuel Presner and Others, Foreword by Hayden White, Stanford: Stanford University Press.
Koselleck, Reinhart (2004), *Futures Past. On the Semantics of Historical Time*, revised version with new introduction by Keith Tribe, New York: Columbia University Press.
Koselleck, Reinhart (2010), *Begriffsgeschichten. Studien zur Semantik und Pragmatic der politischen und soziale Sprache*, Frankfurt: Shrukamp.
Koselleck, Reinhart (2018), *Sediments of Time: On Possible Histories*, edited and translated by Sean Franzel and Stefan-Ludwig Hoffmann, Stanford: Stanford University Press.
Levitt IV, Charles L. (2017), 'Probing the Limits of Crocean Historicism', *The Italianist*, 37 (3): 387–406.
Lianeri, Alexandra (2014), 'A Regime of Untranslatables: Temporalities of Translation and Conceptual History', *History and Theory*, 53 (4): 473–97.
Lorenz, Chris (2022), 'Probing the Limits of Metaphor: On the Stratigraphic Model in History and Geology', in Zoltán Boldizsár Simon and Lars Deile (eds.), *Historical Understanding: Past, Present, and Future*, 203–16, London: Bloomsbury.
Morley, Neville D. G. (2008), 'Das Altertum das sich nicht übertsetzen lässt: Translation and Untranslatability in Ancient History', in Alexandra Lianeri and Vanda Zajko (eds.), *Translation and the Classic: Identity as Change in the History of Culture*, 128–47, Oxford: Oxford University Press.
Moss, Myra E. (1999), 'Croce and Collingwood: Philosophy and History', in Jack D'Amico, Dain Trafton and Massimo Verdicchio (eds.), *The Legacy of Benedetto Croce: Contemporary Critical Views*, 145–62, Toronto: University of Toronto Press.
Moss, Myra E. (2013), 'Benedetto Croce, Historian-Philosopher: Is History Autobiography?', *Bollettino Filosofico*, 28: 253–7.
Müller, Jan Werner (2014), 'On Conceptual History', in Darrin M. McMahon and Samuel Moyn (eds.), *Rethinking Modern European Intellectual History*, 74–93, Oxford: Oxford University Press.

Nord, Christiane (2007), 'Function Plus Loyalty: Ethics in Professional Translation', *Genesis: Revista scientifica do ISAG*, 6: 7–17.
Palonen, Kari (1985), *Politik als Handlungsbegriff. Horizontwandel des Politikbegriffs in Deutschland 1890–1933*, Helsinki: Societas Scientiarium Finnica.
Palonen, Kari (1990), *Die Thematisirung der Politik als Phänomen. Eine Interpretation der Gechichte des Begriffs Politik im Frankreich des 20. Jahrhundert*, Helsinki: Societas Scientiarium Finnica.
Palonen, Kari (1997), 'An Application of Conceptual History to Itself: From Method to Theory in Reinhart Koselleck's Begriffsgeschichte', *Finnish Yearbook of Political Thought*, 1 (1): 39–69.
Palonen, Kari (2004), *Die Entzauberung der Begriffe: Das Umschreiben der politischen Begriffe bei Quentin Skinner und Reinhart Koselleck*, Münster: Lit verlag.
Palonen, Kari (2012), 'Reinhart Koselleck on Translation, Anachronism, and Conceptual Change', in Martin J. Burke and Malvin Richter (eds.), *Why Concepts Matter. Translating Social and Political Thought*, 73–92, Leiden and Boston: Brill.
Palonen, Kari (2014), *Politics and Conceptual Histories. Rhetorical and Temporal Perspectives*, London: Bloomsbury.
Phillips, Ruth B. (2011), *Museum Pieces. Towards the Indigenization of Canadian Museums*, Montreal: McGill Queen's University Press.
Phillips, Ruth B., Elizabeth Edward and Chris Gosden (eds.) (2020), *Sensible Objects: Colonialism, Museums and Material Culture*, 1st edn, 2006, New York: Routledge.
Piccardi, Roberta (ed.) (2002), *Carteggio Croce – Medicus*, Napoli – Bologna: Istituto Italiano per gli sudi filosofici – Il Mulino.
Pocock, John Greville Agard (1985), 'Introduction. The State of the Art', in *Virtue, Commerce, and History: Essays on Political Thought and History, Chiefly in the Eighteenth Century*, 1–34, Cambridge: Cambridge University Press.
Rizzi, Andrea, Birgit Lang and Anthony Pym (eds.) (2019), *What Is Translation History? A Trust-Based Approach*, Cham: Palgrave-Macmillan.
Schmitt, Carl (2007), 'The Age of Neutralization and Depoliticization', in *The Concept of the Political: Expanded Edition*, translated and with an Introduction by George Schwab, with a forward by Tracy B. Strong and Notes by Leo Strauss, Chicago: The University of Chicago Press.
Skinner, Quentin (1969), 'Meaning and Understanding in the History of Ideas', *History and Theory*, 8 (1): 3–53.
Skinner, Quentin (1988), 'Reply to My Critics', in J. Tully (ed.), *Meaning and Context: Quentin Skinner and His Critics*, 235–59, Cambridge: Cambridge University Press (recollected as 'Interpretation, Rationality, Truth', in *Visions of Politics*, 27–56, especially 46–9).
Skinner, Quentin (2002a), 'Meaning and Understanding in the History of Ideas', in *Visions of Politics*, 1 'Regarding Method', 57–89, Cambridge: Cambridge University Press.
Skinner, Quentin (2002b), 'Interpretation and the Understanding of Speech Acts', in *Visions of Politics*, 1 'Regarding Method', 103–27, Cambridge: Cambridge University Press.
Steglich, Sina (2021), 'The Archive as Chronotopos in the Nineteenth Century: Toward a History of Archival Times', *History and Theory*, 60 (2): 234–48.
Steinmetz, Willibald, Michael Freeden and Javier Fernández Sebastián (eds.) (2017), *Conceptual History in the European Space*, New York and Oxford: Berghahn Books.
Stolova, Nataliya I. (2015), *Cognitive Linguistic and Lexical Change: Motion Verbs from Latin to Romance*, Amsterdam – Philadelphia: John Benjamins publishing company.

Tribe, Keith (2015), *The Economy of the Word. Language, History, and Economics*, Oxford: Oxford University Press.
Vázquez, González, Juan Gabriel, Montserrat Martinez Vázquez and Pilar Ron Vaz (eds.) (2006), *The Historical Linguistics – Cognitive Linguistics Interface*, Huelva: Universidad de Huelva.
Vigorelli, Amedeo (ed.) (1991), 'Lettere di Robin George Collingwood a Bendetto Croce (1912–1939)', *Rivista di Filosofia*, 46 (3): 545–63.
Wakabayashy, Judy (2019), 'Time Matters: Conceptual and Methodological Considerations in Translation Timescapes', *Chronotopos*, 1 (1): 23–39.
Weber, Max (2019), *Economy and Society. A New Translation*, edited and translated by Keith Tribe, Oxford: Oxford University Press.
Winters, Margaret E., Heli Tissari and Kathryn Allan (2010), *Historical Cognitive Linguistics*, Berlin: De Gruyter Mouton.
Zammito, John H. (2004), 'Koselleck's Philosophy of Historical Time(s) and the Practice of History', *History and Theory*, 43 (1): 124–35.
Zammito, John H. (2021), 'Koselleck's Time', *History and Theory*, 60 (2): 396–405.
Zammitto, John H. (2015), 'Drilling Down: Can Historians Operationalize Koselleck's Stratigraphical Times?', *Configurations*, 23 (2): 199–215.
Zgusta, Ladislav (1990), 'Onomasiological Change: Sachen-change Reflected by *Worter*', in Edgard C. Polomé (ed.), *Research Guide on Language Change*, Berlin and New York: Mouton de Gruyter.

Name Index

Achilles 34, 57, 62, 67, 104
Adamo, Sergia 11, 21
Adorno, Theodor W. 51, 61–2, 64–5
Adrastus (Phrygian king)
Aeliun Theon 83
Aeschylus 15, 52–5, 62–3, 65–6, 150, 155
Ágel, Vilmos 210
Agnetta, Marco 188
Ajtoni, Zsuzsanna 91, 102
Akashi, Motoko 163–4
Alexander (son of Priam) 27
Allan, Kathryn 213
Allan, Michael 174, 185
Allen, O. Wesley Jr. 75–6, 84, 87
Alonzi, Luigi iii–v, viii, 1, 18, 162, 191, 196, 200, 208–9
Anaktoria 35
Ankersmit, Frank R. 206, 209
Anter, Andreas 117, 119
Apel, Hans 129
Aphrodite (Argimpasa) 41, 97
Apollo 36, 41–3
Apter, Emily 92, 102
Arcesilaus 42
Arendt, Hannah 19, 163
Aristeas of Proconnesus 25
Aristotle 42, 150, 154, 156–8, 165
Armitage, David 142, 163
Armitage, Simon 65
Armstrong, Richard 61
Arnold, Matthew 56
Arrojo, Rosemary 145, 163
Asad, Talal 2, 21
Ásgeirsson, Jón Ma. 88
Asheri, David 44–5
Aslan, Reza 77, 80–7
Aslanyan, Anna 102
Assmann, Aleida 174, 185
Assmann, Jan 97, 102, 174
Astarte 97
Athanasius of Alexandria 86

Athens 54
Atossa (Persian queen) 53–4
Attridge, Harold 75, 81, 84, 87, 89
Atys (son of Croesus) 36
Auer, Ignaz 126
Augustine of Hippo 71, 83
Aune, David E. 82, 87–90
Aurell, Jaume 193, 209
Austin, John 194, 197
Auvrayes-Assays, Clara 72, 87
Azadpour, Lydia 187

Babel, Reinhard 171, 185
Baccus, Gaston 131
Bachmann, Ingeborg 189
Bachmann-Medic, Doris 91, 102
Bacon, Francis 184
Baker, Mona 22–4, 61, 64–5, 67, 87, 145, 163
Bakhtin, Mikhail 14
Bakis (Boetian prophet) 43
Balmer, Josephine 61, 64
Bandia, Paul F. 12, 21
Bara, Jules 133
Barad, Karen 183
Barash, Jeffrey Andrew 19, 21
Barker, Elton 45
Barnstone, Willis 102
Barthes, Roland 13, 153
Bartholomew the Apostle 85
Barthou, Louis 130, 138
Barton, John 15, 52, 60–1, 64
Bassnett, Susan 3, 11, 19, 21, 61, 65, 69–70, 87, 102, 145, 163, 183, 185
Bastin, Georges L. 21
Batchelor, Kathryn 51, 61, 65
Battus 42, 45
Bauckham, Richard 73–5, 77, 82–5, 87
Baudelaire, Charles 19
Beal, Jane, 12, 21
Beattie, Pamela 186

Beauregard, Paul 130, 138
Becker, Fritz 128
Becker, Konrad 186
Becker, Max 128
Beer, Gillian 184–6
Beethoven, Ludwig van 6
Beidelman, Thomas O. 97, 102
Belgum, Kirsten 188
Bellairs, Carlyon 133
Bembo, Pietro 99
Benjamin, John D. 188
Benjamin, Walter 2, 13, 19, 21, 23, 146, 163–4, 166, 188
Bennett, Jane 172, 184, 186, 191
Bennett, Karen v, vi, 15, 69, 70, 81, 87, 176, 186
Bentley, Richard 94, 102
Beowulf 93
Bergwik, Staffan 210
Berman, Antoine 146, 163, 183, 186
Berman, Isabelle 163
Bernier, Christian 87
Bernoulli, Daniel 117
Bertacco, Simona 186
Bettray, Johannes 96, 102
Bevernage, Berber 142, 164
Bewell, Alan 176, 186
Bhabha, Homi 3
Bias of Priene 35
Biton 36
Blamey, Kathleen 19, 23, 89
Blenderhassett, Rowland 126
Blumczynski, Piotr 70, 88
Böhme, Jakob 183
Bonar, Andrew 128
Borchert, Jens 129, 138
Borges, Jorge-Louis 145
Bourdieu, Pierre 13, 102
Bowersock, Glynn 105
Bowie, Andrew 62, 65
Bowring, Richard 95, 102
Bracke, Alexandre 130
Bradsahw Busebee, Mark 21
Brady, Erika 44, 47
Brah, Avtar 22
Brandwood, Steven 44–5
Braudel, Fernand 205
Brecht, Bertold 92
Bredius, Abraham 94, 102

Brennan, Eileen 23
Brentano, Lujo 117, 119
Bromberg, Jacques A. 61, 65
Brown, Peter 101–2
Browne, Dennis 124
Browne, Thomas 174
Bruni, Leonardo 99
Bryan, Christopher 83, 88
Bryce, James 124–5, 138
Bubandt, Nils 189
Buchanan, George 128
Budick, Sanford 89, 102
Buesa Gomez, Carmen 23
Bultmann, Rudolf 81
Burke, Edmund 124, 140
Burke, Martin J. 139–40, 159, 163, 165, 212
Burke, Peter v, vii, ix, 1–2, 10–1, 14, 16, 18, 21, 91–2, 98–105, 141, 145, 162–3, 189, 191, 197–8, 208–9
Burkert, Walter 41, 44–6
Burkett, Delbert 74, 88
Bury, Michael 104
Butcher, Samuel 93
Butler, Shane 65–6
Butterfield, Herbert 98, 103
Byatt, Lucina 104
Byrd, Vance 188
Byrne, Sandie 65, 67
Byrskog, Samuel 82–3, 88

Caesar Julius 86
Caine, Barbara 104
Calhoun, Joshua 176, 186
Callahan, Allen D. 89
Calvin, Jean 101
Cambyses of Persia 31–2, 44–6
Campbell, Gordon 95–6, 103
Campion, Gilbert 126, 139
Cananau, Iulian 204, 209
Canevaro, Mirko 58, 65
Carbonell Cortés, Ovidi 22
Carr, Terry 187
Carson, Anne 185–6
Cartledge, Paul 53, 65, 154, 163
Casaubon, Isaac 94
Cassin, Barbara 87, 92, 103, 155, 163
Cavander, Kenneth 64
Cecil, Hugh 133

Cercel, Larisa 188
Certau, Michel de 8, 13
Cervantes, Miguel de 145
Chakrabarty, Dipesh 101, 103, 148, 163, 168, 186
Chamberlain, Austen 127
Chamberlain, David S. 45–6
Champollion, Jean-François 173–4
Chantraine, Pierre 44, 46
Chapman, George 93, 105
Charles I (King of Scotland and England) 99
Chaucer, Geoffrey 7, 93–5, 103
Chesterman, Andrew 90
Chew, Stephen L. 86, 88
Chou (dynasty) 98
Chrétien de Troyes 103
Christ, Matthew R. 44, 46
Christian (protagonist of *Der Runeberg*) 171, 179–80
Chuang Tzu 98
Cicero, Marcus Tullius 147, 156–7, 160
Cincinnatus, Lucius Quintus 127
Clark, Elizabeth 77, 86, 89
Claussen, Emma 122–3, 139
Clement of Alexandria 82–5
Cleobis 36
Cleomenes 45
Cleon 64
Cleopatra 100
Clifford, James 21
Coghill, Neville 94–5, 103
Cohen, Jeffrey J. 172, 186
Collingwood, Robin G. 8, 18, 152–4, 161, 191–7, 209–11, 213
Confucius 98
Connelly, James 194, 209
Conrad, Sebastian 150, 163
Constantin (Emperor) 78, 93, 105
Conway, Kyle 19, 21
Coombes, Annie E. 12, 22, 200, 209
Corcella, Aldo 45
Cormier, Raymond J. 98, 103
Coseriu, Eugenio 202, 209
Count of Hohenzollern 178
Cowen, Josef 126
Cowper, William 93
Cozzi, Gaetano 105
Cozzi, Luisa 105

Crahay, Roland 45–6
Crick, Malcom 97, 103
Croce, Benedetto 18, 191–5, 197, 208–13
Croesus (king of Lydia) 28, 34–47
Cronin, Michael 18, 167, 169, 172–3, 182–3, 186
Crossan, John Dominic 84
Cunningham, Andrew 188
Curzon, George 127
Cuvier, Georges 170, 177, 183–4, 187–8
Cyrus of Persia 28, 36–9, 44–5

D'Amico, Jack 211
D'hulst, Lieven 12, 22
Dahlen, Olle 135
Dahmen, Pierre 102, 103
Dahrendorf, Ralf 16, 107, 118–19
Damamme, Dominique 131, 139
Damasus I (Pope) 86
Dante, Alighieri 7, 94
Darbo-Peschanski, Catherine 45–6
Darius of Persia 31–4, 54–5
Darwin, Charles 175–6, 180, 184, 186
Daub, Adrian 188
David (King of Israel) 87
De Haan, Nathalie 65
De Landa, Manuel 171, 184, 186
De Pourcq, Maarten 61, 65–6
De' Nobili, Roberto 16, 96, 102
Debray, Régis 173
Deile, Lars 166, 211
Deleuze, Gilles 8
Derrida, Jacques 8, 13, 22, 145–6, 163
Détienne, Marcel 10, 22, 47, 160, 163
Devèze, Marius 130, 138
Dewey, Joana 83, 88
Dibelius, Martin 81
Dilthey, Wilhelm 161
Ditchfield, Simon 97, 103
Dixon, Robert M. W. 44, 46
Dolet, Étienne 198
Donnay, Samuel 133
Dosse, François 100, 103
Dryden, John 91, 102
Duclos, Jacques 131
Dugue de la Fauconnière, Henri Joseph 130
Duling, Dennis C. 74, 86, 88
Dunn, John 149, 150, 154, 163
Durkheim, Émile 110

Name Index 217

Easterling, Pat E. 65
Eco, Umberto 92, 97, 103
Edgeworth, Francis Ysidro 113
Edward, Elizabeth 212
Efstathiou, Athanasios 65
Ekström, Anders 210
Elman, Benjamin A. 93, 103
Éluard, Paul 7
Emde, Hans-Georg 134
Emerson, Ralph Waldo 187
Emmerich, Michael 95, 103
Eschbach, Andreas 189
Esteves Pereira, Margarida 22
Eucken, Rudolf 201–205, 209–210
Euphorbas 63
Euripides 62
Eusebius of Caesarea 72–4, 81–3
Evans, Paul 126, 139
Evans-Pritchard, Edward E. 2, 16, 19, 22, 97, 100, 102–4

Faraguna, Michele 43, 46
Farina, Mario 104
Farnell, David F. 89
Fasano Guarini, Elena 156, 163
Fazio, Bartolomeo 99, 103
Fechner, Gustave Theodor 117
Fenwick, Charles 127
Ferdinand I (King of Naples) 99
Ferdinand the Catholic 192
Fernández Sebastián, Javier 204, 210, 212
Figueira, Thomas 45
Finley, Moses viii, 154, 163
Fioretti, Dino 113–14, 119
Firnberg, Hertha 135
Fischer, Walter 128
Foran, Lisa 19, 22
Foucault, Michel 13, 149
Fox, Charles James 124
Fragnito, Gigliola 95, 103
Franchi, Elena 65
Frank, Manfred 189
Franzel, Sean 164, 185, 187, 205, 211
Fraunhofer, Hedwig 173, 186
Freeden, Michael 212
Frehsee, Heinz 136
Freud, Sigmund 174, 186
Fuentes, Juan Francisco 204, 210, 212
Furnémont, Léon 131

Gabriel, Juan 213
Gadamer, Hans-Georg 144, 161, 202, 206, 210–11
Gaeta, Franco 94, 104
Galen of Pergamon 93
Galton, Francis 113
Gambier, Yves 21, 145, 164
Gan, Elain 189
Garbo, Gunnar 135
Gardt, Andreas 210
Gasperi, Carlos 179, 186
Geeraerts, Dirk 205, 210
Geertz, Clifford 97, 103
Geertz, Hildred 100, 101, 104
Geiger, Jeffrey viii
Genji 95, 102–3
Gentzler, Edwin 13, 22, 70, 88
Gera, Deborah Levine 45–6
Gerhardsson, Birger 77, 88
Gerht, Hans 108
Gerstenmaier, Eugen 129
Geryon (giant) 33
Giangiulio, Maurizio 58, 65, 67
Gilio da Fabriano 99, 104
Gillespie, Carol vi
Ginzburg, Carlo 192
Glynn, Dylan 205, 210
Godley, Alfred Denis 31, 44, 46
Goering, Timothy 210
Goethe, Johann Wolfgang von 110, 174–5, 187–9
Goldberg, Hans-Peter 126, 139
Goldhill, Simon 141, 164
Goodbody, Alex 170, 186
Gopal, Pryiamvada 51, 65
Gosden, Chris 212
Gosh, Amitav 168, 186
Gosh, Ranjan 164
Gradl, Johann Baptist 135
Grafton, Anthony 93–4, 104
Graziosi, Barbara 65
Greenwood, Emily 58–60, 63, 65
Griesbach, Johann Jakob 71
Griffith, Frank Kingsely 128
Grimm, Jacob Ludwig Karl 108, 189
Grimm, Wilhelm Karl 108, 189
Groves, Jason 168, 178, 180–1, 186
Gucciardini, Francesco 98, 104
Guillery, Jules 133

Guldin, Rainer 11, 22
Gundelfinger, Friedrich 189
Gundry, Robert H. 83, 88
Gunning, Tom 185–6
Guterman, Norbert 189

Habermas, Jürgen 108
Hacking, Ian 112, 119, 196, 210
Halbwachs, Maurice 65
Hall, Edith 15, 52, 54–5, 62–5
Hall, Peter 64
Halverson, Sandra L. 23
Hammersen, Walter 136
Hampsher-Monk, Iain 155, 164, 211
Hanke, Edith 118–19
Hansen, Mogen Herman 122, 139
Haraway, Donna 180, 183, 186
Harden, Theo 22
Harding, Sue-Ann 19, 22
Hardwick, Lorna v, vi, 49, 50, 58, 60–6, 141, 162, 164
Harloe, Katherine 58, 66
Harrington, James 123, 139
Harris, Paul A. 185, 187
Harrison, Stephen J. vi, 65–7
Harrison, Thomas 43–6, 54, 62–3, 65–6
Harrison, Tony 65–7
Hartley, Leslie P. 98, 104
Hartog, François 208, 210
Hass-Zumkehr, Ulrike 210
Hawkins, John David 30, 46
Haywood, Jan 44, 46, 62, 66
Heaney, Seamus 62, 66
Heather, Swanson 189
Hector 57
Hedeman, Anne 12, 22
Hegel, Georg Wilhelm Friedrich 193, 195
Hegesippus the Nazarene 85
Heidegger, Martin 144, 146, 164, 208
Heidelberger, Michael 118, 120
Heiskanen, Jaakko 204, 210
Helen of Troy 27–8, 39
Helleputte, Joris 130–31
Henderson, Alexander 118
Hendrix, Holland Lee 87
Henenkeland, Karl A. E. 22
Henry de Navarre 123
Heracles (Hercules) 33
Herda, Alexander 43, 46

Hermans, Theo 11–13, 22, 64, 88, 141, 153, 155, 164
Hernes, Tor 12, 22
Herodotus v, 14, 25–47, 52, 63, 65, 67
Hesiod 32
Hesk, Jon 60, 66
Hestia 41
Heyvaert, Stefan 186
Hilti, Palmer 187
Hippocrates 93
Hobbes, Thomas 93, 121, 140
Hock, Ronald F. 73, 88
Hoffmann, Ernst T. A. 189
Hoffmann, Stephan Ludwig 164, 185, 187, 205, 211
Hofmann, Michael 91–2, 104
Hog, Quintin 128
Hogan, Patrick James 133
Hollis, Martin 195, 210
Hollman, Alexander 44, 46
Holmes, Brooke 62, 66
Homer vi, 15, 32, 55–8, 63, 65, 92–3, 104–5, 175
Hong, Wenjie 21–2
Honoré, Anthony M. 70, 88
Hoppe, Stephan 12, 22
Hornblower, Simon 66
Hotman, François 99, 104
Howland, Douglas 12, 22
Huber, Johannes 127
Hübinger, Ganglof 107, 119
Hume, David 100, 104
Humphrey, Chris 103
Hutton, James 175, 184, 187
Huyssen, Andreas 183, 187, 200, 210
Hymans, Paul 133

Ignatius of Antioch 85
Iózwikowska, Wanda 163–4
Irenaeus of Lyon 72, 79, 81, 83
Isaiah of Jerusalem 84
Iser, Wolfgang 89, 102
Israel, Hephzibah 191, 199, 210

Jackson, Andrew 124
Jakobson, Roman 5, 19, 22, 173, 187, 204, 210
James I (King of Scotland and England) 95, 103–4

Janda, Richard 205, 210
Jardine, Nicholas 188
Jaurès, Jean 130
Jeanneret, François 131
Jérôme (saint) 20, 69, 81, 83, 99
Jesus 15, 69–90
Jiheng, Yao 93
John the Baptist 71
John the Evangelist 70–5, 79, 81–2, 86–7
Johnson, Peter 194, 209, 210
Johnston, David 70, 87
Jordheim, Helge 21–2, 147, 161, 164, 205–7, 210
Joseph, Bryan D. 210
Josephus Flavius 85
Józwikowska, Wanda 163–4
Justine, Martin 83

Karamanou, Ioanna 65–6
Kaufman, Rachel 209, 211
Kauppi, Niilo vii
Kearney, Richard 23
Kelber, Werner H. 83, 88
Kelley, Donald 99, 104
Kelly, Louis G. 69, 88
Kenward, Claire 67
Keynes, John Maynard 113, 118–20
Kielmeyer, Karl Friedrich 170, 187
Kindt, Julia 45–6
Kingsbury, Jack Dean 84, 88
Kinslansky, Mark 123, 140
Kirchberg, Jutta 45–6
Kirkwood, David 134
Kleinberg, Ethan 161–2, 164
Kleiner, Viktor 134
Klingsohr (poet) 170
Klooster, Jacqueline 62, 66
Kneller, Jane 188
Koester, Helmut 73–5, 77, 79, 82–3, 87–8, 90
Kohlmeier, Herbert 135
Kohn, Ayelet 183, 189
Koselleck, Reinhart 16–18, 121, 136, 139, 142, 144, 147, 159–64, 178, 184–5, 187, 200–12
Krasilnikov, Jens A. 66
Krempl, Matthias 135
Kreuger, Frederick H. 94, 104
Krimmer, Elizabeth 188

Krishna Mehrotra, Arvind 12, 22
Kubler, George 205
Kuhiwczak, Piotr viii
Kuin, Inger N. I. 62, 66
Kürzinger, Josef 74, 88
Kuzniar, Alice 171, 179, 185, 187

Lacotte, Charles Eugène 131
Laird, A. G. 45–6
Lambert, José 70, 88
Lamprecht, Karl 110
Lang, Andrew 93
Lang, Birgit 198, 212
Lange, Friedrich A. 117
Laplace, Pierre-Simon 113
Large, Duncan 92, 104, 163–4
Lassman, Peter 140
Lauche, Jacques 130
Laurence, French 123–4
Lawson, Wilfrid 133
Le Cunff, Anne-Laure 83, 88
Le Guin, Ursula 18, 167, 172, 184, 187
Le Guin, Ursula K. 18, 167, 172, 184, 187
Leach, Stephen 209
Lee, Christine 58, 65–6
Lee, Holland 87
Lee, Jennie 128
Lefevere, André 11, 19, 21–2, 70, 75, 78, 88–9, 145, 163–4
Legge-Bourge, Harry 128
Lehmann, Hartmut 164, 211
Leibniz, Gottfried Wilhelm von 148, 150
Lemonnier, Maurice 131
Levasseur, Florentin 130
Levitt IV, Charles L. 208, 211
Lewis, Clive S. 92, 104
Lexis, Wilhelm 116–17, 119
Lianeri, Alexandra v, viii, 17, 50, 61, 67, 141, 155, 159, 161–2, 164–5, 191, 206, 208, 211
Liapis, Vayos 66
Lienhard, Godfrey 97, 104
Linde, Ingo 185
Littau, Karin v, viii, 17–18, 167, 169, 187
Liu, Lydia H. 148, 164
Livy (Titus Livius) 156
Lizardo, Omar 107–8, 120
Lloyd, Alan 45
Lloyd, Howell 104

Logue, Christopher 63, 65, 67
Longley, Michael 62
Loraux, Nicole 100, 101, 104
Lorenz, Chris 142, 164, 205, 211
Loriga, Sabina 19, 22
Louis XI (King of France) 192
Louis XIV (King of France) vii, 197, 209
Lovejoy, Arthur 17, 149–51, 162, 164–5, 194
Lowenthal, David 98, 104
Luhmann, Niklas 11
Luke the Evangelist 15, 70–2, 75–6, 79–84, 87–90
Lukes, Steven 210
Lukhsu (Carian deity) 25
Luna-Fabritius, Adriana vii
Luptowits, Michael 136
Luther, Martin 20
Lyell, Charles 175–6, 180, 184, 187
Lyotard, François 13
Lyxes (father of Herodotus) 25

MacDonald, Ramsay 128, 133
Mac Sweeney, Naoíse 52, 62, 66–7
Macedo, Ana Gabriela 19, 22
Macfarlane, Alan 2, 23
Machiavelli, Niccoló 123, 153, 156, 163, 166
Macintosh, Fiona 65, 67
Mack, Burton L. 78, 82, 85–9
Mackie, Hillary Susan 45–6
MacLachlan, Bonnie 44, 46
Macquisten, Frederick 134
Macualay, Thomas 101, 102
Mähl, Hans-Joachim 187
Mahoney, Dennis 171, 184, 187
Maitland, Sarah ix, 4–5, 23
Maleta, Alfred 134
Malinowski, Bonisław 2, 19, 97, 101, 104
Mallarmé, Stéphan 6
Mandell, Sara 43, 46
Manheim, Ralph 188
Mani (prophet) 85
Mantegna, Andrea 99
Marais, Kobus 87, 173, 183, 187
Marcion of Pontus 82–5
Marcus, George E. 21
Marcuse, Herbert 108
Marett, Robert Ranulf 19

Mark the Evangelist 15, 70–85, 88–90, 98
Martin, Dibelius 81
Martín, Muñoz 14, 21, 23–4
Martin, Richard P. v, vi, 14, 25, 44, 46
Martindale, Charles 141, 165
Martínez Barmejo, Saúl 92, 104
Martínez Vázquez, Montserrat 213
Mary Magdalene 85
Mary the Virgin 85
Matthew the Evangelist 15, 70–6, 79–84, 88–9
Matzner, Sebastian 62, 67
Maxwell, James Clerk 113
McConnell, Justine 67
McCormack, Thomas J. 209
McGill, John 83, 89
McKnight, Edgar V. 88
McMahon, Darrin M. 149, 165, 211
Medea 39
Medicus, Fritz 192, 212
Mehering, Reinhard 117, 119
Mehne, Philipp 184, 189
Meier, Christian 122, 139
Mellowes, Marilyn 74–5, 79, 82, 84, 86, 89
Menard, Pierre 145
Menzel, Wolfgang 117
Methuen, Charlotte 103
Meyer, Eduard 16, 110–19
Meylaerts, Reine 87
Micah (prophet) 87
Miletti, Lorenzo 45–6
Milton, John 150
Ming (Chinese dynasty) 93
Mjoen, Alf 133
Moeser, Marion C. 73, 83, 89
Mogford, Rhodri ix
Mommsen, Wolfgang J. 118–19, 140
Montaigne, Michel de 6, 95
Moreno, Alfonso 45
Morgan, Ella S. 189
Mori, Luca 107, 119
Morley, Neville D. G. 10, 23, 58, 64–7, 145, 165, 208, 211
Morris, William 93
Morrison, Blake 62, 67
Morrison, Herbert 128
Moses 74, 88

Moss, Myra 208, 211
Moyn, Samuel 149, 165, 211
Moynihan, Patrick Berkely 128
Müller, Jan Werner 204, 211
Muñoz Martin, Ricardo 14, 21, 23–4
Muñoz-Calvo, Micaela 19, 23
Munson, Rosaria 39–41, 44–6
Murray, Christopher 66
Murray, Oswyn 45
Murray, Pomerance 186
Muslow, Alun 13, 20, 163

Nabougodi, Mathelinda 19, 23
Neale, John 101, 104
Neumann, Birgit 102
Newman, Francis 93, 104
Neyrey, Jerome S. J. 82, 89
Ngugi wa Thiong'o 59–60, 67
Nicodemus 85
Nicolson, Adam 95, 104
Nietzsche, Friedrich 92, 102, 188
Niranjana, Tejaswini 3
Nocek, Adam J. 187
Nokkala, Ere vii
Nord, Christiane 198, 212
Norrby, Sören 135
Nørskov, Vinnie 66
Novalis (Fredrich von Hardenberg) 18, 167–188
Nunning, Ansgar 102

Offerlé, Michel 139
O'Day, Gail R. 87, 89
O'Keeffe, Brian 182, 182, 188
Oleart, Álvaro vii
Olivier, Laurent 142, 166
Origen of Alexandria 82–3
Ormrod, Mark W. 103
Osborn, Marijane 21
Ostrogorski, Moisei 125, 139
Ostwald, Martin 45, 47
Oswald, Alice 15, 52, 55–8, 63, 65, 67
Ottenheim, Konrad A. 22
Outram, Dorinda 184, 188
Ovid 91, 102
Oz-Salzberger, Fania 148, 165

Pagden, Anthony 165
Pagels, Elaine 77, 81, 86, 89

Pakenham, Frank 128
Palonen, Kari v, vii, 16–18, 107, 119, 121–6, 136, 139, 153, 159–60, 165, 200–7, 209, 212
Pálsson, Gisli 97, 104
Panyassis (unle or cousin of Herodotus) 25, 43
Papenheim, Martin 123, 139
Papias of Hierapolis 72–4, 83
Parikka, Jussi 180, 181, 183, 185, 188
Parry, Adam 93, 104
Parsons, Talcott 16, 108–9, 118
Pasternak, Boris 101
Paul of Tarsus 75–81, 84–7
Paul, André 87
Paul, Georgina 57, 63, 67
Pawson, David 76, 89
Pearson, Karl 113
Peck, Andy 89
Peirce, Charles Sanders 20, 173
Pellauer, David 19, 23, 89
Pelling, Christopher 66
Pender, Elizabeth 63, 65
Periander 37
Pericles 59–60
Pernau, Margrit 159, 165–6
Perrin, Norman 82, 89
Peter the Apostle 72–4, 82–3, 85, 87
Peter, Friedrich 135
Peters, John Durham 181, 183–5, 188
Petersen, David L. 87, 89
Petrarch, Francis 103, 156
Pettersson, Axel Georg 135
Pfannkuchen, Antje 174, 183, 188
Phalaris of Akragas 94, 102
Phillips, Mark ix, 98, 102–4, 142, 165
Phillips, Ruth B. ix, 200, 209, 212
Philo Judaeus 83
Phrynicos 52–4
Piccardi, Roberta 192, 212
Pickford, Henry W. 64
Pindar 32–3
Piper, Ronald A. 82, 89
Pisistratus 44
Pitt, William 124
Pittacus of Mytilene 35
Plato 6, 26, 41, 64, 149, 150
Plunkitt of Tammany Hall 124, 139
Plunkitt, George W. 124

Po-chia Hsia, Ronnie vii, 21, 102–4, 209
Pocock, John G. A. 17–8, 99, 104, 139, 144, 155–8, 160, 162, 164–5, 196–7, 199, 202, 204, 207, 212
Poisson, Siméon Denis 113
Pole, David Graham 128
Polomé, Edgard C. 213
Polybius 156–7
Polycarp of Smyrna 72
Polymnestus of Thera 42
Pomerance, Murray 186
Pomian, Krysztof 205
Pope, Alexander 93
Porębski, Mieczysław 93, 105
Porter, James vi
Porter, Theodore M. 112–3, 119
Poseidon (Thagimasadas) 41
Poussin, Nicolas 103
Presner, Todd Samuel 164, 211
Priam 55
Procles (king of Sparta) 37–8
Proietti, Giorgia 53, 63, 65, 67
Protesilaus 57
Psammetichus (king of Egypt) 28–9, 38, 41
Pym, Anthony 12, 23, 198, 212
Pythia 36, 38, 42

Qing (Chinese dynasty) 93
Queiroz de Barros, Rita 24
Quetelet, Adolphe 112

Racine, Jean 6
Radcliffe-Brown, Alfred R. 2, 19
Radicioni, Maura 87, 186
Rancière, Jacques 143–4, 162, 165
Rao, Ennio 103
Raubitschek, Anthony vi
Raubitschek, Isabelle vi
Rauth, Eric 186
Recker, Marie-Louise 129, 139
Redlich, Josef 126, 139
Refini, Eugenio 141, 165
Regoliosi, Mariangela 105
Rendall, Steven 2, 23
Rengakos, Antonios 58, 67
Renger, Anne-Marie 129
Rheinberger, Hans-Jörg 205
Ricci, Matteo 16, 96, 102

Richardson, Carol 104
Richardson, Catherine
Richardson, Edmund 66
Richter, Eugen 126
Richter, Julia 12, 23
Richter, Melvin 139–40, 153, 159–60, 163–5, 211–12
Ricouer, Paul 5, 8–10, 19–23, 86, 89, 144
Rieu, Émile 93
Rigby, Kate 170, 181, 185, 188
Rijser, David 65
Ringer, Fritz 117, 119
Rizzi, Andrea 198, 212
Robinson, Douglas 185, 188
Rockhill, Gabriel 165
Roelcke, Thorsten 210
Rojo, Ana 21, 23
Rosbotham, Samuel 134
Rose, Marilyn Gaddis 164
Rosier-Catach, Irène 87
Rosman, Abraham 23
Rossi, Caroline 22
Roth, Gunther 108, 118, 120
Roussellier, Nicolas 129, 139
Rubel, Paula G. 19, 23
Rubiés, Joan Pau 96, 105
Rudwick, Martin 183–4, 188
Rundle, Christopher 12, 22–3
Runia, Eelco 161, 165
Rupke, Nicholas 178, 188
Rushdie, Salman 97, 101, 105

Sachsenmaier, Dominic 159, 165–6
Saldanha, Gabriela 23–4, 61, 67, 145, 163
Sallis, John 148–9, 166
Samoyoult, Tiphaine 100, 105
Sanneh, Lamin 97, 105
Santos, Spenser 12, 23
Sappho 35
Sarpi, Paolo 101, 103, 105
Saunders, Stanley P. 74, 84, 89
Schaber, Steven C. 174, 188
Schaumann, Caroline 188
Schelling, Friedrich Wilhelm Joseph von 174–5, 180, 188–9
Schelling, Karl Friedrich August 189
Scheuchzer, Johann Jakob 177, 184
Scheyven, Raymond 131

Schieder, Wolfgang 139, 211
Schirripa, Pino 44, 47
Schlegel, August Wilhelm 188
Schlegel, Friedrich von 169
Schleiermacher, Fredrich 91–2, 105, 144, 155
Schluchter, Wolfgang 140
Schmidt, Helmut 134
Schmidt, Karl Ludwig 73, 89
Schmitt, Carl 107, 119–21, 139, 193, 195, 212
Schober, Kurt 136
Schröter, Jens 83, 89
Schultz, Majken 12, 22
Schulz, Gerhard 187
Schwab, George 212
Sebeok, Thomas A. 44, 47
Secord, James 187
Selinger, William 123, 140
Sellin, Volker 139, 211
Seppel, Marten vii
Serra, Renato 192
Sesostris (Rameses II) 29–30
Shakespeare, William 7, 95–6, 100–1, 105
Shelley, Percy B. 183
Shils, Edward 108
Shklovski, Viktor 92
Sica, Alan vii
Sidiropoulos, Avra 66
Siebeck, Paul 118, 192
Silva, Gisele 87, 186
Simon, Zoltán Boldizsár 144, 148, 166, 211
Simonides of Ceos 185
Sinyavksy, Andrei 101
Skårman, Bo 135
Skidelsky, Robert 118, 120
Skinner, Quentin 17–18, 121, 124, 129, 140, 144, 149, 152–6, 162–6, 194–7, 212
Sköld, Per Edvin 135
Smith, Adam viii
Smith, Ben C. 71, 89
Smith, Mark 102, 105
Smith, Samuel 127
Snell, Henry 134
Snell-Hornby, Mary 3, 11, 23
Soares, Carmen 45
Socrates 26, 75
Soldat-Jaffe, Tatiana 186

Solon 35–8, 45
Sommella, Valentina 163
Song (Chinese dynasty) 93
Sophocles 62, 67, 150
Speirs, Donald 140
Spelman, Henry 100, 105
Speziali, Carlo 132
Spicer, Andrew 103
Spiegel, Gabrielle 98, 105
Sprick, Philip 140
Stambaugh, Joan 164
Stark, Whitney 184
Stead, Henry 62, 67
Steffens, Heinrich 167, 189
Steglich, Sina 200, 212
Steiner, George 5–7, 9–10, 19, 23–4, 69, 89, 145, 166, 182, 189
Steinmetz, Willibald 124, 140, 159, 166, 204, 212
Stensen, Niels (Nicolaus Steno) 205
Stierle, Karlheinz 81, 89
Stigler, Stephen M. 112–3, 120
Stolova, Nataliya I. 205, 212
Strachey, James 186
Strand, Michael 107–8, 120
Sträng, Gunnar 135
Strauss, Leo 165, 212
Stray, Christopher vi
Strobel, Käte 136
Strong, Tracy B. 212
Struthers Malbon, Elizabeth 88
Stuart Mill, John 118
Sturge, Kate 19, 24
Sullivan, Heather I. 181, 188–9
Sundberg, Ingrid 135
Suppan, Walter 135
Süssmilch, Johann Peter 112
Syloson (governor of Samos) 33–4
Szeman, Imre 182, 189

Tamm, Marek 142, 166, 183, 189
Tang dynasty 91
Tanizaki, Junichirō 95
Tarkasnawa (king of Myra) 30, 46
Taru, Haapala vii
Telecleides, 44
Tellus 36
Terlinden, George 131
Tertullian, 82–5

Theodosius (Emperor) 78
Theophilus 76, 79, 84
Thomas the Apostle 71, 79, 85, 89
Thomas, Julia Adeney 105
Thomas, Keith 100, 105
Thomas, Robert L. 74, 89
Thompson, Edward P. 161, 166
Thompson, Faith 99, 105
Thompson, Richard 75, 84, 87, 90
Thrue Djurslev, Christian 66
Thuchydides 15, 52, 58–61, 64–7, 84
Tieck, Ludwig 169–71, 177, 179–81, 186–7, 189
Tilmans, Karin 211
Tissari, Heli 213
Toury, Gideon 70, 78, 86, 90, 153, 166
Trafton, Dain 211
Tribe, Keith v, vii, ix, 16, 66, 107, 118, 120, 164, 191, 196, 201, 209–13
Trimble, Gail 67
Trivedi, Harish 3, 24
Trollope, Anthony 93
Tsakmakis, Antonis 58, 67
Tsing, Anna 184, 189
Tully, James 152, 166, 212
Turchetti, Mario 123, 140
Turkka, Tapani 123, 140
Turner, Richard 187

Ullrich, Sebastian 128, 140
Underwood, Simeon 93, 105

Valla, Lorenzo 93–4, 99, 103, 105
van der Dussen, Jan 208–209
van Deusen, Nancy 88
van Doorslaer, Luc 21, 145, 164
van Gorp, Hendrik 70, 88
van Meegeren, Han 94
van Vree, Frank 211
Vandiver, Elizabeth vi, 63, 66–7
Vansina, Jan 26, 47
Vaz, Pilar Ron 213
Vázquez, González 213
Velz, John W. 100, 105
Venus 97
Venuti, Lawrence 3, 19–20, 24, 91–2, 105, 157, 166
Verdicchio, Massimo 211
Verhaegen, Eugène 132

Vermeer, Hans 80, 90
Vermeer, Johannes 94, 102, 104
Vernant, Jean-Pierre 44, 47
Verne, Jules 189
Vico, Giambattista 191
Vidal Claramonte, Maria Carmen África 12–13, 20–1, 24, 91, 105
Vigorelli, Amedeo 192, 213
Virgil 62, 91
Viroli, Maurizio 163
von Bismarck, Otto 125–6, 139
von Hardenberg, Friedrich see Novalis
von Humboldt, Wilhelm 155, 163
von Kries, Johannes 16, 112–19
von Merkatz, Hans-Joachim 128
von Ofterdingen, Heinrich 169, 170, 184, 187
von Philippovich, Eugen 117
von Schelting, Alexander 107, 120
von Stein, Charlotte 111
von Steinheil, Carl August 117

Wagemann, Johannes 140
Wakabayashi, Judy 208, 213
Walcott, Derek 62, 67
Waley, Arthur 98, 105
Warner, Rex 64
Waterfield, Robin 26, 44, 47
Watnebryn, Olaf 134
Weber, Ernst Heinrich 117
Weber, Marianne 109
Weber, Max vii, 16, 107–22, 125, 127, 129, 138, 140, 201, 203, 205, 213
Wedén, Sven 135
Wehn, Karin 185
Weiler, Christina 184, 189
Weissbrod, Rachel 183, 189
West, Stephanie 44, 47
Whistler, Daniel 187
White, Henry Graham 134
White, Hyden 8, 13, 20, 192, 206, 211
White, Michael L. 73–5, 77, 82–4, 87–90
Williams, Bernard 154, 166
Wilson, Bryan R. 201
Wilson, Cecil 134
Winckelmann, Johannes 108, 117, 120
Windham, William 124
Winters, Margaret E. 205, 213
Withalm, Hermann 135

Witte, Arndt 22
Wittgenstein, Ludwig 194
Wittich, Claus 108, 118, 120
Wolf, Friedrich August 175
Wood, David W. 188
Wortsman, Peter 189
Wrede, William 82, 89
Wright Mills, Charles 108, 163

Xerxes of Persia 37, 53–5
Xiao, Kairong 14, 24

Yaeger, Patricia 182, 189
Yates, David C. 62, 67
Yates, Frances 94, 105
Yi, Chen 21, 24
Yule, George Udny 113

Zabell, Sandy 113, 120
Zajko, Vanda 66, 141, 164–5, 211
Zammito, John H. 205–6, 213
Zedler, Johann Heinrich 108
Zeus 36–7, 41, 43
Zevaès, Alexandre 130
Zgusta, Ladislav 205, 210
Ziegler, Heide 104
Zimmermann, Isolde 123, 129, 140
Zincke, Georg Heinrich 108
Ziolkowski, Theodore 184, 189
Zorn, Harry 163
Zulima (captive Saracen) 170
Zutshi, Chitralekha 12, 24
Zwemer, Samuel 95, 105